THE LEGEND OF ZELDA™

Ocarina of Time

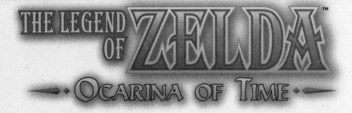

OCARINA OF TIME — THE GAME

The Legend of Zelda™ *: Ocarina of Time* was developed for the Nintendo 64 game platform and originally released in 1998 as part of *The Legend of Zelda*™ series of games. *Ocarina of Time* became a huge success, selling over 7 million units worldwide and winning several industry awards.

AKIRA HIMEKAWA

Link's adventure begins!! There are hardly ever any main characters that are so strong, cool and kind! Anyway, I poured on lots of love ♥ when I drew this manga! OK, everyone, together with Link, let's play the *Ocarina of Time* and warp to Hyrule and the world of *The Legend of Zelda*™!

Akira Himekawa is the collaboration of two women, A. Honda and S. Nagano. Together they have created nine manga adventures featuring Link and the popular video game world of *The Legend of Zelda*™, including *Ocarina of Time*, *Oracle of Seasons* and *Four Swords*. Their most recent work, *Legend of Zelda*™: *Phantom Hourglass*, is serialized in *Shogaku Rokunensei*.

THE LEGEND OF ZELDA™

— OCARINA OF TIME —

PART 1

Perfect Square Edition

STORY & ART BY
AKIRA HIMEKAWA

TM & © 2008 Nintendo.
© 2000 Akira HIMEKAWA/Shogakukan
All rights reserved.
Original Japanese edition
"ZELDA NO DENSETSU - TOKI NO OCARINA - JOU"
published by SHOGAKUKAN Inc.
English translation rights in the United States of America, Canada,
United Kingdom, Ireland, Australia and New Zealand
arranged with SHOGAKUKAN.

Translation/John Werry, Honyaku Center Inc.
English Adaptation/Steven "Stan!" Brown
Touch-up Art & Lettering/John Hunt
Cover & Interior Design/Izumi Hirayama
Editor/Mike Montesa

Printed in the U.S.A.

Published by VIZ Media, LLC
P.O. Box 77010
San Francisco, CA 94107

16
First printing, October 2008
Sixteenth printing, June 2017

PARENTAL ADVISORY
LEGEND OF ZELDA is
rated A and is suitable
for readers of all ages.
ratings.viz.com

www.viz.com

www.perfectsquare.com

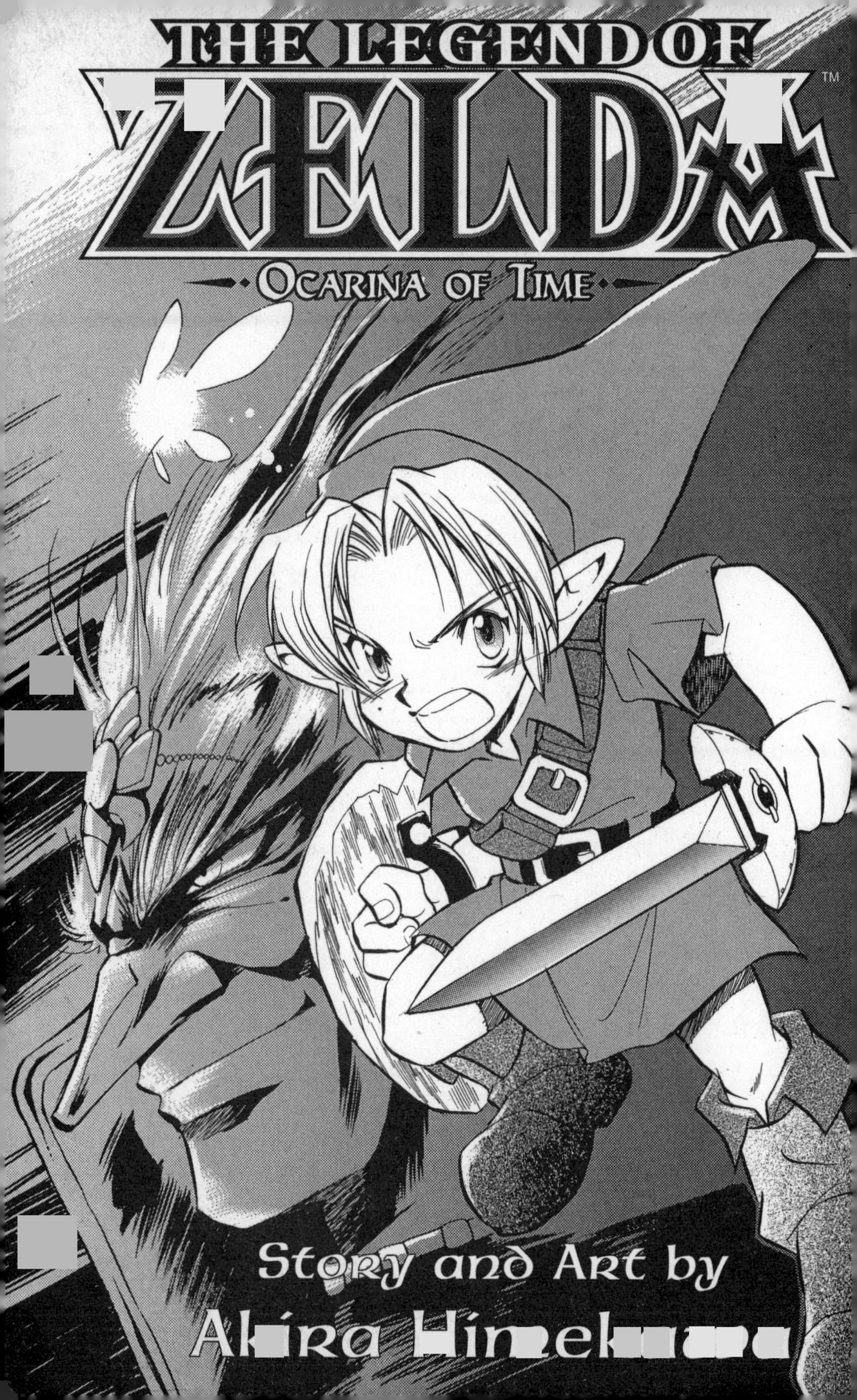
THE LEGEND OF
ZELDA™
OCARINA OF TIME
Story and Art by

THE LEGEND OF ZELDA™

OCARINA OF TIME

PART 1

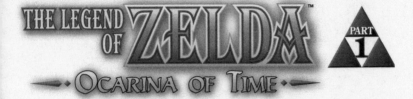

CONTENTS

OCARINA OF TIME

HERO OF TIME

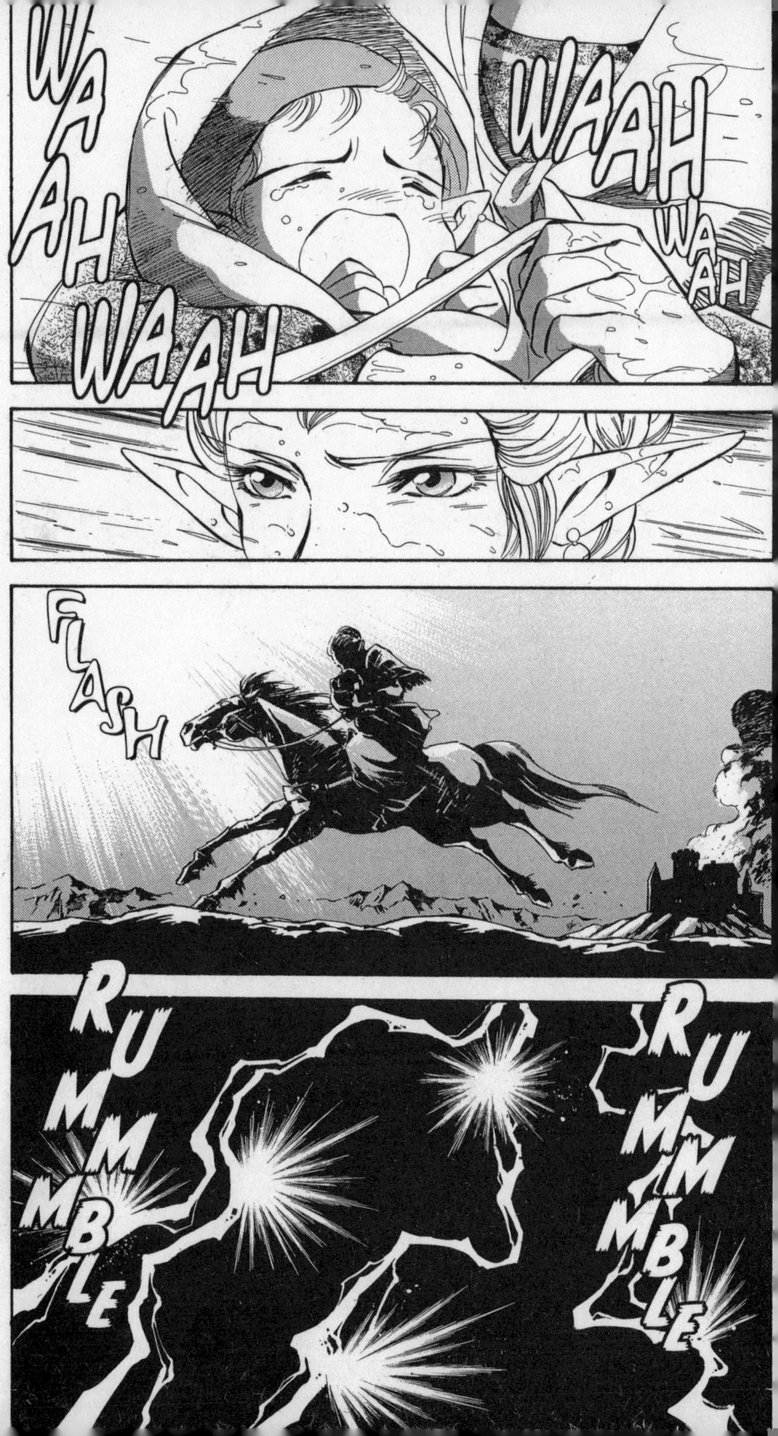
WAAH
WAAH
WAAH
WAAH
FLASH
RUMMMBLE
RUMMMBLE

OCARINA OF TIME

CHAPTER 1 THE GREAT DEKU TREE INCIDENT

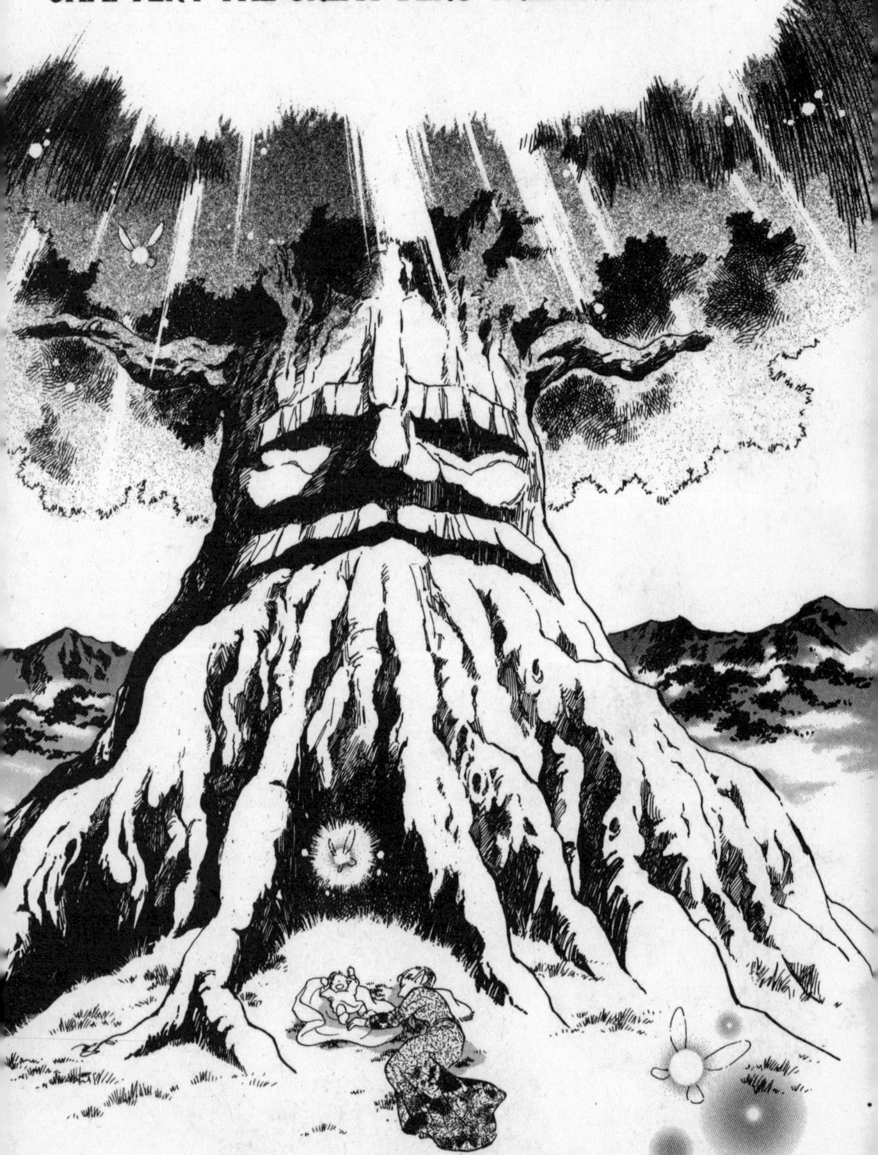

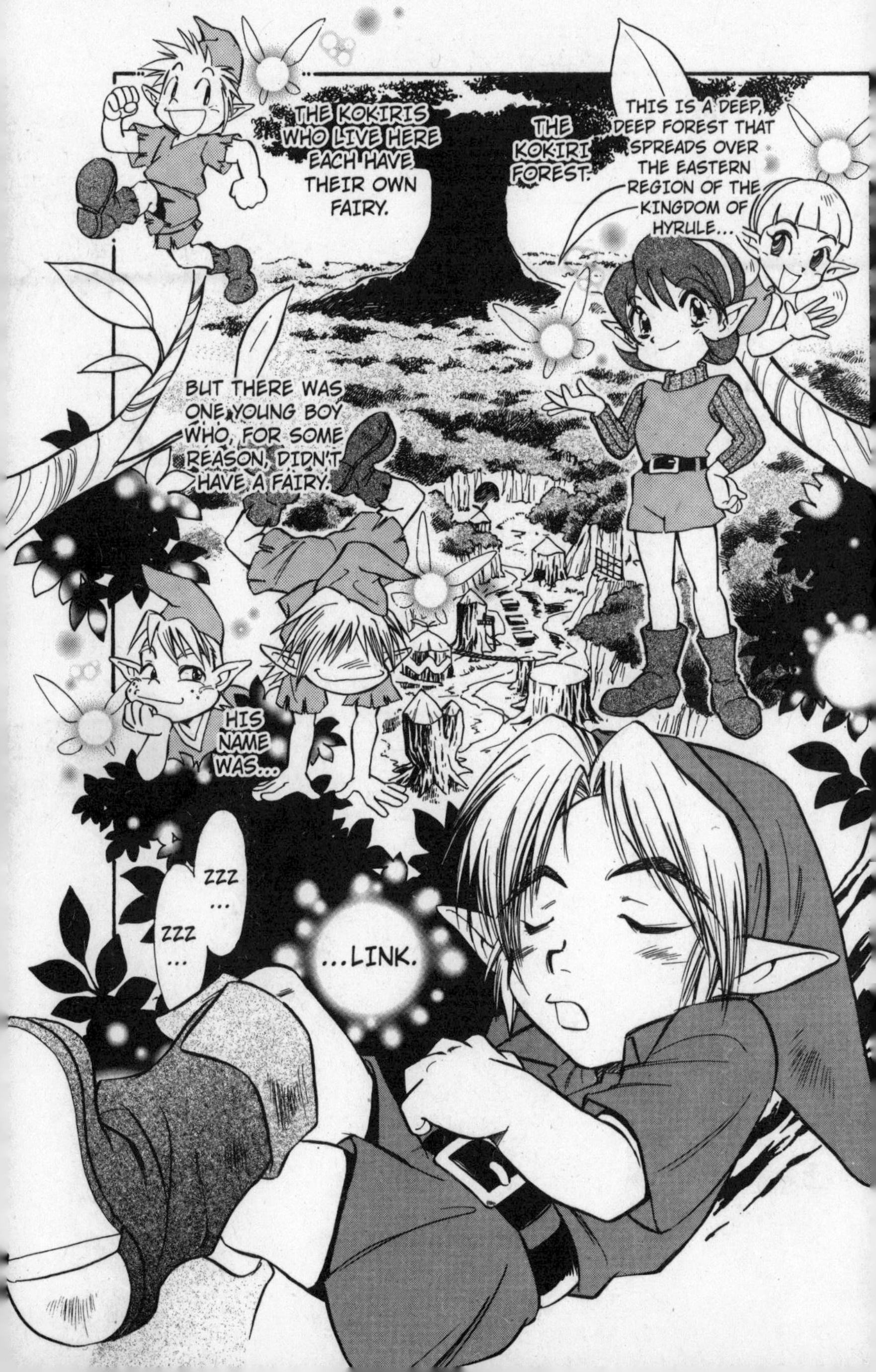
THIS IS A DEEP, DEEP FOREST THAT SPREADS OVER THE EASTERN REGION OF THE KINGDOM OF HYRULE...
THE KOKIRI FOREST.
THE KOKIRIS WHO LIVE HERE EACH HAVE THEIR OWN FAIRY.
BUT THERE WAS ONE YOUNG BOY WHO, FOR SOME REASON, DIDN'T HAVE A FAIRY.
HIS NAME WAS...
...LINK.
ZZZ ... ZZZ ...

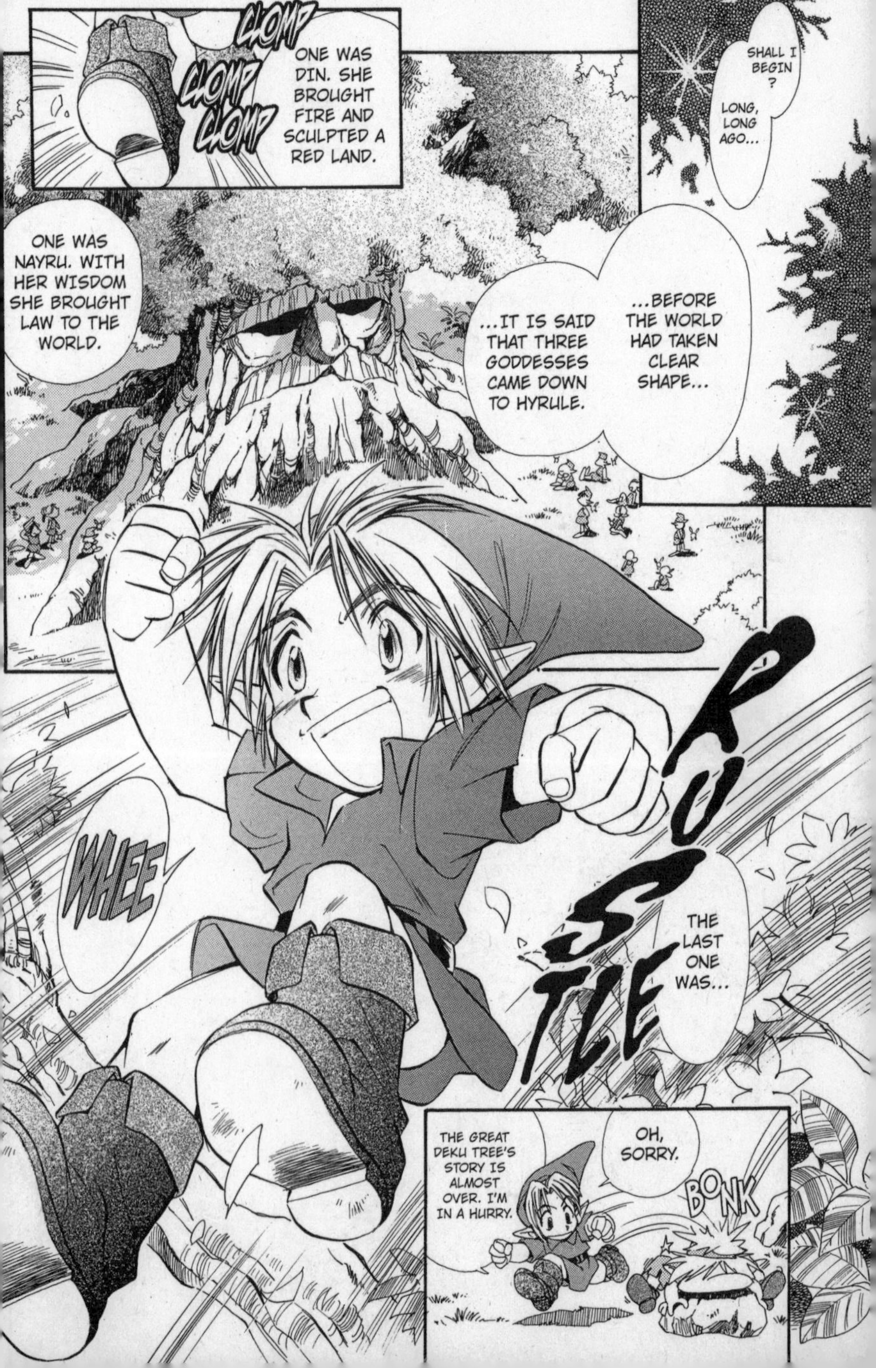
SHALL I BEGIN?
LONG, LONG AGO...
...BEFORE THE WORLD HAD TAKEN CLEAR SHAPE...
...IT IS SAID THAT THREE GODDESSES CAME DOWN TO HYRULE.
CLOMP CLOMP CLOMP
ONE WAS DIN. SHE BROUGHT FIRE AND SCULPTED A RED LAND.
ONE WAS NAYRU. WITH HER WISDOM SHE BROUGHT LAW TO THE WORLD.
RUSTLE
THE LAST ONE WAS...
WHEE
OH, SORRY.
THE GREAT DEKU TREE'S STORY IS ALMOST OVER. I'M IN A HURRY.
BONK

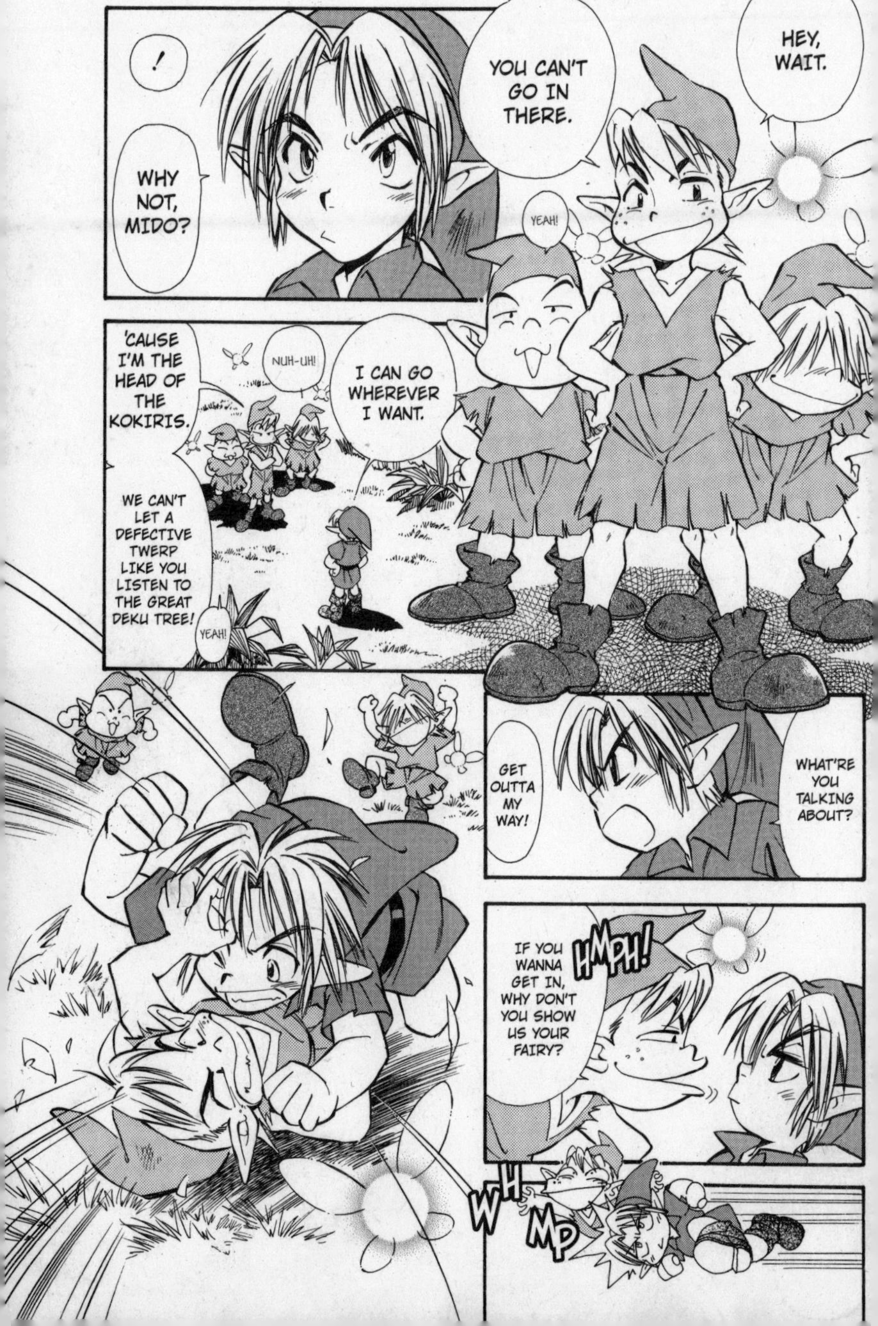
HEY, WAIT.
YOU CAN'T GO IN THERE.
YEAH!
!
WHY NOT, MIDO?
I CAN GO WHEREVER I WANT.
NUH-UH!
'CAUSE I'M THE HEAD OF THE KOKIRIS.
WE CAN'T LET A DEFECTIVE TWERP LIKE YOU LISTEN TO THE GREAT DEKU TREE!
YEAH!
WHAT'RE YOU TALKING ABOUT?
GET OUTTA MY WAY!
IF YOU WANNA GET IN, WHY DON'T YOU SHOW US YOUR FAIRY?
HMPH!
WHMP

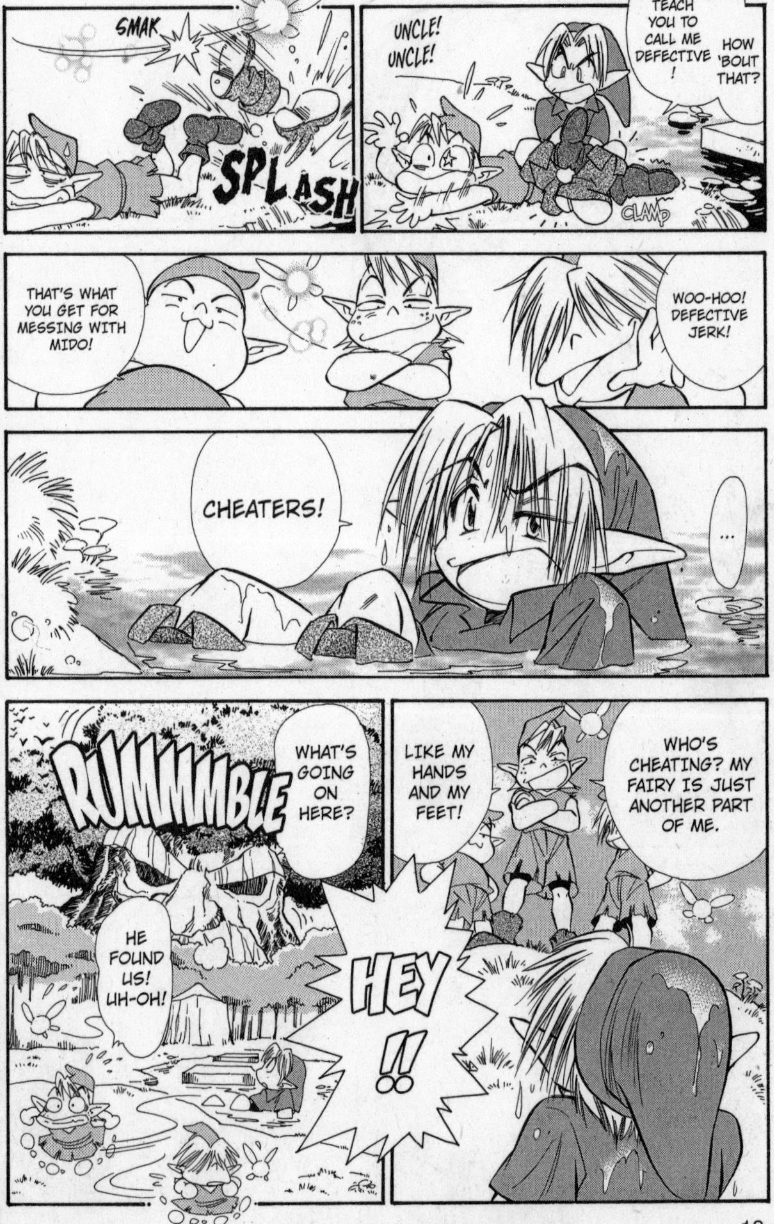
THAT'LL TEACH YOU TO CALL ME DEFECTIVE!
HOW 'BOUT THAT?
UNCLE! UNCLE!
CLAMP
SMAK
SPLASH
WOO-HOO! DEFECTIVE JERK!
THAT'S WHAT YOU GET FOR MESSING WITH MIDO!
...
CHEATERS!
WHO'S CHEATING? MY FAIRY IS JUST ANOTHER PART OF ME.
LIKE MY HANDS AND MY FEET!
HEY!!
WHAT'S GOING ON HERE?
RUMMMBLE
HE FOUND US! UH-OH!

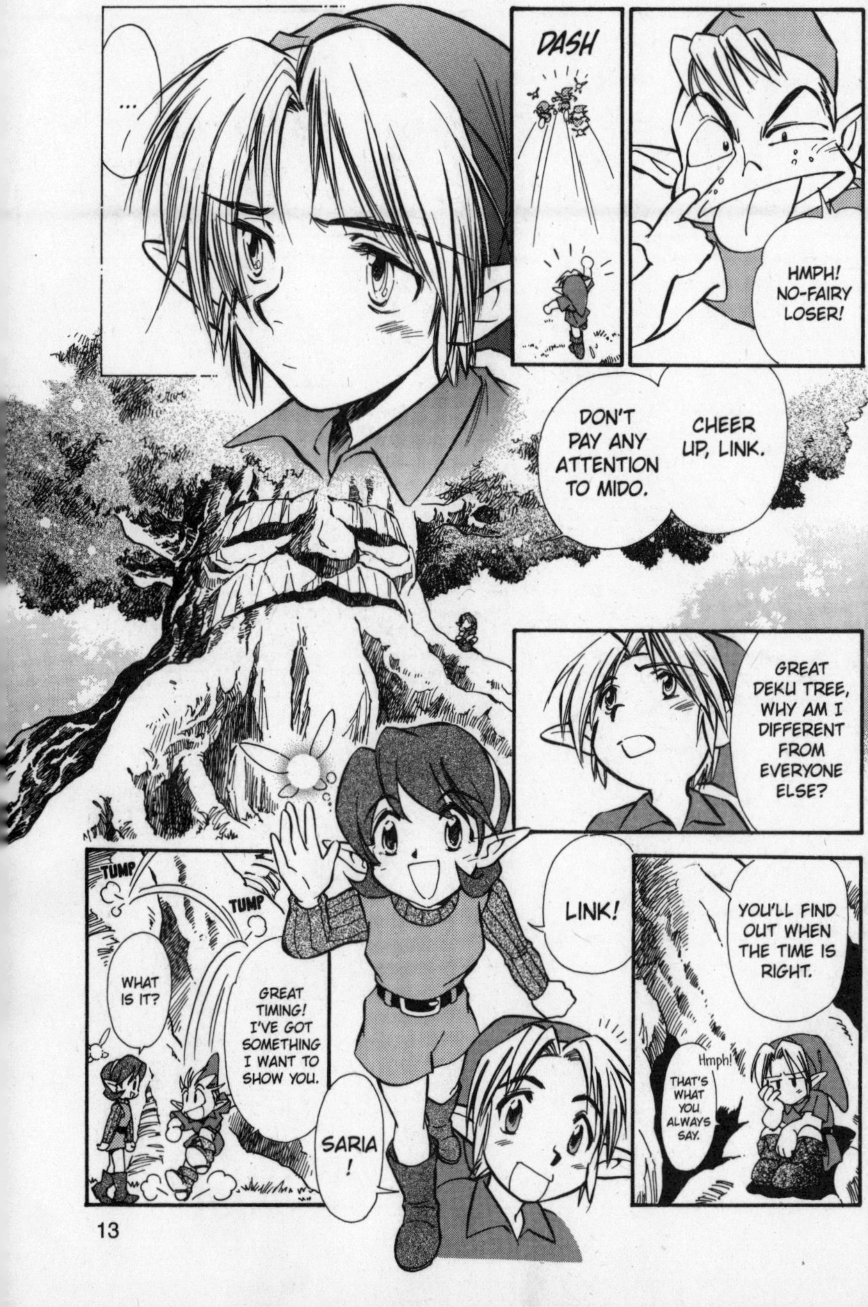
HMPH! NO-FAIRY LOSER!
DASH
...
CHEER UP, LINK.
DON'T PAY ANY ATTENTION TO MIDO.
GREAT DEKU TREE, WHY AM I DIFFERENT FROM EVERYONE ELSE?
YOU'LL FIND OUT WHEN THE TIME IS RIGHT.
Hmph!
THAT'S WHAT YOU ALWAYS SAY.
LINK!
SARIA!
TUMP
TUMP
GREAT TIMING! I'VE GOT SOMETHING I WANT TO SHOW YOU.
WHAT IS IT?

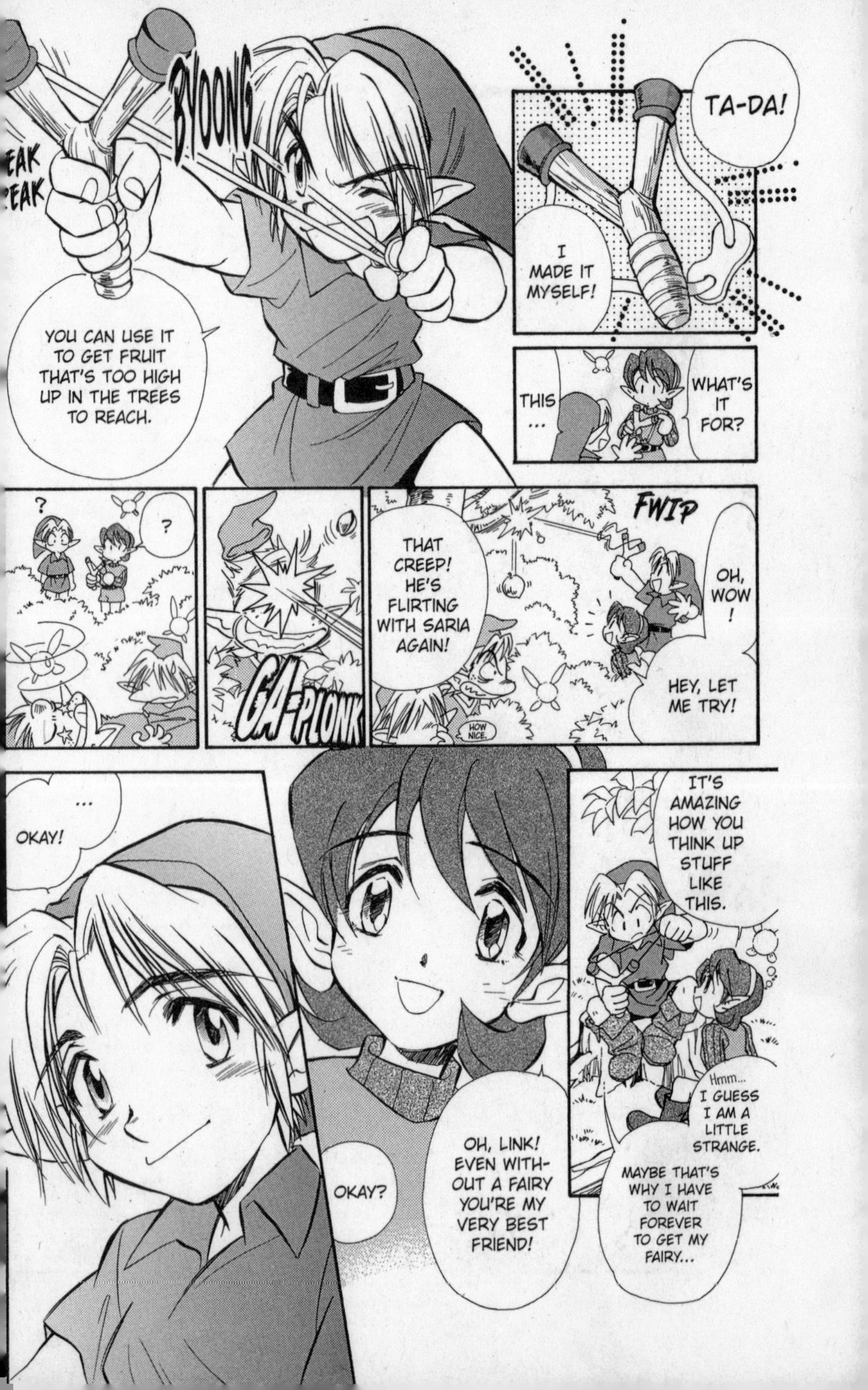

TA-DA!
I MADE IT MYSELF!
WHAT'S IT FOR?
THIS ...
BYOONG
EAK
EAK
YOU CAN USE IT TO GET FRUIT THAT'S TOO HIGH UP IN THE TREES TO REACH.
FWIP
OH, WOW!
HEY, LET ME TRY!
THAT CREEP! HE'S FLIRTING WITH SARIA AGAIN!
HOW NICE.
GA-PLONK
?
?
IT'S AMAZING HOW YOU THINK UP STUFF LIKE THIS.
Hmm... I GUESS I AM A LITTLE STRANGE.
MAYBE THAT'S WHY I HAVE TO WAIT FOREVER TO GET MY FAIRY...
OH, LINK! EVEN WITH-OUT A FAIRY YOU'RE MY VERY BEST FRIEND!
OKAY?
...
OKAY!

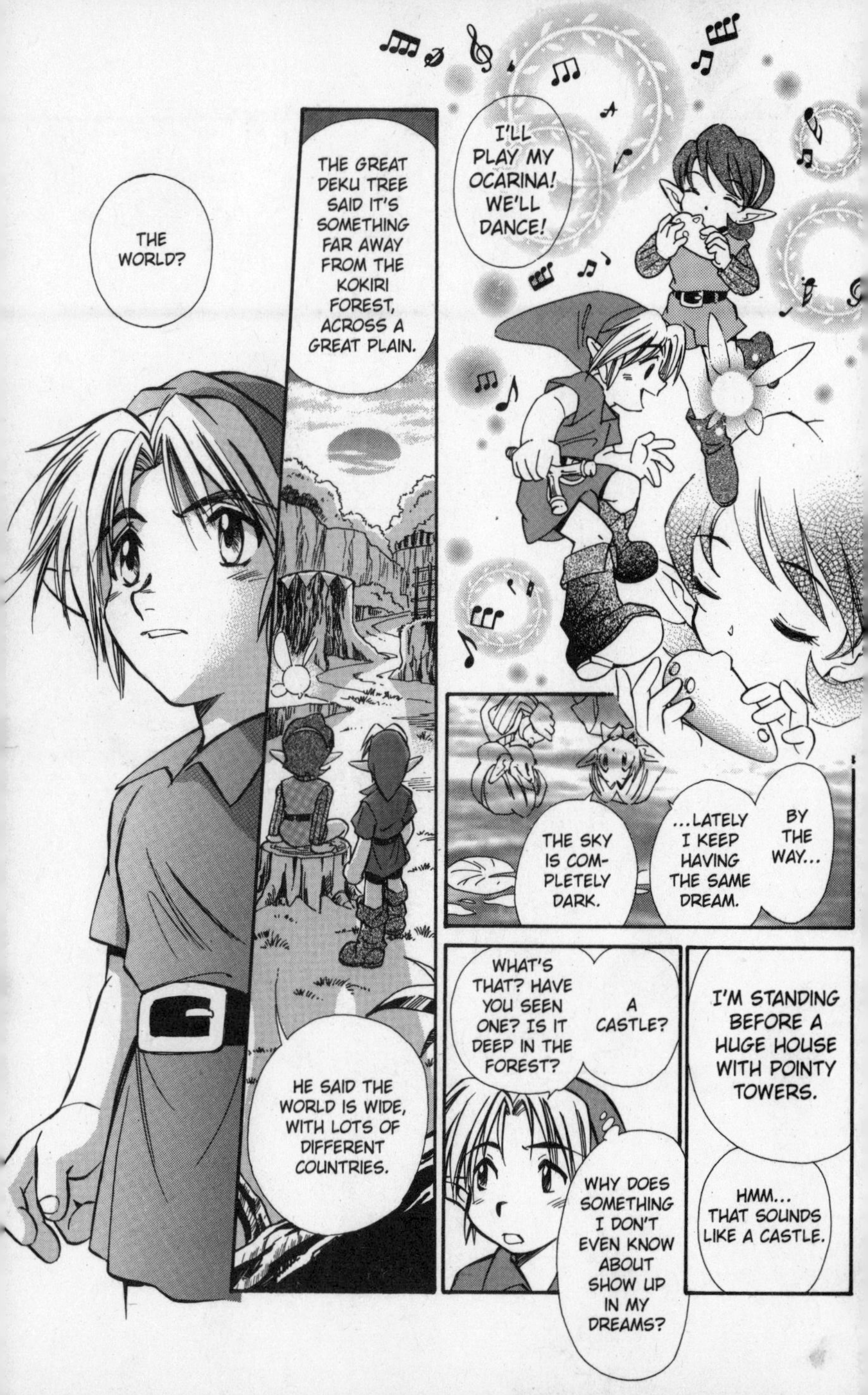
I'LL PLAY MY OCARINA! WE'LL DANCE!
BY THE WAY...
...LATELY I KEEP HAVING THE SAME DREAM.
THE SKY IS COMPLETELY DARK.
I'M STANDING BEFORE A HUGE HOUSE WITH POINTY TOWERS.
HMM... THAT SOUNDS LIKE A CASTLE.
A CASTLE?
WHAT'S THAT? HAVE YOU SEEN ONE? IS IT DEEP IN THE FOREST?
WHY DOES SOMETHING I DON'T EVEN KNOW ABOUT SHOW UP IN MY DREAMS?
THE GREAT DEKU TREE SAID IT'S SOMETHING FAR AWAY FROM THE KOKIRI FOREST, ACROSS A GREAT PLAIN.
HE SAID THE WORLD IS WIDE, WITH LOTS OF DIFFERENT COUNTRIES.
THE WORLD?

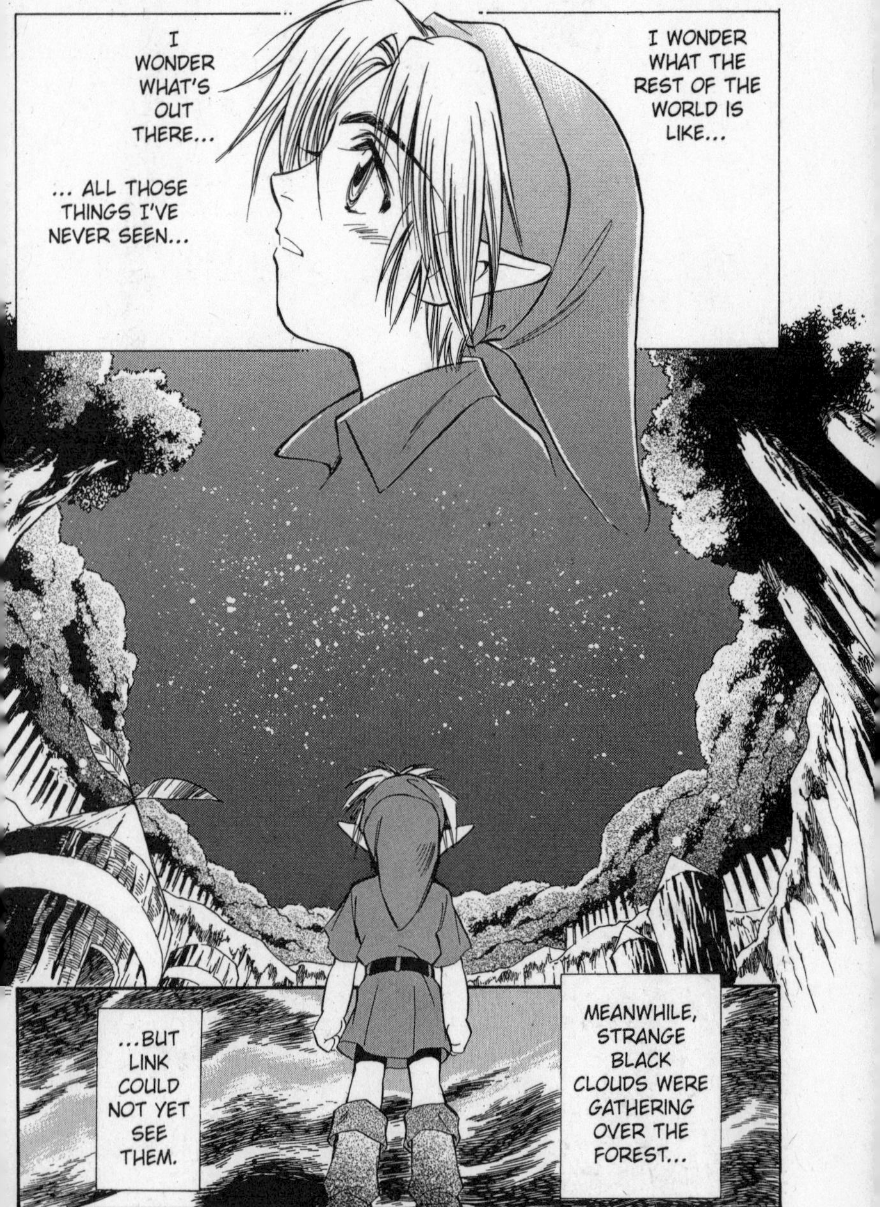
I WONDER WHAT THE REST OF THE WORLD IS LIKE...
I WONDER WHAT'S OUT THERE...
... ALL THOSE THINGS I'VE NEVER SEEN...
MEANWHILE, STRANGE BLACK CLOUDS WERE GATHERING OVER THE FOREST...
...BUT LINK COULD NOT YET SEE THEM.

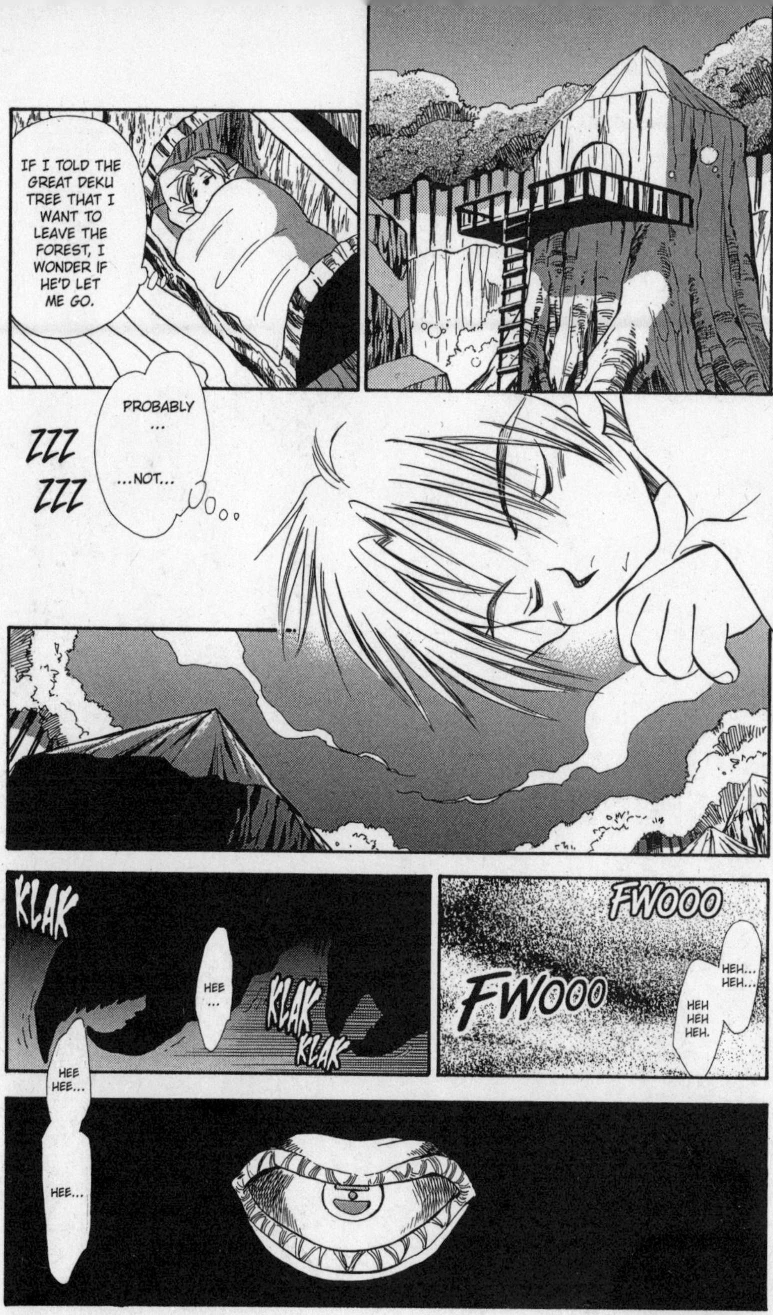
IF I TOLD THE GREAT DEKU TREE THAT I WANT TO LEAVE THE FOREST, I WONDER IF HE'D LET ME GO.
PROBABLY ... ...NOT...
ZZZ ZZZ
FWOOO
HEH... HEH... HEH HEH HEH.
FWOOO
KLAK
HEE...
KLAK KLAK
HEE HEE...
HEE...

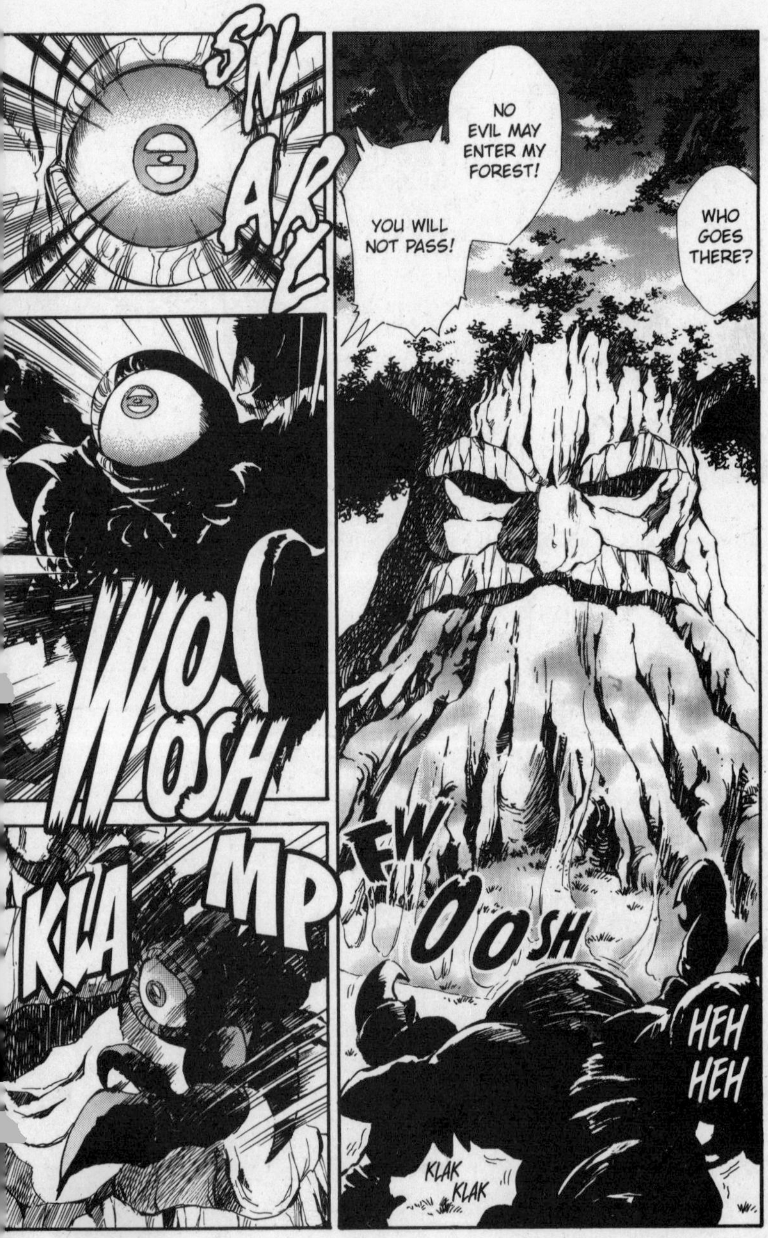
WHO GOES THERE?
NO EVIL MAY ENTER MY FOREST!
YOU WILL NOT PASS!
FWOOSH
HEH HEH
KLAK KLAK
SNARL
WOOSH
KLAMP

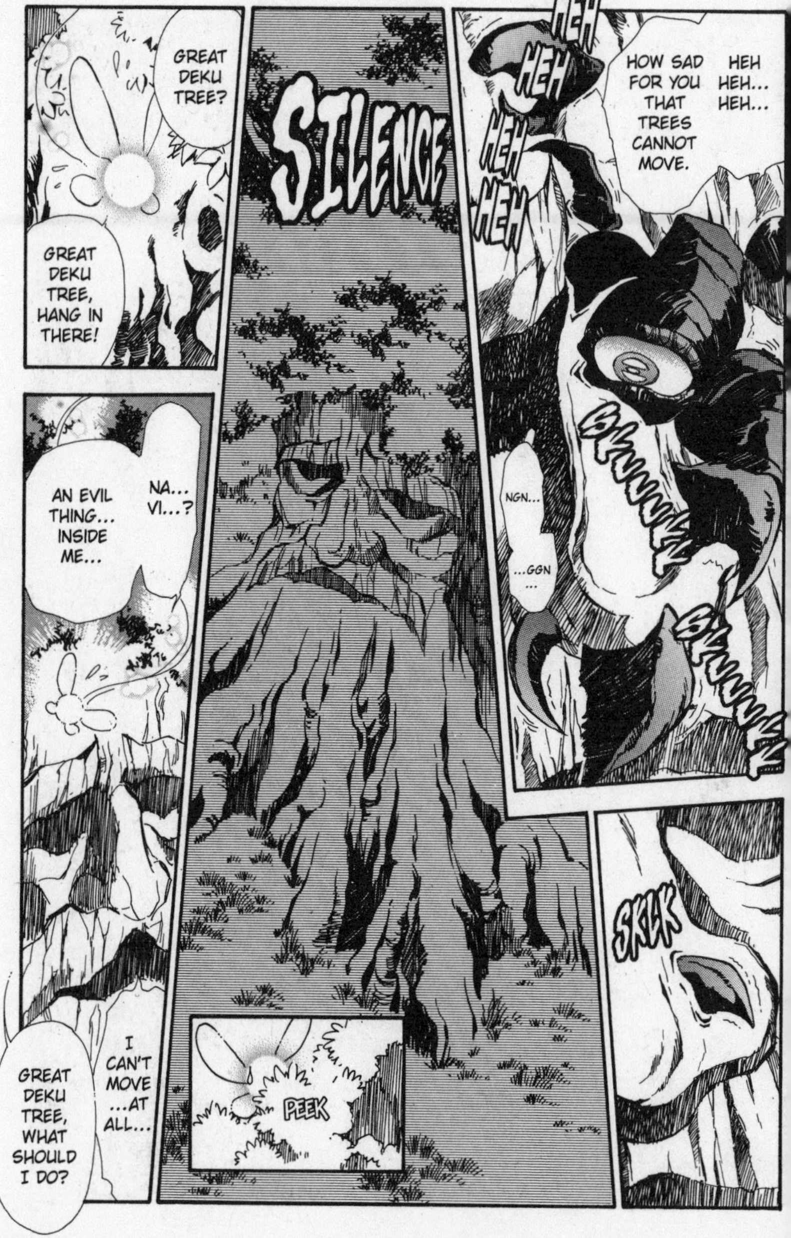
HEH HEH... HEH...
HOW SAD FOR YOU THAT TREES CANNOT MOVE.
HEH HEH HEH HEH
NGN...
...GGN ...
SKLK
SILENCE
PEEK
GREAT DEKU TREE?
GREAT DEKU TREE, HANG IN THERE!
NA... VI...?
AN EVIL THING... INSIDE ME...
I CAN'T MOVE ...AT ALL...
GREAT DEKU TREE, WHAT SHOULD I DO?

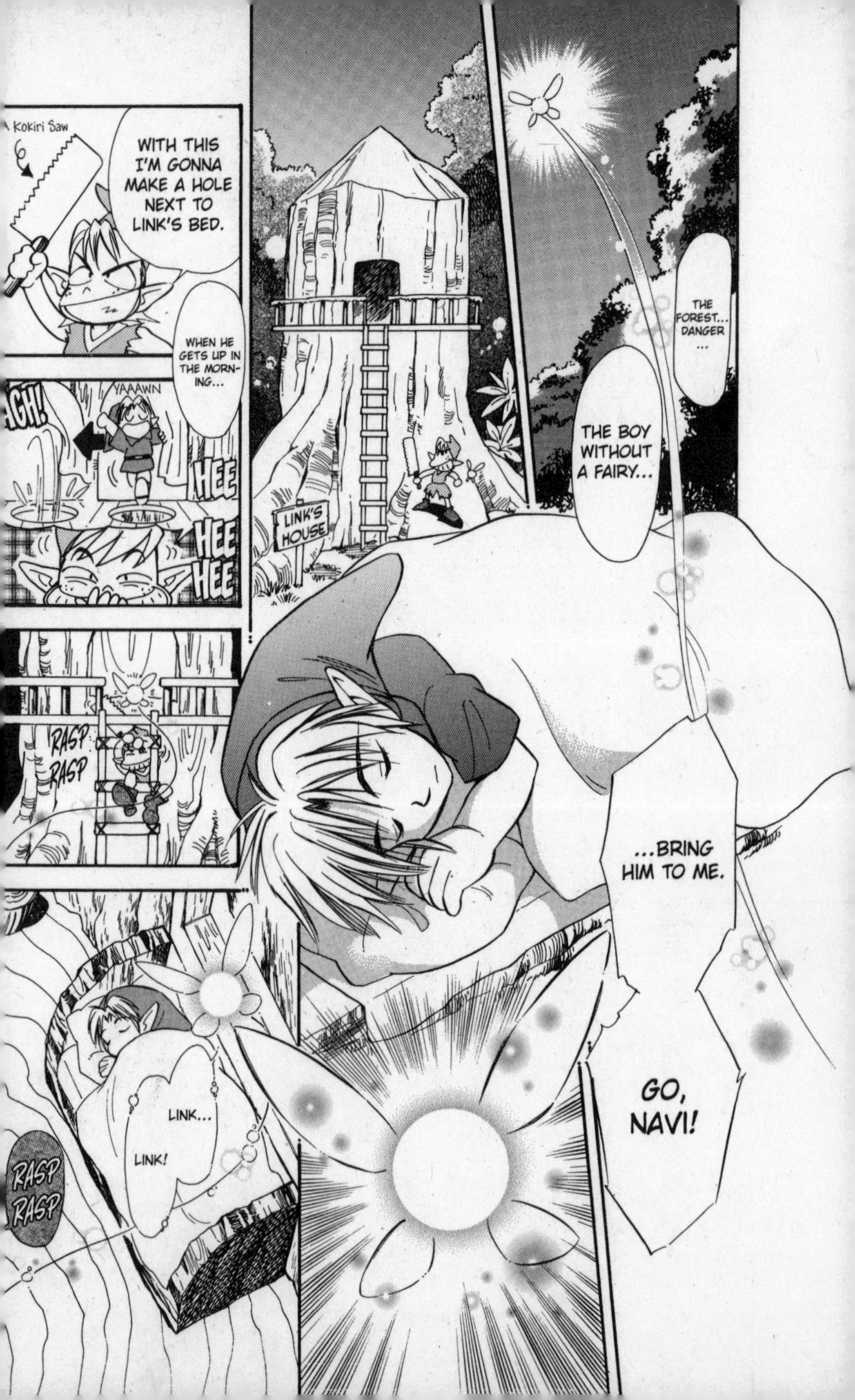
THE FOREST... DANGER ...
THE BOY WITHOUT A FAIRY...
...BRING HIM TO ME.
GO, NAVI!
LINK'S HOUSE
A Kokiri Saw
WITH THIS I'M GONNA MAKE A HOLE NEXT TO LINK'S BED.
WHEN HE GETS UP IN THE MORNING...
YAAAWN
GH!
HEE HEE HEE
RASP RASP
LINK...
LINK!
RASP RASP

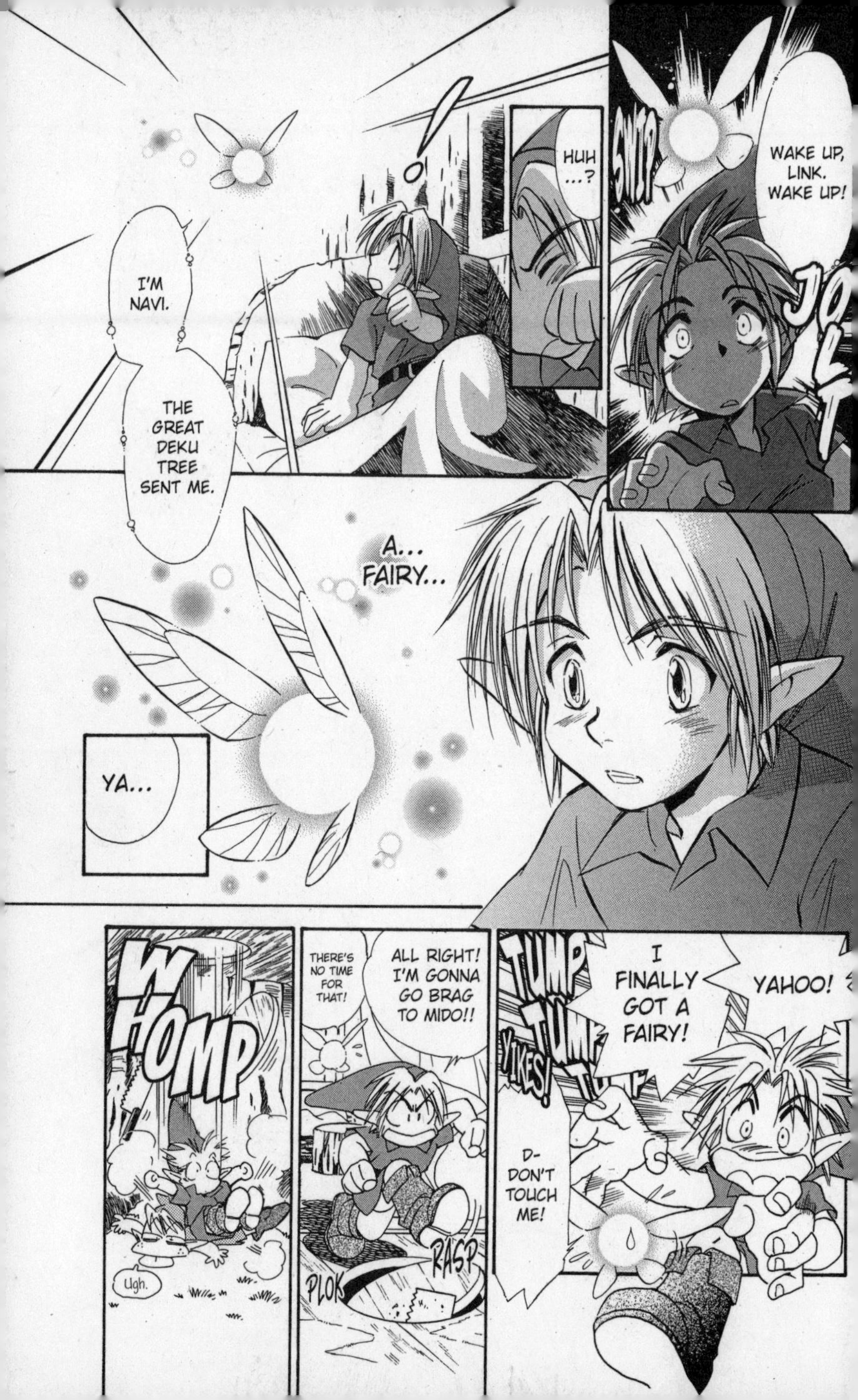
WAKE UP, LINK. WAKE UP!
JOLT
HUH ...?
!
I'M NAVI.
THE GREAT DEKU TREE SENT ME.
A... FAIRY...
YA...
YAHOO!
I FINALLY GOT A FAIRY!
TUMP TUMP TUMP
YIKES!
D-DON'T TOUCH ME!
ALL RIGHT! I'M GONNA GO BRAG TO MIDO!!
THERE'S NO TIME FOR THAT!
RASP
PLOK
WHOMP
Ugh.

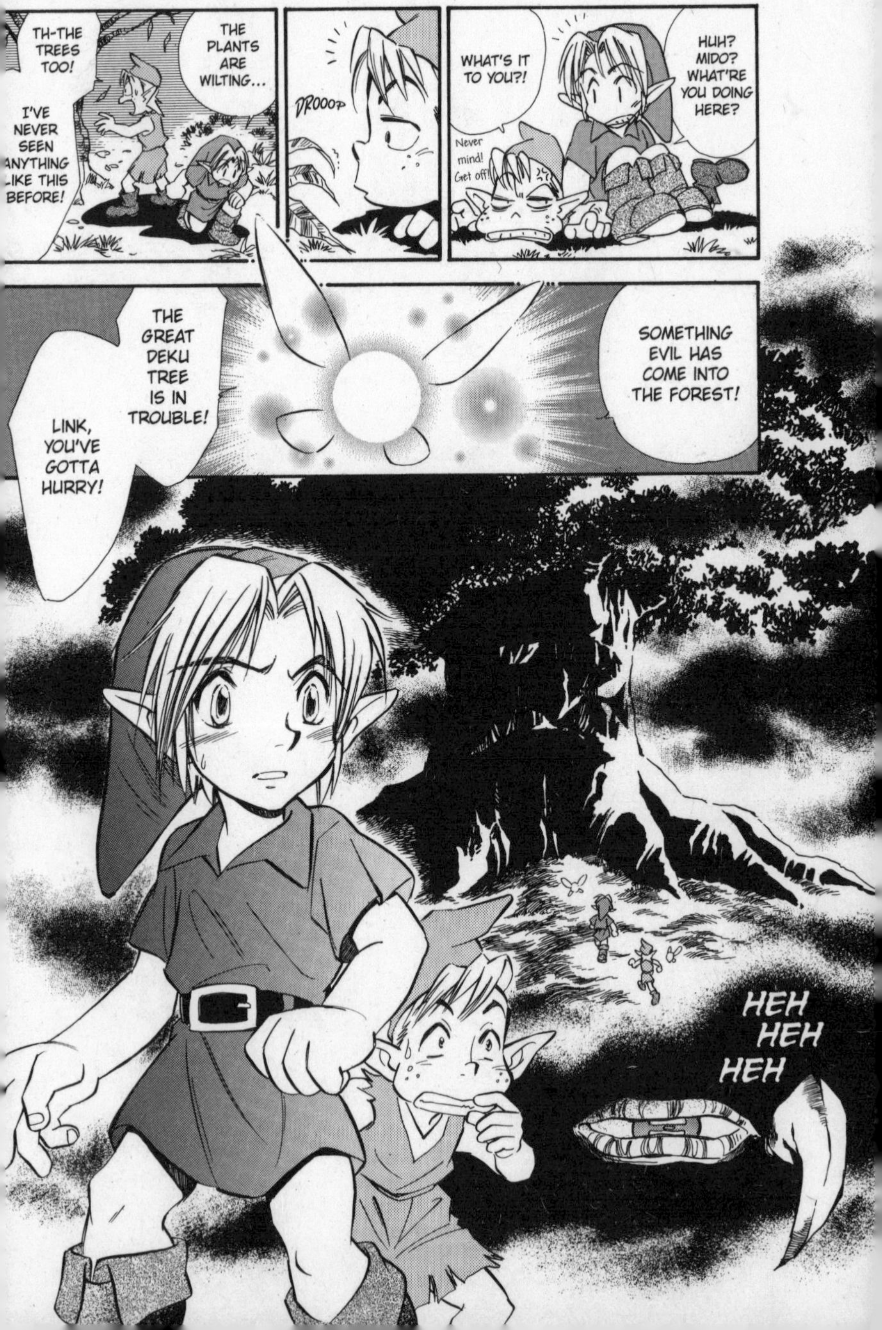
HUH? MIDO? WHAT'RE YOU DOING HERE?
WHAT'S IT TO YOU?!
Never mind! Get off!
DROOOP
THE PLANTS ARE WILTING...
TH-THE TREES TOO!
I'VE NEVER SEEN ANYTHING LIKE THIS BEFORE!
SOMETHING EVIL HAS COME INTO THE FOREST!
THE GREAT DEKU TREE IS IN TROUBLE!
LINK, YOU'VE GOTTA HURRY!
HEH HEH HEH

BONUS ILLUSTRATION 1

A ROUGH SKETCH HIMEKAWA SENSEI DREW BEFORE THE SERIES

CHAPTER 2
LINK'S JOURNEY BEGINS

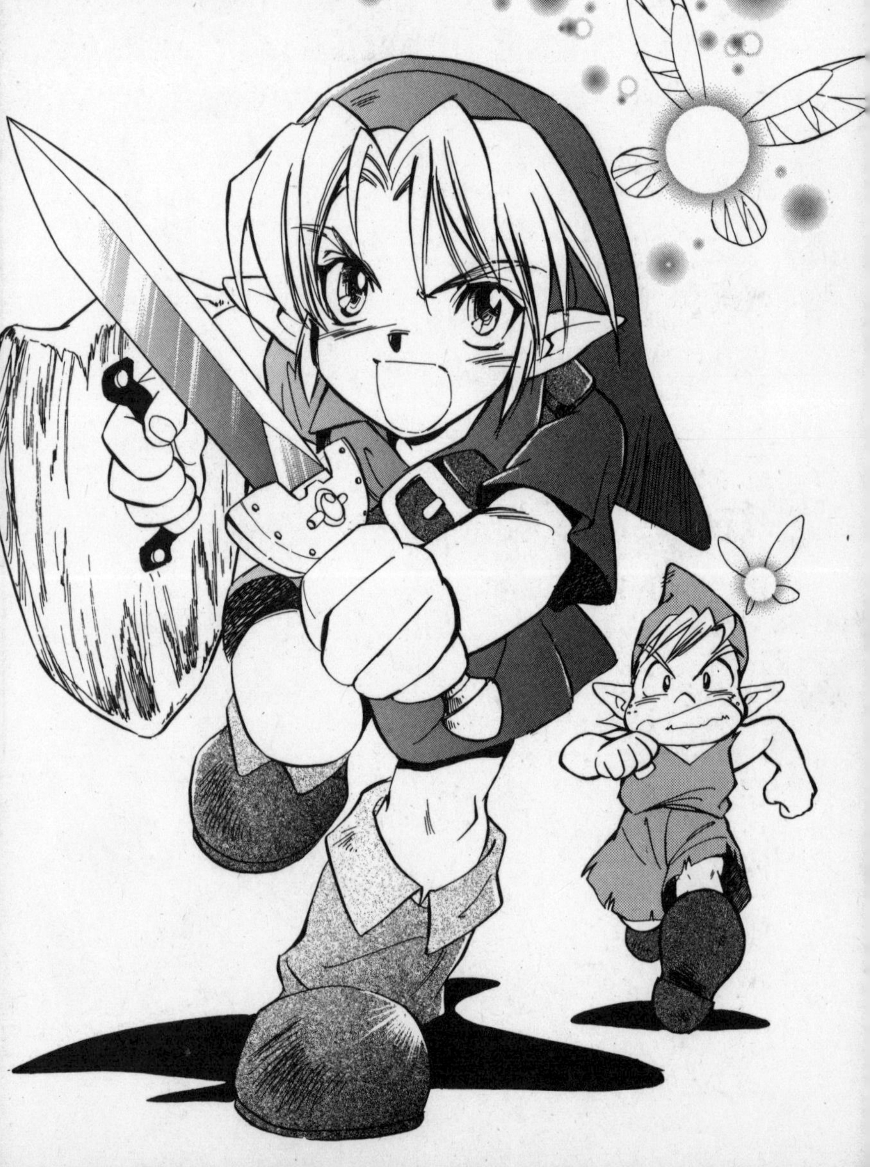

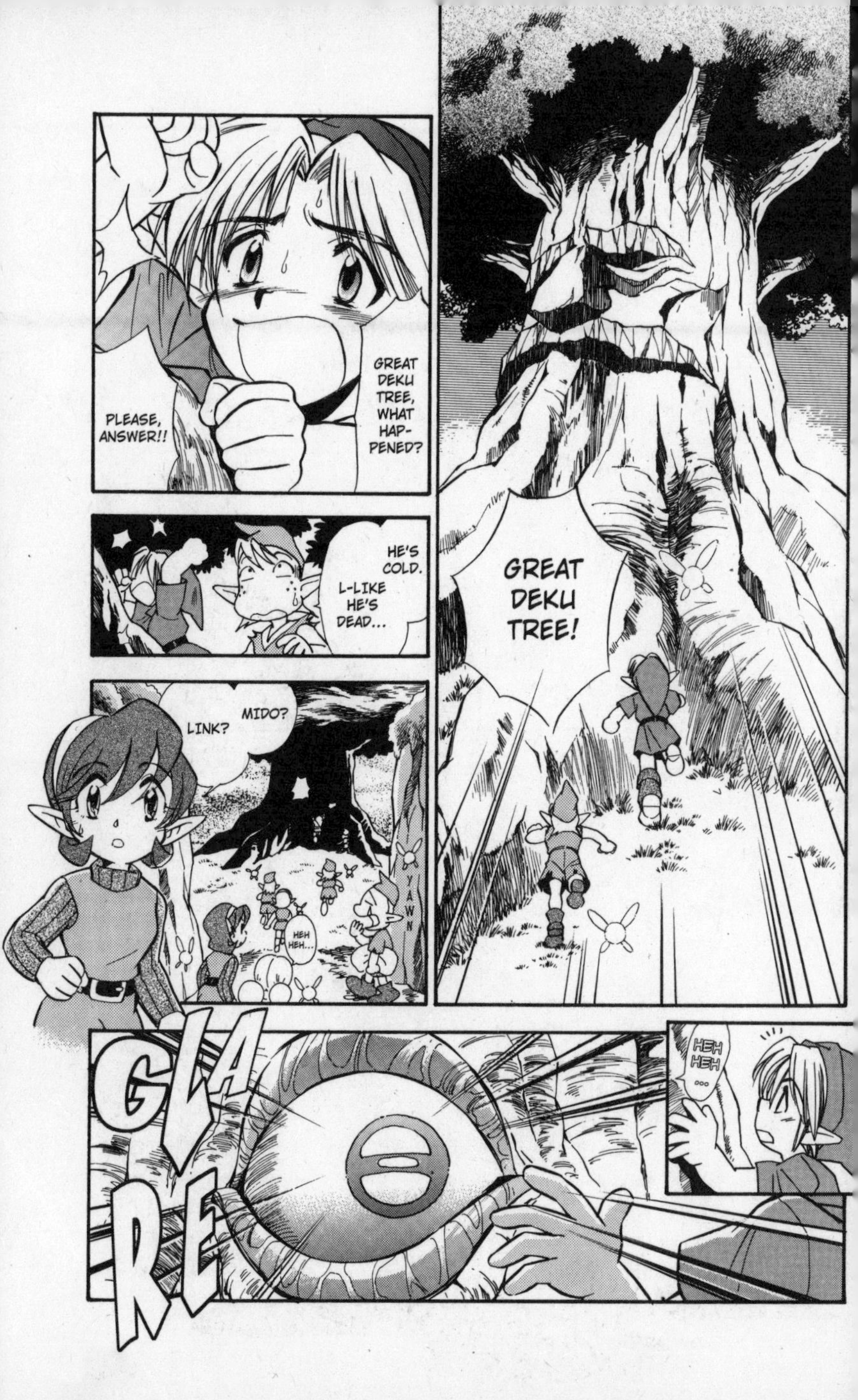
GREAT DEKU TREE!
GREAT DEKU TREE, WHAT HAP-PENED?
PLEASE, ANSWER!!
HE'S COLD.
L-LIKE HE'S DEAD...
MIDO?
LINK?
YAWN
HEH HEH...
HEH HEH ...
GLARE

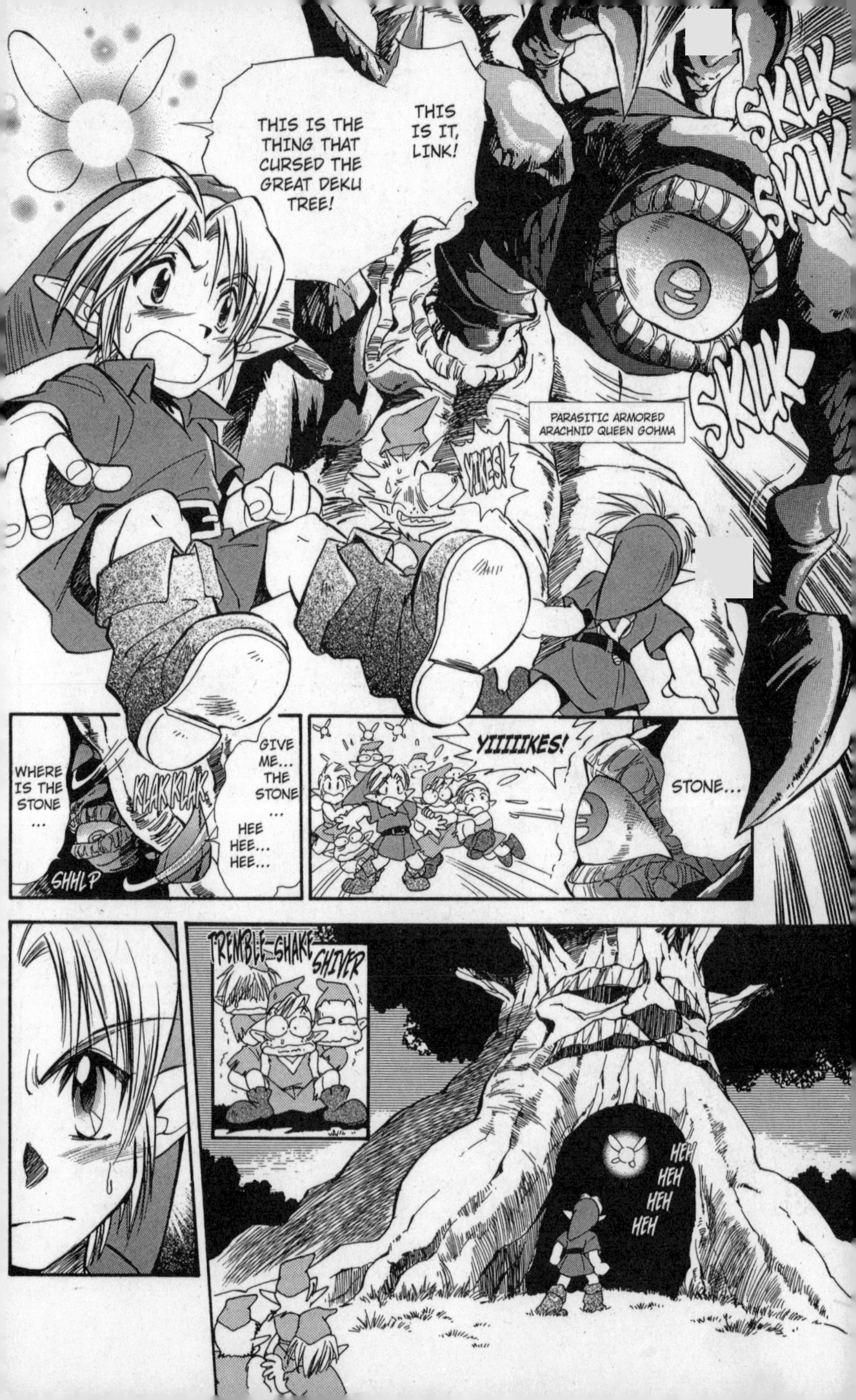
SKLK
SKLK
SKLK
THIS IS IT, LINK!
THIS IS THE THING THAT CURSED THE GREAT DEKU TREE!
PARASITIC ARMORED ARACHNID QUEEN GOHMA
YIKES!
STONE...
YIIIIIKES!
GIVE ME... THE STONE...
HEE HEE... HEE...
KLAK KLAK
WHERE IS THE STONE...
SHHLP
HEH HEH HEH HEH
TREMBLE-SHAKE
SHIVER

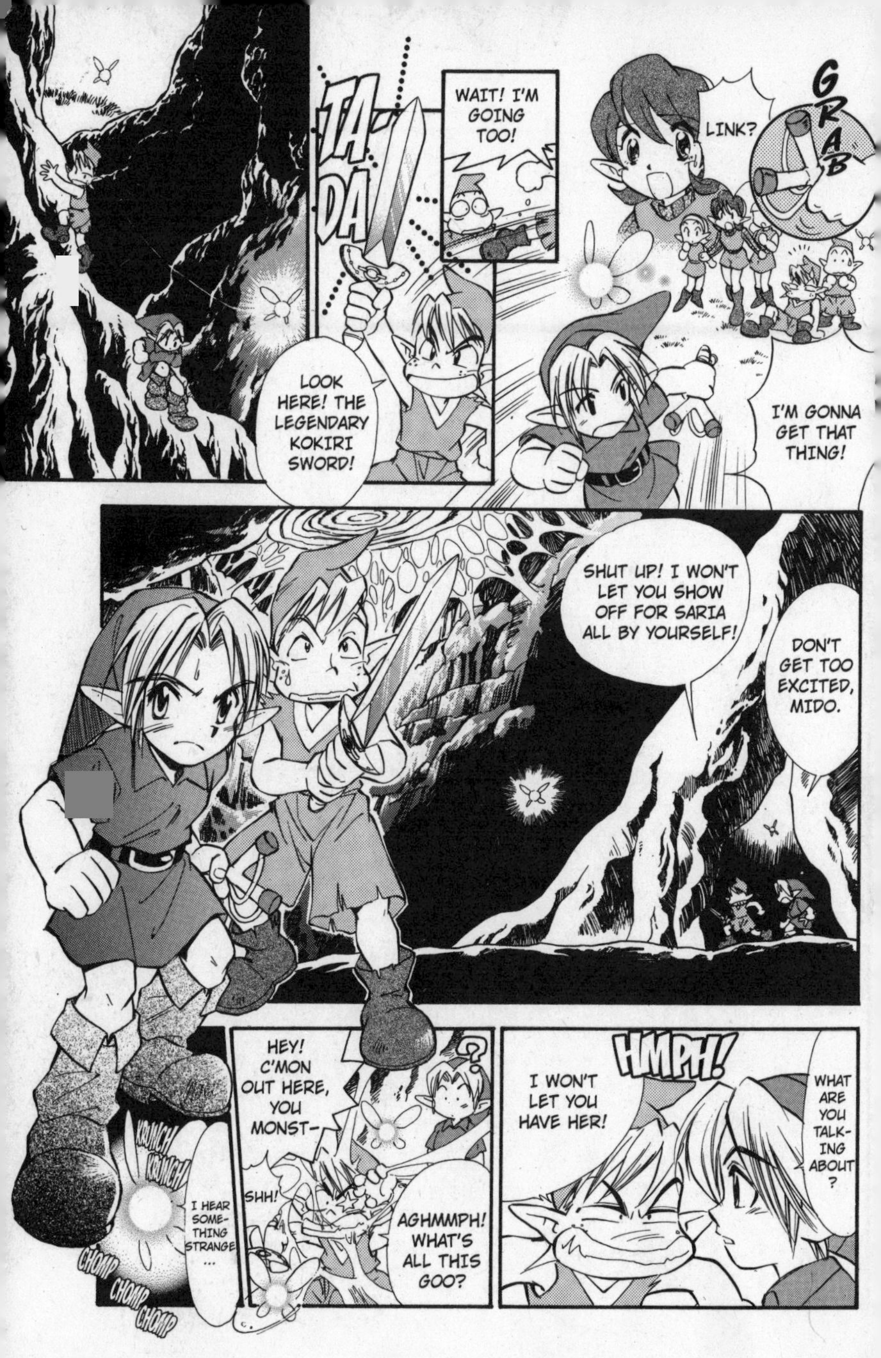
LINK?
GRAB
I'M GONNA GET THAT THING!
WAIT! I'M GOING TOO!
TA-DA
LOOK HERE! THE LEGENDARY KOKIRI SWORD!
DON'T GET TOO EXCITED, MIDO.
SHUT UP! I WON'T LET YOU SHOW OFF FOR SARIA ALL BY YOURSELF!
WHAT ARE YOU TALK-ING ABOUT?
HMPH!
I WON'T LET YOU HAVE HER!
HEY! C'MON OUT HERE, YOU MONST-
SHH!
AGHMMPH! WHAT'S ALL THIS GOO?
KRUNCH KRUNCH
I HEAR SOME-THING STRANGE ...
CHOMP CHOMP CHOMP

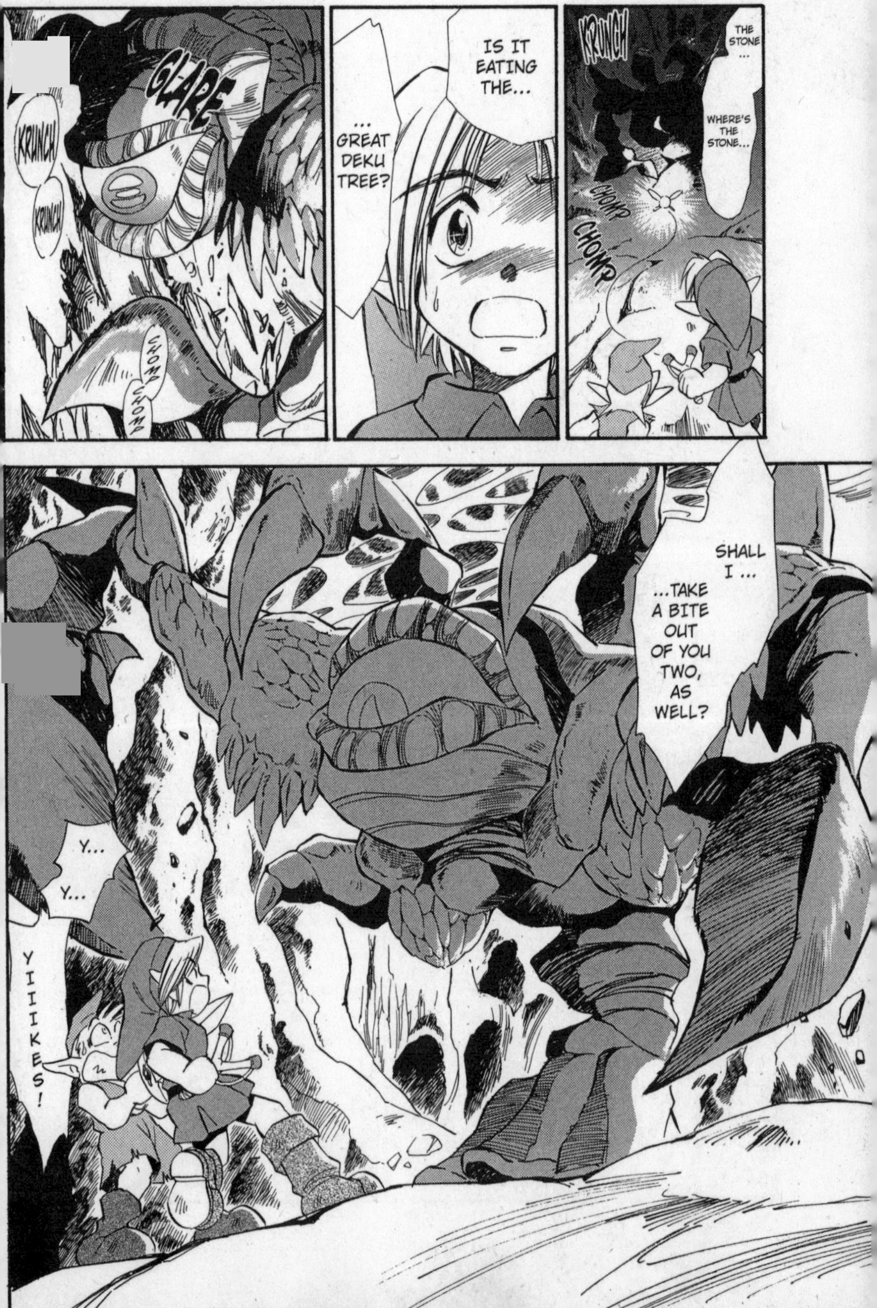
KRUNCH
THE STONE...
WHERE'S THE STONE...
CHOMP
CHOMP
IS IT EATING THE...
...GREAT DEKU TREE?
GLARE
KRUNCH
KRUNCH
CHOMP CHOMP
SHALL I...
...TAKE A BITE OUT OF YOU TWO, AS WELL?
Y...
Y...
YIIIKES!

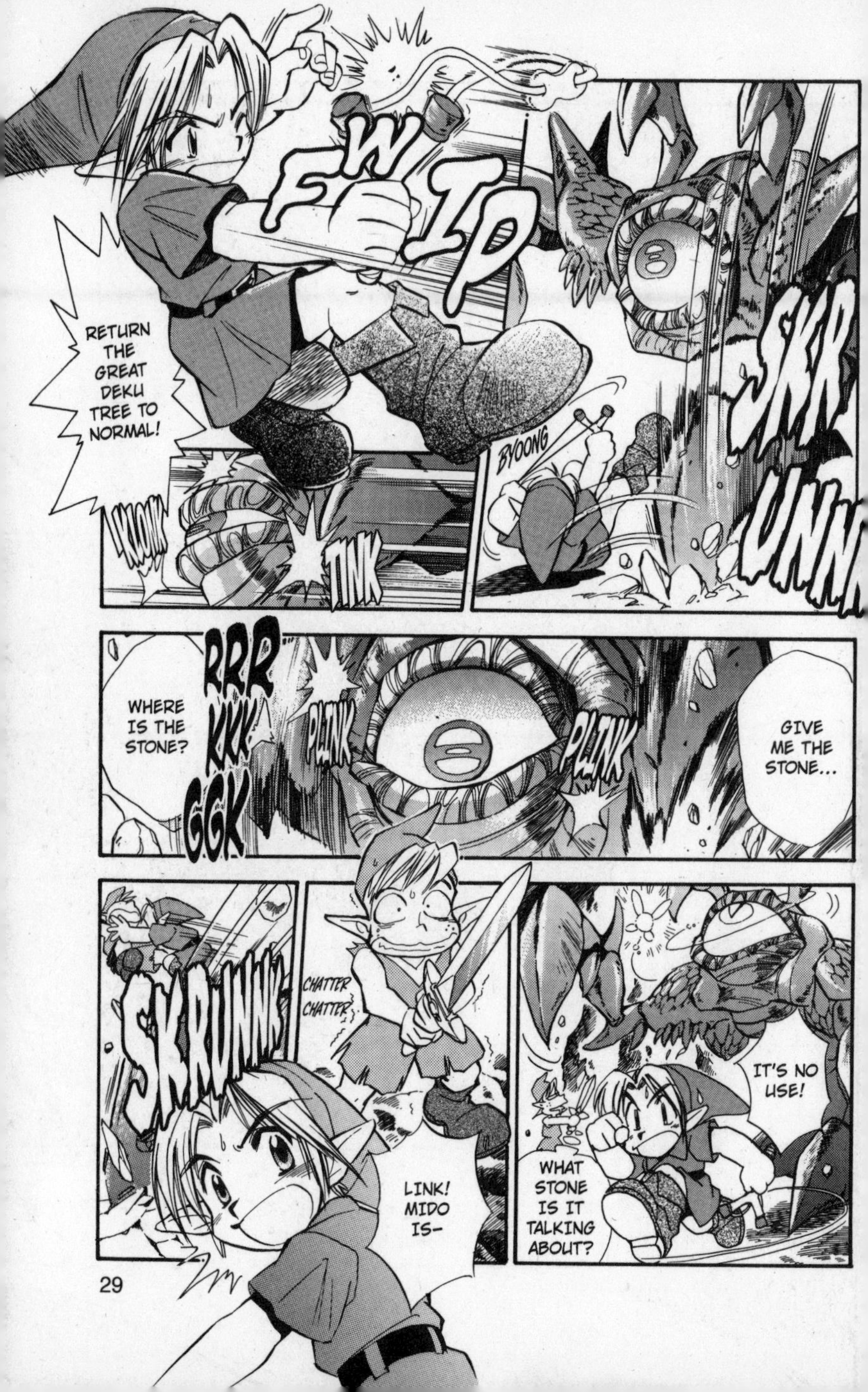
FWIP
SKRUNN
BYOONG
RETURN THE GREAT DEKU TREE TO NORMAL!
KRONK
TINK
GIVE ME THE STONE...
PLINK
PLINK
RRRKKKGGK
WHERE IS THE STONE?
IT'S NO USE!
WHAT STONE IS IT TALKING ABOUT?
CHATTER CHATTER
SKRUNNK
LINK! MIDO IS-

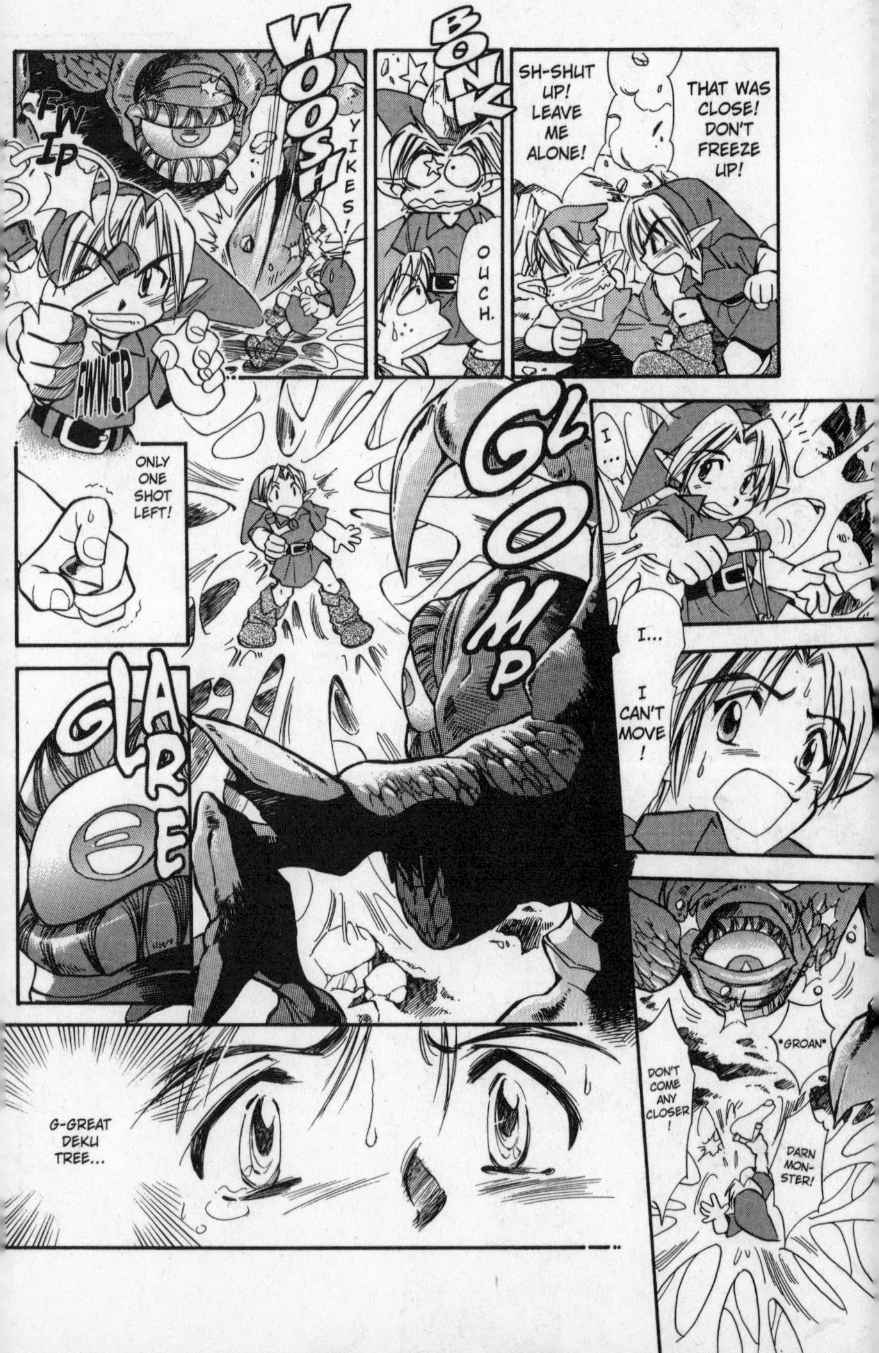
THAT WAS CLOSE! DON'T FREEZE UP!
SH-SHUT UP! LEAVE ME ALONE!
BONK
OUCH.
WOOSH
YIKES!
FWIP
FWWIP
I...
GLOMP
ONLY ONE SHOT LEFT!
I...
I CAN'T MOVE!
GLARE
GROAN
DARN MON-STER!
DON'T COME ANY CLOSER!
G-GREAT DEKU TREE...

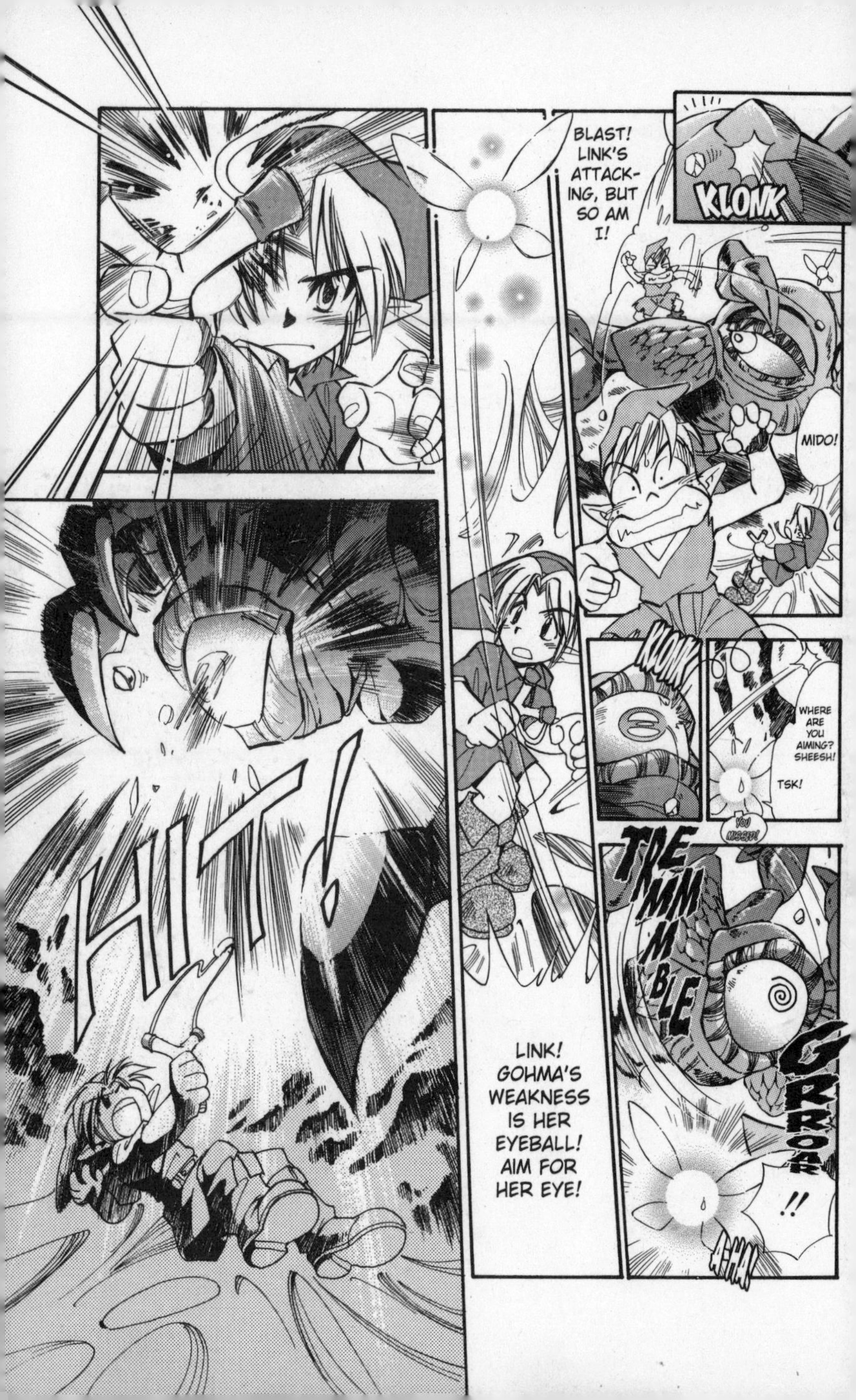
KLONK
MIDO!
KLONK
WHERE ARE YOU AIMING? SHEESH!
TSK!
YOU MISSED!
TREMMMMBLE
GRRROAR
!!
AHA!
BLAST! LINK'S ATTACKING, BUT SO AM I!
LINK! GOHMA'S WEAKNESS IS HER EYEBALL! AIM FOR HER EYE!
HIT!

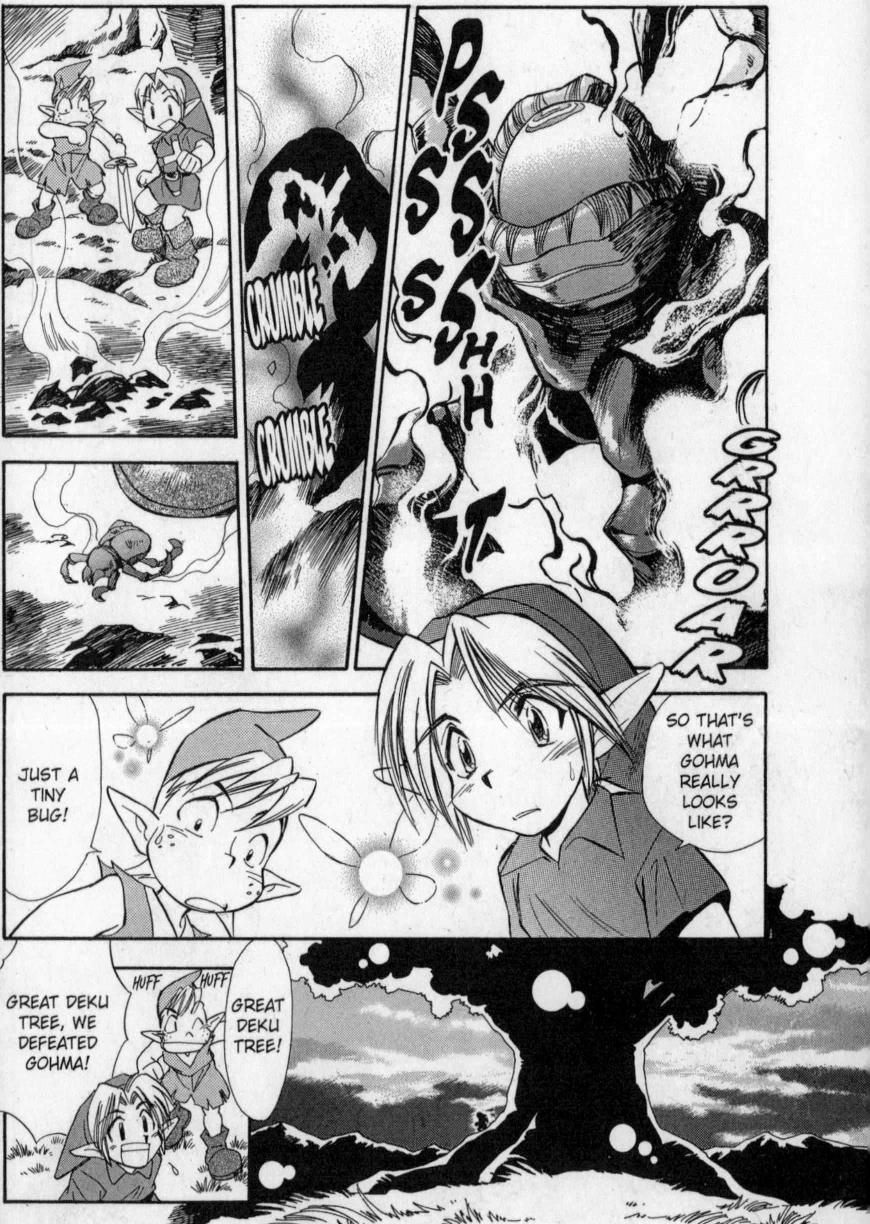
PSSSSSHHT
GRRROAR
CRUMBLE
CRUMBLE
SO THAT'S WHAT GOHMA REALLY LOOKS LIKE?
JUST A TINY BUG!
GREAT DEKU TREE!
HUFF
HUFF
GREAT DEKU TREE, WE DEFEATED GOHMA!

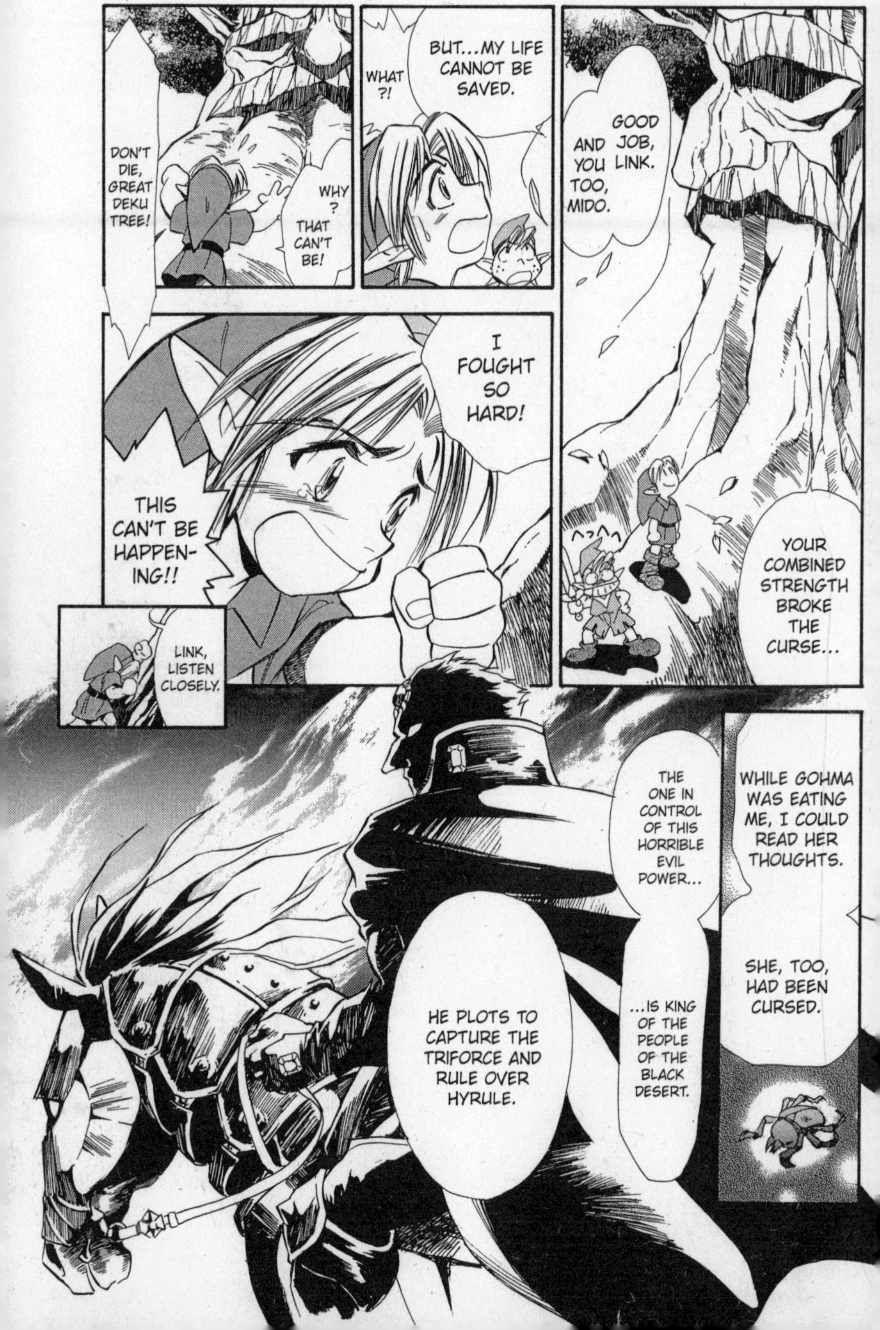
GOOD JOB, LINK.
AND YOU TOO, MIDO.
YOUR COMBINED STRENGTH BROKE THE CURSE...
BUT...MY LIFE CANNOT BE SAVED.
WHAT?!
WHY? THAT CAN'T BE!
DON'T DIE, GREAT DEKU TREE!
I FOUGHT SO HARD!
THIS CAN'T BE HAPPENING!!
LINK, LISTEN CLOSELY.
WHILE GOHMA WAS EATING ME, I COULD READ HER THOUGHTS.
SHE, TOO, HAD BEEN CURSED.
THE ONE IN CONTROL OF THIS HORRIBLE EVIL POWER...
...IS KING OF THE PEOPLE OF THE BLACK DESERT.
HE PLOTS TO CAPTURE THE TRIFORCE AND RULE OVER HYRULE.

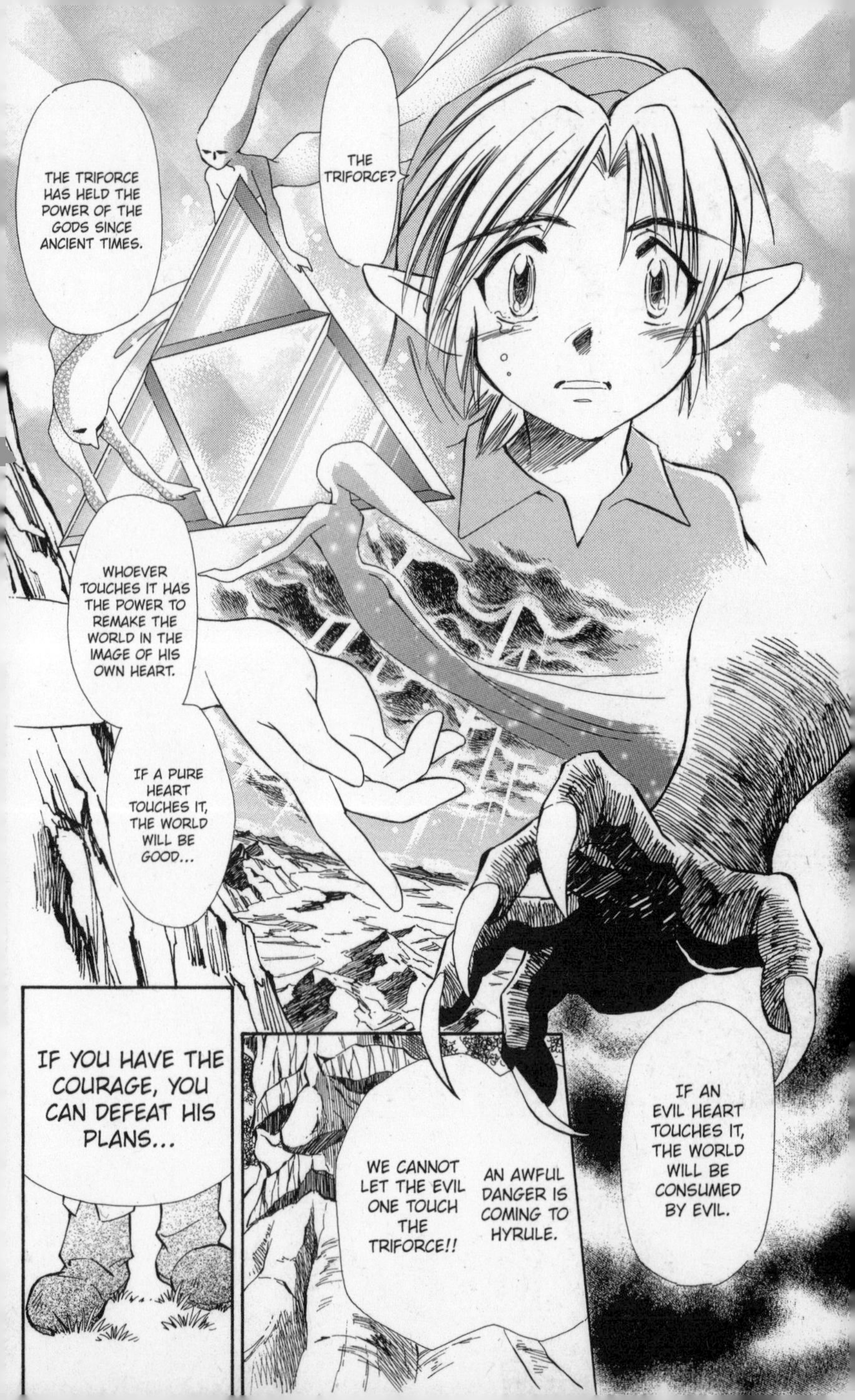
THE TRIFORCE?
THE TRIFORCE HAS HELD THE POWER OF THE GODS SINCE ANCIENT TIMES.
WHOEVER TOUCHES IT HAS THE POWER TO REMAKE THE WORLD IN THE IMAGE OF HIS OWN HEART.
IF A PURE HEART TOUCHES IT, THE WORLD WILL BE GOOD...
IF AN EVIL HEART TOUCHES IT, THE WORLD WILL BE CONSUMED BY EVIL.
AN AWFUL DANGER IS COMING TO HYRULE.
WE CANNOT LET THE EVIL ONE TOUCH THE TRIFORCE!!
IF YOU HAVE THE COURAGE, YOU CAN DEFEAT HIS PLANS...

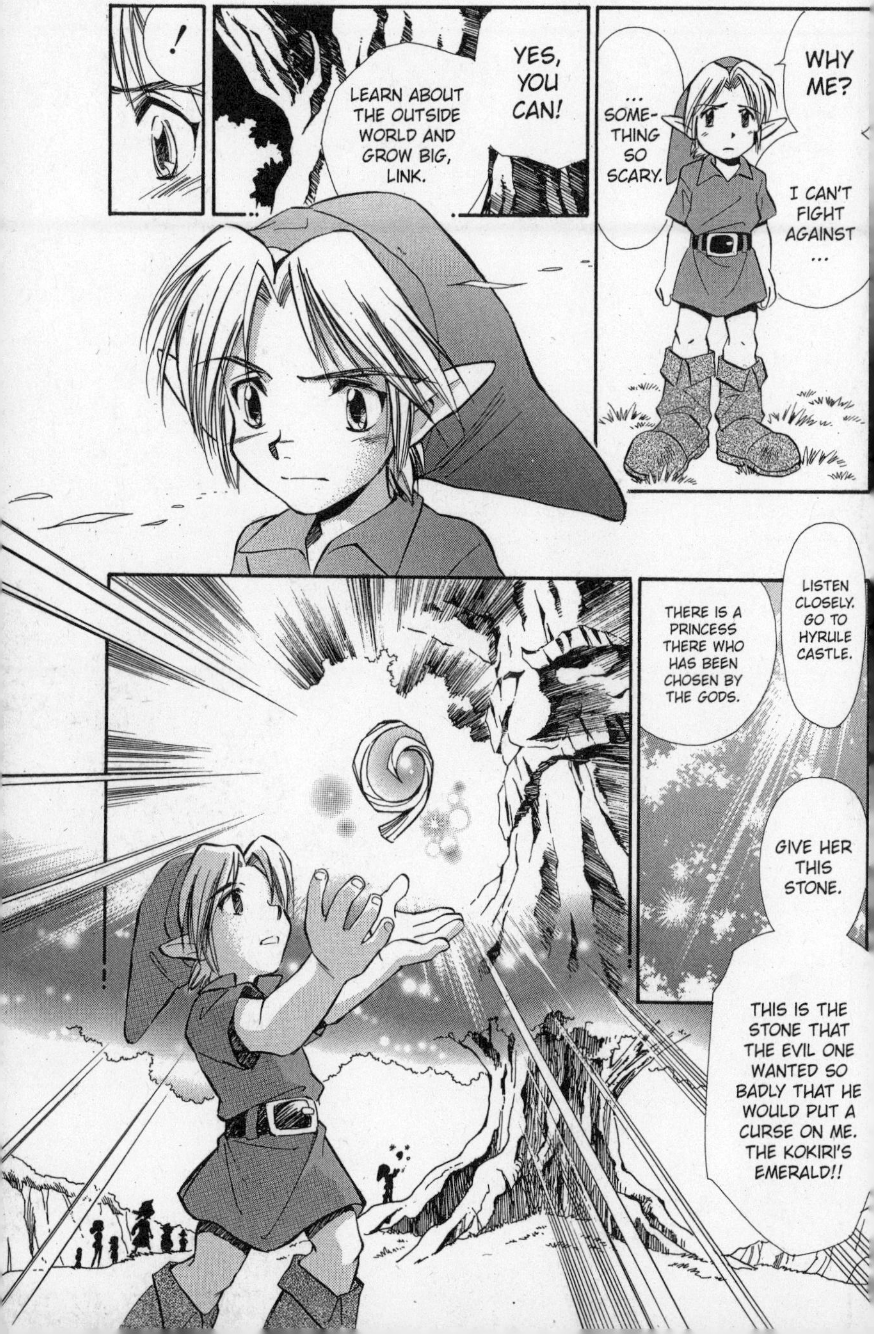
WHY ME?
I CAN'T FIGHT AGAINST ...
... SOMETHING SO SCARY.
YES, YOU CAN!
LEARN ABOUT THE OUTSIDE WORLD AND GROW BIG, LINK.
!
LISTEN CLOSELY. GO TO HYRULE CASTLE.
THERE IS A PRINCESS THERE WHO HAS BEEN CHOSEN BY THE GODS.
GIVE HER THIS STONE.
THIS IS THE STONE THAT THE EVIL ONE WANTED SO BADLY THAT HE WOULD PUT A CURSE ON ME. THE KOKIRI'S EMERALD!!

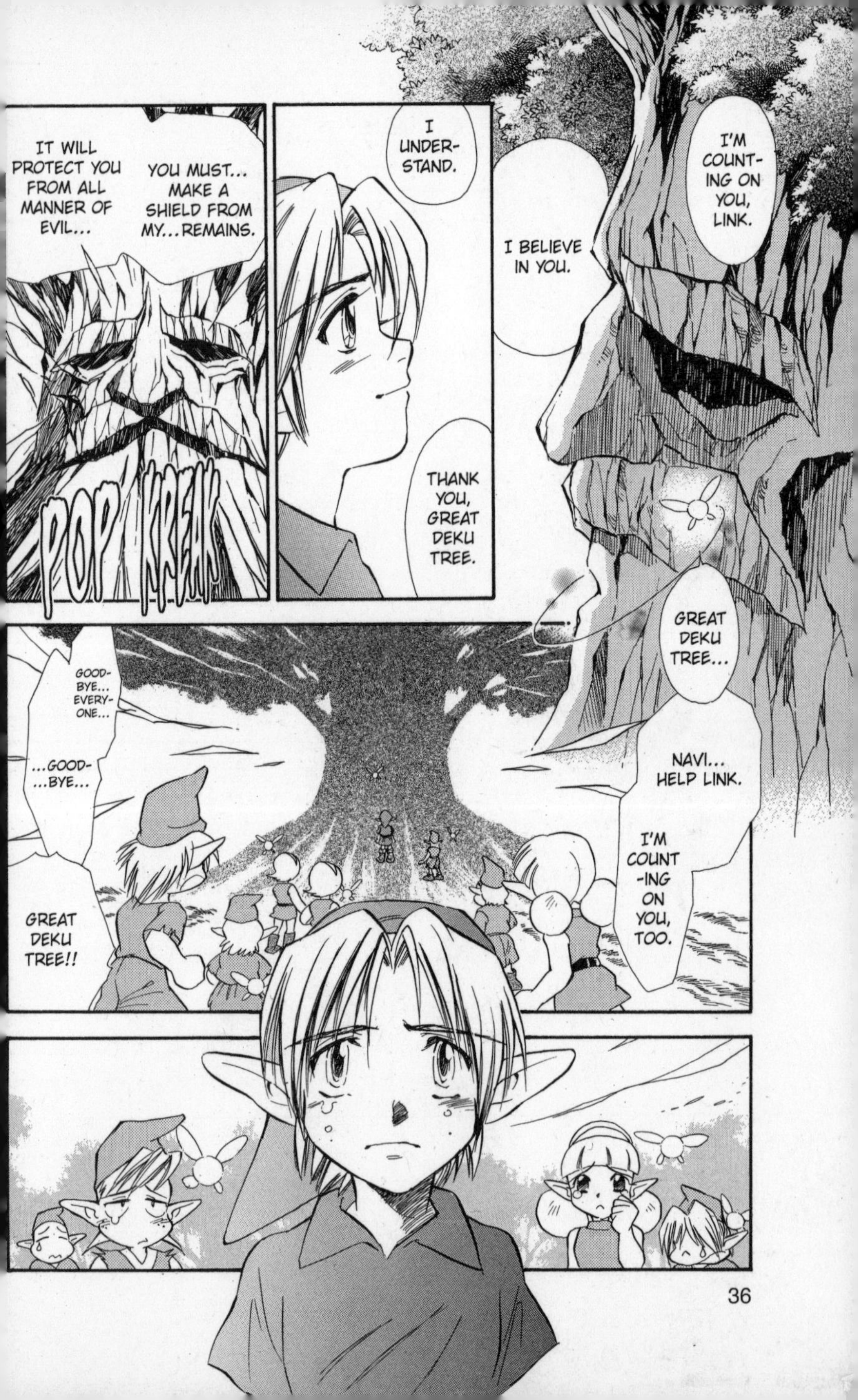
I'M COUNTING ON YOU, LINK.
I BELIEVE IN YOU.
GREAT DEKU TREE...
NAVI... HELP LINK.
I'M COUNTING ON YOU, TOO.
I UNDERSTAND.
THANK YOU, GREAT DEKU TREE.
YOU MUST... MAKE A SHIELD FROM MY... REMAINS.
IT WILL PROTECT YOU FROM ALL MANNER OF EVIL...
POP KREAK
GOODBYE... EVERYONE...
...GOOD- ...BYE...
GREAT DEKU TREE!!

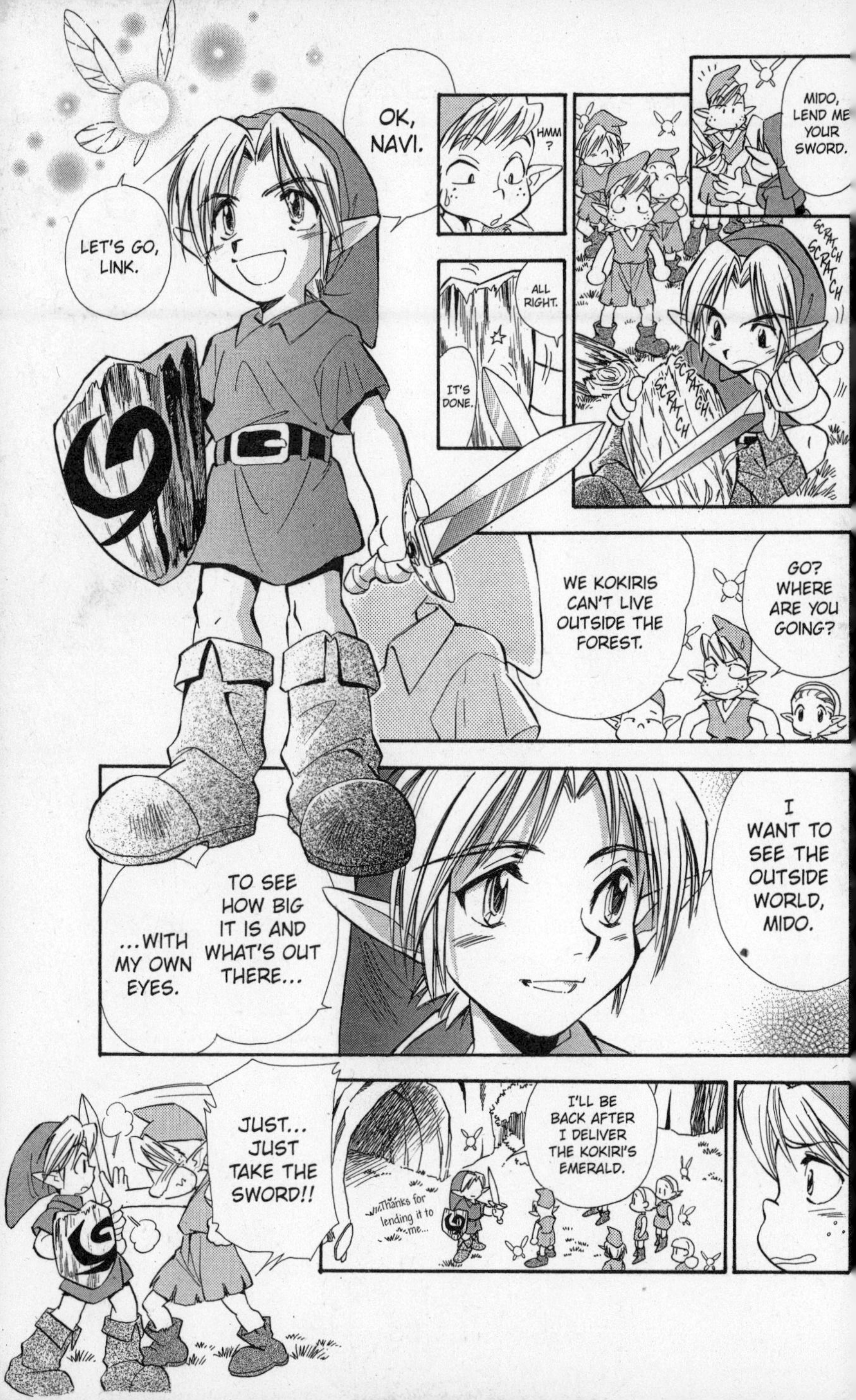
MIDO, LEND ME YOUR SWORD.
SCRATCH SCRATCH
SCRATCH SCRATCH
HMM ?
ALL RIGHT.
IT'S DONE.
OK, NAVI.
LET'S GO, LINK.
GO? WHERE ARE YOU GOING?
WE KOKIRIS CAN'T LIVE OUTSIDE THE FOREST.
I WANT TO SEE THE OUTSIDE WORLD, MIDO.
TO SEE HOW BIG IT IS AND WHAT'S OUT THERE...
...WITH MY OWN EYES.
I'LL BE BACK AFTER I DELIVER THE KOKIRI'S EMERALD.
Thanks for lending it to me...
JUST... JUST TAKE THE SWORD!!

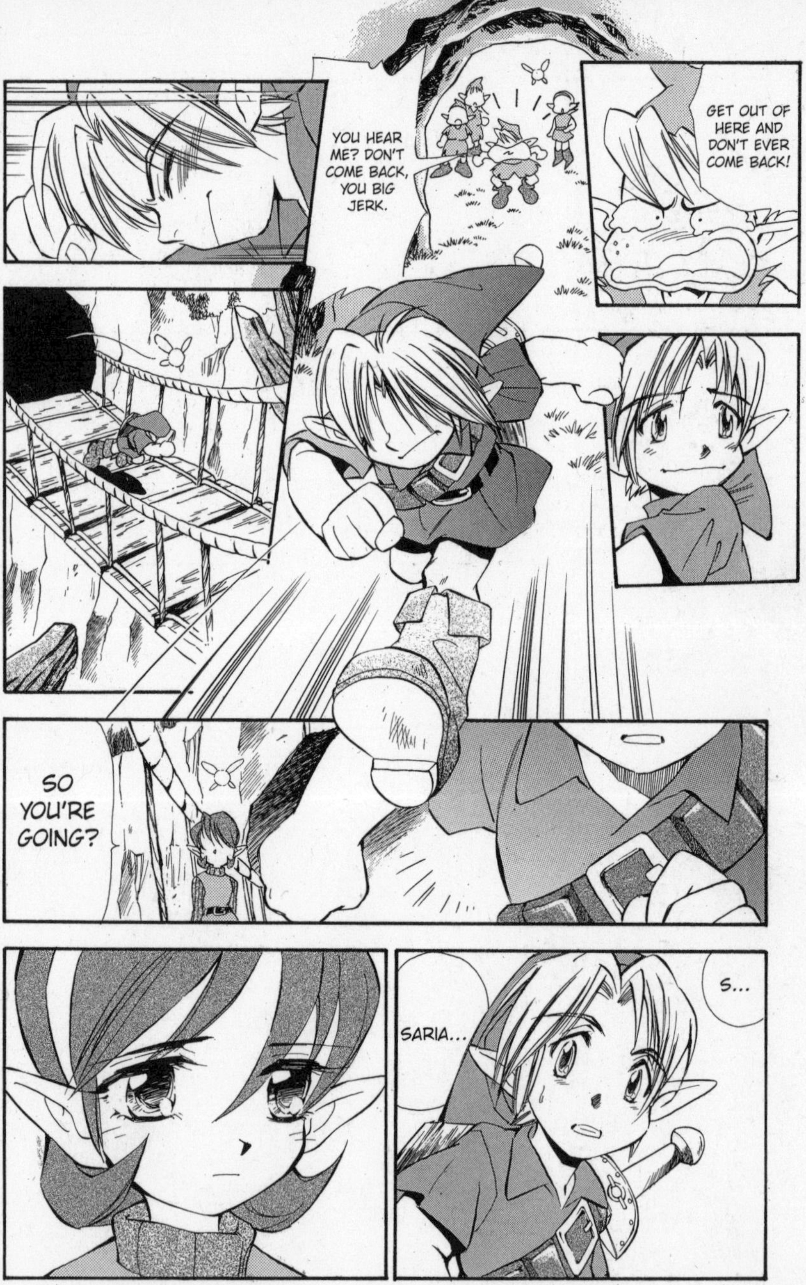
GET OUT OF HERE AND DON'T EVER COME BACK!
YOU HEAR ME? DON'T COME BACK, YOU BIG JERK.
SO YOU'RE GOING?
S...
SARIA...

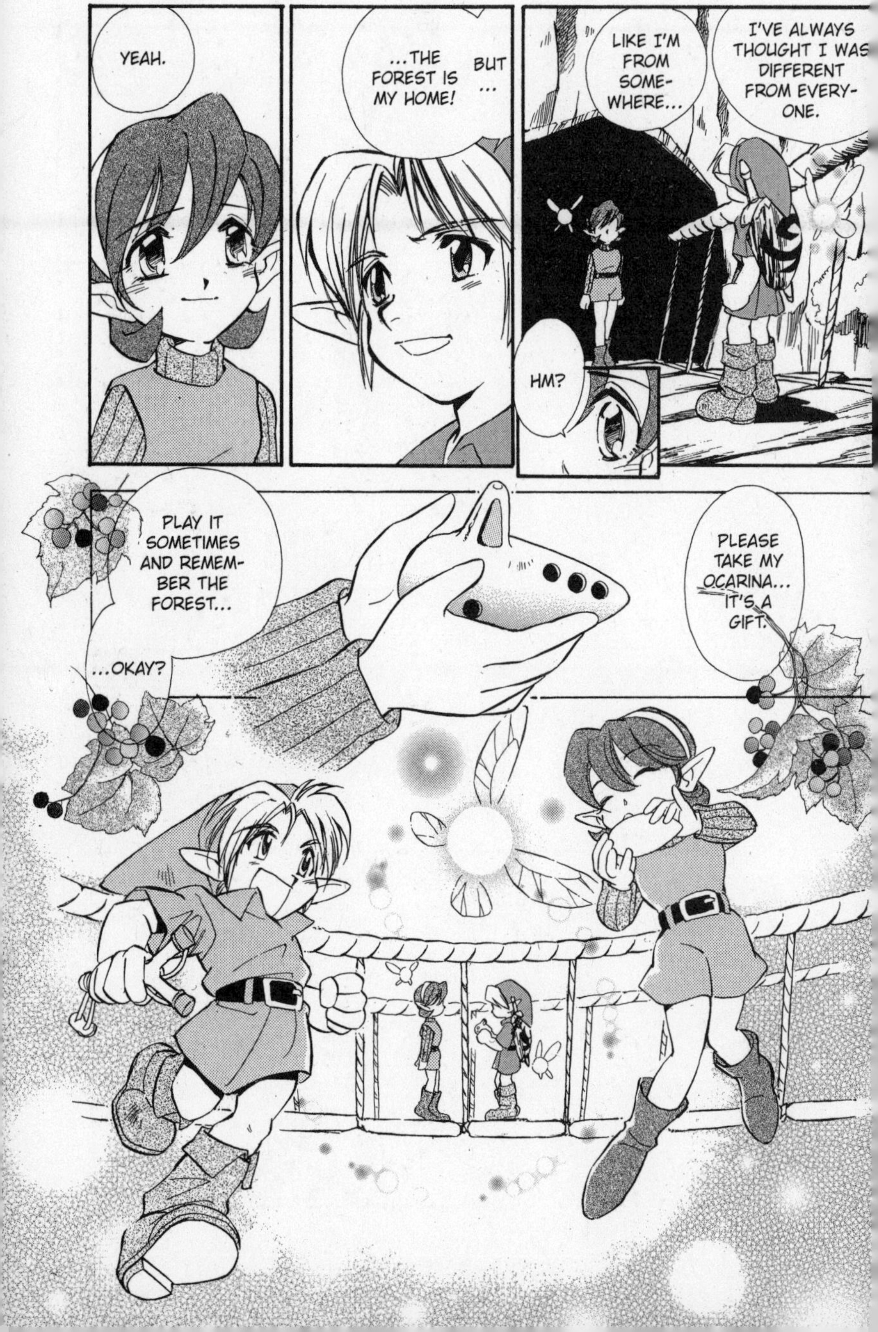
I'VE ALWAYS THOUGHT I WAS DIFFERENT FROM EVERYONE.
LIKE I'M FROM SOMEWHERE...
HM?
BUT...
...THE FOREST IS MY HOME!
YEAH.
PLEASE TAKE MY OCARINA... IT'S A GIFT.
PLAY IT SOMETIMES AND REMEMBER THE FOREST...
...OKAY?

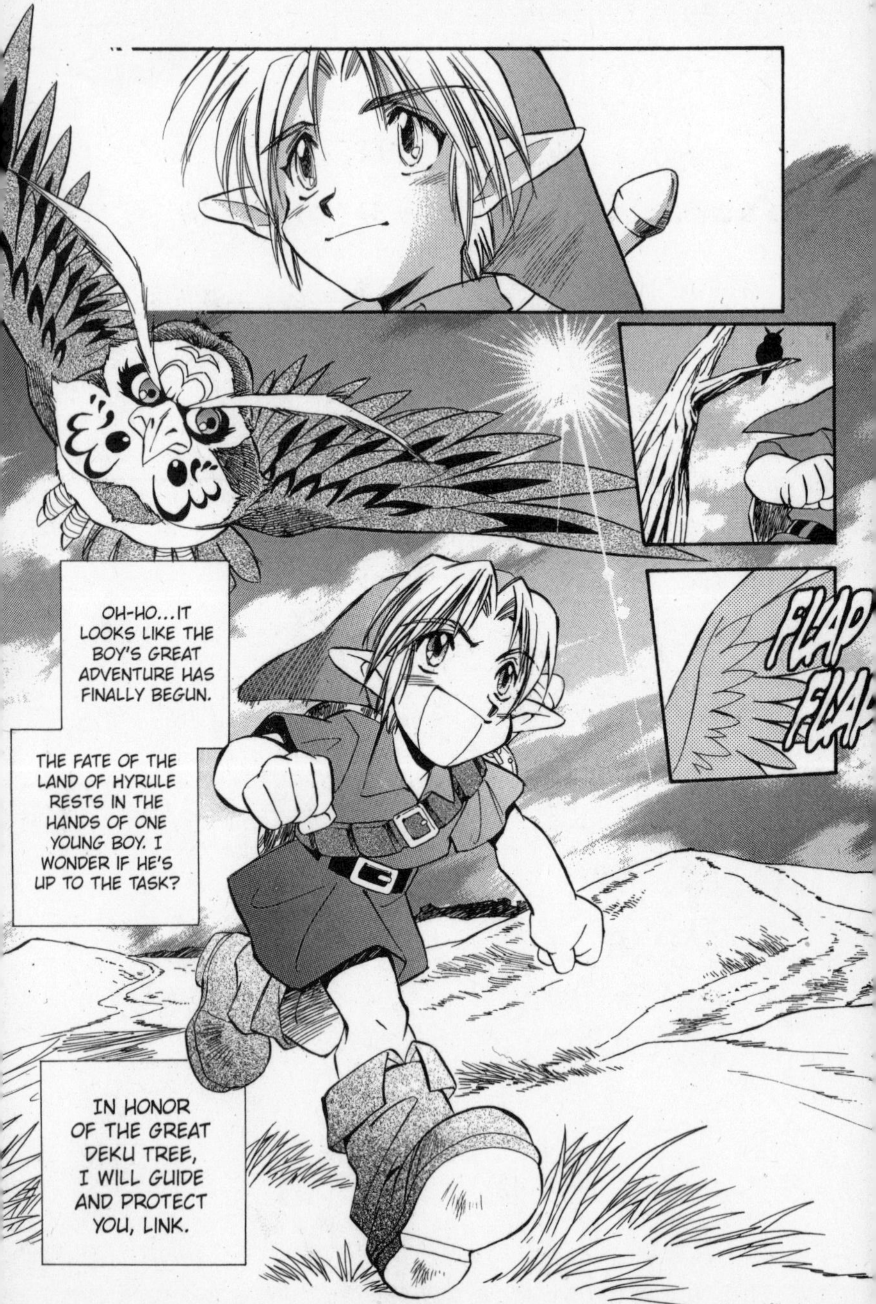
FLAP
FLA-
OH-HO...IT LOOKS LIKE THE BOY'S GREAT ADVENTURE HAS FINALLY BEGUN.
THE FATE OF THE LAND OF HYRULE RESTS IN THE HANDS OF ONE YOUNG BOY. I WONDER IF HE'S UP TO THE TASK?
IN HONOR OF THE GREAT DEKU TREE, I WILL GUIDE AND PROTECT YOU, LINK.

BONUS ILLUSTRATION 2

THIS ROUGH SKETCH WAS DRAWN BEFORE THE SERIES BEGAN.

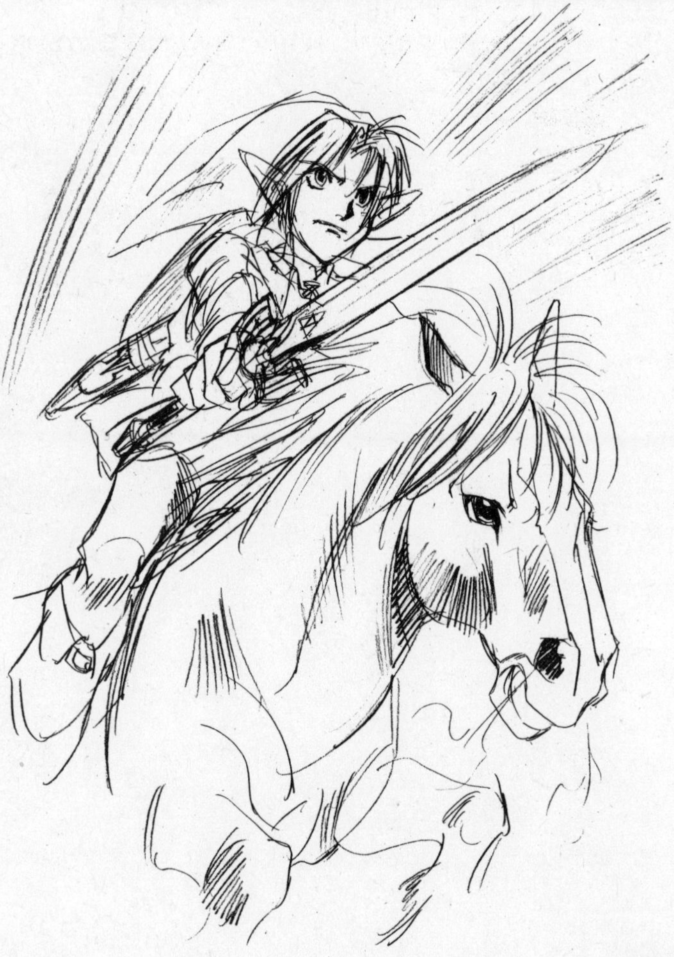

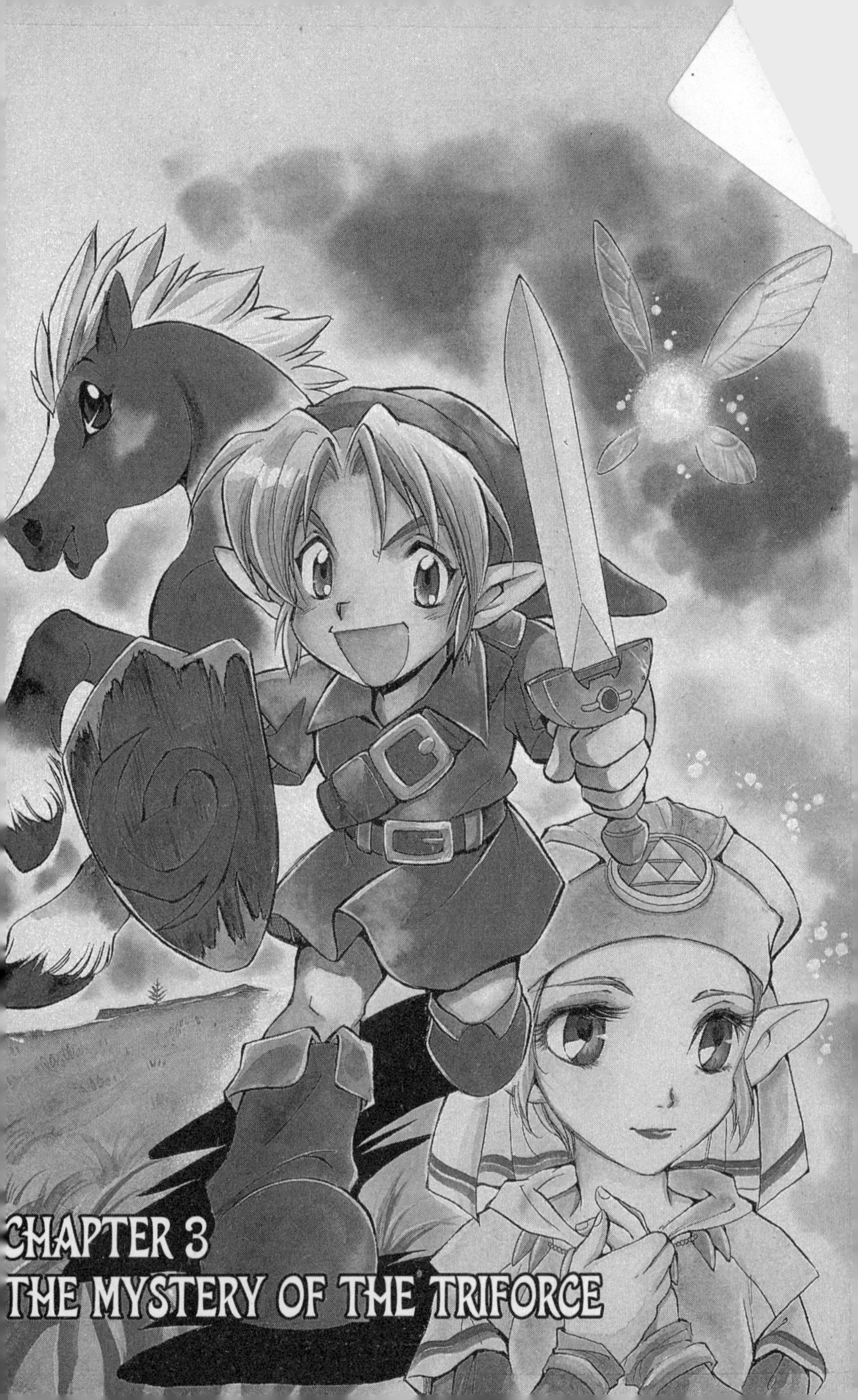

CHAPTER 3
THE MYSTERY OF THE TRIFORCE

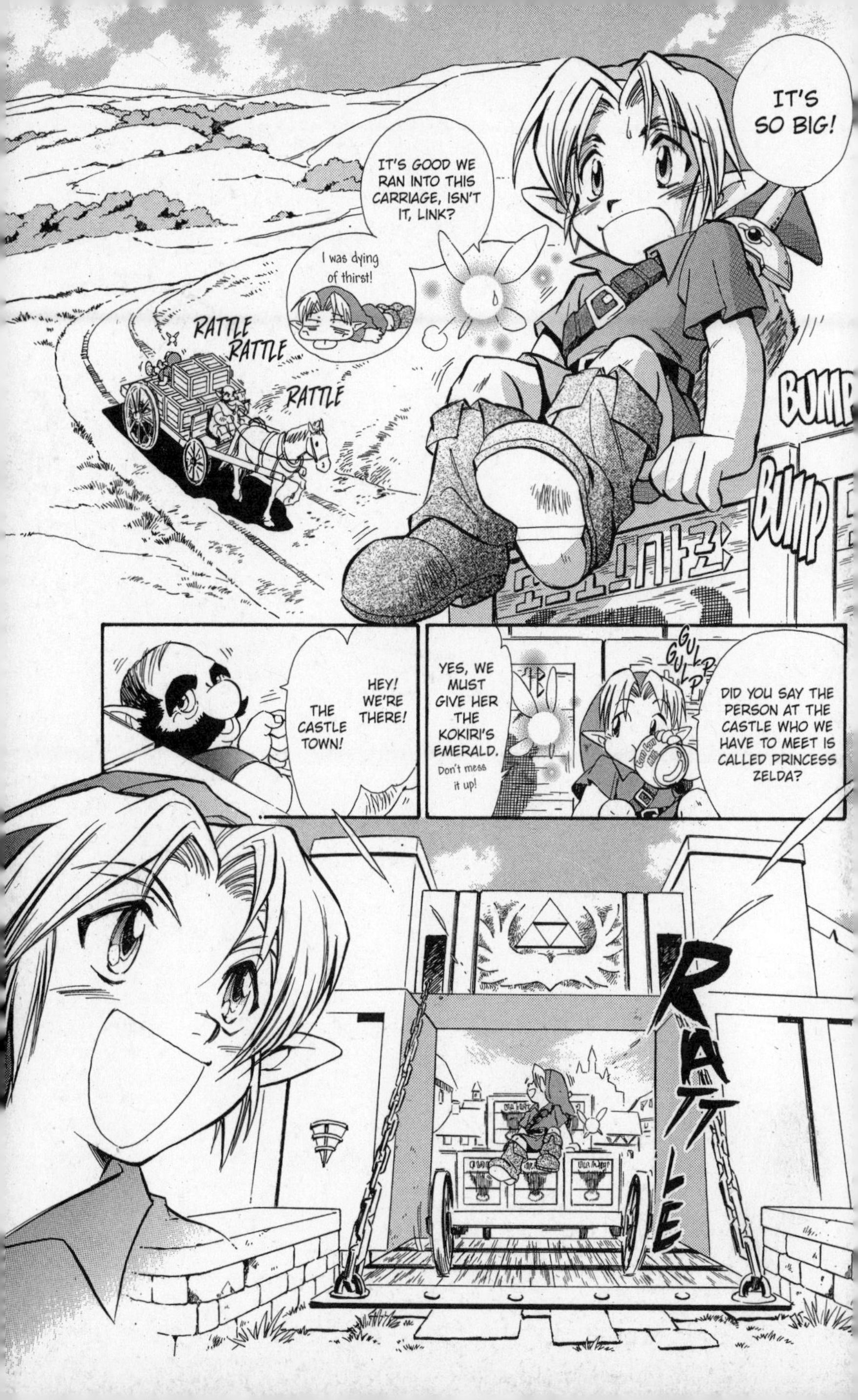
IT'S SO BIG!
BUMP
BUMP
IT'S GOOD WE RAN INTO THIS CARRIAGE, ISN'T IT, LINK?
I was dying of thirst!
RATTLE RATTLE
RATTLE
GULP GULP
DID YOU SAY THE PERSON AT THE CASTLE WHO WE HAVE TO MEET IS CALLED PRINCESS ZELDA?
YES, WE MUST GIVE HER THE KOKIRI'S EMERALD.
Don't mess it up!
HEY! WE'RE THERE!
THE CASTLE TOWN!
RATTLE

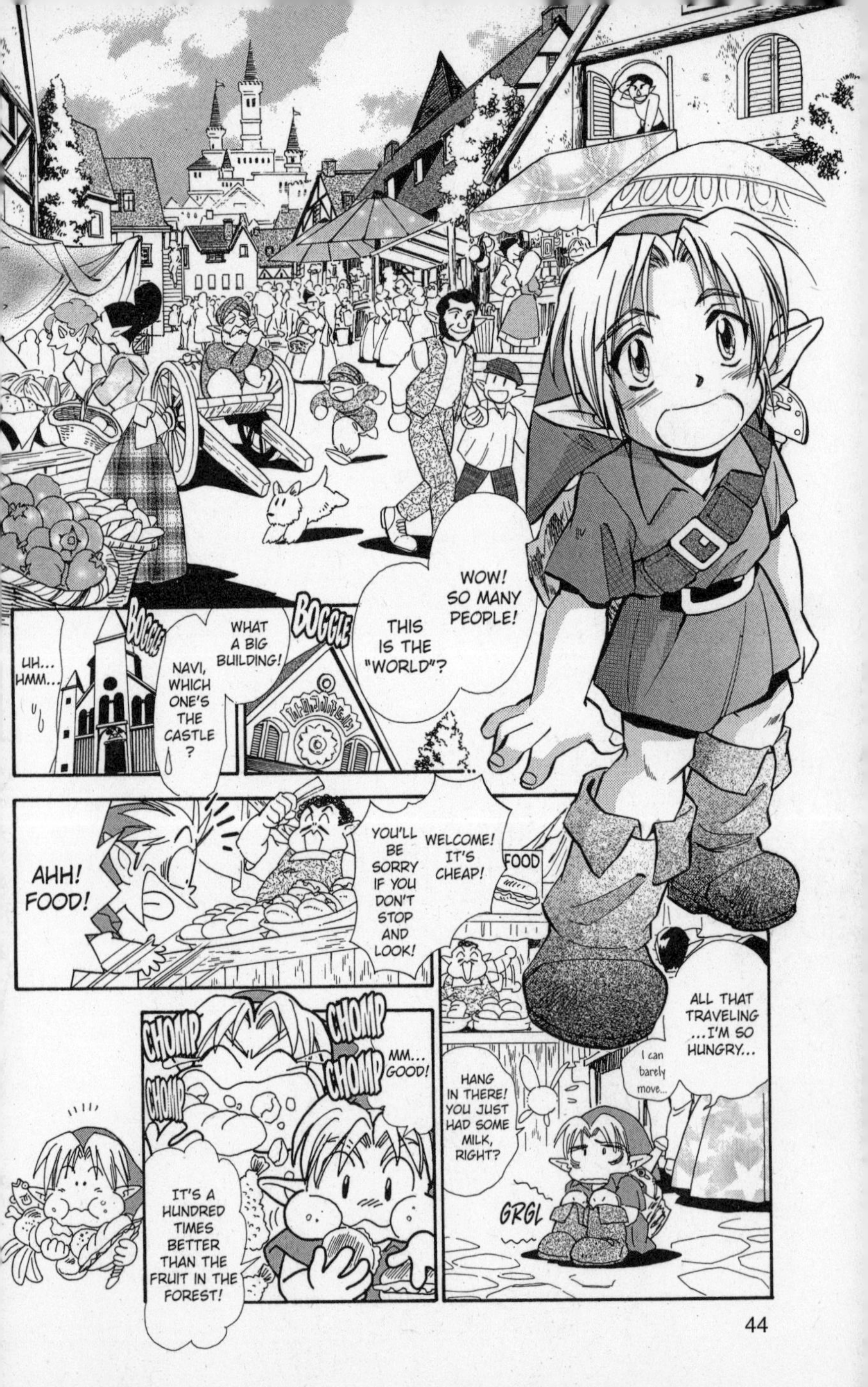
WOW! SO MANY PEOPLE!
THIS IS THE "WORLD"?
BOGGLE
WHAT A BIG BUILDING!
BOGGLE
NAVI, WHICH ONE'S THE CASTLE?
UH... HMM...
ALL THAT TRAVELING ...I'M SO HUNGRY...
I can barely move...
HANG IN THERE! YOU JUST HAD SOME MILK, RIGHT?
GRGL
WELCOME! IT'S CHEAP!
YOU'LL BE SORRY IF YOU DON'T STOP AND LOOK!
FOOD
AHH! FOOD!
CHOMP
CHOMP
MM... GOOD!
CHOMP
CHOMP
IT'S A HUNDRED TIMES BETTER THAN THE FRUIT IN THE FOREST!

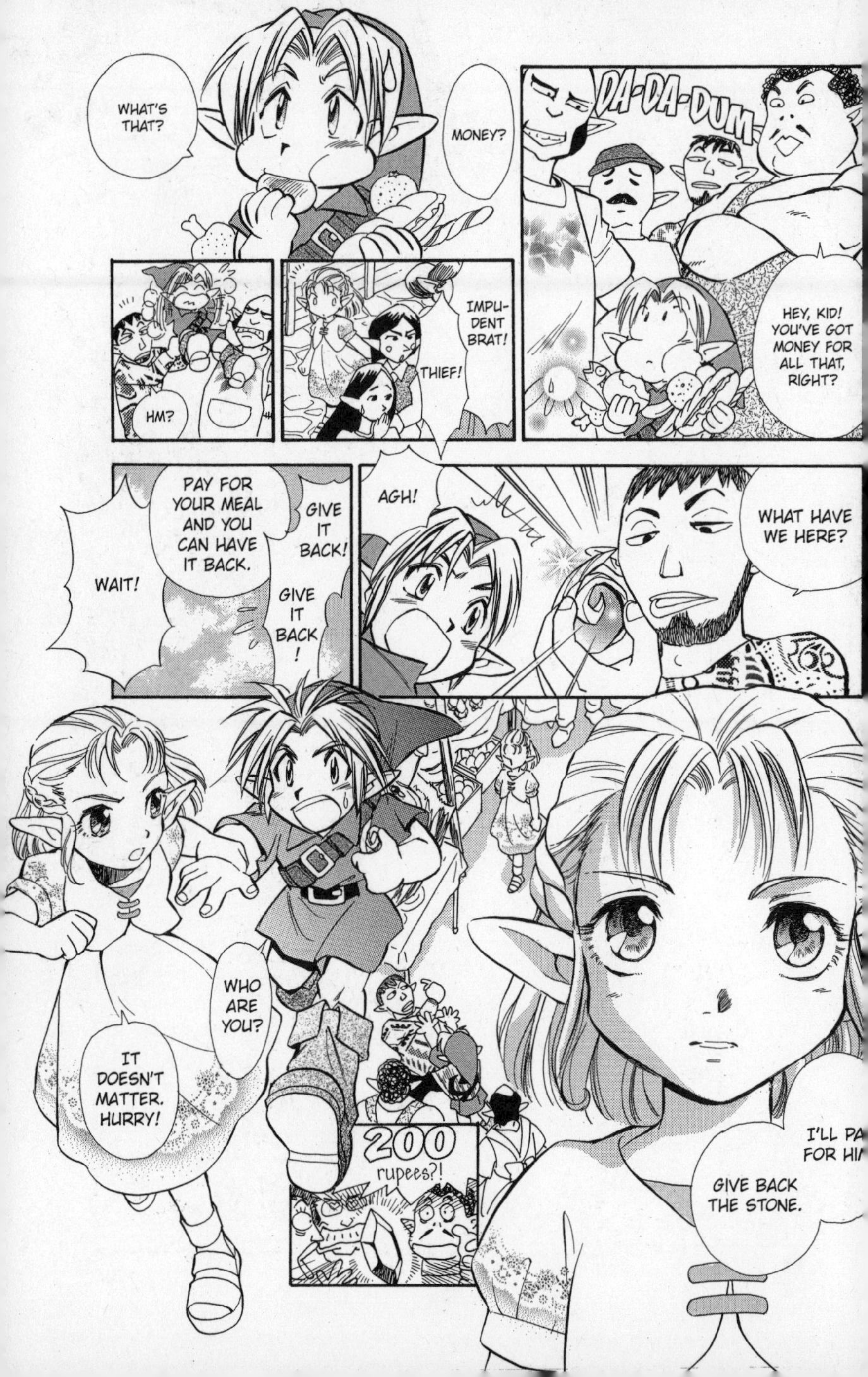
DA-DA-DUM
HEY, KID! YOU'VE GOT MONEY FOR ALL THAT, RIGHT?
MONEY?
WHAT'S THAT?
IMPU-DENT BRAT!
THIEF!
HM?
WHAT HAVE WE HERE?
AGH!
GIVE IT BACK!
GIVE IT BACK!
PAY FOR YOUR MEAL AND YOU CAN HAVE IT BACK.
WAIT!
I'LL PA FOR HI
GIVE BACK THE STONE.
200 rupees?!
WHO ARE YOU?
IT DOESN'T MATTER. HURRY!

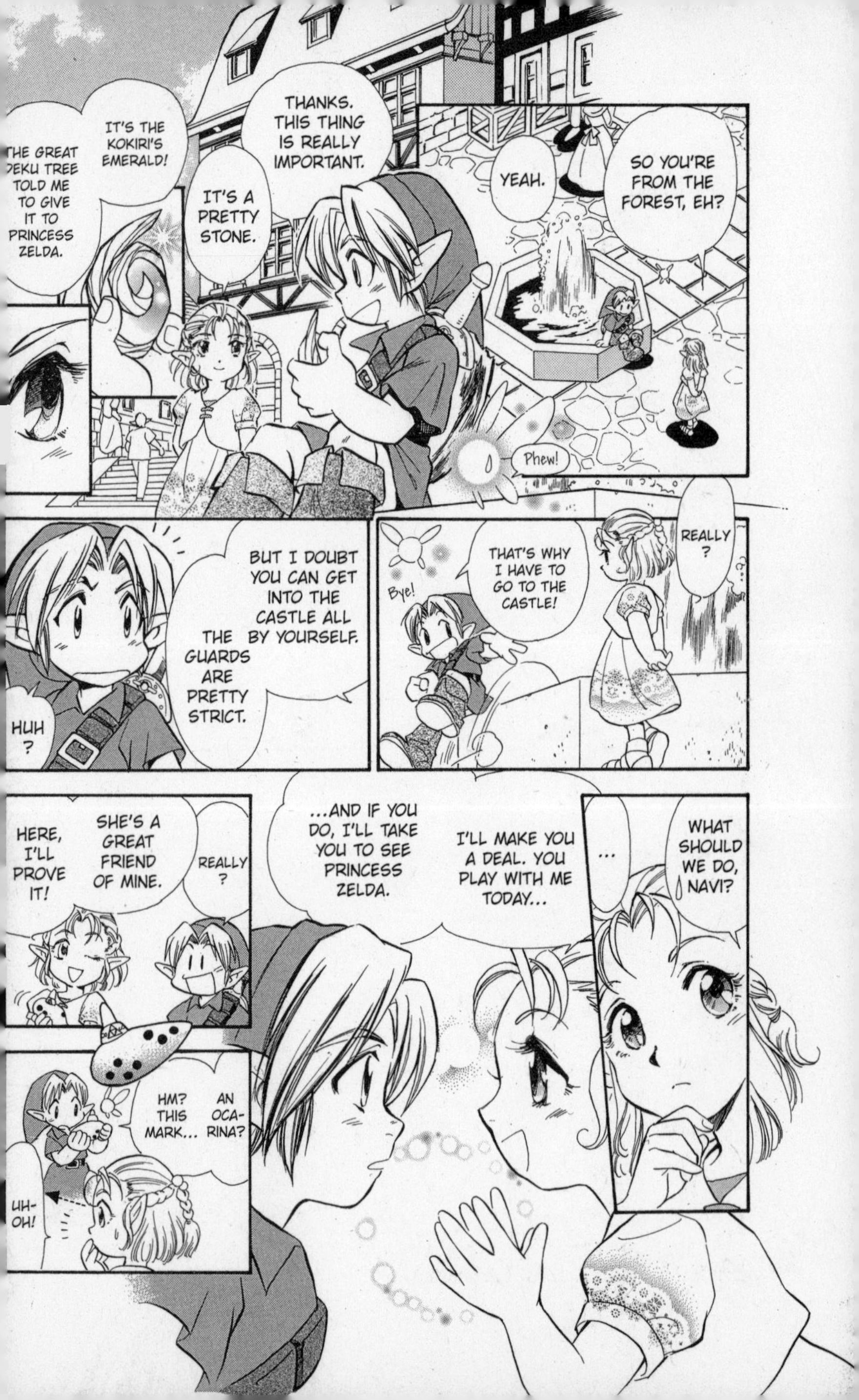

SO YOU'RE FROM THE FOREST, EH?
YEAH.
Phew!
THANKS. THIS THING IS REALLY IMPORTANT.
IT'S A PRETTY STONE.
IT'S THE KOKIRI'S EMERALD!
THE GREAT DEKU TREE TOLD ME TO GIVE IT TO PRINCESS ZELDA.
REALLY ?
THAT'S WHY I HAVE TO GO TO THE CASTLE!
Bye!
BUT I DOUBT YOU CAN GET INTO THE CASTLE ALL BY YOURSELF.
THE GUARDS ARE PRETTY STRICT.
HUH ?
WHAT SHOULD WE DO, NAVI?
...
I'LL MAKE YOU A DEAL. YOU PLAY WITH ME TODAY...
...AND IF YOU DO, I'LL TAKE YOU TO SEE PRINCESS ZELDA.
REALLY ?
SHE'S A GREAT FRIEND OF MINE.
HERE, I'LL PROVE IT!
AN OCA-RINA?
HM? THIS MARK...
UH-OH!

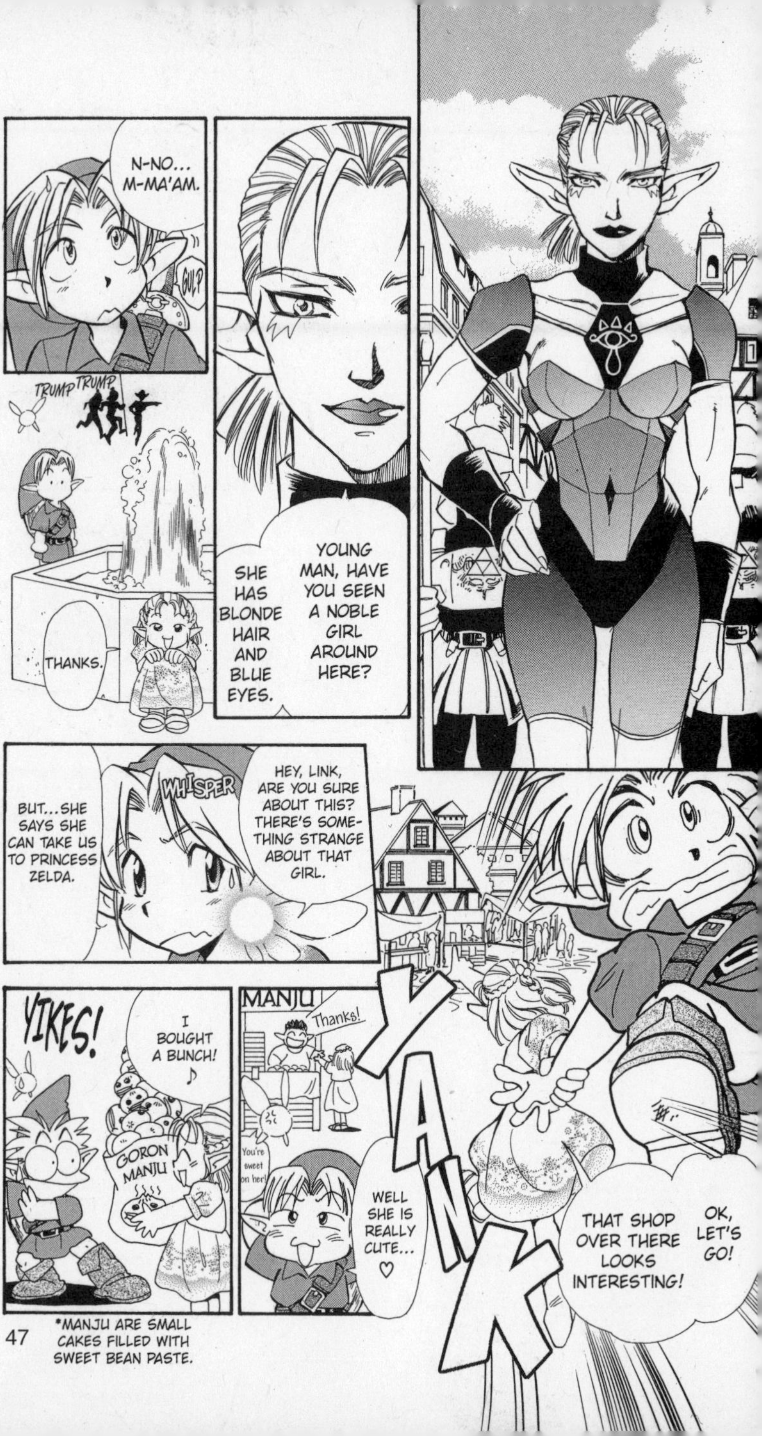
YOUNG MAN, HAVE YOU SEEN A NOBLE GIRL AROUND HERE?
SHE HAS BLONDE HAIR AND BLUE EYES.
N-NO... M-MA'AM.
GULP
TRUMP TRUMP
THANKS.
YANK
OK, LET'S GO!
THAT SHOP OVER THERE LOOKS INTERESTING!
HEY, LINK, ARE YOU SURE ABOUT THIS? THERE'S SOME-THING STRANGE ABOUT THAT GIRL.
WHISPER
BUT...SHE SAYS SHE CAN TAKE US TO PRINCESS ZELDA.
MANJU
Thanks!
You're sweet on her!
WELL SHE IS REALLY CUTE... ♡
YIKES!
I BOUGHT A BUNCH! ♪
GORON MANJU

*MANJU ARE SMALL CAKES FILLED WITH SWEET BEAN PASTE.

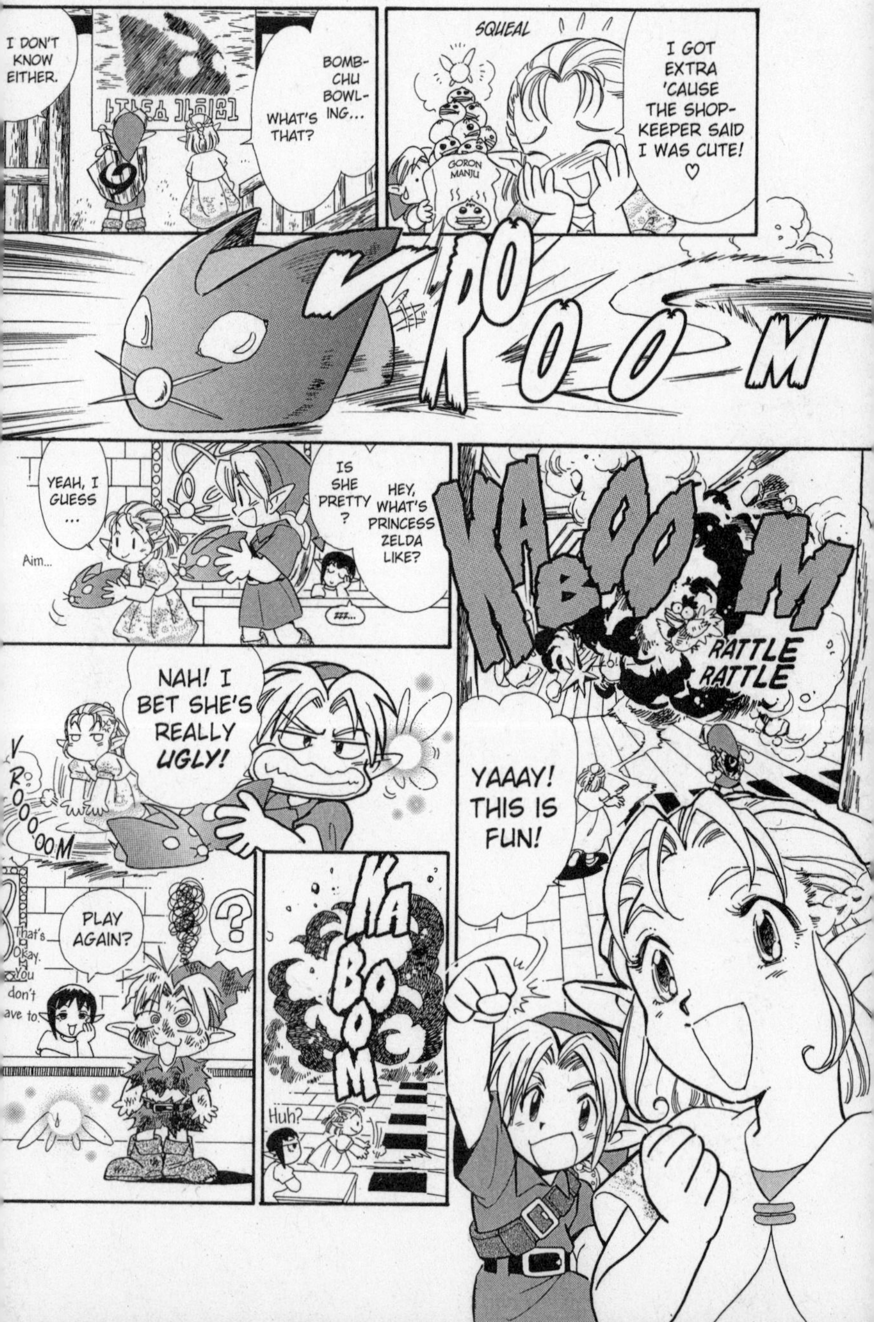
SQUEAL
I GOT EXTRA 'CAUSE THE SHOP-KEEPER SAID I WAS CUTE! ♡
GORON MANJU
BOMB-CHU BOWL-ING...
WHAT'S THAT?
I DON'T KNOW EITHER.
VROOOOM
KABOOM
RATTLE RATTLE
YAAAY! THIS IS FUN!
HEY, WHAT'S PRINCESS ZELDA LIKE?
IS SHE PRETTY?
YEAH, I GUESS...
Aim...
zzz...
NAH! I BET SHE'S REALLY UGLY!
VROOOOOM
KABOOM
Huh?
?
PLAY AGAIN?
That's okay. You don't ave to.

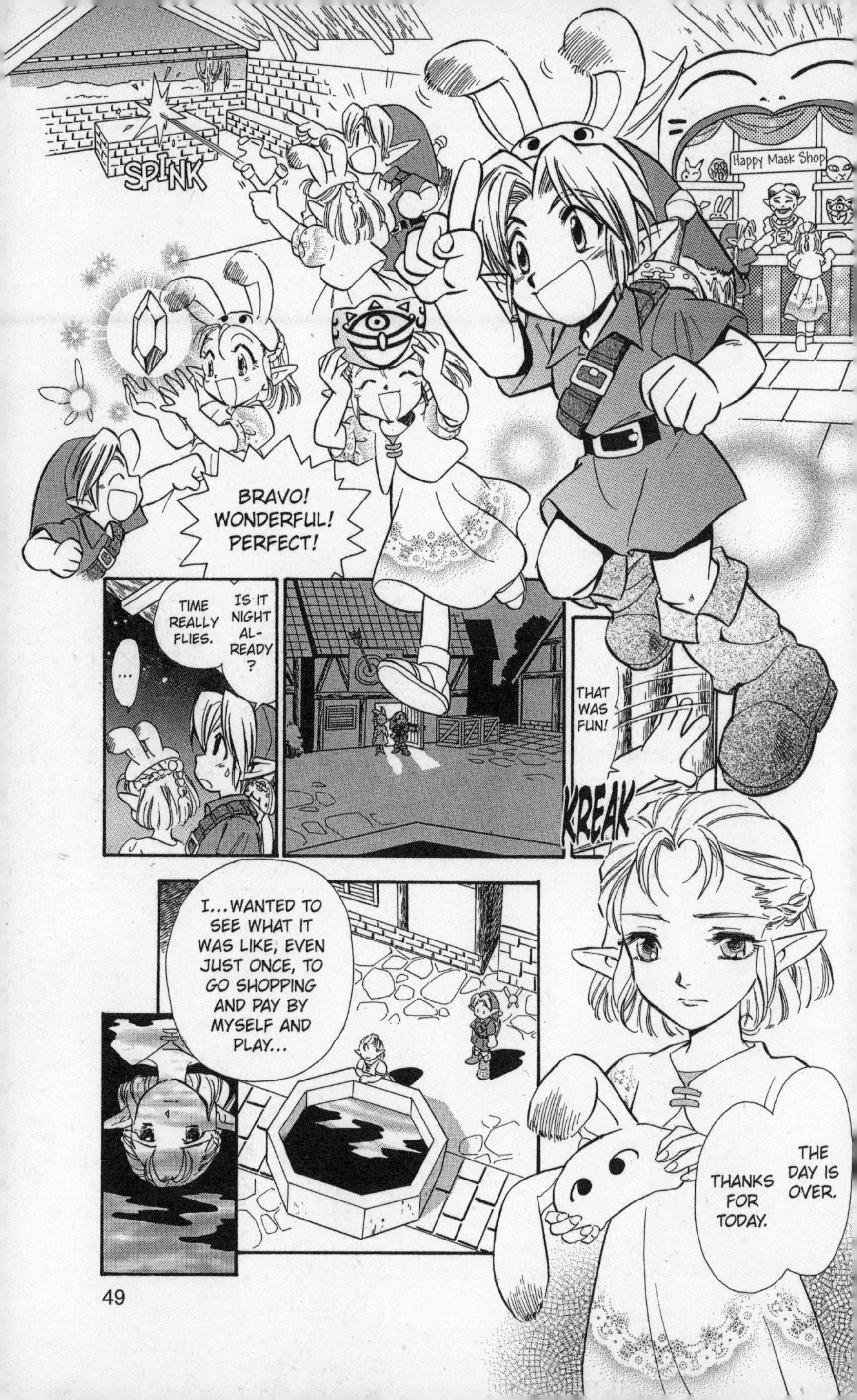
Happy Mask Shop
SPINK
BRAVO! WONDERFUL! PERFECT!
THAT WAS FUN!
KREAK
IS IT NIGHT AL-READY?
TIME REALLY FLIES.
...
THE DAY IS OVER.
THANKS FOR TODAY.
I...WANTED TO SEE WHAT IT WAS LIKE, EVEN JUST ONCE, TO GO SHOPPING AND PAY BY MYSELF AND PLAY...

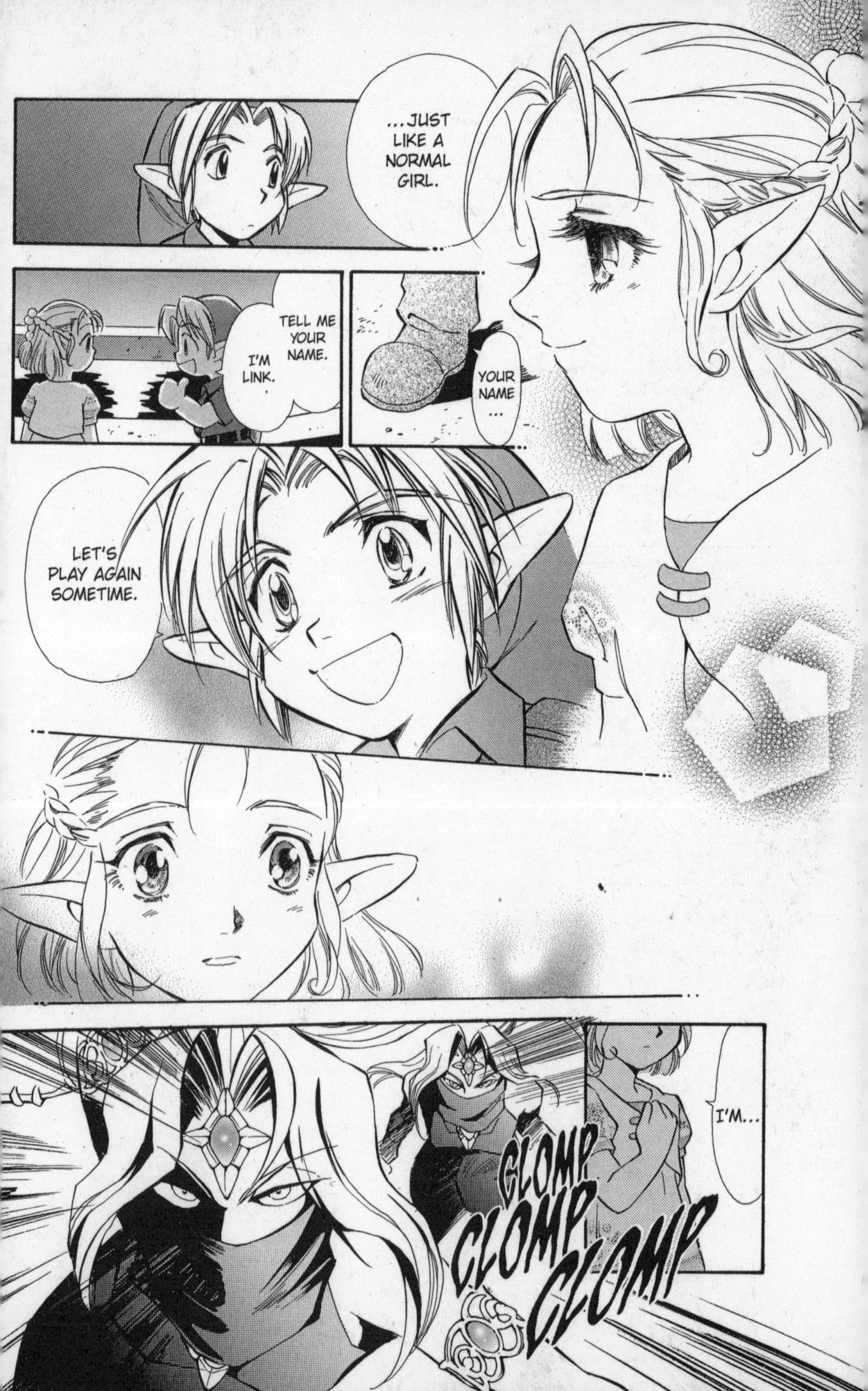
...JUST LIKE A NORMAL GIRL.
YOUR NAME ...
TELL ME YOUR NAME.
I'M LINK.
LET'S PLAY AGAIN SOMETIME.
I'M...
CLOMP
CLOMP
CLOMP

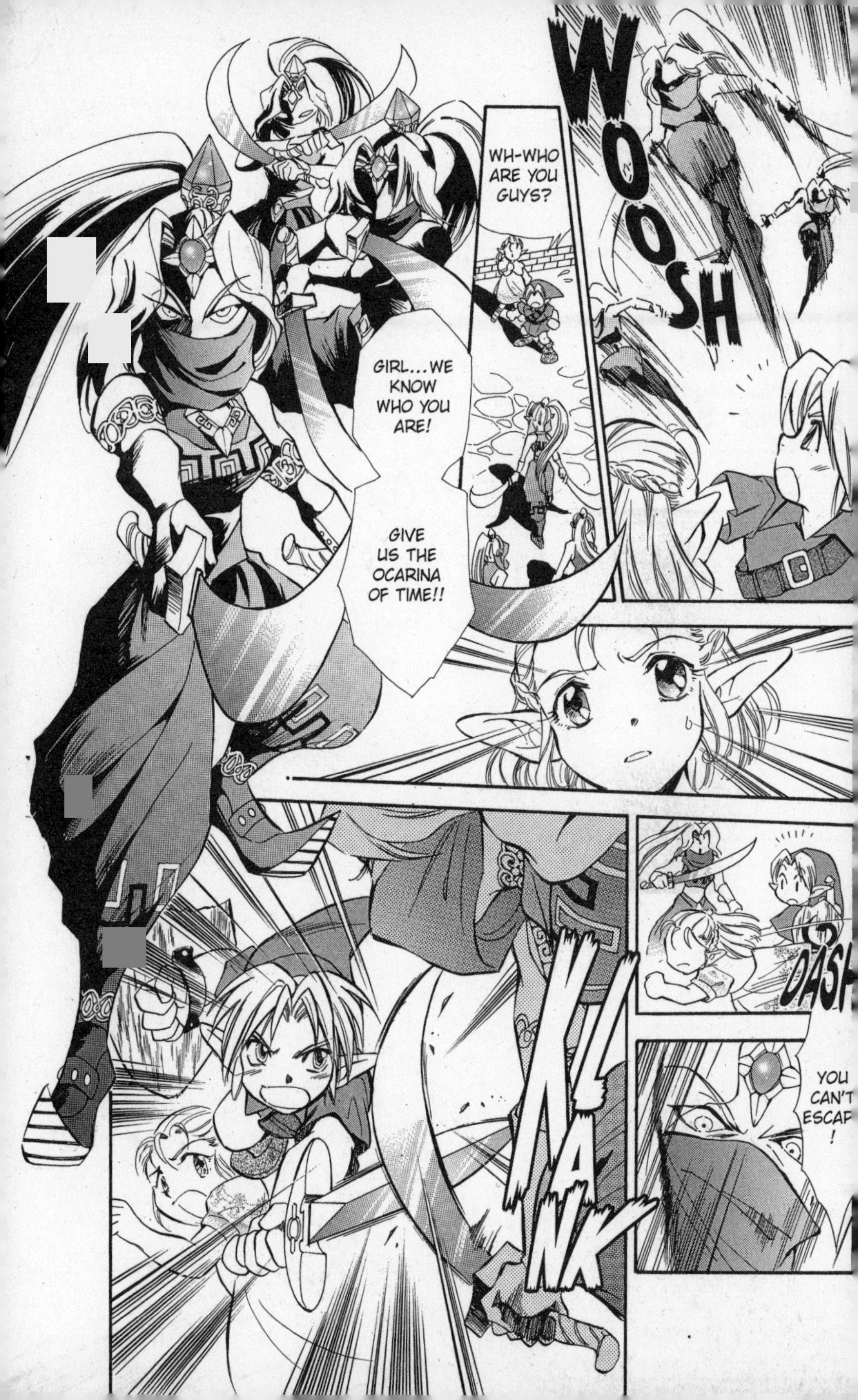
WOOSH
WH-WHO ARE YOU GUYS?
GIRL...WE KNOW WHO YOU ARE!
GIVE US THE OCARINA OF TIME!!
DASH
YOU CAN'T ESCAP !
WHANK

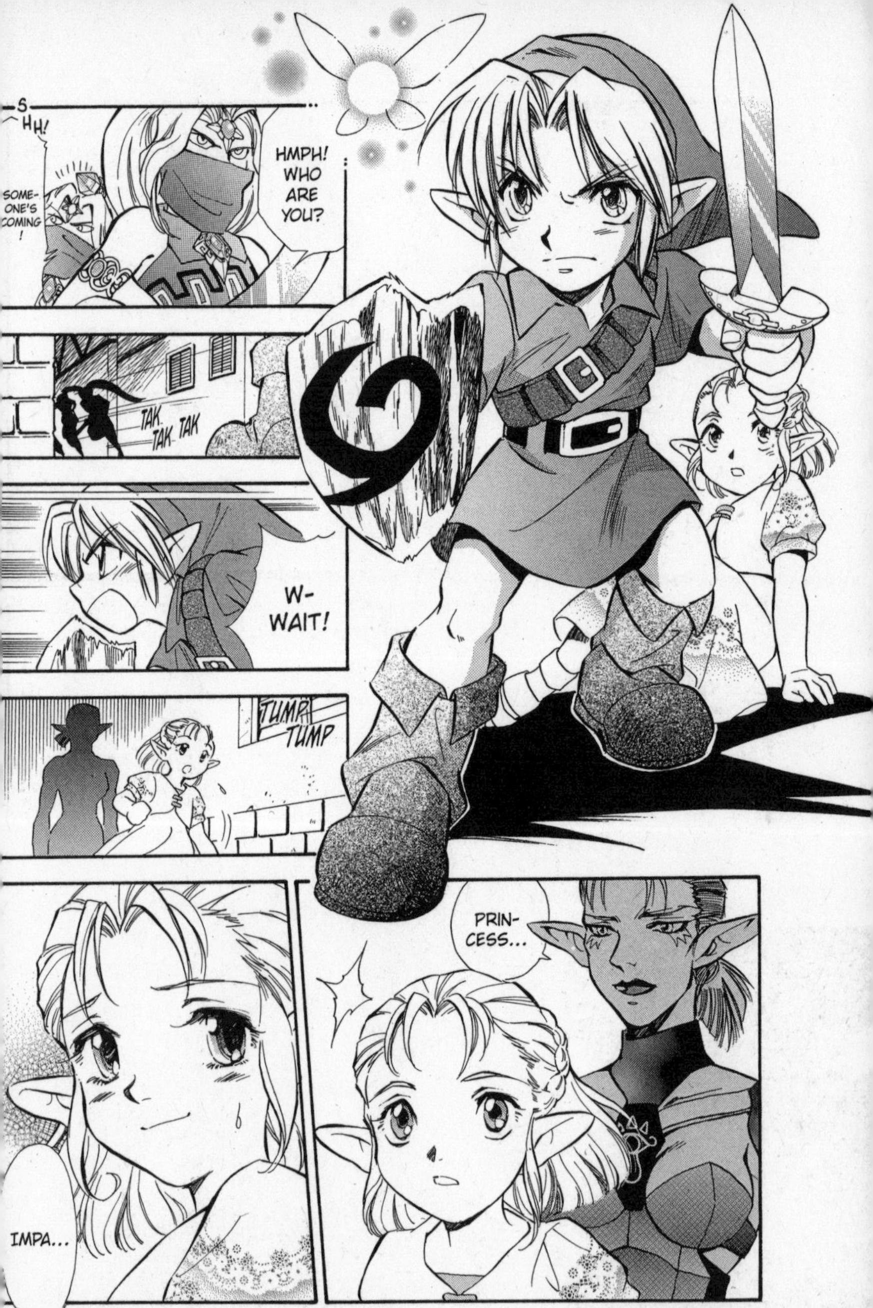
HMPH! WHO ARE YOU?
S-HH!
SOME-ONE'S COMING!
TAK TAK TAK
W-WAIT!
TUMP TUMP
PRIN-CESS...
IMPA...

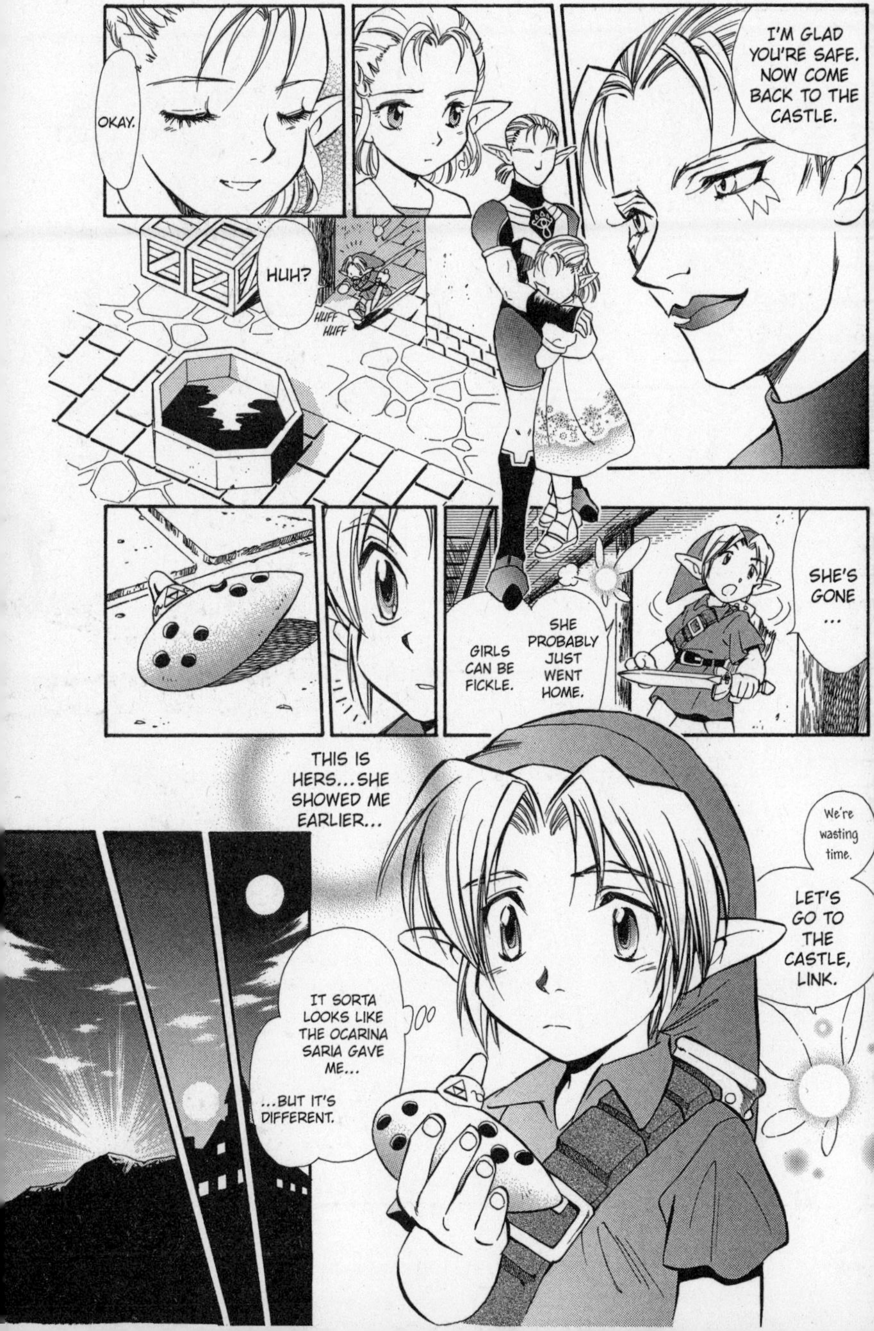
I'M GLAD YOU'RE SAFE. NOW COME BACK TO THE CASTLE.
OKAY.
HUH?
HUFF HUFF
SHE'S GONE...
SHE PROBABLY JUST WENT HOME.
GIRLS CAN BE FICKLE.
THIS IS HERS...SHE SHOWED ME EARLIER...
We're wasting time.
LET'S GO TO THE CASTLE, LINK.
IT SORTA LOOKS LIKE THE OCARINA SARIA GAVE ME...
...BUT IT'S DIFFERENT.

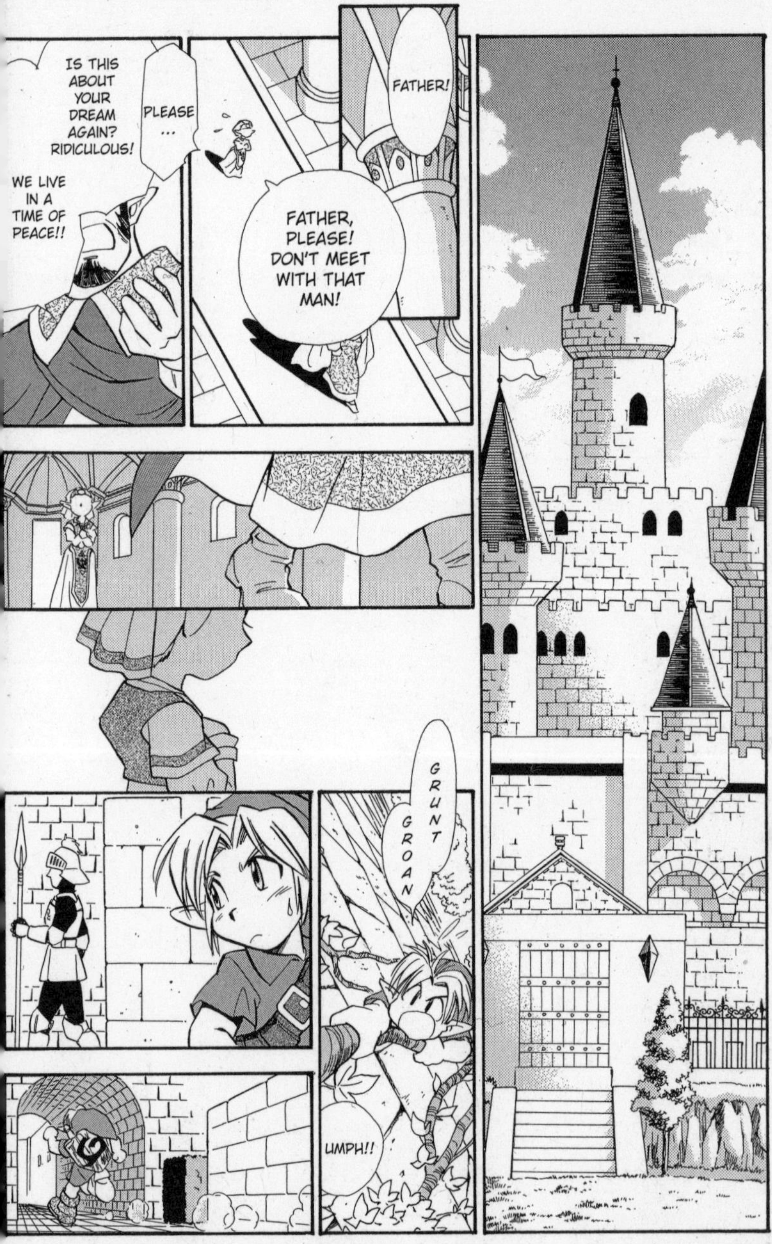
FATHER!
FATHER, PLEASE! DON'T MEET WITH THAT MAN!
PLEASE ...
IS THIS ABOUT YOUR DREAM AGAIN? RIDICULOUS!
WE LIVE IN A TIME OF PEACE!!
GRUNT
GROAN
UMPH!!

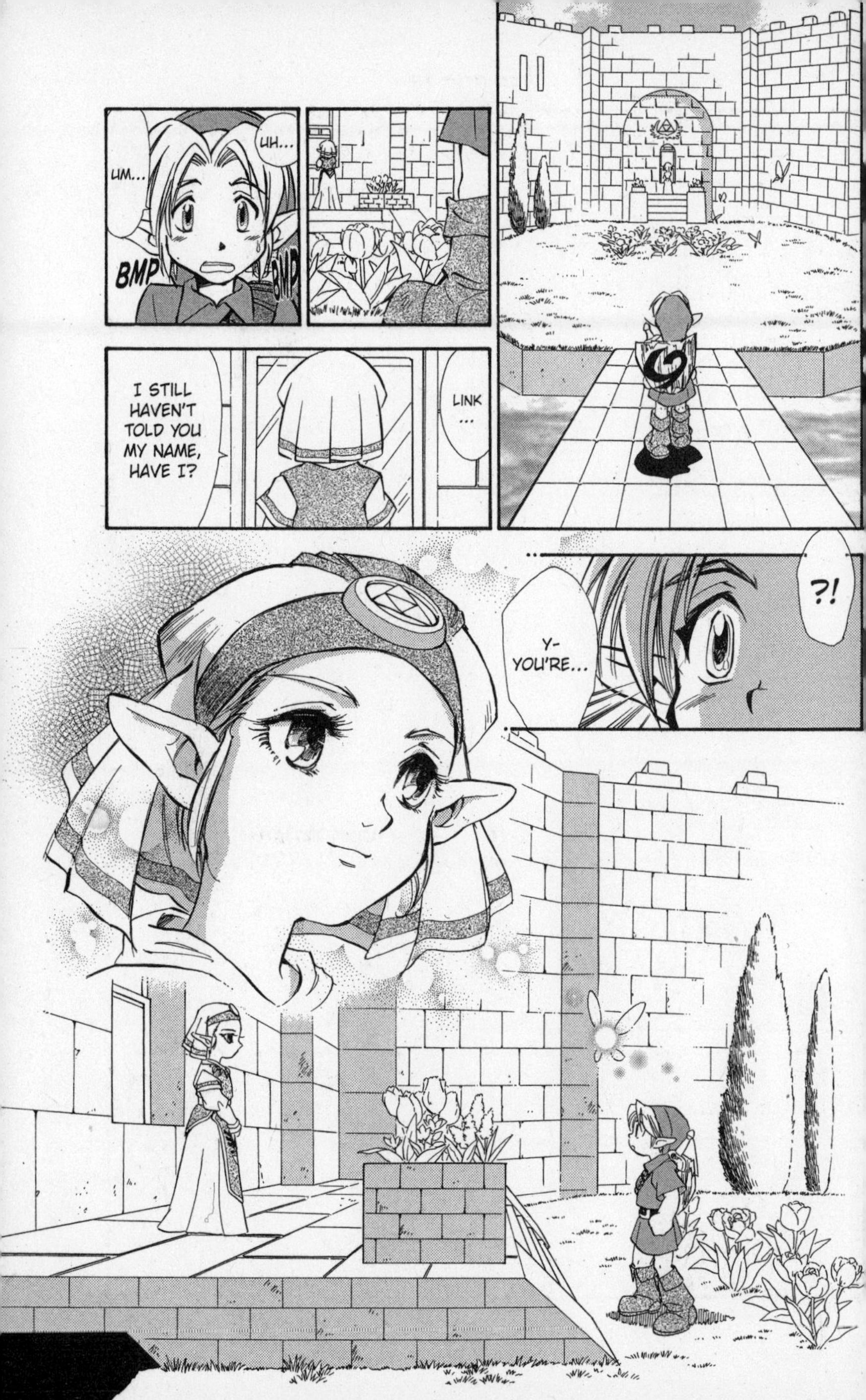
UH...
UM...
BMP
BMP
LINK ...
I STILL HAVEN'T TOLD YOU MY NAME, HAVE I?
?!
Y- YOU'RE...

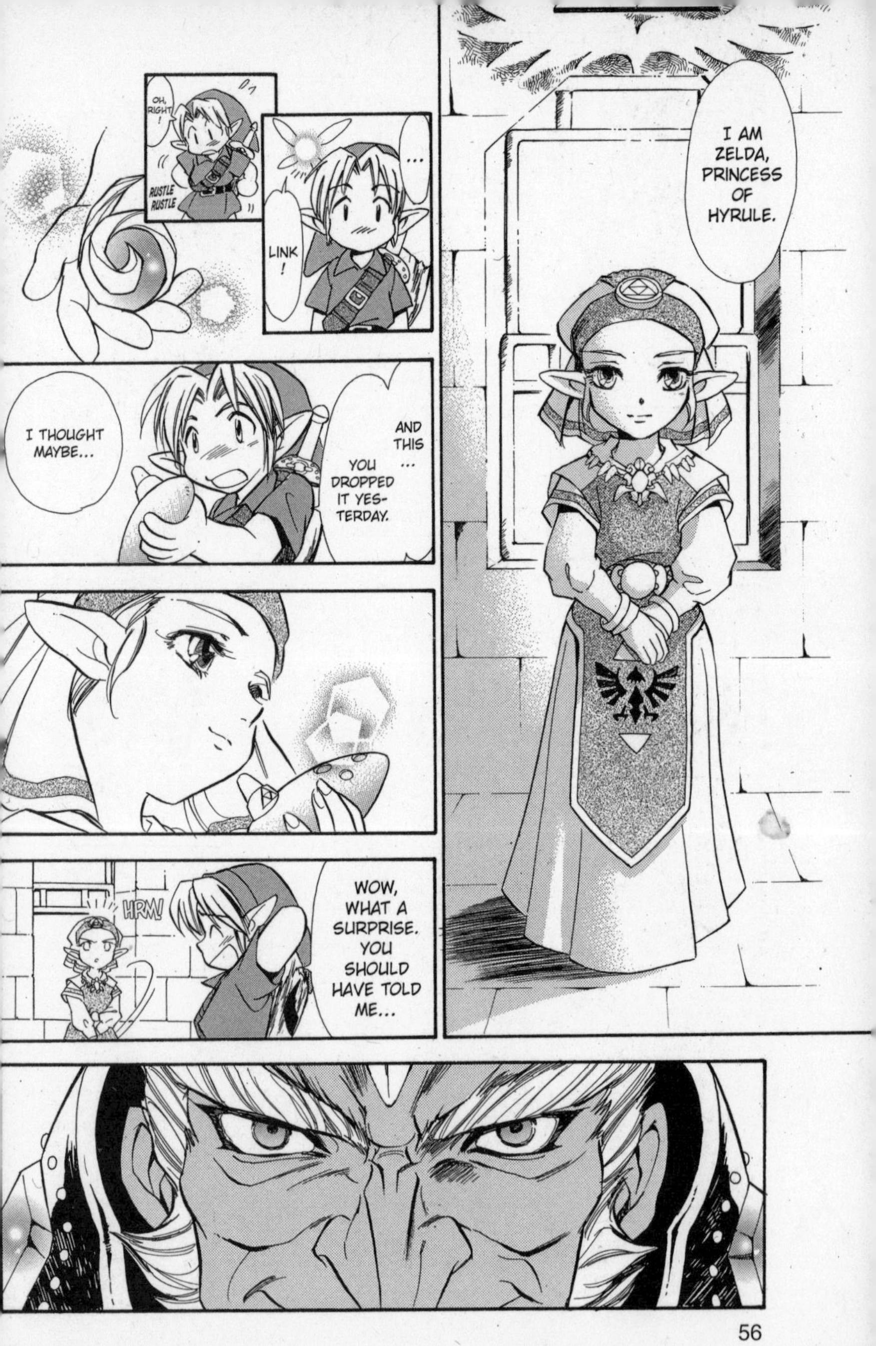
I AM ZELDA, PRINCESS OF HYRULE.
...
LINK!
OH, RIGHT!
RUSTLE RUSTLE
AND THIS...
YOU DROPPED IT YES-TERDAY.
I THOUGHT MAYBE...
WOW, WHAT A SURPRISE. YOU SHOULD HAVE TOLD ME...
HRM!

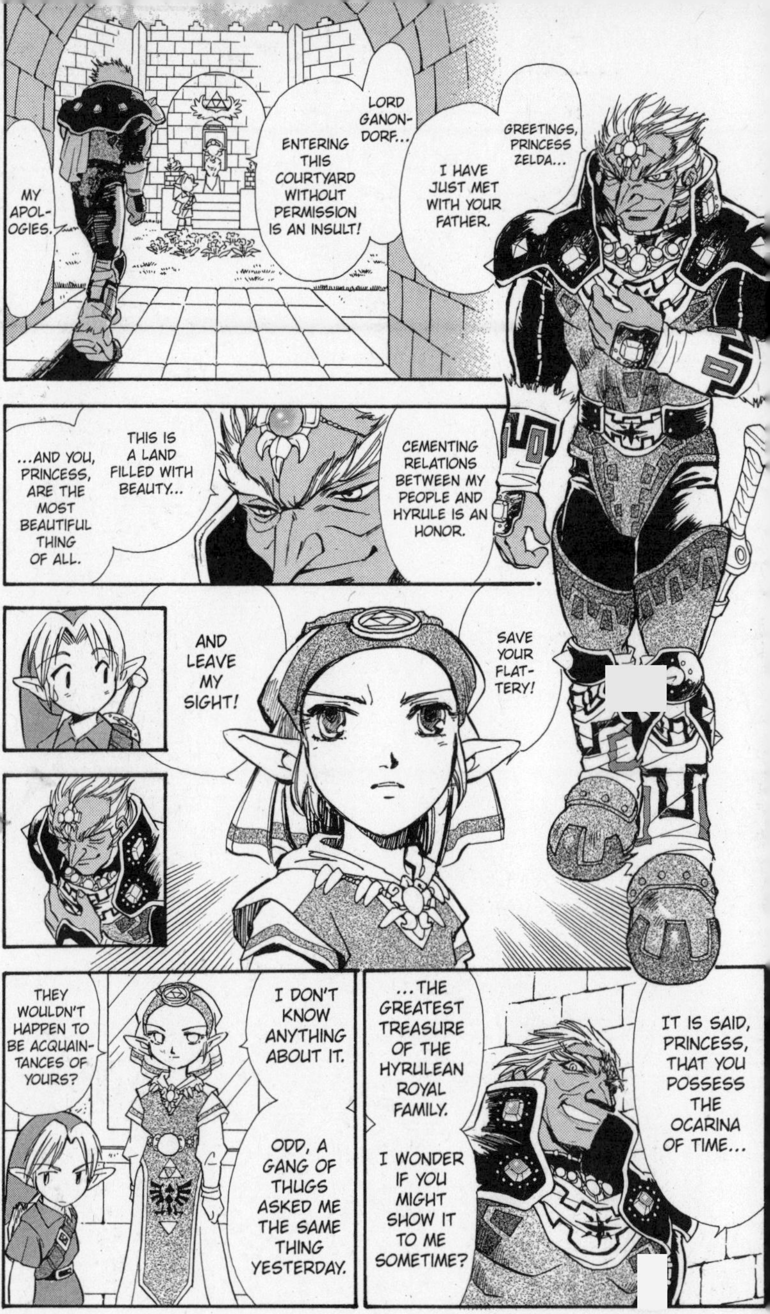
GREETINGS, PRINCESS ZELDA...
I HAVE JUST MET WITH YOUR FATHER.
LORD GANON-DORF...
ENTERING THIS COURTYARD WITHOUT PERMISSION IS AN INSULT!
MY APOL-OGIES.
CEMENTING RELATIONS BETWEEN MY PEOPLE AND HYRULE IS AN HONOR.
THIS IS A LAND FILLED WITH BEAUTY...
...AND YOU, PRINCESS, ARE THE MOST BEAUTIFUL THING OF ALL.
SAVE YOUR FLAT-TERY!
AND LEAVE MY SIGHT!
IT IS SAID, PRINCESS, THAT YOU POSSESS THE OCARINA OF TIME...
...THE GREATEST TREASURE OF THE HYRULEAN ROYAL FAMILY.
I WONDER IF YOU MIGHT SHOW IT TO ME SOMETIME?
I DON'T KNOW ANYTHING ABOUT IT.
ODD, A GANG OF THUGS ASKED ME THE SAME THING YESTERDAY.
THEY WOULDN'T HAPPEN TO BE ACQUAIN-TANCES OF YOURS?

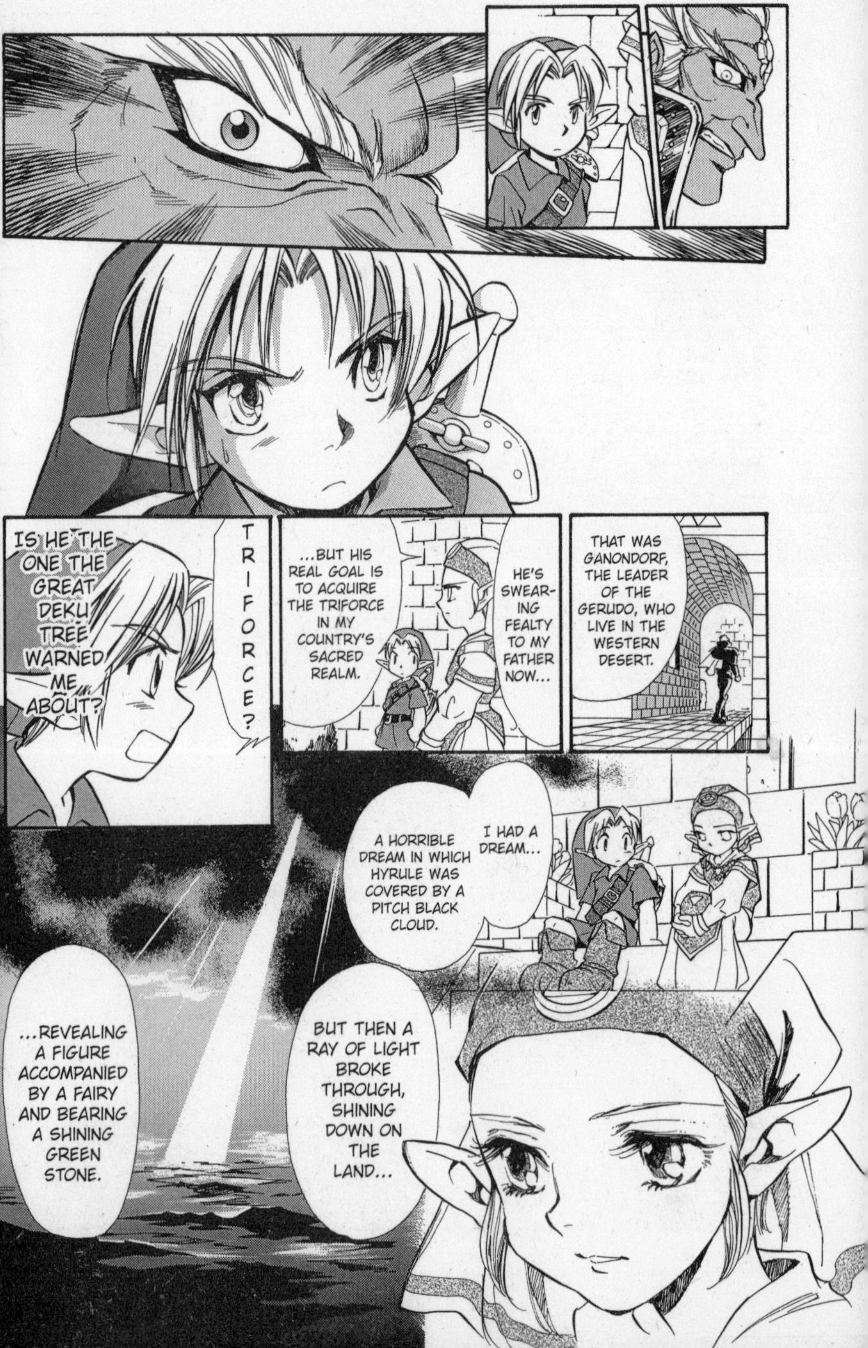
THAT WAS GANONDORF, THE LEADER OF THE GERUDO, WHO LIVE IN THE WESTERN DESERT.
HE'S SWEAR-ING FEALTY TO MY FATHER NOW...
...BUT HIS REAL GOAL IS TO ACQUIRE THE TRIFORCE IN MY COUNTRY'S SACRED REALM.
TRIFORCE?
IS HE THE ONE THE GREAT DEKU TREE WARNED ME ABOUT?
I HAD A DREAM...
A HORRIBLE DREAM IN WHICH HYRULE WAS COVERED BY A PITCH BLACK CLOUD.
BUT THEN A RAY OF LIGHT BROKE THROUGH, SHINING DOWN ON THE LAND...
...REVEALING A FIGURE ACCOMPANIED BY A FAIRY AND BEARING A SHINING GREEN STONE.

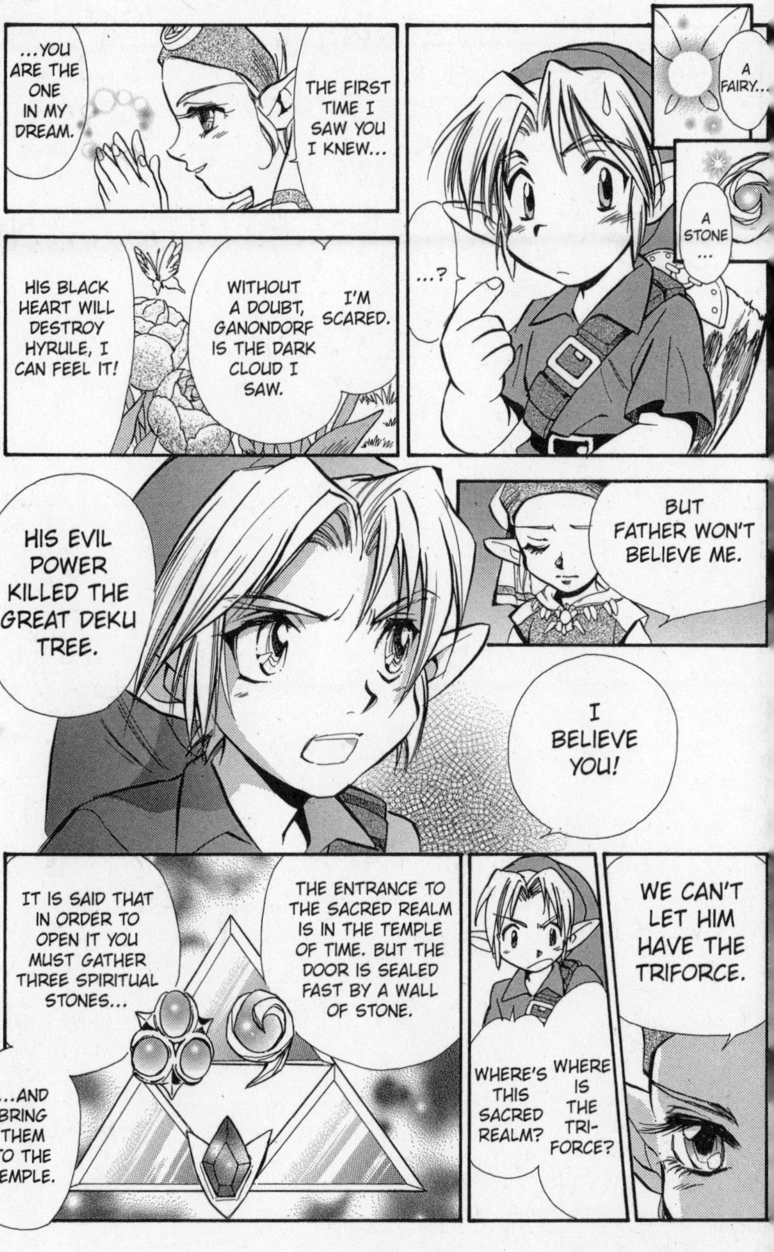

...?
A FAIRY...
A STONE...
...YOU ARE THE ONE IN MY DREAM.
THE FIRST TIME I SAW YOU I KNEW...
I'M SCARED.
WITHOUT A DOUBT, GANONDORF IS THE DARK CLOUD I SAW.
HIS BLACK HEART WILL DESTROY HYRULE, I CAN FEEL IT!
BUT FATHER WON'T BELIEVE ME.
I BELIEVE YOU!
HIS EVIL POWER KILLED THE GREAT DEKU TREE.
WE CAN'T LET HIM HAVE THE TRIFORCE.
WHERE IS THE TRI-FORCE?
WHERE'S THIS SACRED REALM?
THE ENTRANCE TO THE SACRED REALM IS IN THE TEMPLE OF TIME. BUT THE DOOR IS SEALED FAST BY A WALL OF STONE.
IT IS SAID THAT IN ORDER TO OPEN IT YOU MUST GATHER THREE SPIRITUAL STONES...
...AND BRING THEM TO THE TEMPLE.

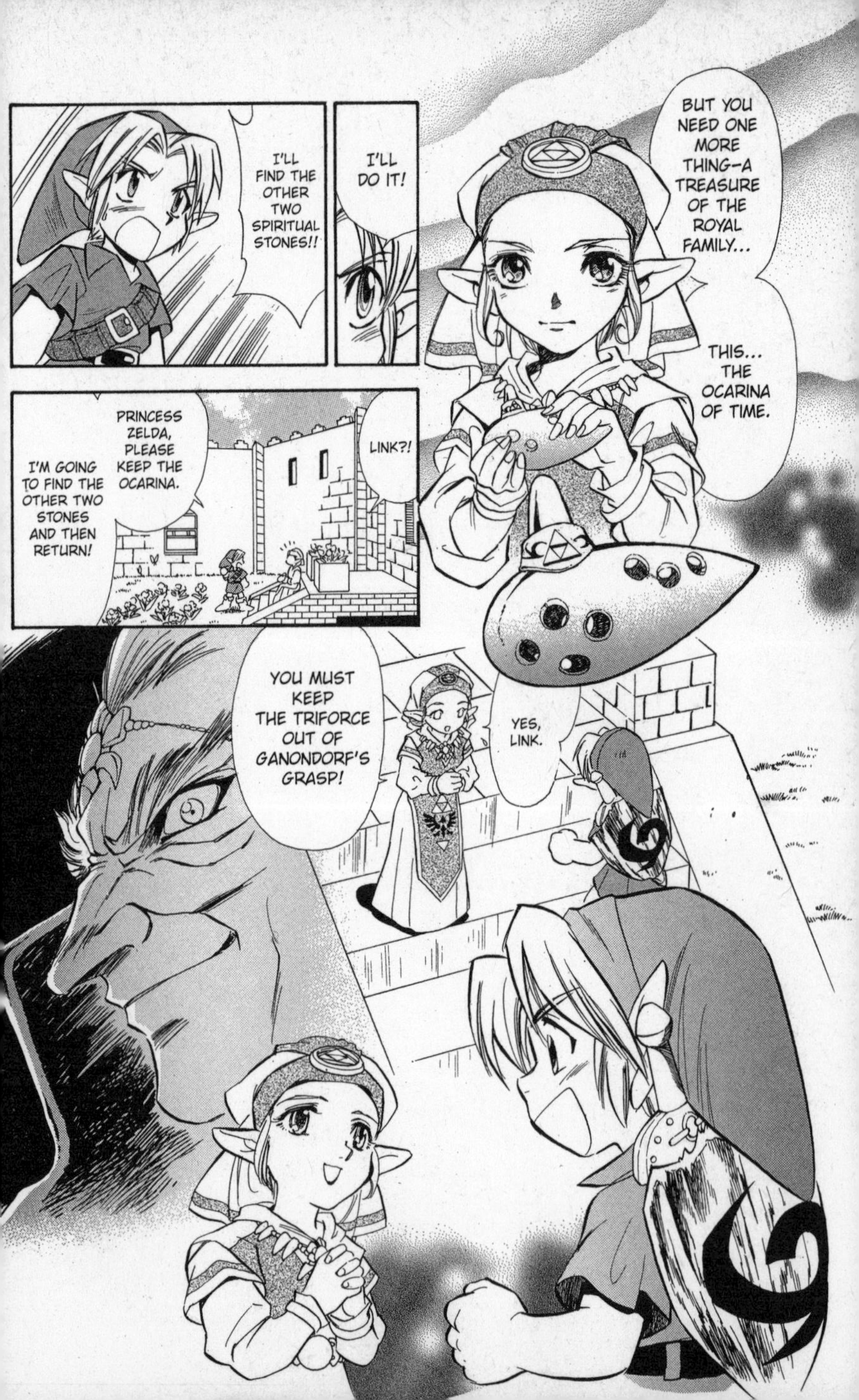
BUT YOU NEED ONE MORE THING—A TREASURE OF THE ROYAL FAMILY...
THIS... THE OCARINA OF TIME.
I'LL DO IT!
I'LL FIND THE OTHER TWO SPIRITUAL STONES!!
LINK?!
PRINCESS ZELDA, PLEASE KEEP THE OCARINA.
I'M GOING TO FIND THE OTHER TWO STONES AND THEN RETURN!
YOU MUST KEEP THE TRIFORCE OUT OF GANONDORF'S GRASP!
YES, LINK.

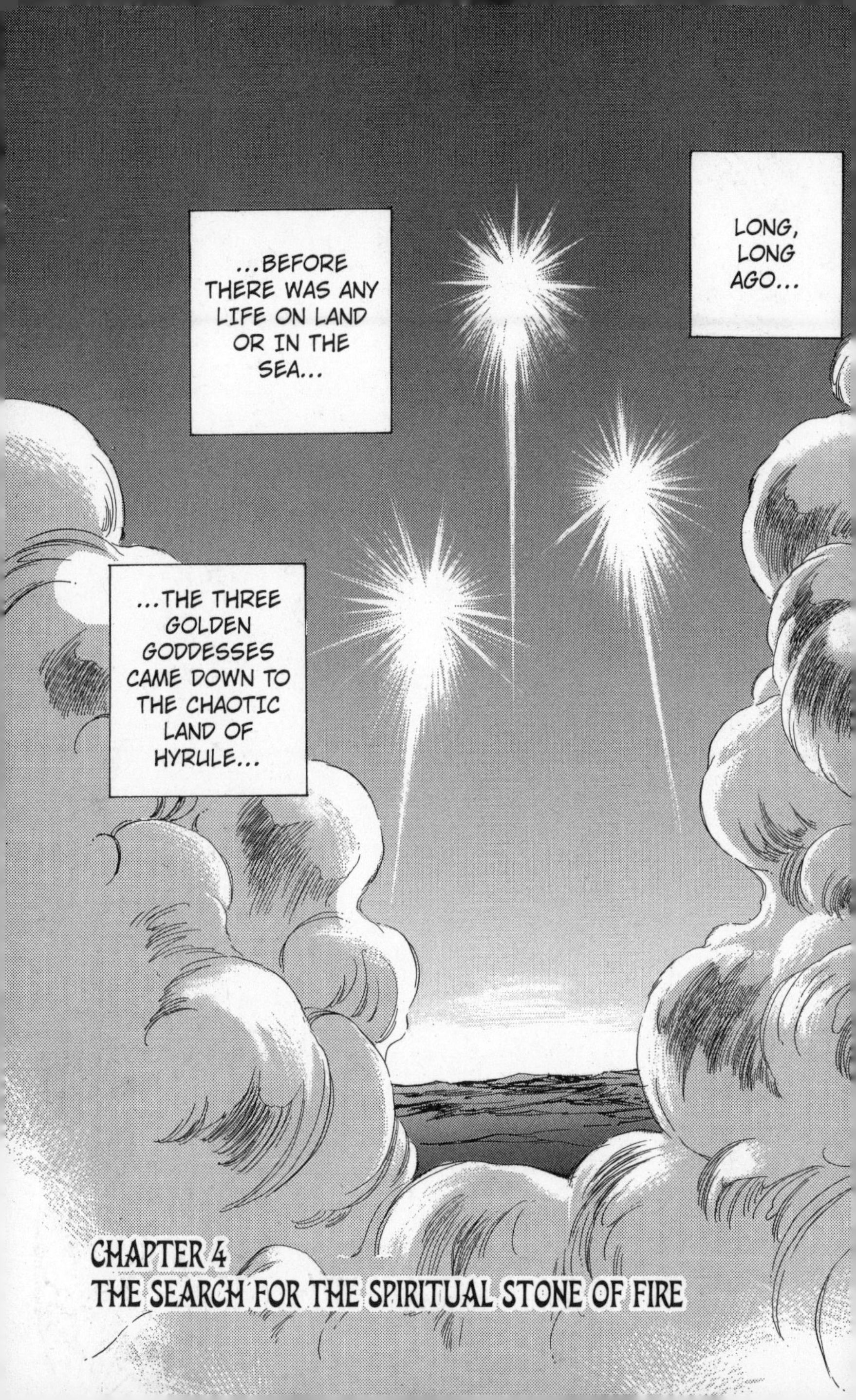
LONG, LONG AGO...
...BEFORE THERE WAS ANY LIFE ON LAND OR IN THE SEA...
...THE THREE GOLDEN GODDESSES CAME DOWN TO THE CHAOTIC LAND OF HYRULE...
CHAPTER 4
THE SEARCH FOR THE SPIRITUAL STONE OF FIRE

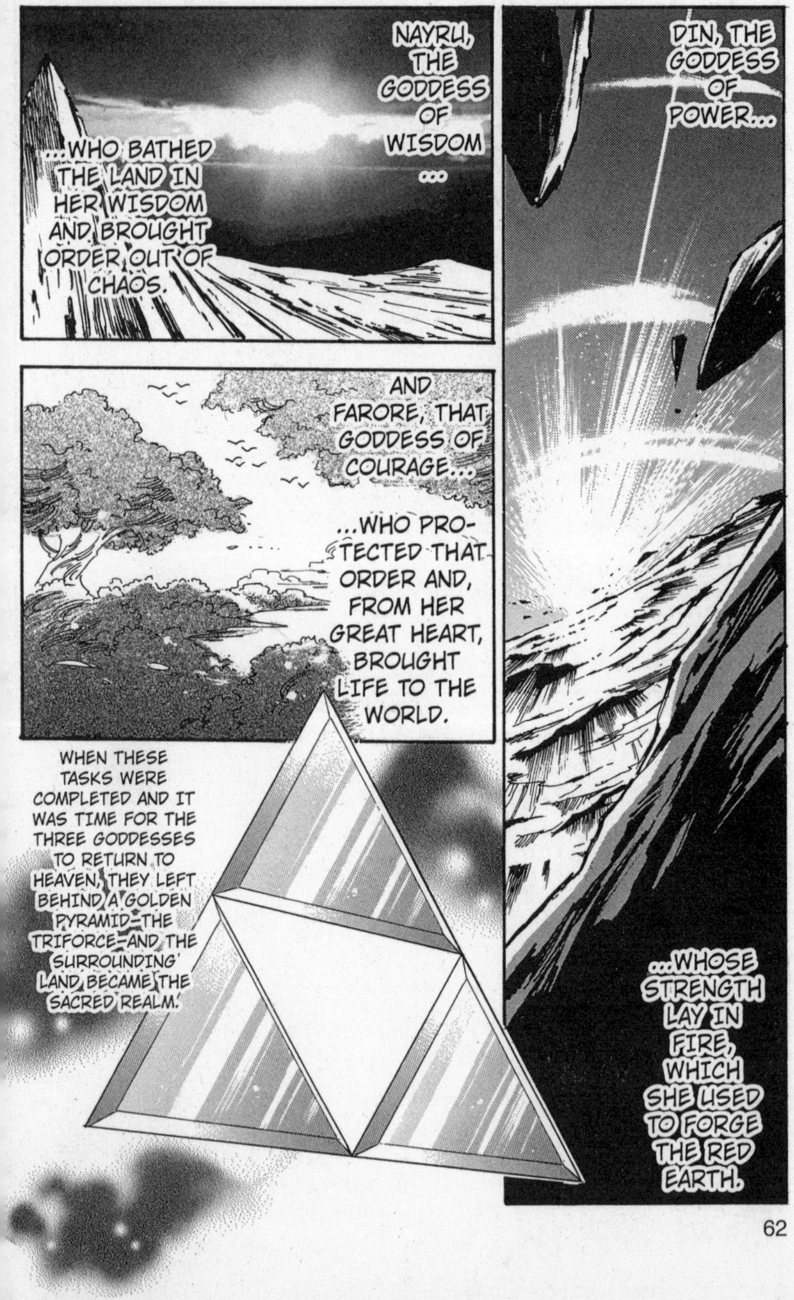
DIN, THE GODDESS OF POWER...
...WHOSE STRENGTH LAY IN FIRE, WHICH SHE USED TO FORGE THE RED EARTH.
NAYRU, THE GODDESS OF WISDOM...
...WHO BATHED THE LAND IN HER WISDOM AND BROUGHT ORDER OUT OF CHAOS.
AND FARORE, THAT GODDESS OF COURAGE...
...WHO PROTECTED THAT ORDER AND, FROM HER GREAT HEART, BROUGHT LIFE TO THE WORLD.
WHEN THESE TASKS WERE COMPLETED AND IT WAS TIME FOR THE THREE GODDESSES TO RETURN TO HEAVEN, THEY LEFT BEHIND A GOLDEN PYRAMID—THE TRIFORCE—AND THE SURROUNDING LAND BECAME THE SACRED REALM.

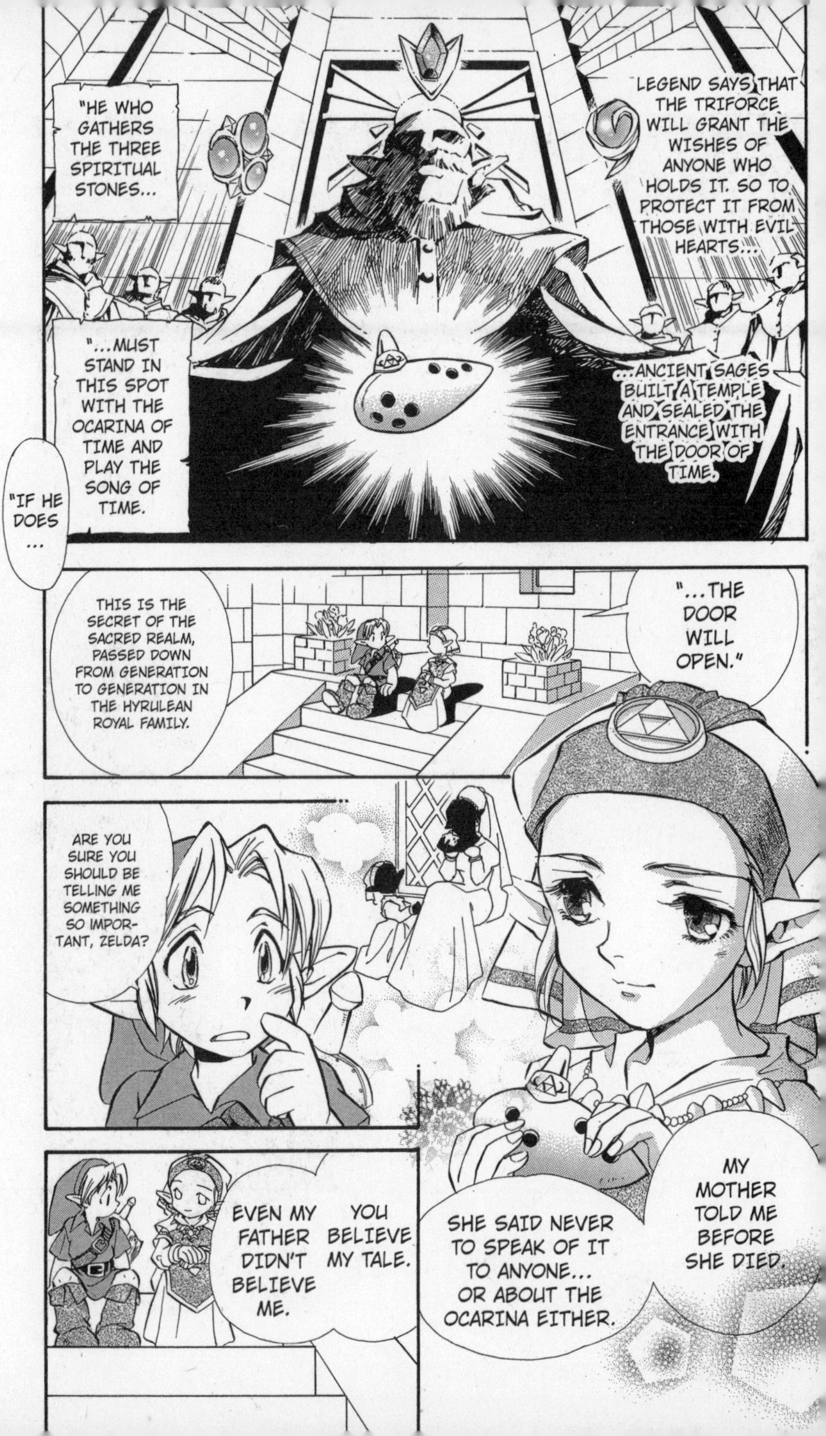
LEGEND SAYS THAT THE TRIFORCE WILL GRANT THE WISHES OF ANYONE WHO HOLDS IT. SO TO PROTECT IT FROM THOSE WITH EVIL HEARTS...
...ANCIENT SAGES BUILT A TEMPLE AND SEALED THE ENTRANCE WITH THE DOOR OF TIME.
"HE WHO GATHERS THE THREE SPIRITUAL STONES...
"...MUST STAND IN THIS SPOT WITH THE OCARINA OF TIME AND PLAY THE SONG OF TIME.
"IF HE DOES...
"...THE DOOR WILL OPEN."
THIS IS THE SECRET OF THE SACRED REALM, PASSED DOWN FROM GENERATION TO GENERATION IN THE HYRULEAN ROYAL FAMILY.
ARE YOU SURE YOU SHOULD BE TELLING ME SOMETHING SO IMPORTANT, ZELDA?
MY MOTHER TOLD ME BEFORE SHE DIED.
SHE SAID NEVER TO SPEAK OF IT TO ANYONE... OR ABOUT THE OCARINA EITHER.
EVEN MY FATHER DIDN'T BELIEVE ME. YOU BELIEVE MY TALE.

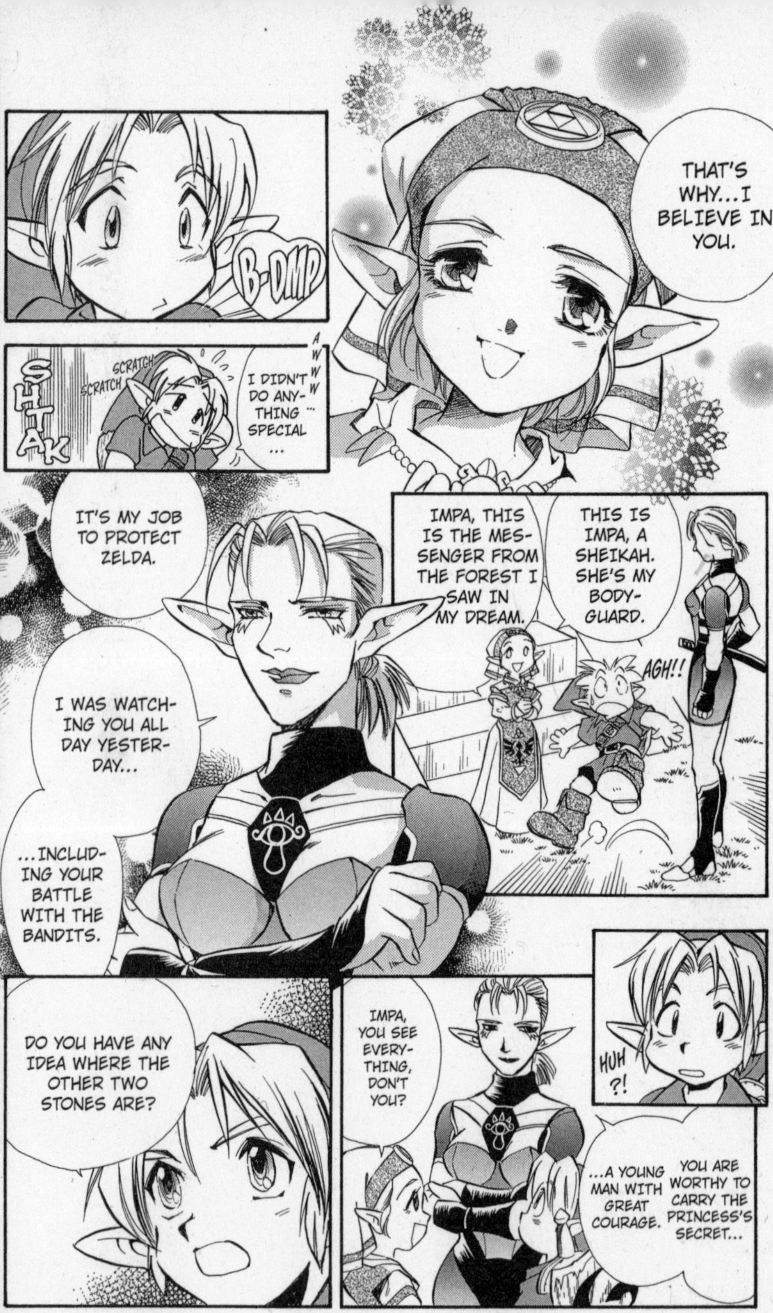
THAT'S WHY...I BELIEVE IN YOU.
B-DMP
AWWW...
I DIDN'T DO ANY-THING SPECIAL...
SCRATCH SCRATCH
SHTAK
THIS IS IMPA, A SHEIKAH. SHE'S MY BODY-GUARD.
IMPA, THIS IS THE MES-SENGER FROM THE FOREST I SAW IN MY DREAM.
AGH!!
IT'S MY JOB TO PROTECT ZELDA.
I WAS WATCH-ING YOU ALL DAY YESTER-DAY...
...INCLUD-ING YOUR BATTLE WITH THE BANDITS.
HUH ?!
YOU ARE WORTHY TO CARRY THE PRINCESS'S SECRET...
...A YOUNG MAN WITH GREAT COURAGE.
IMPA, YOU SEE EVERY-THING, DON'T YOU?
DO YOU HAVE ANY IDEA WHERE THE OTHER TWO STONES ARE?

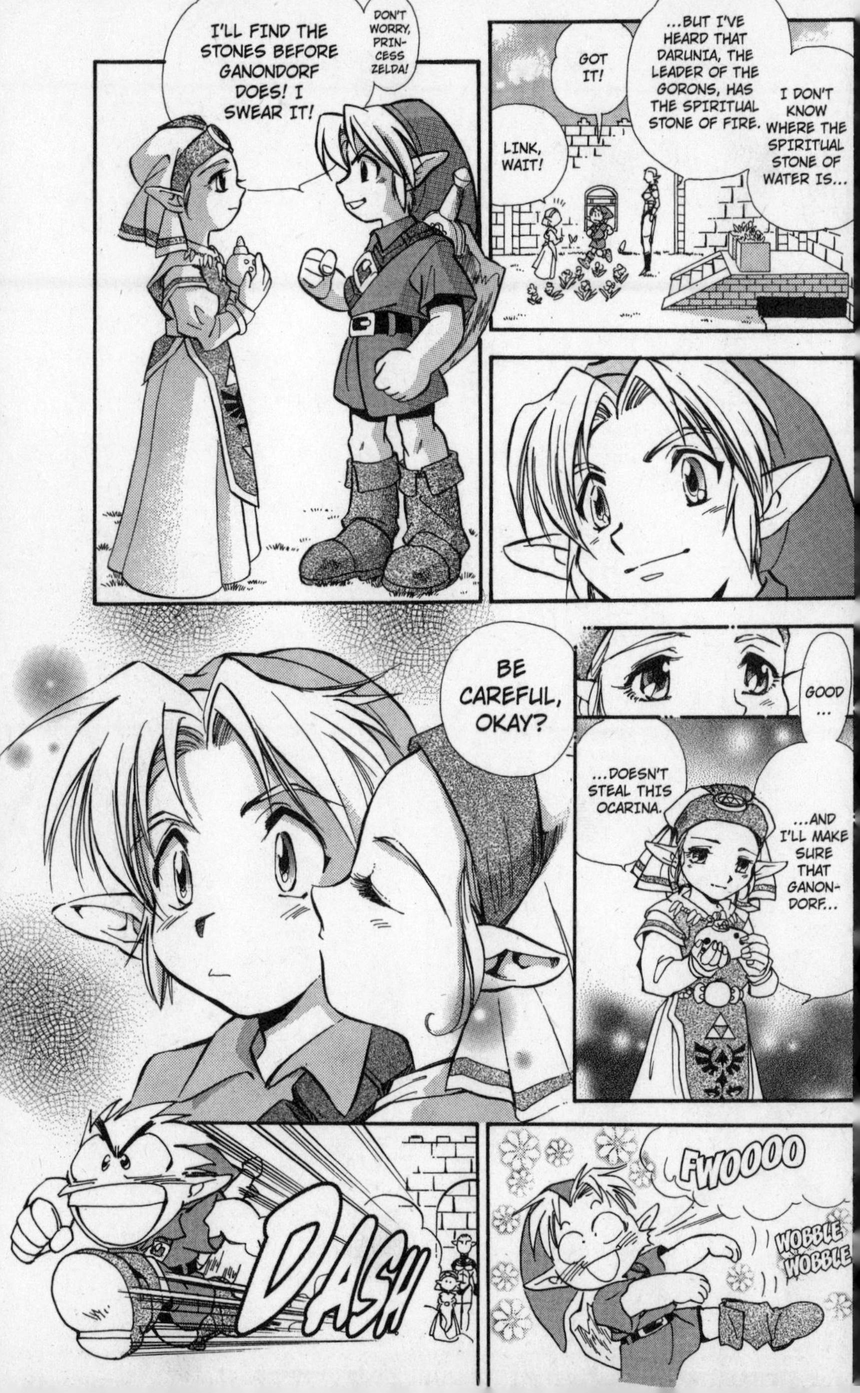
I DON'T KNOW WHERE THE SPIRITUAL STONE OF WATER IS...
...BUT I'VE HEARD THAT DARUNIA, THE LEADER OF THE GORONS, HAS THE SPIRITUAL STONE OF FIRE.
GOT IT!
LINK, WAIT!
DON'T WORRY, PRIN-CESS ZELDA!
I'LL FIND THE STONES BEFORE GANONDORF DOES! I SWEAR IT!
GOOD...
...AND I'LL MAKE SURE THAT GANON-DORF...
...DOESN'T STEAL THIS OCARINA.
BE CAREFUL, OKAY?
FWOOOO
WOBBLE WOBBLE
DASH

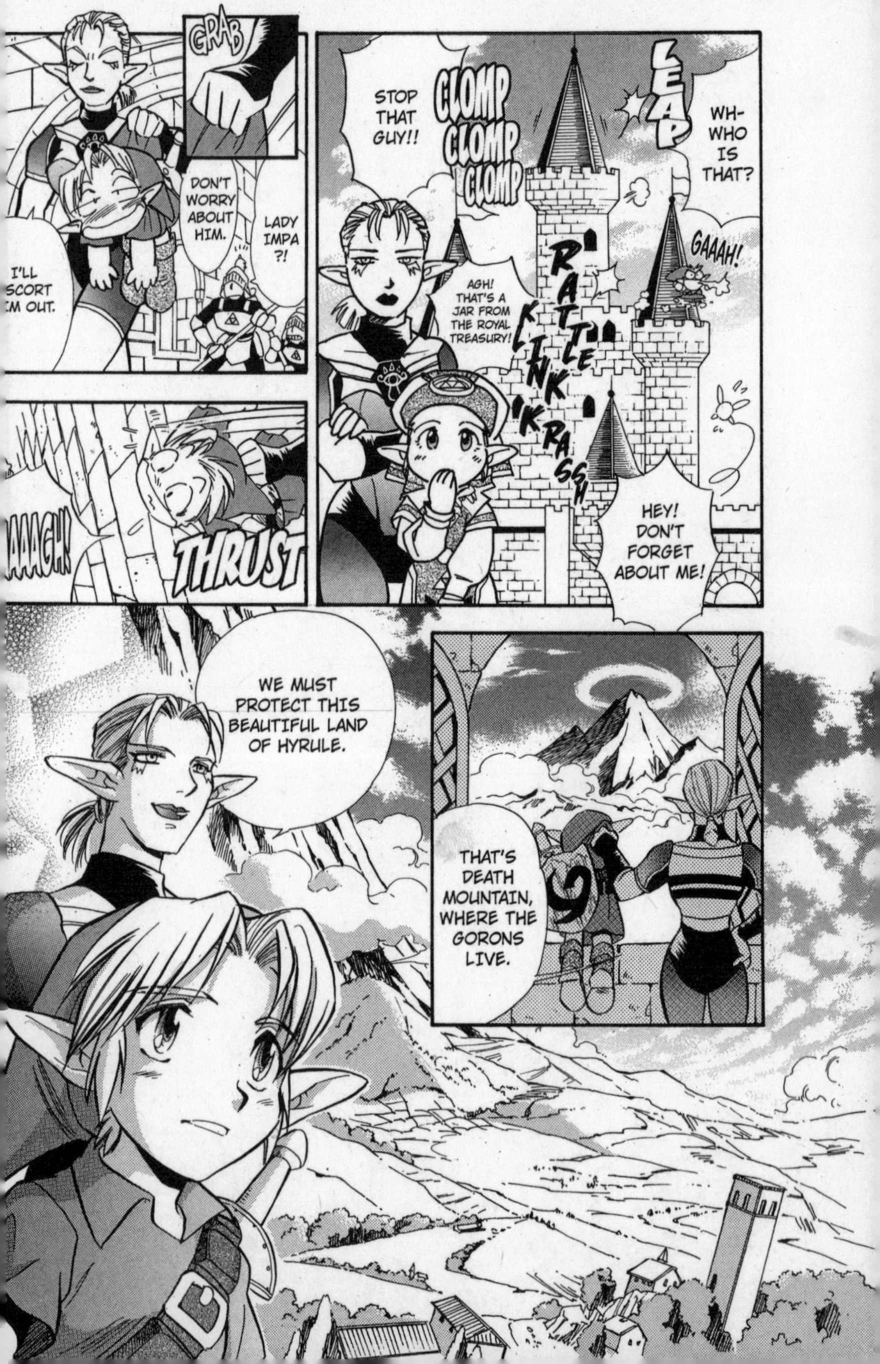
WH- WHO IS THAT?
LEAP
GAAAH!
CLOMP CLOMP CLOMP
STOP THAT GUY!!
RATTLE
KLINK
KRASSH
AGH! THAT'S A JAR FROM THE ROYAL TREASURY!
HEY! DON'T FORGET ABOUT ME!
GRAB
LADY IMPA ?!
DON'T WORRY ABOUT HIM.
I'LL
SCORT
IM OUT.
THRUST
AAAAGH!
THAT'S DEATH MOUNTAIN, WHERE THE GORONS LIVE.
WE MUST PROTECT THIS BEAUTIFUL LAND OF HYRULE.

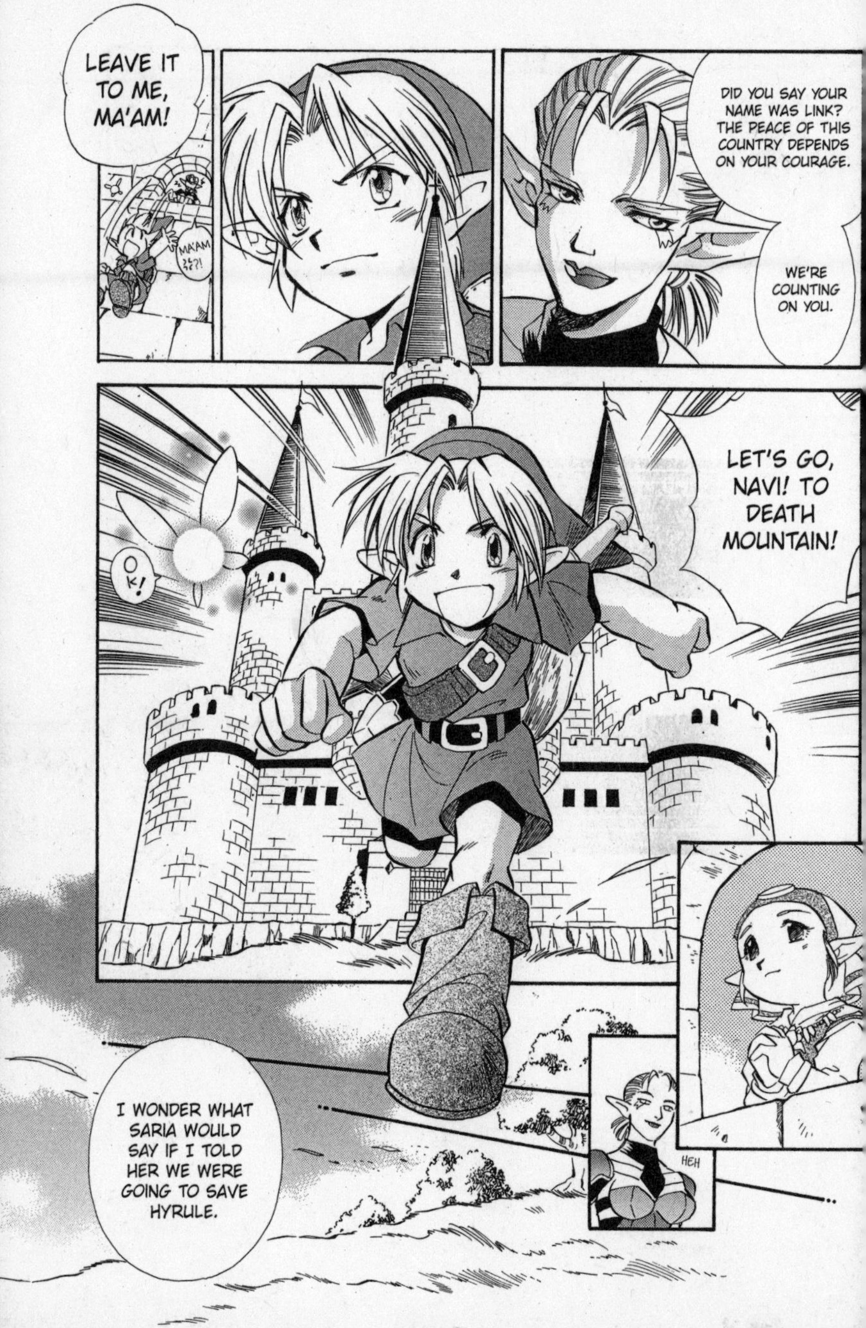
DID YOU SAY YOUR NAME WAS LINK? THE PEACE OF THIS COUNTRY DEPENDS ON YOUR COURAGE.
WE'RE COUNTING ON YOU.
LEAVE IT TO ME, MA'AM!
MA'AM
LET'S GO, NAVI! TO DEATH MOUNTAIN!
OK!
HEH
I WONDER WHAT SARIA WOULD SAY IF I TOLD HER WE WERE GOING TO SAVE HYRULE.

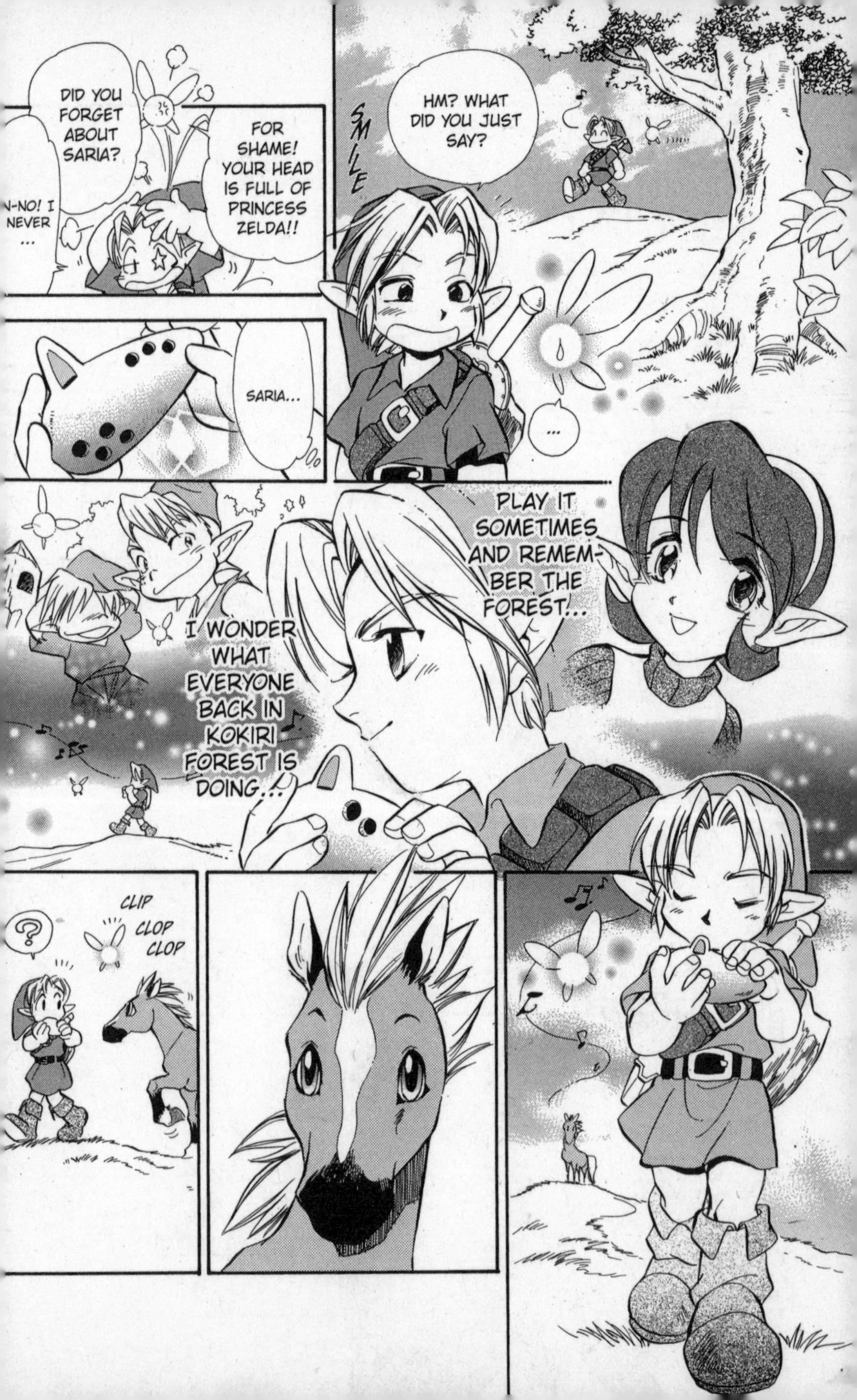
SMILE
HM? WHAT DID YOU JUST SAY?
...
FOR SHAME! YOUR HEAD IS FULL OF PRINCESS ZELDA!!
DID YOU FORGET ABOUT SARIA?
N-NO! I NEVER ...
SARIA...
PLAY IT SOMETIMES AND REMEMBER THE FOREST...
I WONDER WHAT EVERYONE BACK IN KOKIRI FOREST IS DOING...
CLIP CLOP CLOP
?

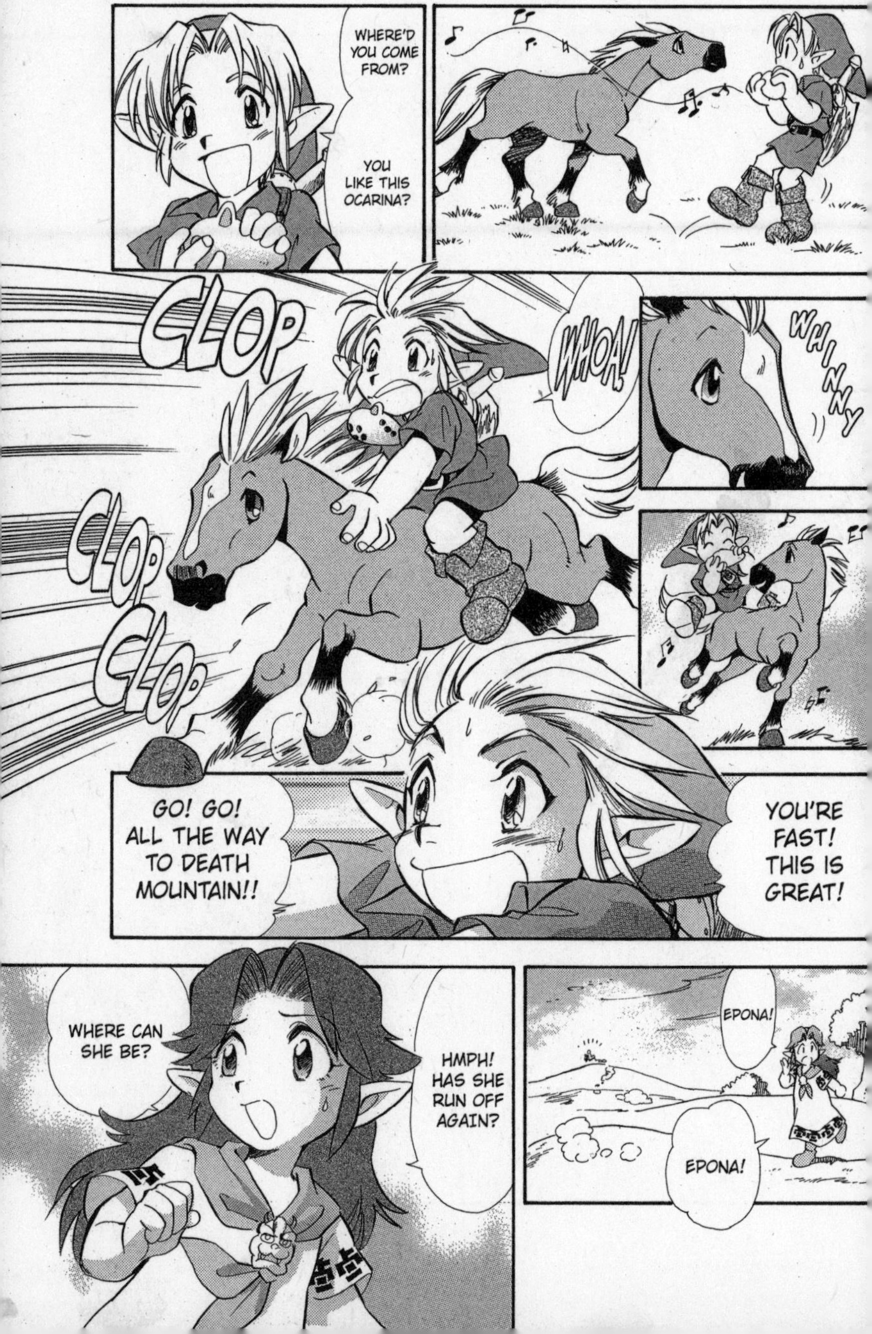
WHERE'D YOU COME FROM?
YOU LIKE THIS OCARINA?
WHINNY
WHOA!
CLOP
CLOP
CLOP
YOU'RE FAST! THIS IS GREAT!
GO! GO! ALL THE WAY TO DEATH MOUNTAIN!!
EPONA!
EPONA!
HMPH! HAS SHE RUN OFF AGAIN?
WHERE CAN SHE BE?

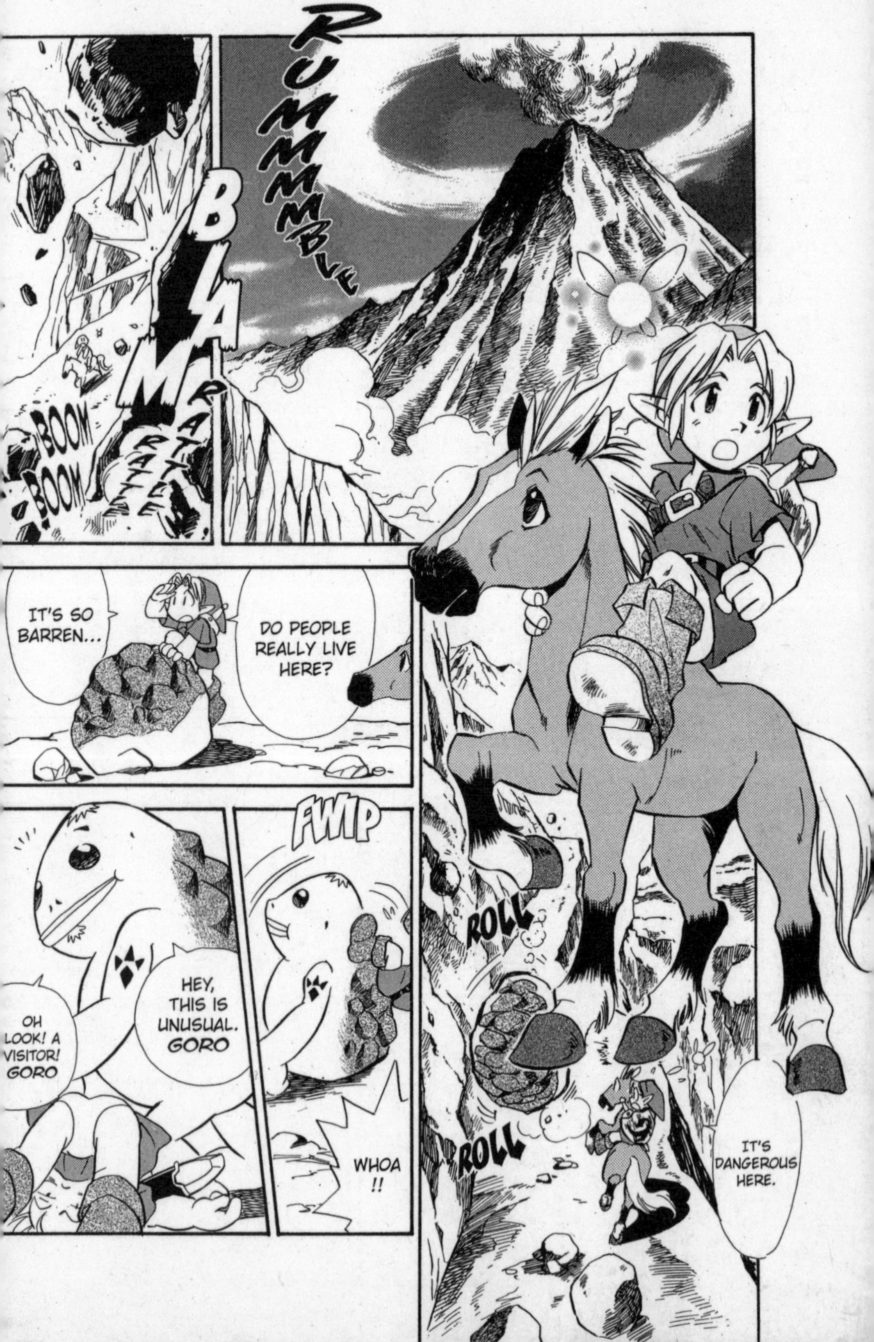
RUMMMMBLE
BLAM
RATTLE RATTLE
BOOM BOOM
ROLL
ROLL
IT'S DANGEROUS HERE.
DO PEOPLE REALLY LIVE HERE?
IT'S SO BARREN...
FWIP
HEY, THIS IS UNUSUAL. GORO
WHOA !!
OH LOOK! A VISITOR! GORO

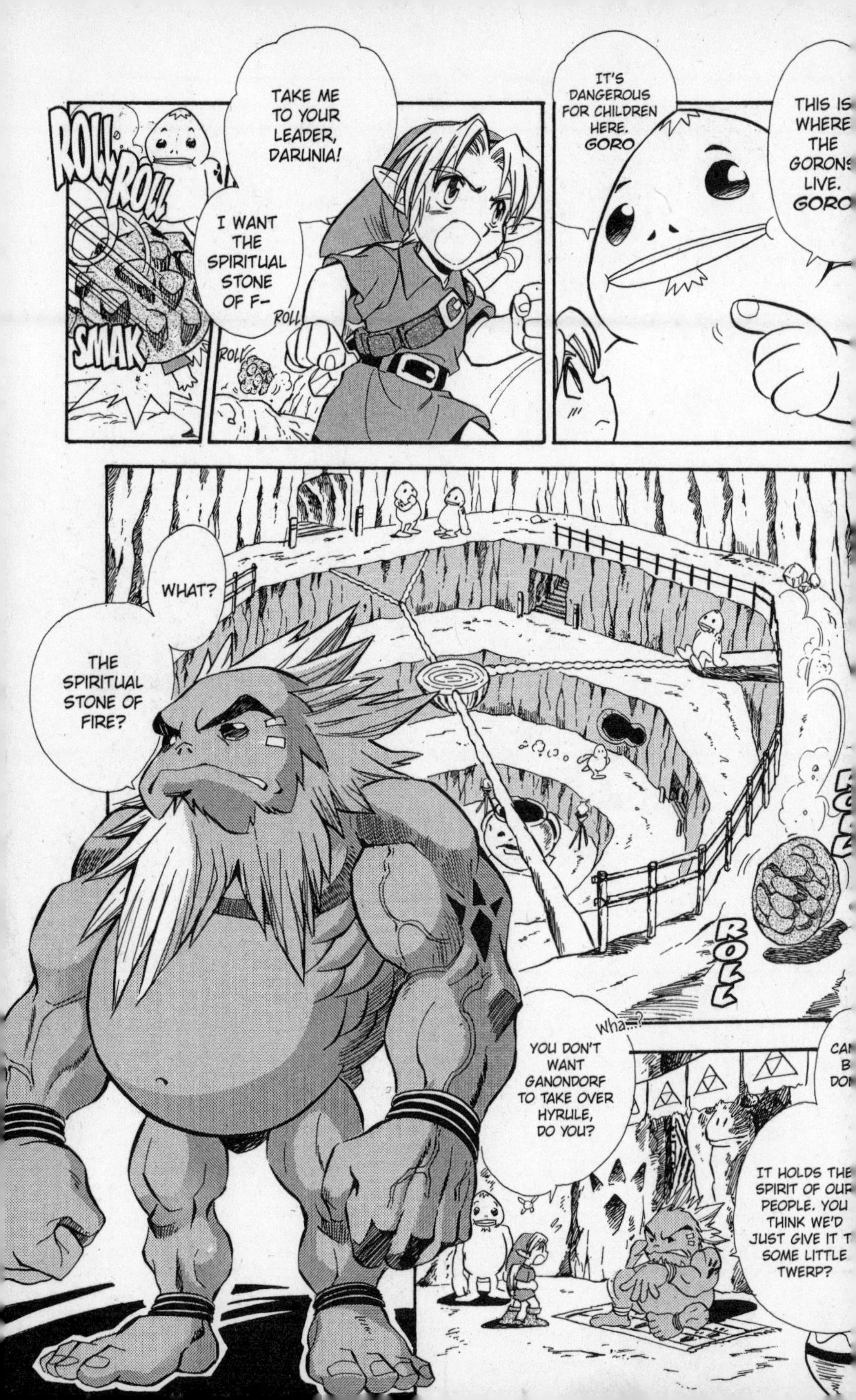
THIS IS WHERE THE GORONS LIVE. GORO
IT'S DANGEROUS FOR CHILDREN HERE. GORO
TAKE ME TO YOUR LEADER, DARUNIA!
I WANT THE SPIRITUAL STONE OF F—
ROLL
ROLL
ROLL ROLL
SMAK
WHAT?
THE SPIRITUAL STONE OF FIRE?
ROLL
ROLL
Wha...?
YOU DON'T WANT GANONDORF TO TAKE OVER HYRULE, DO YOU?
IT HOLDS THE SPIRIT OF OUR PEOPLE. YOU THINK WE'D JUST GIVE IT T SOME LITTLE TWERP?

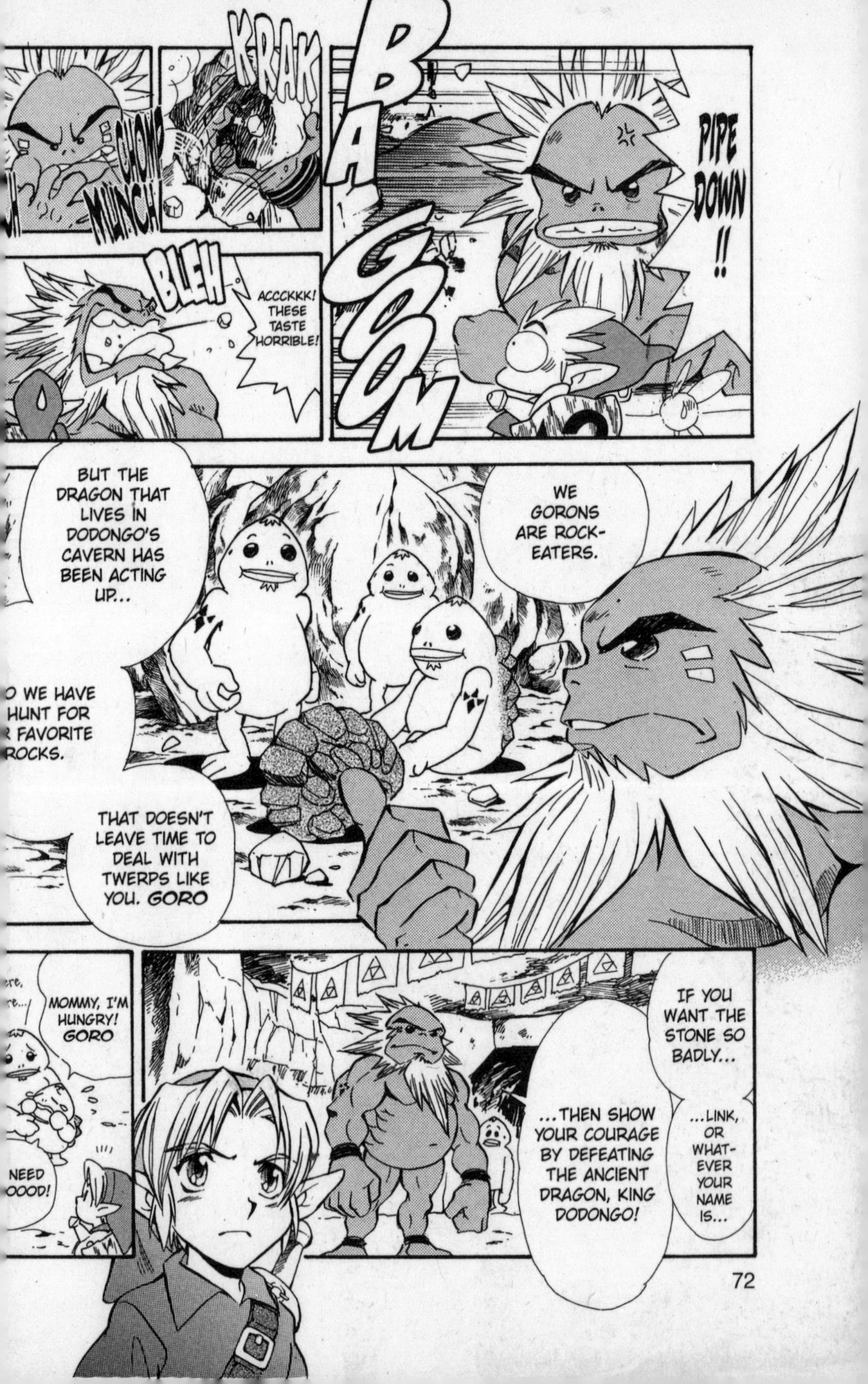
BAGOOM
PIPE DOWN!!
KRAK
CHOMP MUNCH
BLEH
ACCCKKK! THESE TASTE HORRIBLE!
WE GORONS ARE ROCK-EATERS.
BUT THE DRAGON THAT LIVES IN DODONGO'S CAVERN HAS BEEN ACTING UP...
O WE HAVE HUNT FOR R FAVORITE ROCKS.
THAT DOESN'T LEAVE TIME TO DEAL WITH TWERPS LIKE YOU. GORO
IF YOU WANT THE STONE SO BADLY...
...LINK, OR WHAT-EVER YOUR NAME IS...
...THEN SHOW YOUR COURAGE BY DEFEATING THE ANCIENT DRAGON, KING DODONGO!
MOMMY, I'M HUNGRY! GORO
NEED OOOD!

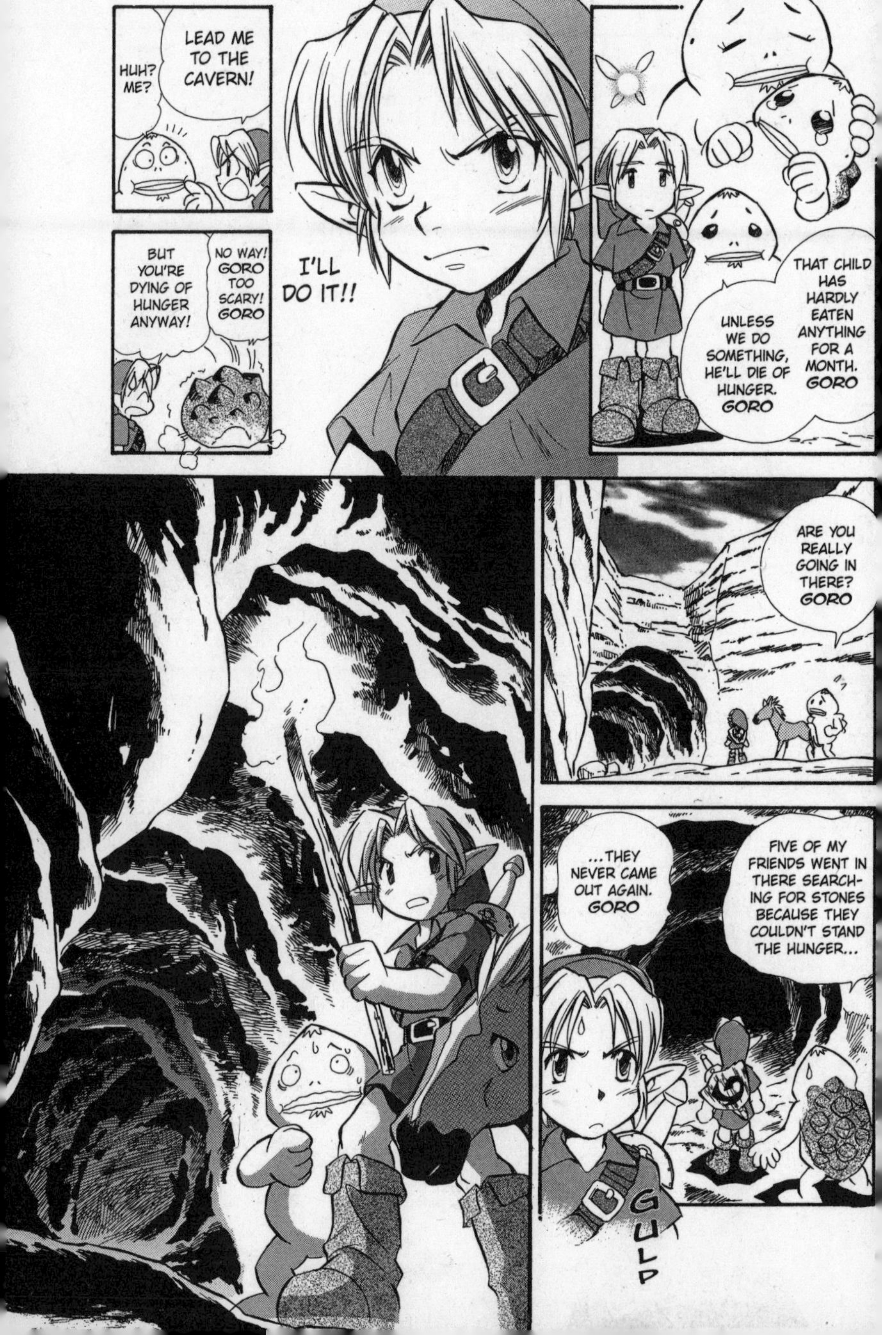
THAT CHILD HAS HARDLY EATEN ANYTHING FOR A MONTH. GORO
UNLESS WE DO SOMETHING, HE'LL DIE OF HUNGER. GORO
LEAD ME TO THE CAVERN!
HUH? ME?
NO WAY! GORO TOO SCARY! GORO
BUT YOU'RE DYING OF HUNGER ANYWAY!
I'LL DO IT!!
ARE YOU REALLY GOING IN THERE? GORO
FIVE OF MY FRIENDS WENT IN THERE SEARCHING FOR STONES BECAUSE THEY COULDN'T STAND THE HUNGER...
...THEY NEVER CAME OUT AGAIN. GORO
GULP

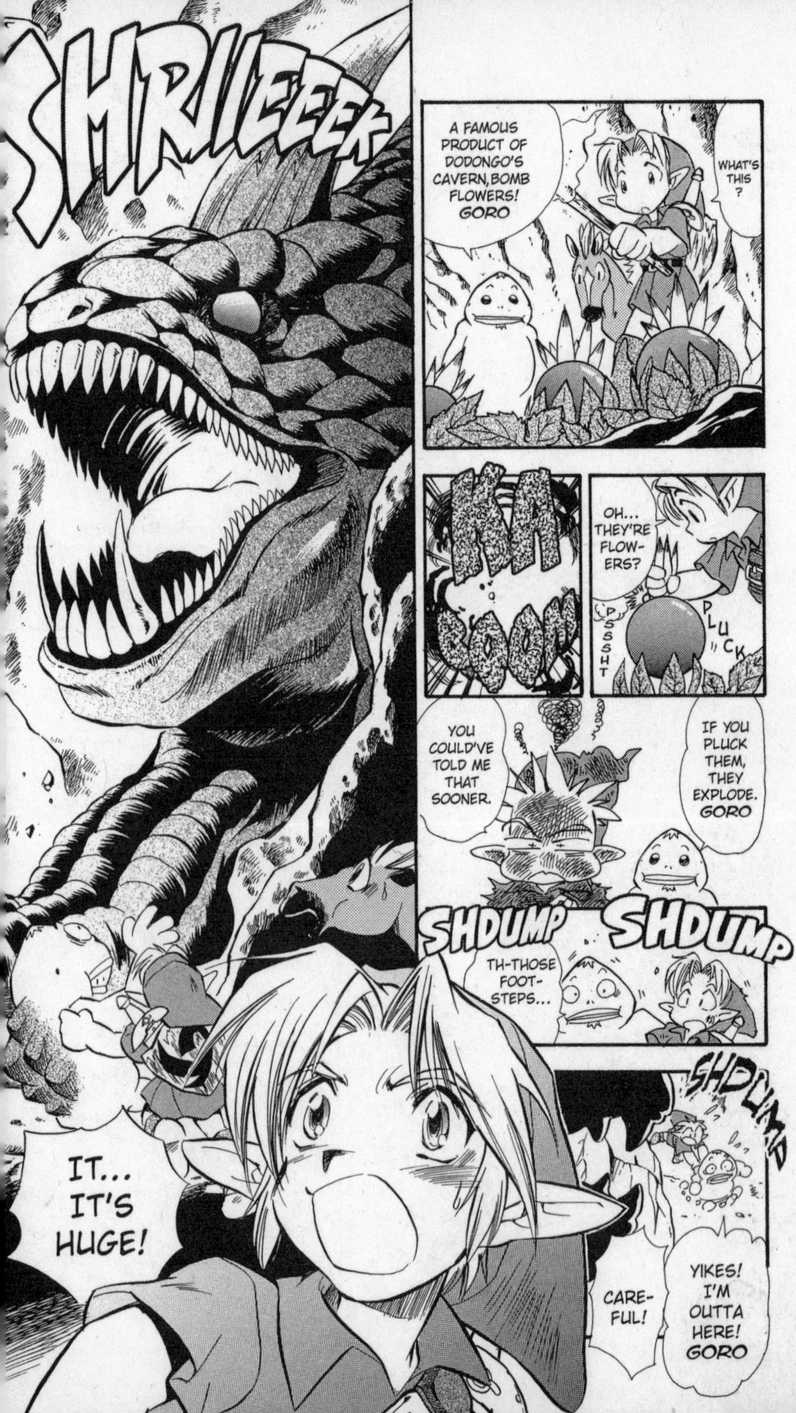
WHAT'S THIS?
A FAMOUS PRODUCT OF DODONGO'S CAVERN, BOMB FLOWERS! GORO
OH... THEY'RE FLOWERS?
PSSSHT
PLUCK
KA-BOOM
IF YOU PLUCK THEM, THEY EXPLODE. GORO
YOU COULD'VE TOLD ME THAT SOONER.
SHDUMP
SHDUMP
TH-THOSE FOOT-STEPS...
SHDUMP
YIKES! I'M OUTTA HERE! GORO
CARE-FUL!
SHRIIEEEK
IT... IT'S HUGE!

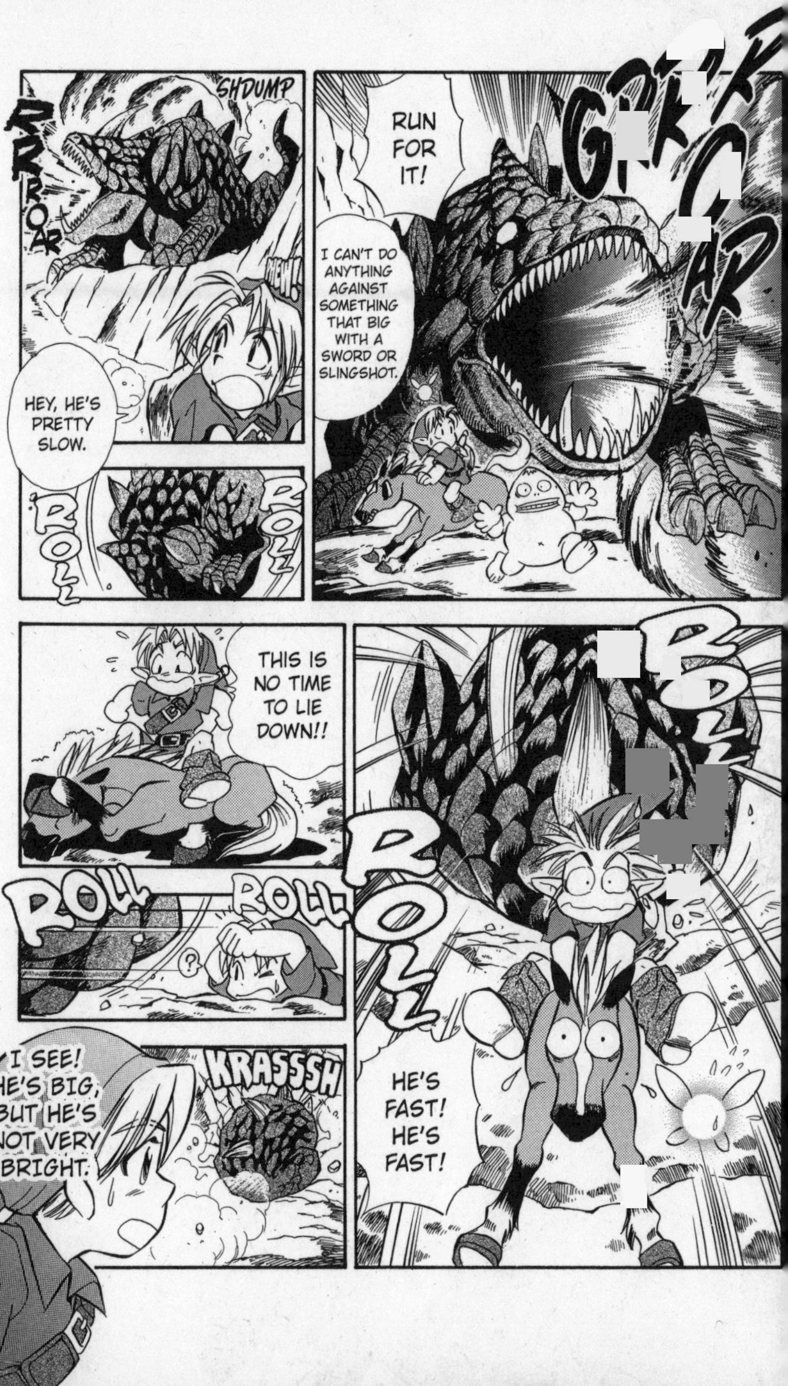
RUN FOR IT!
I CAN'T DO ANYTHING AGAINST SOMETHING THAT BIG WITH A SWORD OR SLINGSHOT.
SHDUMP
RRRROAR
PHEW!
HEY, HE'S PRETTY SLOW.
ROLL
ROLL
ROLL
HE'S FAST! HE'S FAST!
THIS IS NO TIME TO LIE DOWN!!
ROLL
ROLL
?
KRASSSH
I SEE! HE'S BIG, BUT HE'S NOT VERY BRIGHT.

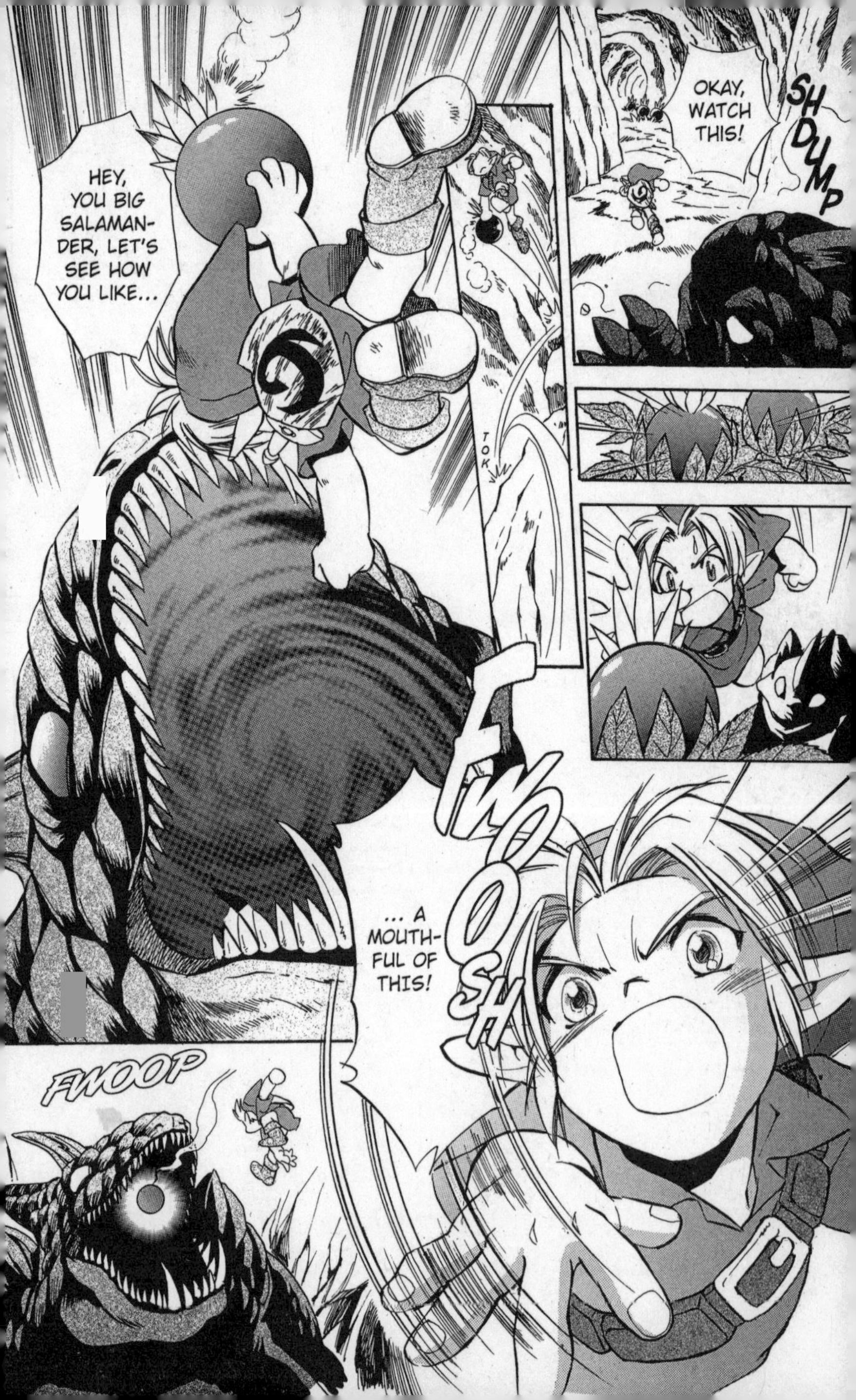
OKAY, WATCH THIS!
SHDUMP
TOK
HEY, YOU BIG SALAMANDER, LET'S SEE HOW YOU LIKE...
FWOOSH
... A MOUTHFUL OF THIS!
FWOOP

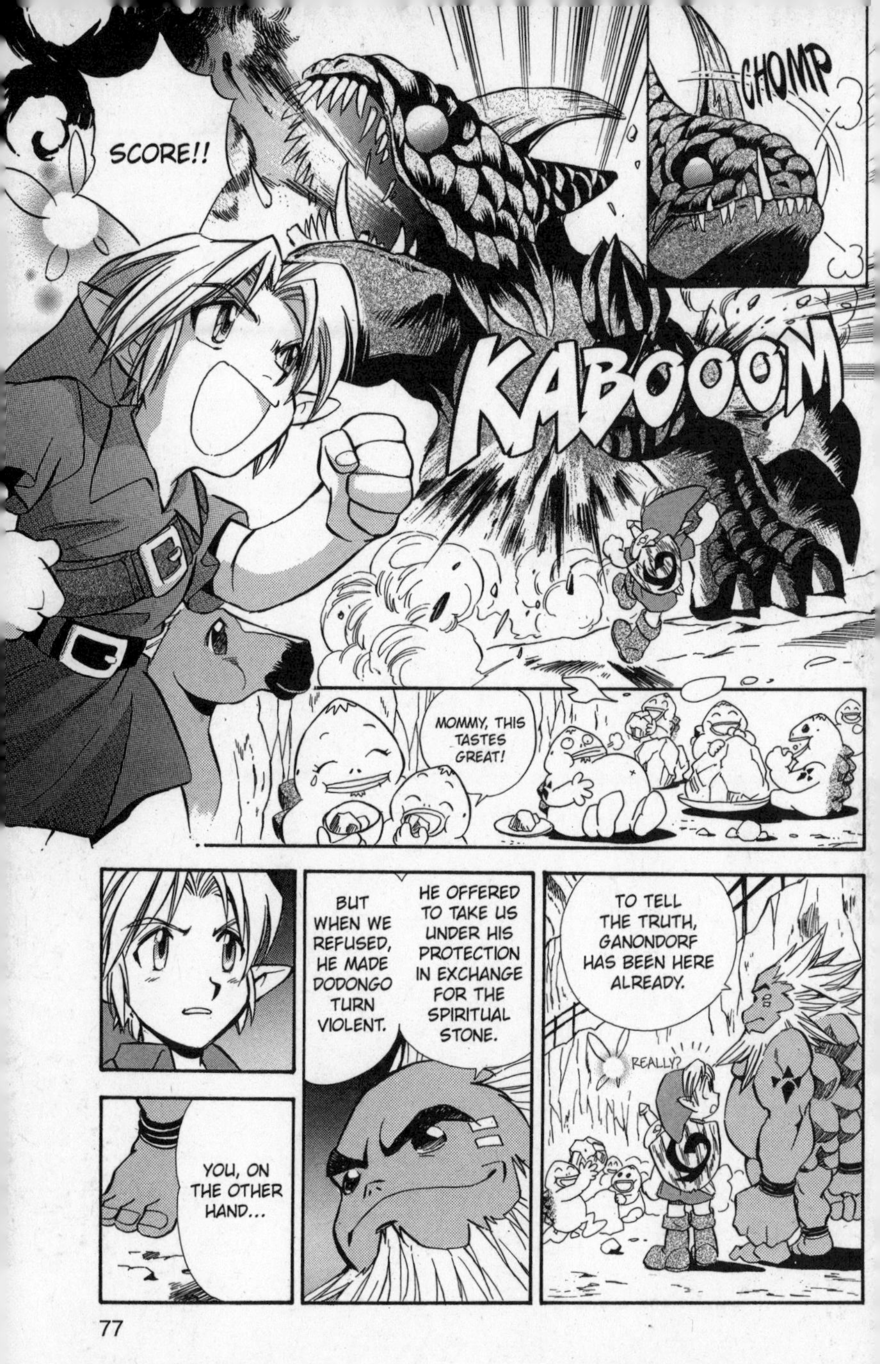
CHOMP
KABOOOM
SCORE!!
MOMMY, THIS TASTES GREAT!
TO TELL THE TRUTH, GANONDORF HAS BEEN HERE ALREADY.
REALLY?
HE OFFERED TO TAKE US UNDER HIS PROTECTION IN EXCHANGE FOR THE SPIRITUAL STONE.
BUT WHEN WE REFUSED, HE MADE DODONGO TURN VIOLENT.
YOU, ON THE OTHER HAND...

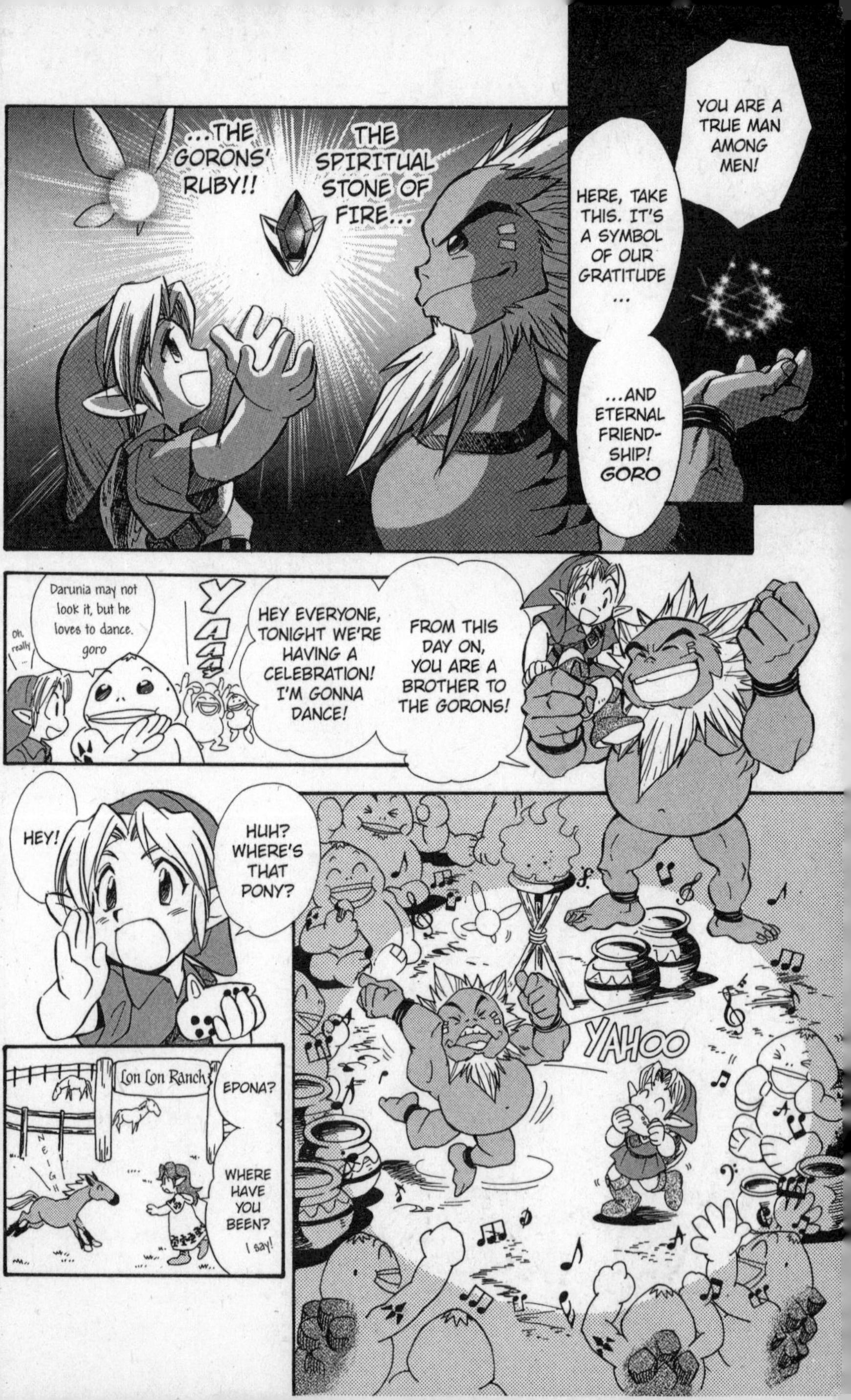
YOU ARE A TRUE MAN AMONG MEN!
HERE, TAKE THIS. IT'S A SYMBOL OF OUR GRATITUDE ...
...AND ETERNAL FRIEND-SHIP! GORO
THE SPIRITUAL STONE OF FIRE...
...THE GORONS' RUBY!!
FROM THIS DAY ON, YOU ARE A BROTHER TO THE GORONS!
HEY EVERYONE, TONIGHT WE'RE HAVING A CELEBRATION! I'M GONNA DANCE!
YAAAY
Darunia may not look it, but he loves to dance. goro
Oh, really ...
YAHOO
HUH? WHERE'S THAT PONY?
HEY!
EPONA?
WHERE HAVE YOU BEEN?
I say!
Lon Lon Ranch
NEIGH

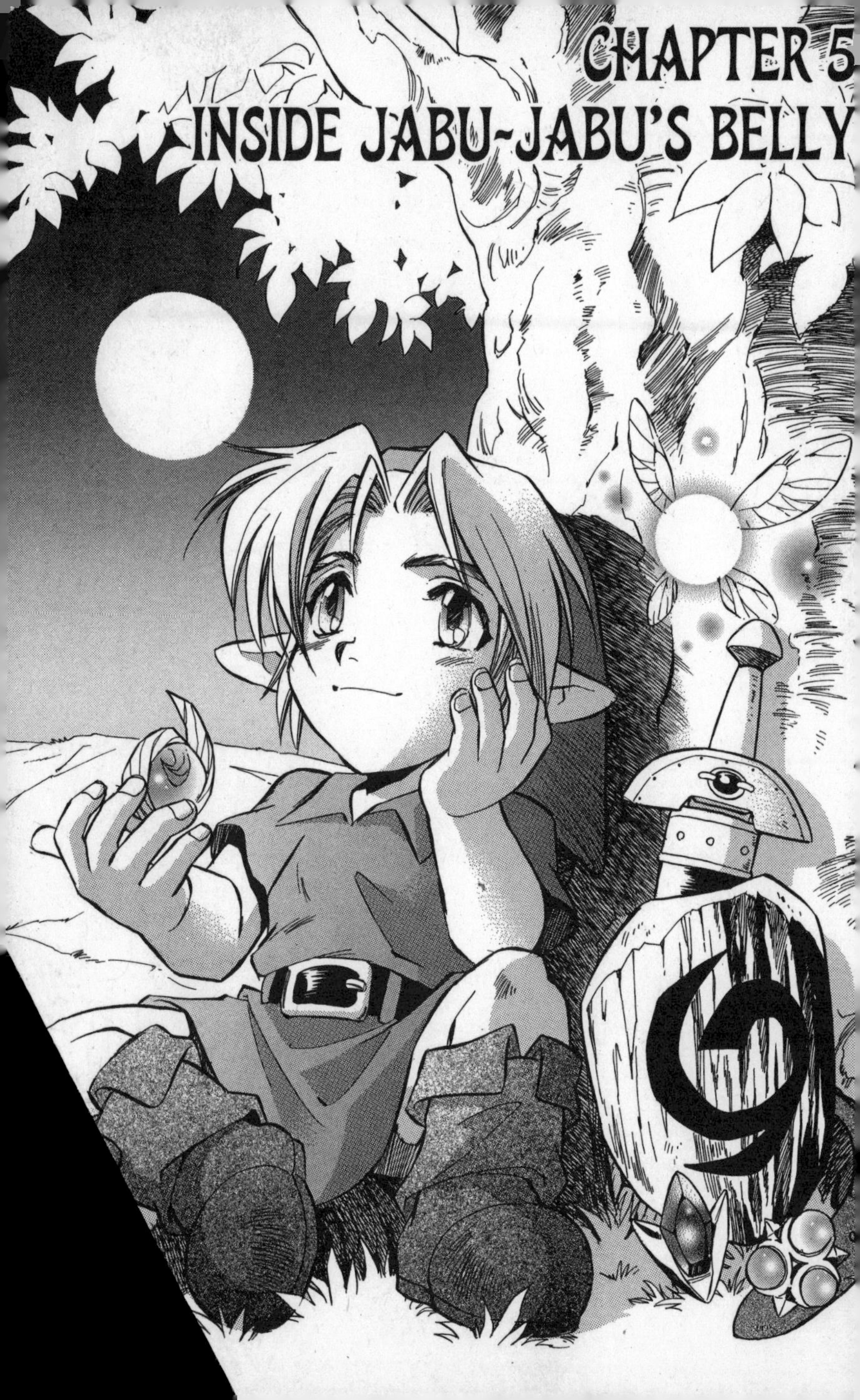
CHAPTER 5
INSIDE JABU-JABU'S BELLY

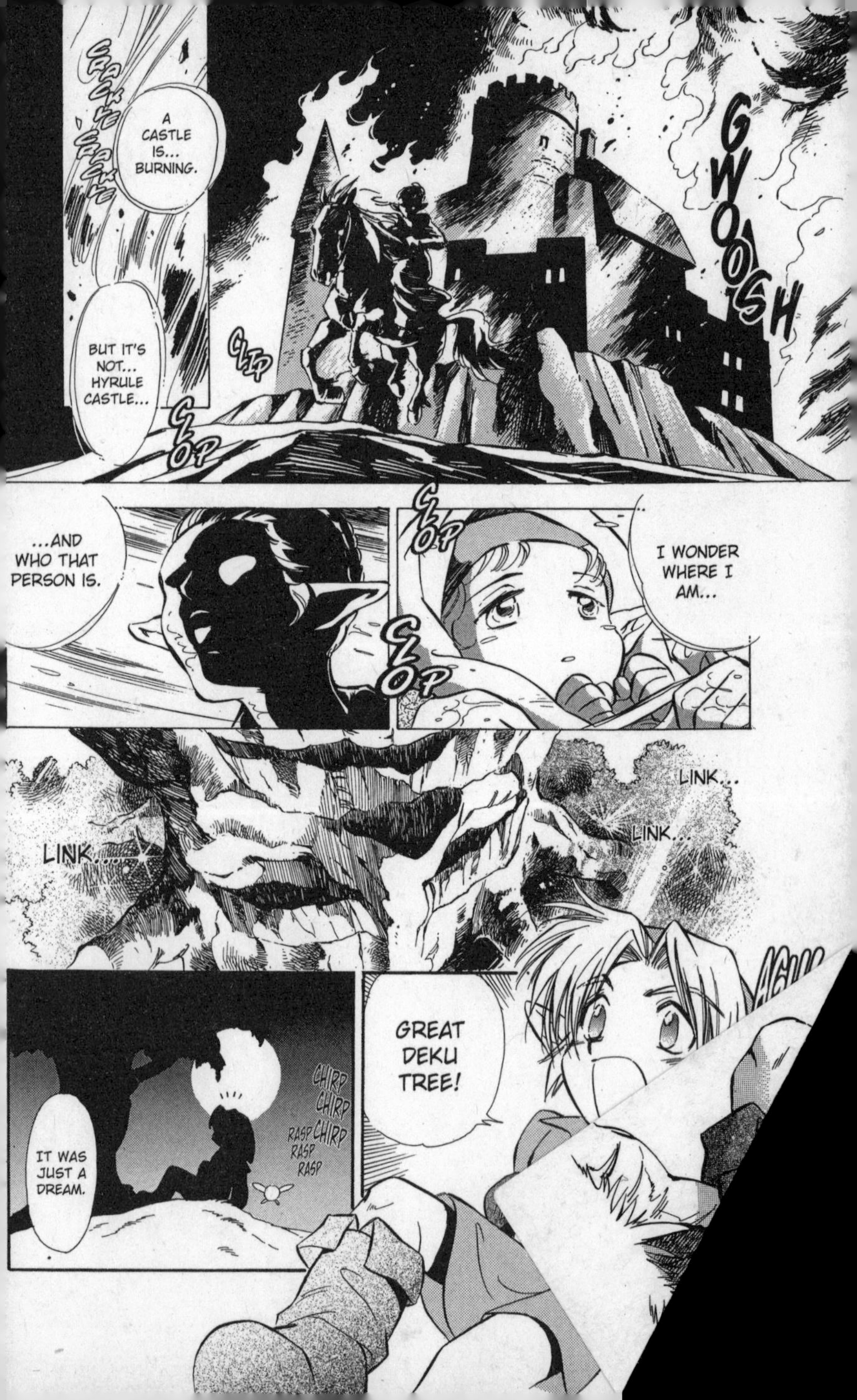
GWOOSH
CRACKLE CRACKLE
A CASTLE IS... BURNING.
CLIP
BUT IT'S NOT... HYRULE CASTLE...
CLOP
I WONDER WHERE I AM...
CLOP
CLOP
...AND WHO THAT PERSON IS.
LINK...
LINK...
LINK...
GREAT DEKU TREE!
CHIRP CHIRP CHIRP
RASP RASP RASP
IT WAS JUST A DREAM.

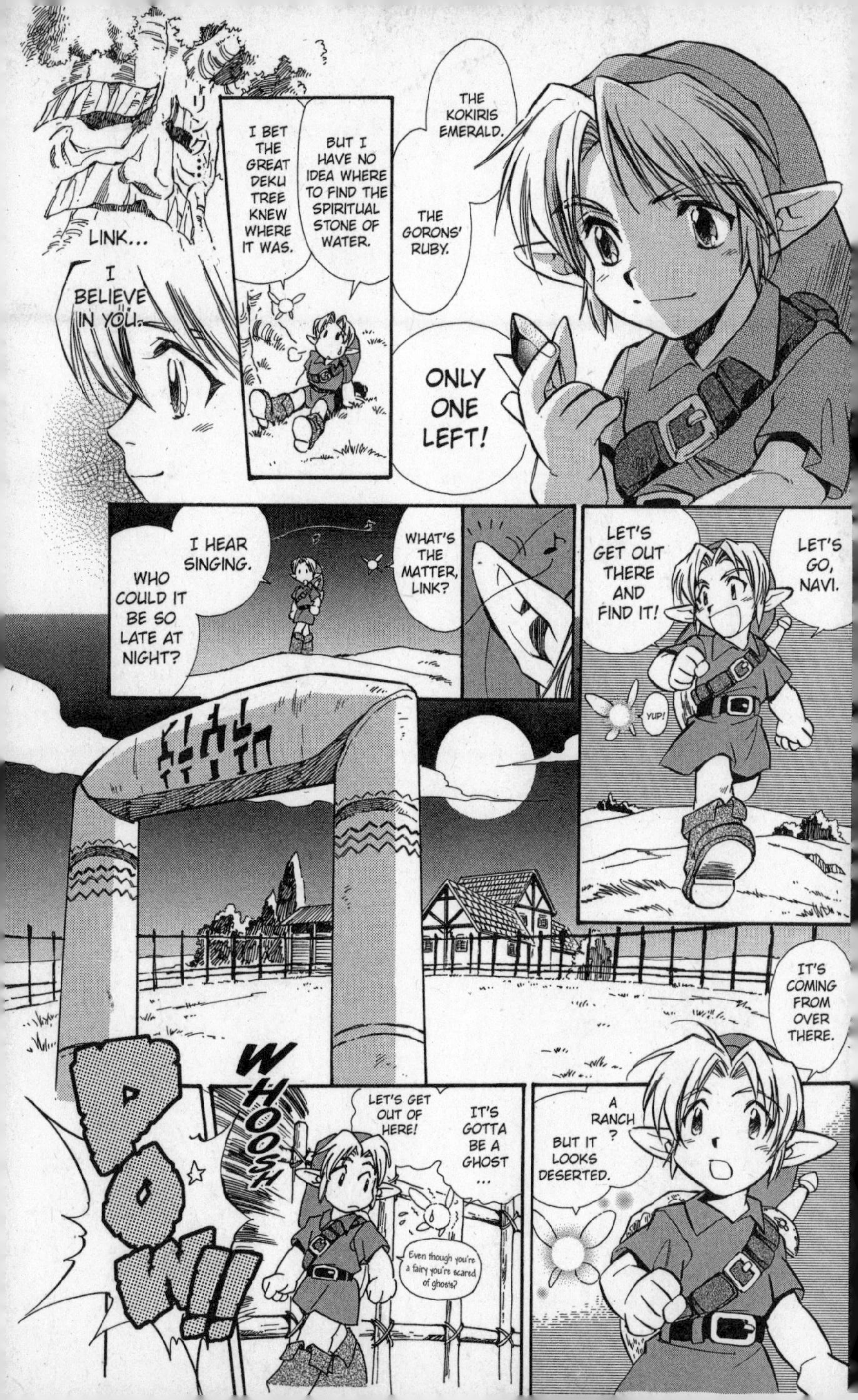
THE KOKIRIS EMERALD.
THE GORONS' RUBY.
ONLY ONE LEFT!
BUT I HAVE NO IDEA WHERE TO FIND THE SPIRITUAL STONE OF WATER.
I BET THE GREAT DEKU TREE KNEW WHERE IT WAS.
LINK...
I BELIEVE IN YOU.
LET'S GO, NAVI.
LET'S GET OUT THERE AND FIND IT!
YUP!
WHAT'S THE MATTER, LINK?
I HEAR SINGING.
WHO COULD IT BE SO LATE AT NIGHT?
IT'S COMING FROM OVER THERE.
A RANCH?
BUT IT LOOKS DESERTED.
IT'S GOTTA BE A GHOST...
LET'S GET OUT OF HERE!
Even though you're a fairy you're scared of ghosts?
WHOOSH
POW!!

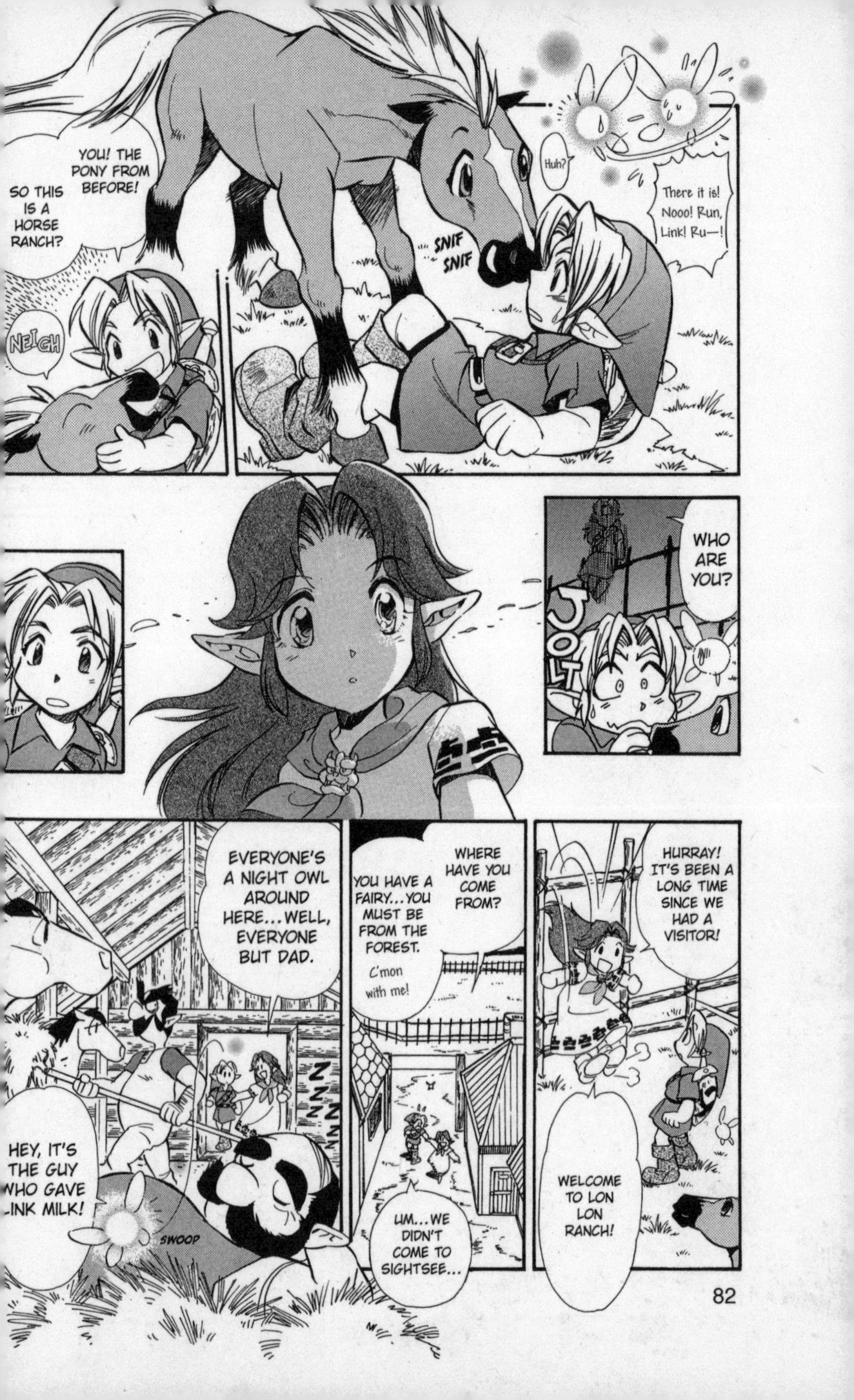

Huh?
There it is! Nooo! Run, Link! Ru—!
SNIF SNIF
YOU! THE PONY FROM BEFORE!
SO THIS IS A HORSE RANCH?
NEIGH
WHO ARE YOU?
JOLT
HURRAY! IT'S BEEN A LONG TIME SINCE WE HAD A VISITOR!
WELCOME TO LON LON RANCH!
WHERE HAVE YOU COME FROM?
YOU HAVE A FAIRY...YOU MUST BE FROM THE FOREST.
C'mon with me!
UM...WE DIDN'T COME TO SIGHTSEE...
EVERYONE'S A NIGHT OWL AROUND HERE...WELL, EVERYONE BUT DAD.
ZZZ
HEY, IT'S THE GUY WHO GAVE LINK MILK!
SWOOP

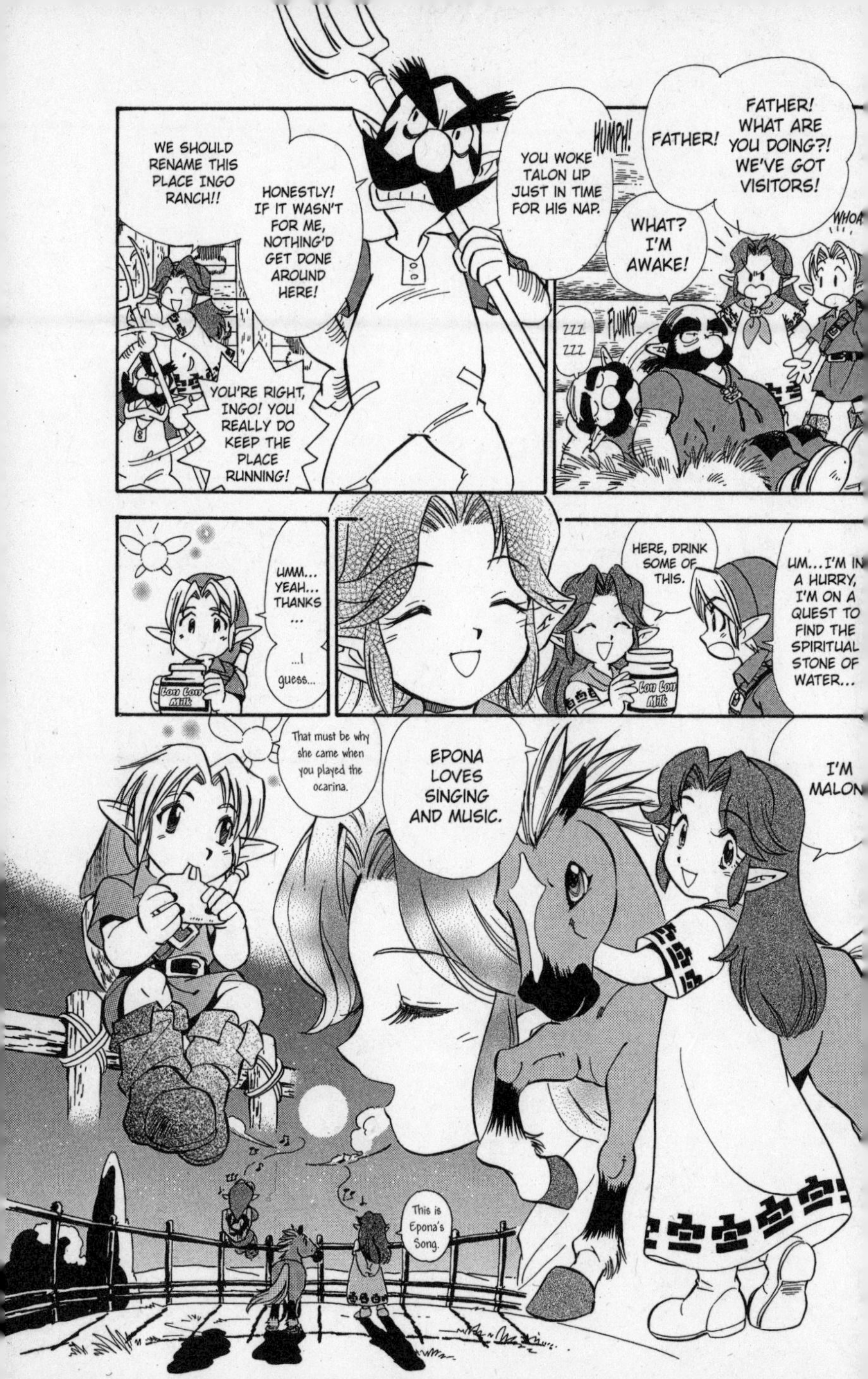
FATHER! WHAT ARE YOU DOING?! WE'VE GOT VISITORS!
FATHER!
WHOA
WHAT? I'M AWAKE!
ZZZ ZZZ
FLUMP
YOU WOKE TALON UP JUST IN TIME FOR HIS NAP.
HUMPH!
HONESTLY! IF IT WASN'T FOR ME, NOTHING'D GET DONE AROUND HERE!
WE SHOULD RENAME THIS PLACE INGO RANCH!!
YOU'RE RIGHT, INGO! YOU REALLY DO KEEP THE PLACE RUNNING!
UM...I'M IN A HURRY, I'M ON A QUEST TO FIND THE SPIRITUAL STONE OF WATER...
HERE, DRINK SOME OF THIS.
Lon Lon Milk
UMM... YEAH... THANKS ...
...I guess...
Lon Lon Milk
I'M MALON
EPONA LOVES SINGING AND MUSIC.
That must be why she came when you played the ocarina.
This is Epona's Song.

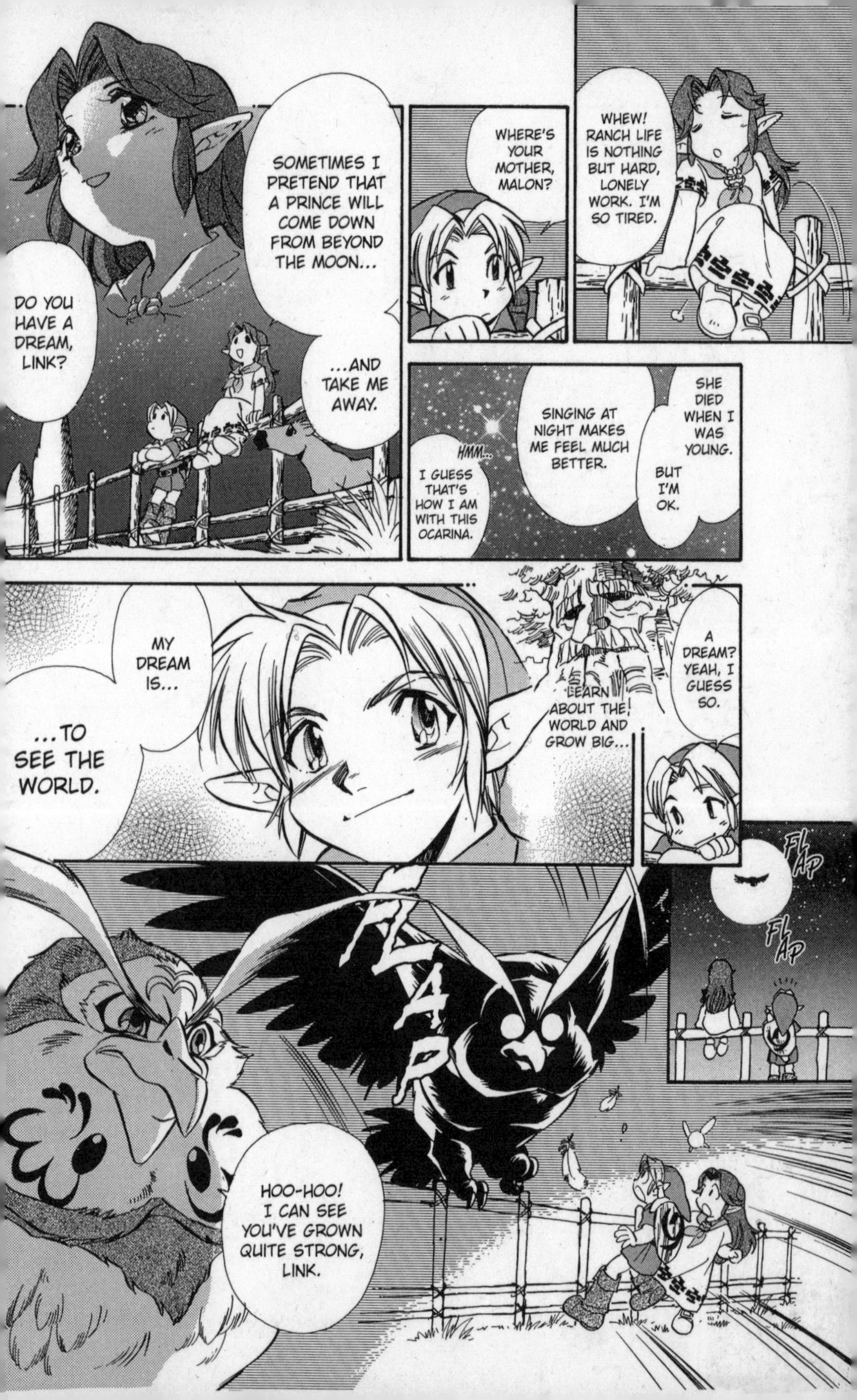
WHEW! RANCH LIFE IS NOTHING BUT HARD, LONELY WORK. I'M SO TIRED.
WHERE'S YOUR MOTHER, MALON?
SHE DIED WHEN I WAS YOUNG.
BUT I'M OK.
SINGING AT NIGHT MAKES ME FEEL MUCH BETTER.
HMM...
I GUESS THAT'S HOW I AM WITH THIS OCARINA.
SOMETIMES I PRETEND THAT A PRINCE WILL COME DOWN FROM BEYOND THE MOON...
...AND TAKE ME AWAY.
DO YOU HAVE A DREAM, LINK?
A DREAM? YEAH, I GUESS SO.
LEARN ABOUT THE WORLD AND GROW BIG...
MY DREAM IS...
...TO SEE THE WORLD.
FLAP
FLAP
FLAP
HOO-HOO! I CAN SEE YOU'VE GROWN QUITE STRONG, LINK.

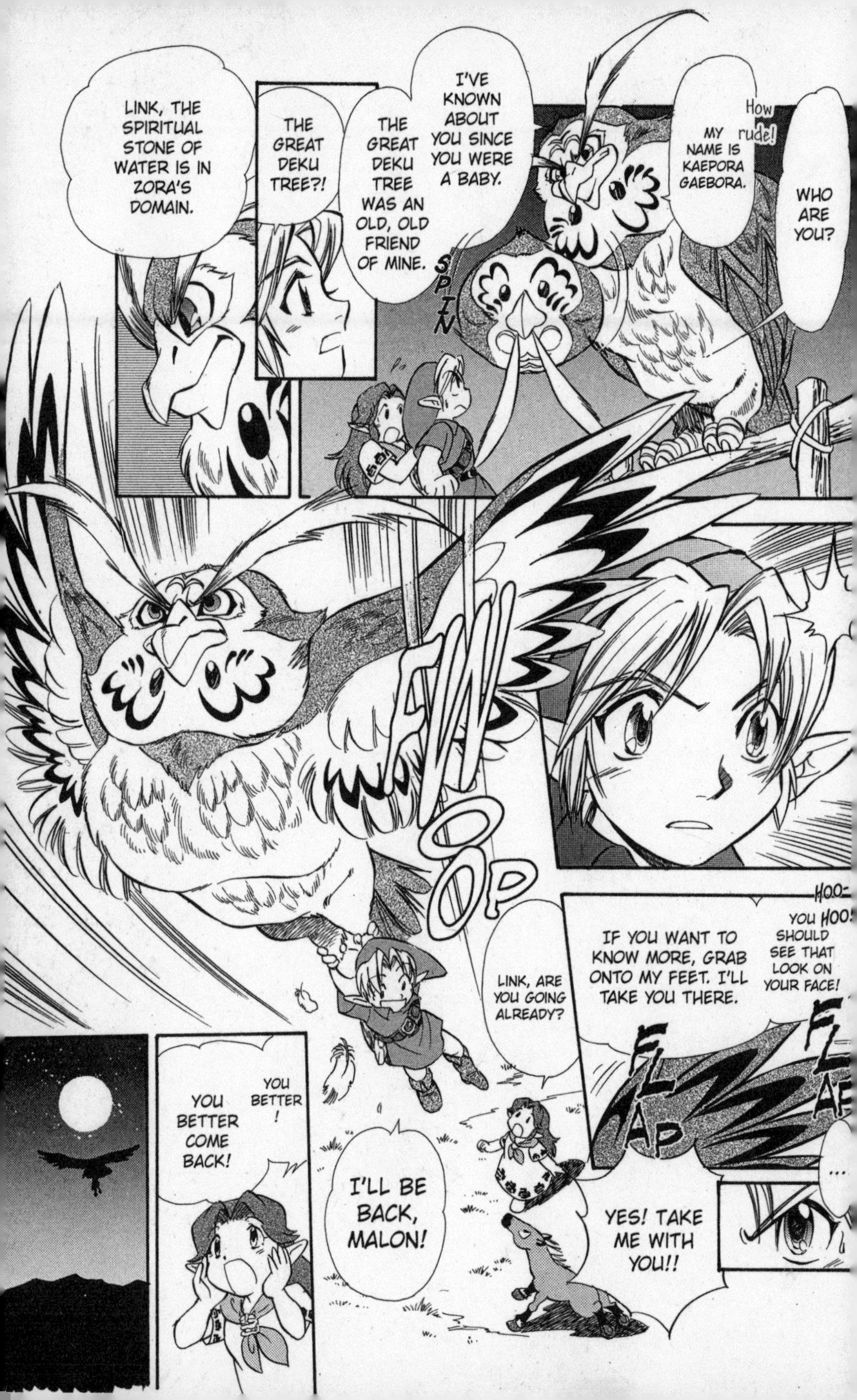

WHO ARE YOU?
How rude!
MY NAME IS KAEPORA GAEBORA.
SPIN
I'VE KNOWN ABOUT YOU SINCE YOU WERE A BABY.
THE GREAT DEKU TREE WAS AN OLD, OLD FRIEND OF MINE.
THE GREAT DEKU TREE?!
LINK, THE SPIRITUAL STONE OF WATER IS IN ZORA'S DOMAIN.
WOOP
HOO-HOO!
YOU SHOULD SEE THAT LOOK ON YOUR FACE!
IF YOU WANT TO KNOW MORE, GRAB ONTO MY FEET. I'LL TAKE YOU THERE.
FLAP
FLAP
...
YES! TAKE ME WITH YOU!!
LINK, ARE YOU GOING ALREADY?
I'LL BE BACK, MALON!
YOU BETTER!
YOU BETTER COME BACK!

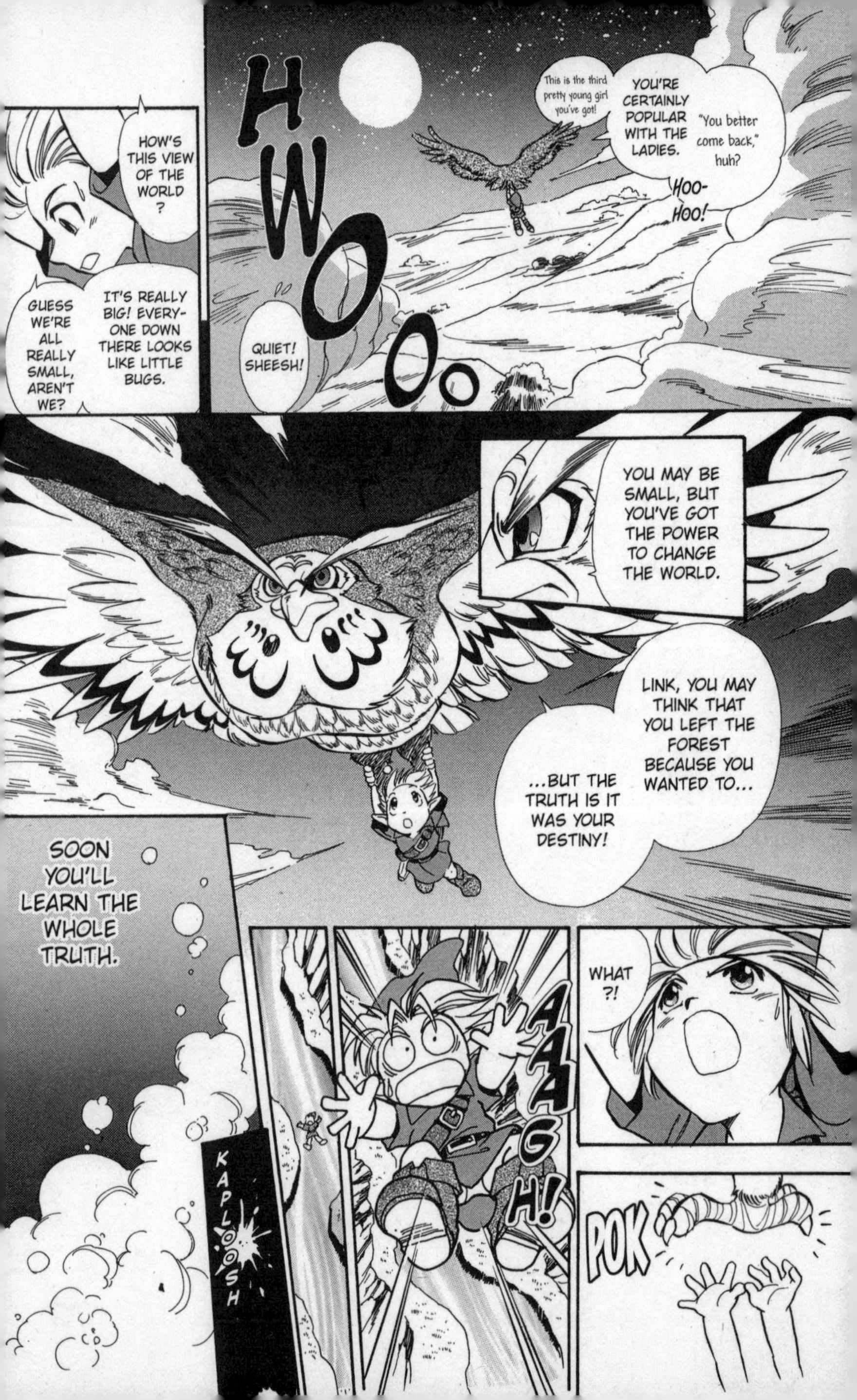
"You better come back," huh?
YOU'RE CERTAINLY POPULAR WITH THE LADIES.
This is the third pretty young girl you've got!
HOO-HOO!
HWOOOO
QUIET! SHEESH!
HOW'S THIS VIEW OF THE WORLD?
IT'S REALLY BIG! EVERYONE DOWN THERE LOOKS LIKE LITTLE BUGS.
GUESS WE'RE ALL REALLY SMALL, AREN'T WE?
YOU MAY BE SMALL, BUT YOU'VE GOT THE POWER TO CHANGE THE WORLD.
LINK, YOU MAY THINK THAT YOU LEFT THE FOREST BECAUSE YOU WANTED TO...
...BUT THE TRUTH IS IT WAS YOUR DESTINY!
SOON YOU'LL LEARN THE WHOLE TRUTH.
WHAT?!
POK
AAAGH!
KAPLOOSH

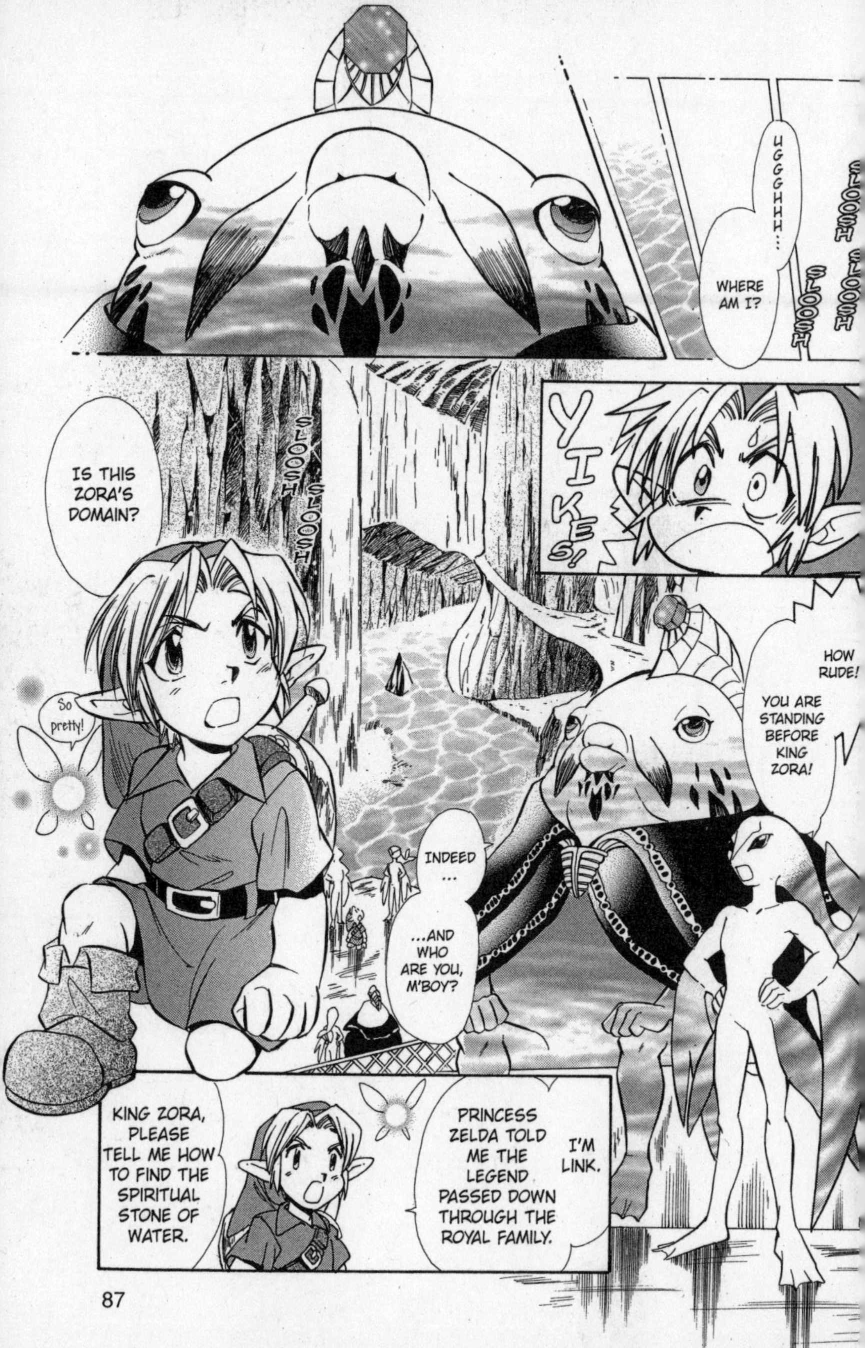
UGGGHHH...
WHERE AM I?
SLOOSH SLOOSH
SLOOSH
YIKES!
IS THIS ZORA'S DOMAIN?
SLOOSH
SLOOSH
So pretty!
HOW RUDE!
YOU ARE STANDING BEFORE KING ZORA!
INDEED ...
...AND WHO ARE YOU, M'BOY?
I'M LINK.
PRINCESS ZELDA TOLD ME THE LEGEND PASSED DOWN THROUGH THE ROYAL FAMILY.
KING ZORA, PLEASE TELL ME HOW TO FIND THE SPIRITUAL STONE OF WATER.

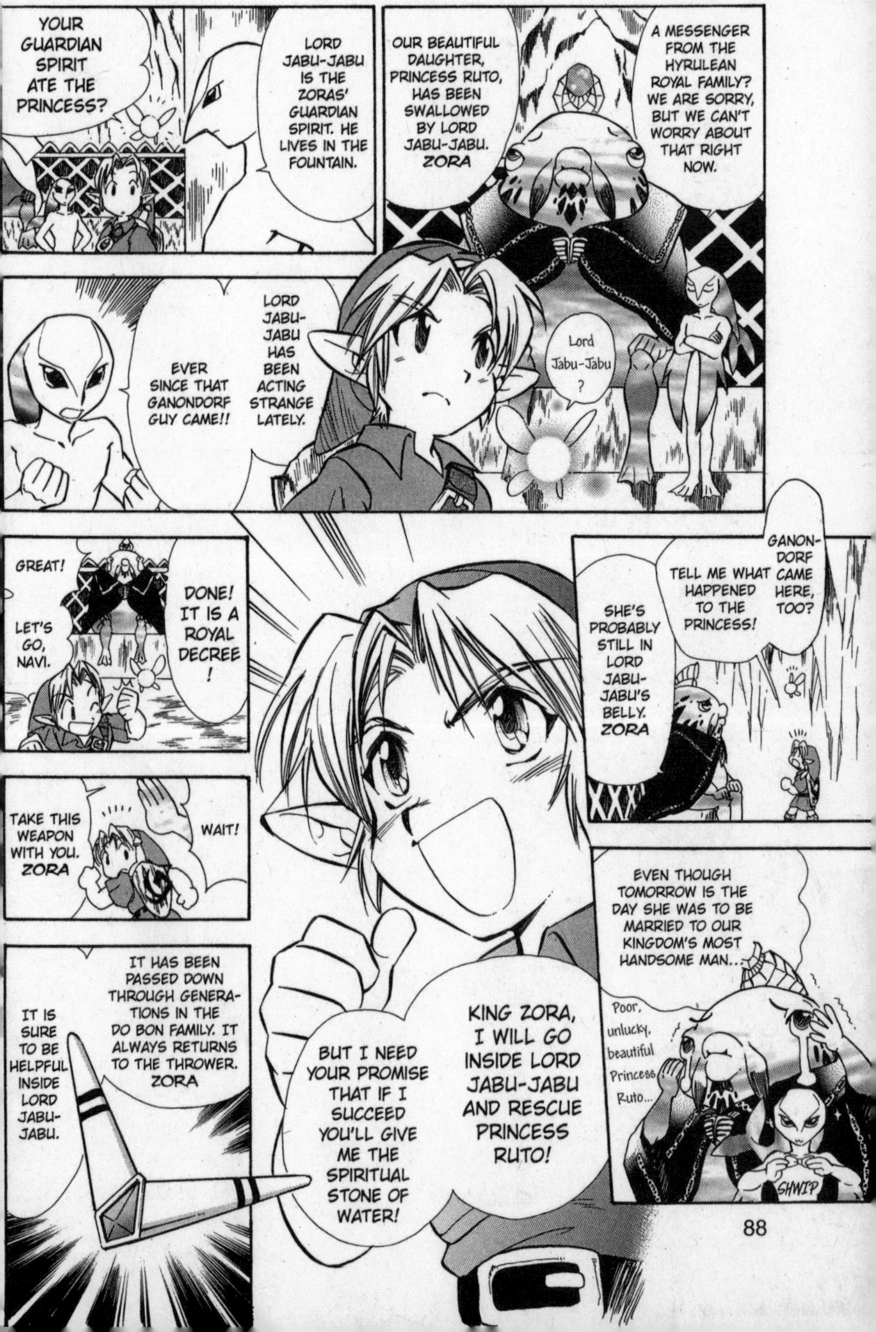
A MESSENGER FROM THE HYRULEAN ROYAL FAMILY? WE ARE SORRY, BUT WE CAN'T WORRY ABOUT THAT RIGHT NOW.
OUR BEAUTIFUL DAUGHTER, PRINCESS RUTO, HAS BEEN SWALLOWED BY LORD JABU-JABU. ZORA
LORD JABU-JABU IS THE ZORAS' GUARDIAN SPIRIT. HE LIVES IN THE FOUNTAIN.
YOUR GUARDIAN SPIRIT ATE THE PRINCESS?
Lord Jabu-Jabu?
LORD JABU-JABU HAS BEEN ACTING STRANGE LATELY.
EVER SINCE THAT GANONDORF GUY CAME!!
GANONDORF CAME HERE, TOO?
TELL ME WHAT HAPPENED TO THE PRINCESS!
SHE'S PROBABLY STILL IN LORD JABU-JABU'S BELLY. ZORA
EVEN THOUGH TOMORROW IS THE DAY SHE WAS TO BE MARRIED TO OUR KINGDOM'S MOST HANDSOME MAN...
Poor, unlucky, beautiful Princess Ruto...
SHWIP
KING ZORA, I WILL GO INSIDE LORD JABU-JABU AND RESCUE PRINCESS RUTO!
BUT I NEED YOUR PROMISE THAT IF I SUCCEED YOU'LL GIVE ME THE SPIRITUAL STONE OF WATER!
DONE! IT IS A ROYAL DECREE!
GREAT!
LET'S GO, NAVI.
WAIT!
TAKE THIS WEAPON WITH YOU. ZORA
IT HAS BEEN PASSED DOWN THROUGH GENERATIONS IN THE DO BON FAMILY. IT ALWAYS RETURNS TO THE THROWER. ZORA
IT IS SURE TO BE HELPFUL INSIDE LORD JABU-JABU.

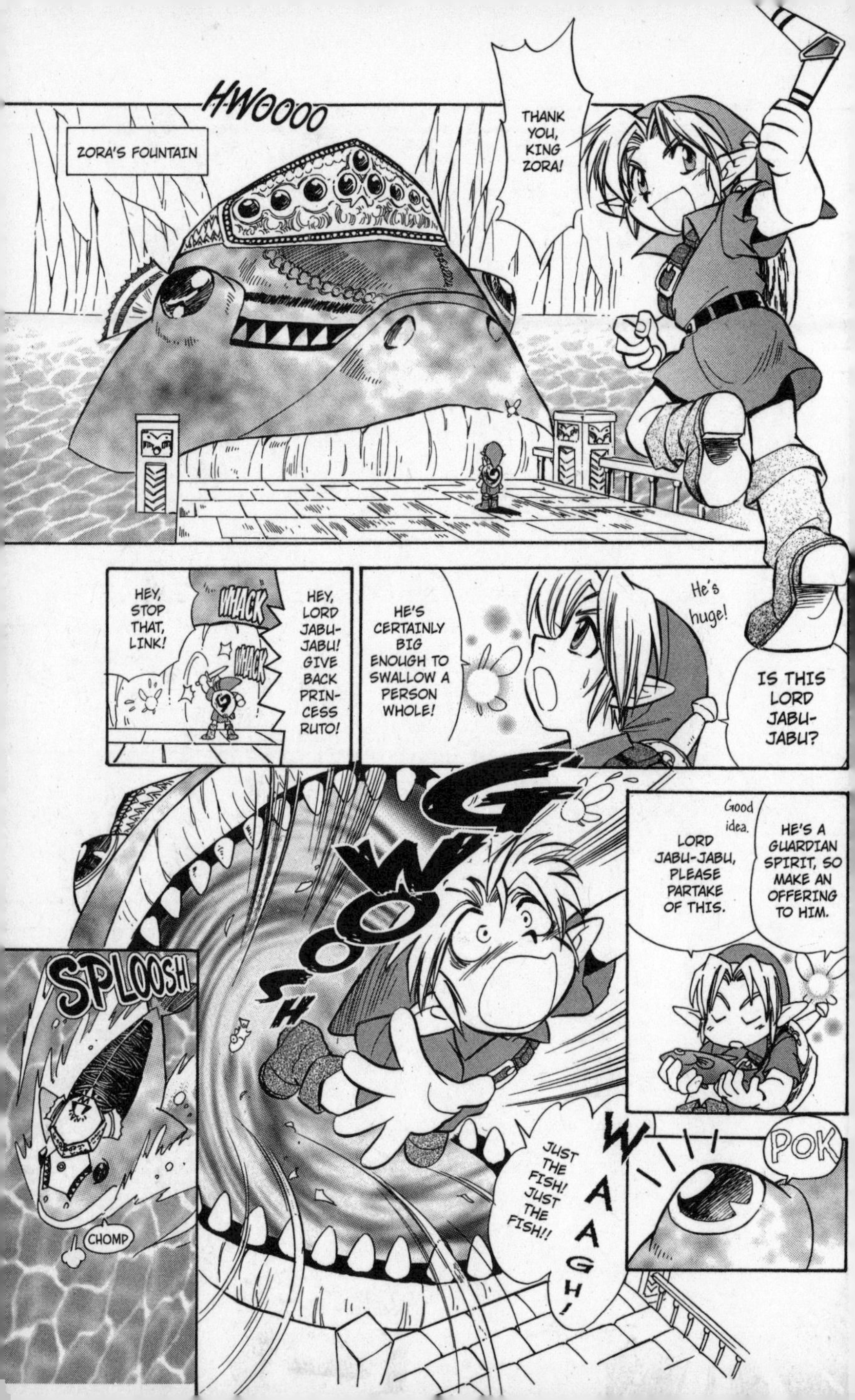
THANK YOU, KING ZORA!
H-WOOOO
ZORA'S FOUNTAIN
IS THIS LORD JABU-JABU?
He's huge!
HE'S CERTAINLY BIG ENOUGH TO SWALLOW A PERSON WHOLE!
HEY, LORD JABU-JABU! GIVE BACK PRINCESS RUTO!
WHACK
WHACK
HEY, STOP THAT, LINK!
HE'S A GUARDIAN SPIRIT, SO MAKE AN OFFERING TO HIM.
Good idea.
LORD JABU-JABU, PLEASE PARTAKE OF THIS.
POK
WAAAGH!
JUST THE FISH! JUST THE FISH!!
SPLOOSH
CHOMP

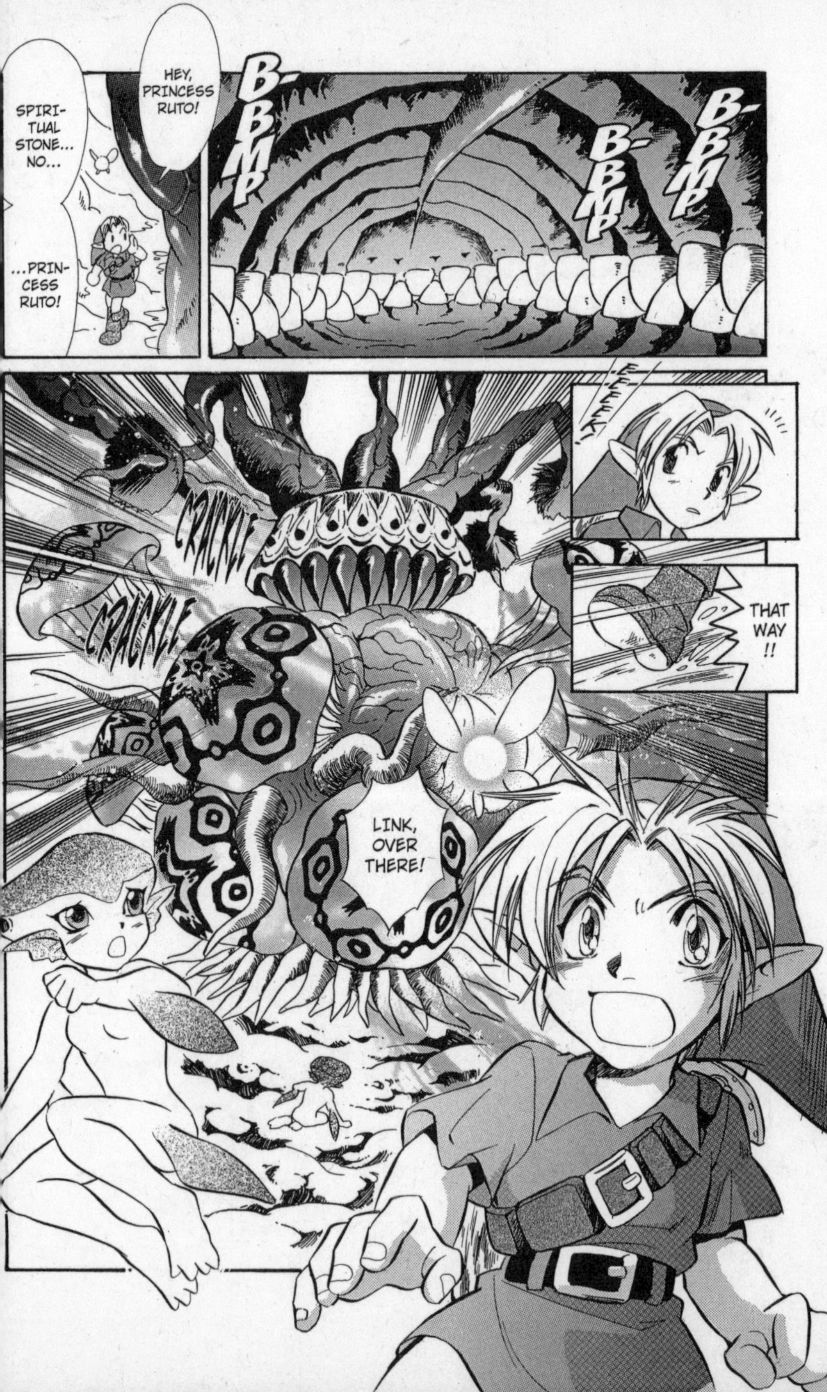
B-BBMP
B-BBMP
B-BBMP
HEY, PRINCESS RUTO!
SPIRITUAL STONE... NO...
...PRINCESS RUTO!
EEEEK!
THAT WAY !!
CRACKLE
CRACKLE
LINK, OVER THERE!

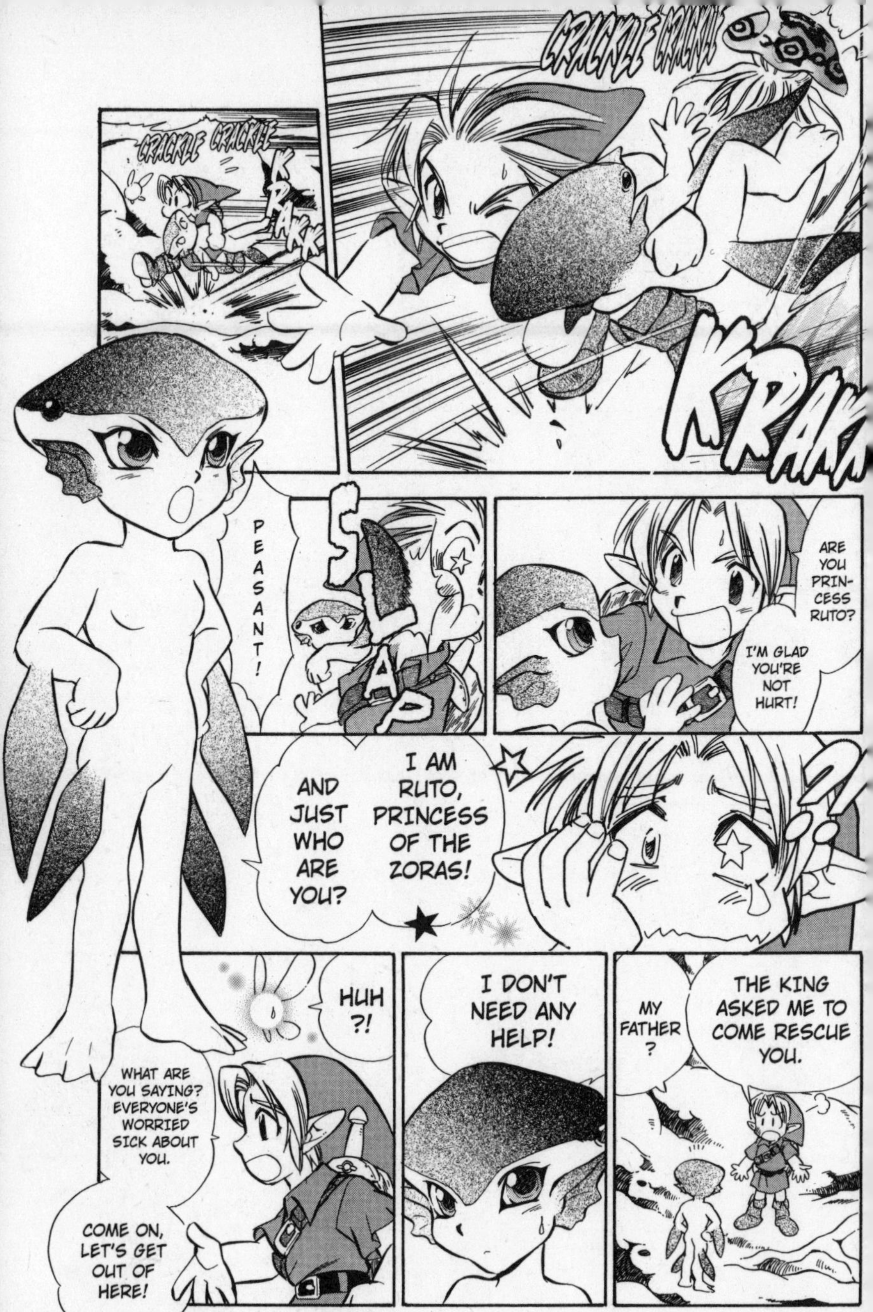
CRACKLE CRACK!!
KRAK
CRACKLE CRACKLE
KRAKK
ARE YOU PRINCESS RUTO?
I'M GLAD YOU'RE NOT HURT!
SLAP
PEASANT!
?!
I AM RUTO, PRINCESS OF THE ZORAS!
AND JUST WHO ARE YOU?
THE KING ASKED ME TO COME RESCUE YOU.
MY FATHER?
I DON'T NEED ANY HELP!
HUH?!
WHAT ARE YOU SAYING? EVERYONE'S WORRIED SICK ABOUT YOU.
COME ON, LET'S GET OUT OF HERE!

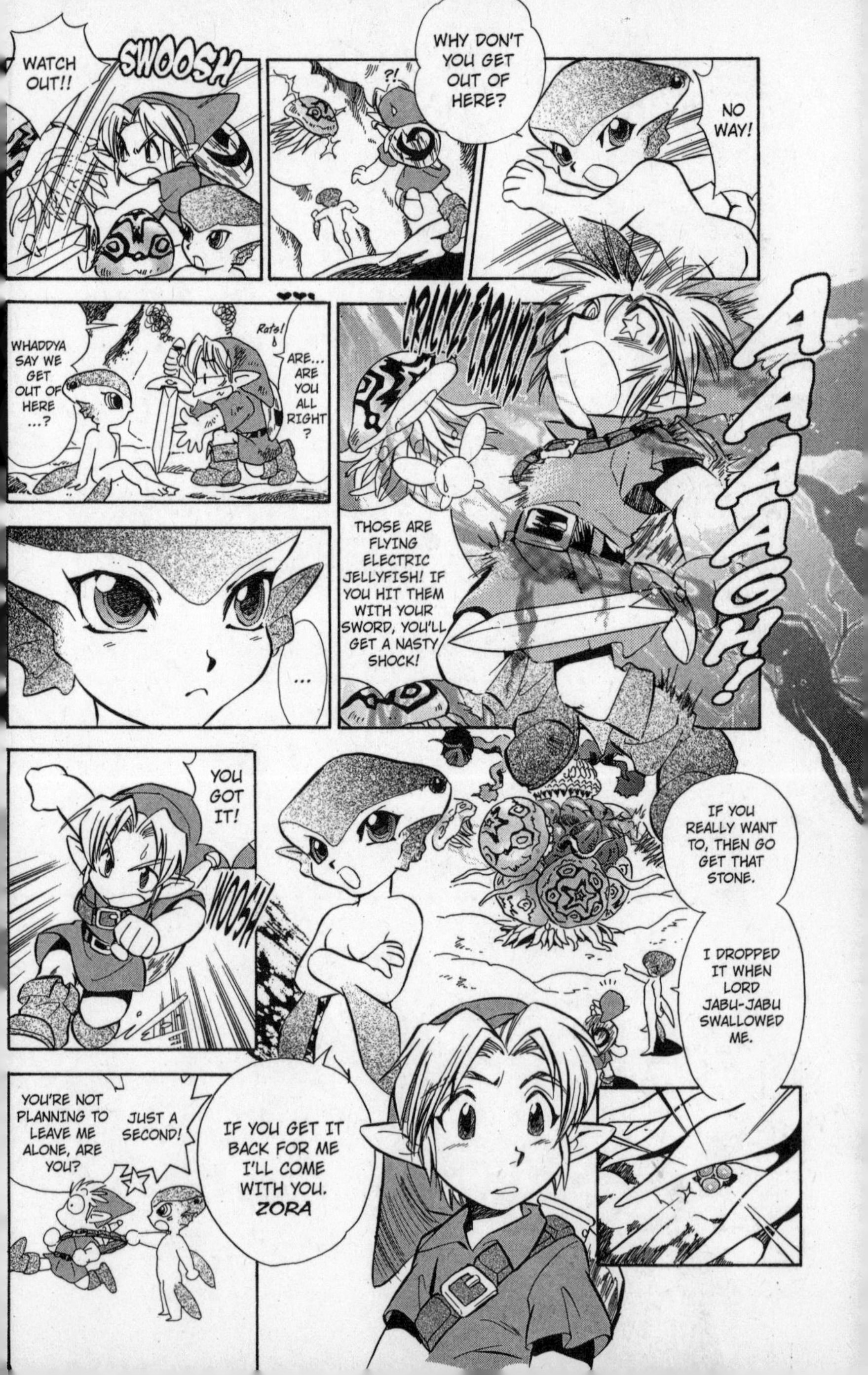
WHY DON'T YOU GET OUT OF HERE?
NO WAY!
?!
WATCH OUT!!
SWOOSH
AAAAAGH!
CRACKLE CRACKLE
THOSE ARE FLYING ELECTRIC JELLYFISH! IF YOU HIT THEM WITH YOUR SWORD, YOU'LL GET A NASTY SHOCK!
Rats!
ARE... ARE YOU ALL RIGHT?
WHADDYA SAY WE GET OUT OF HERE ...?
...
IF YOU REALLY WANT TO, THEN GO GET THAT STONE.
I DROPPED IT WHEN LORD JABU-JABU SWALLOWED ME.
YOU GOT IT!
WOOSH
IF YOU GET IT BACK FOR ME I'LL COME WITH YOU.
ZORA
JUST A SECOND!
YOU'RE NOT PLANNING TO LEAVE ME ALONE, ARE YOU?

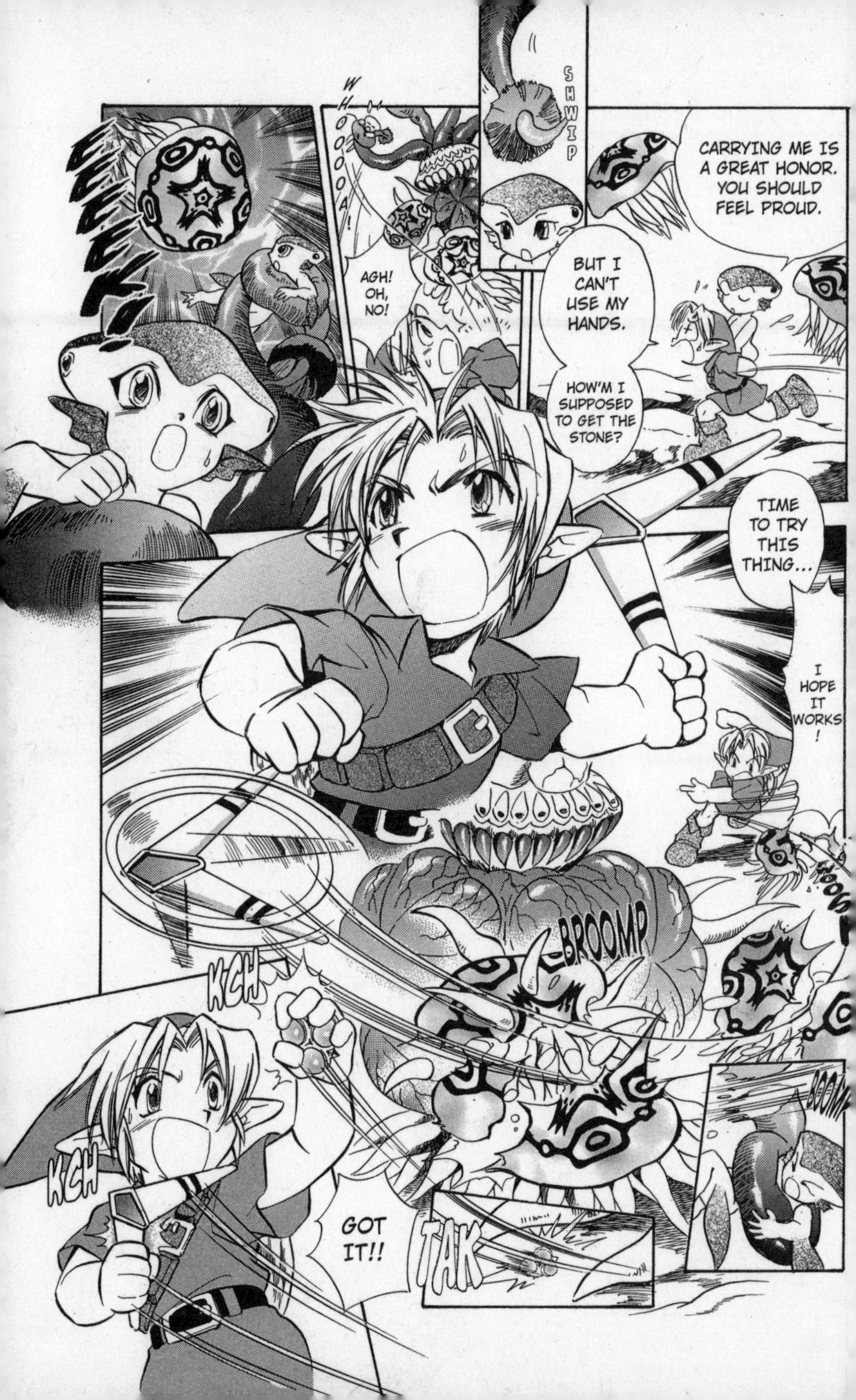
SHWIP
CARRYING ME IS A GREAT HONOR. YOU SHOULD FEEL PROUD.
BUT I CAN'T USE MY HANDS.
HOW'M I SUPPOSED TO GET THE STONE?
WHOOOOOA!
AGH! OH, NO!
TIME TO TRY THIS THING...
I HOPE IT WORKS!
BROOMP
KCH
KCH
BOOM
TAK
GOT IT!!

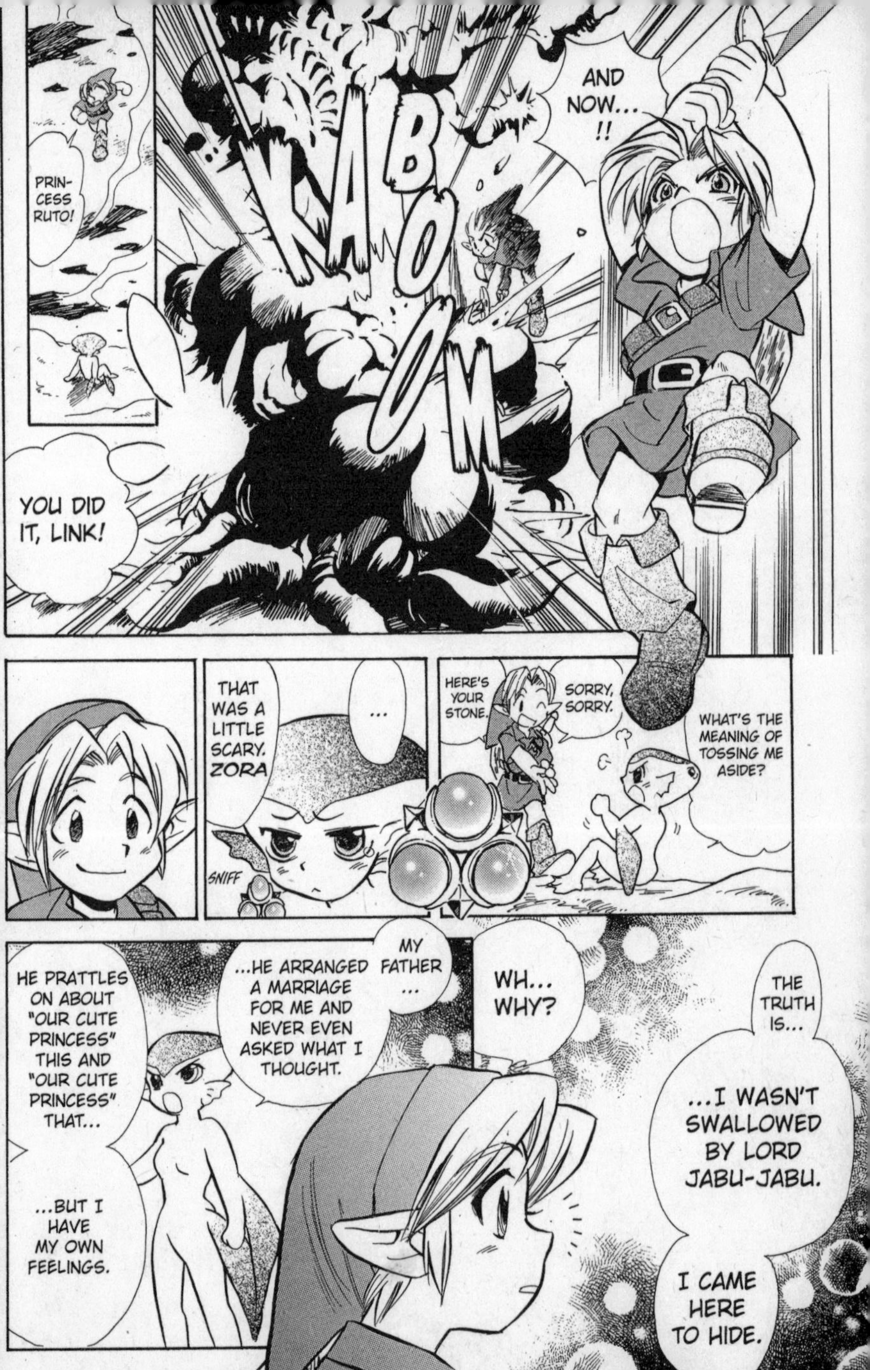
AND NOW... !!
KABOOM
PRIN-CESS RUTO!
YOU DID IT, LINK!
WHAT'S THE MEANING OF TOSSING ME ASIDE?
SORRY, SORRY.
HERE'S YOUR STONE.
...
THAT WAS A LITTLE SCARY.
ZORA
SNIFF
THE TRUTH IS...
...I WASN'T SWALLOWED BY LORD JABU-JABU.
I CAME HERE TO HIDE.
WH... WHY?
MY FATHER ...
...HE ARRANGED A MARRIAGE FOR ME AND NEVER EVEN ASKED WHAT I THOUGHT.
HE PRATTLES ON ABOUT "OUR CUTE PRINCESS" THIS AND "OUR CUTE PRINCESS" THAT...
...BUT I HAVE MY OWN FEELINGS.

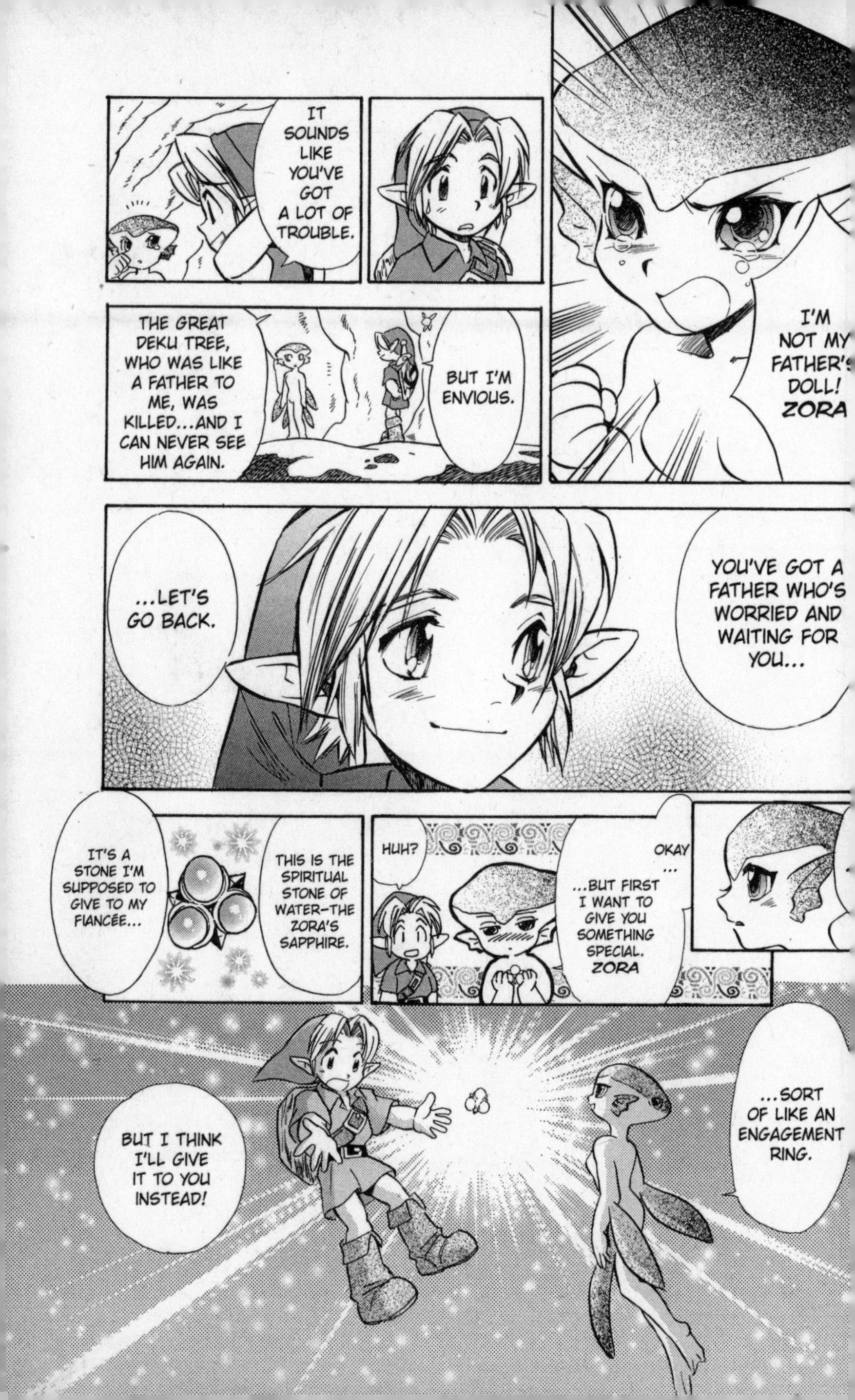
I'M NOT MY FATHER'S DOLL! ZORA
IT SOUNDS LIKE YOU'VE GOT A LOT OF TROUBLE.
BUT I'M ENVIOUS.
THE GREAT DEKU TREE, WHO WAS LIKE A FATHER TO ME, WAS KILLED...AND I CAN NEVER SEE HIM AGAIN.
YOU'VE GOT A FATHER WHO'S WORRIED AND WAITING FOR YOU...
...LET'S GO BACK.
OKAY ...
...BUT FIRST I WANT TO GIVE YOU SOMETHING SPECIAL. ZORA
HUH?
THIS IS THE SPIRITUAL STONE OF WATER—THE ZORA'S SAPPHIRE.
IT'S A STONE I'M SUPPOSED TO GIVE TO MY FIANCÉE...
...SORT OF LIKE AN ENGAGEMENT RING.
BUT I THINK I'LL GIVE IT TO YOU INSTEAD!

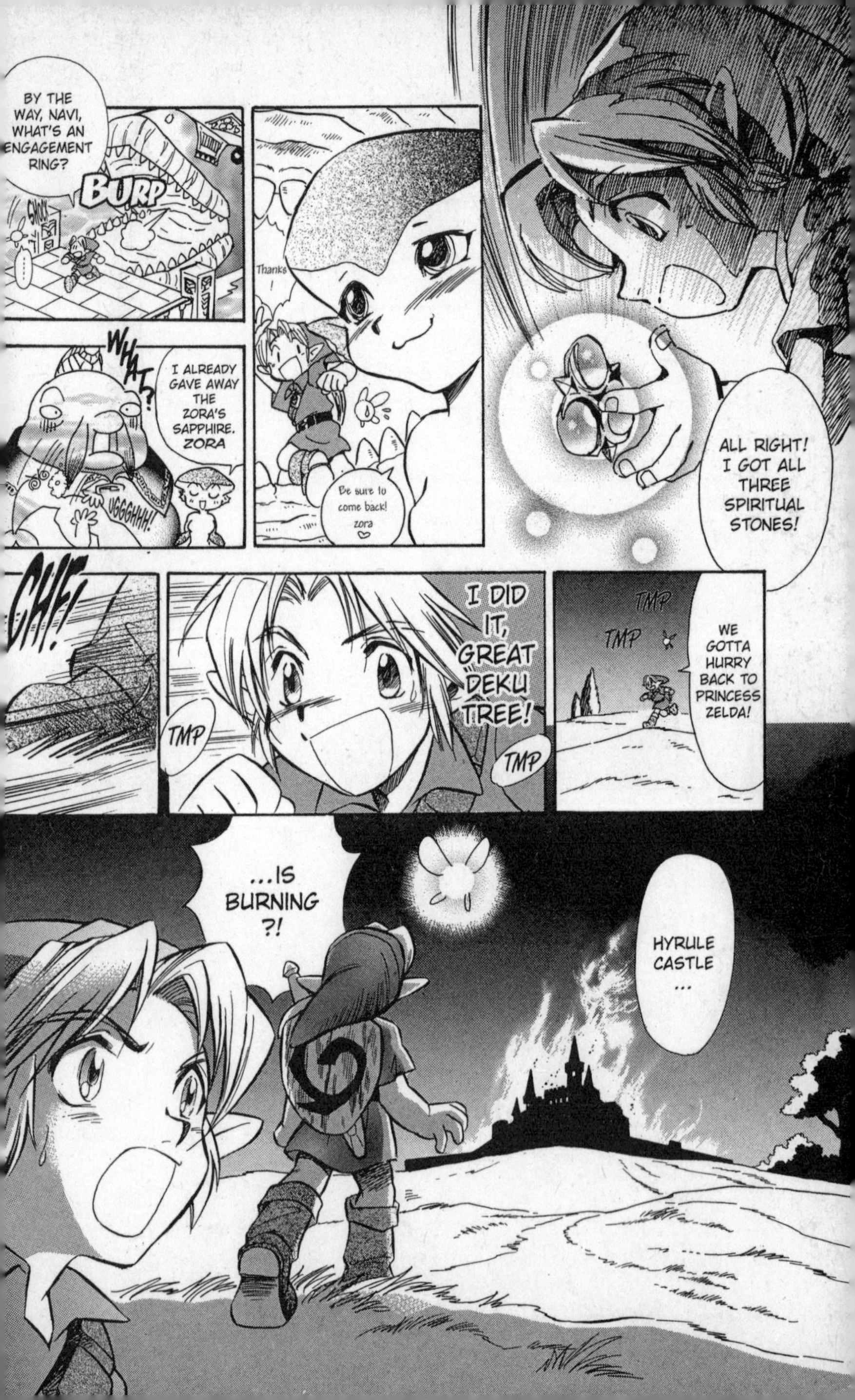
ALL RIGHT! I GOT ALL THREE SPIRITUAL STONES!
Thanks!
Be sure to come back! zora
BY THE WAY, NAVI, WHAT'S AN ENGAGEMENT RING?
BURP
SHOCK
...
WHAT?
I ALREADY GAVE AWAY THE ZORA'S SAPPHIRE. ZORA
UGGGHHH!
TMP
TMP
WE GOTTA HURRY BACK TO PRINCESS ZELDA!
I DID IT, GREAT DEKU TREE!
TMP
TMP
CHF!
HYRULE CASTLE ...
...IS BURNING?!

CHAPTER 6 THE HERO OF TIME IS BORN

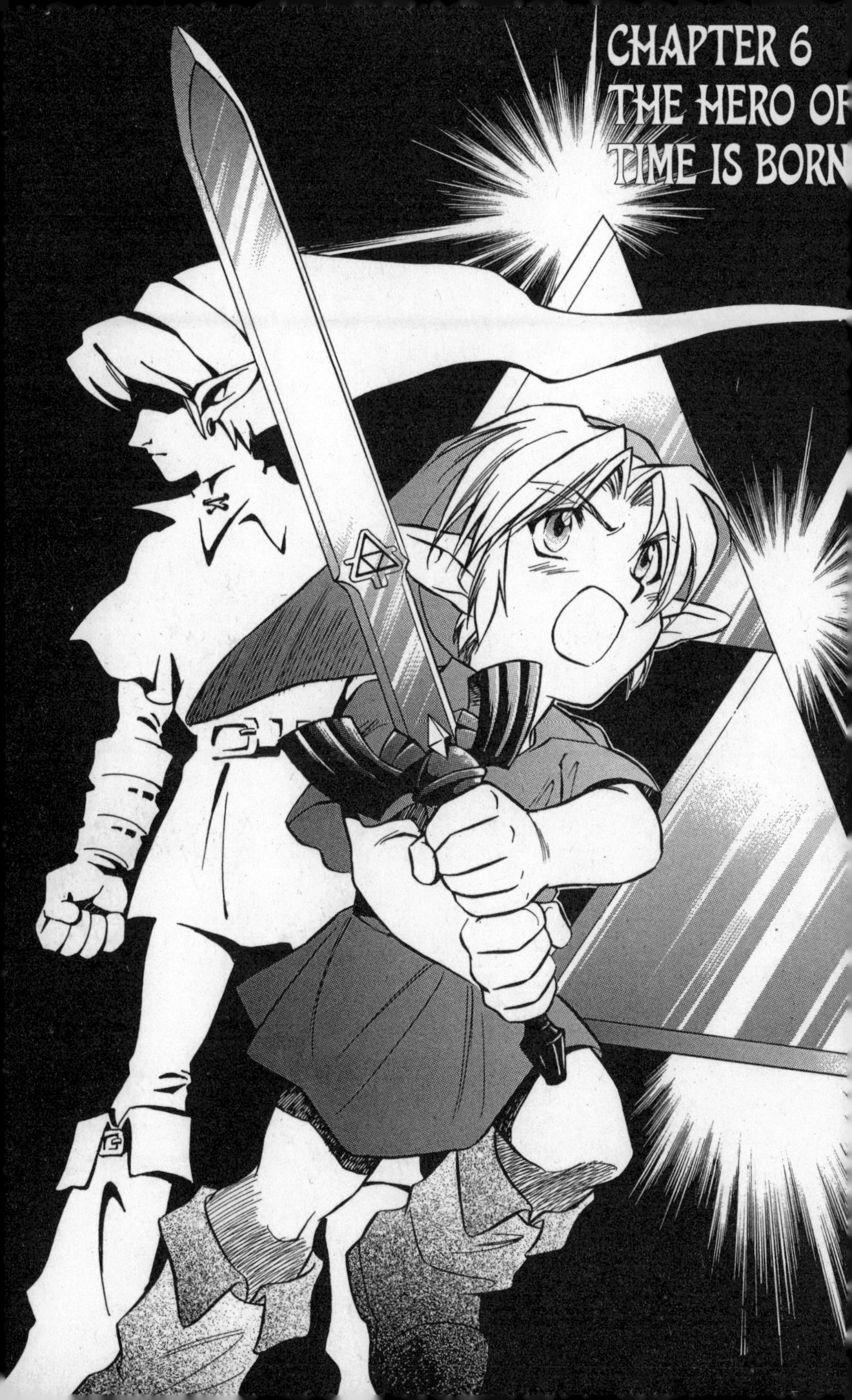

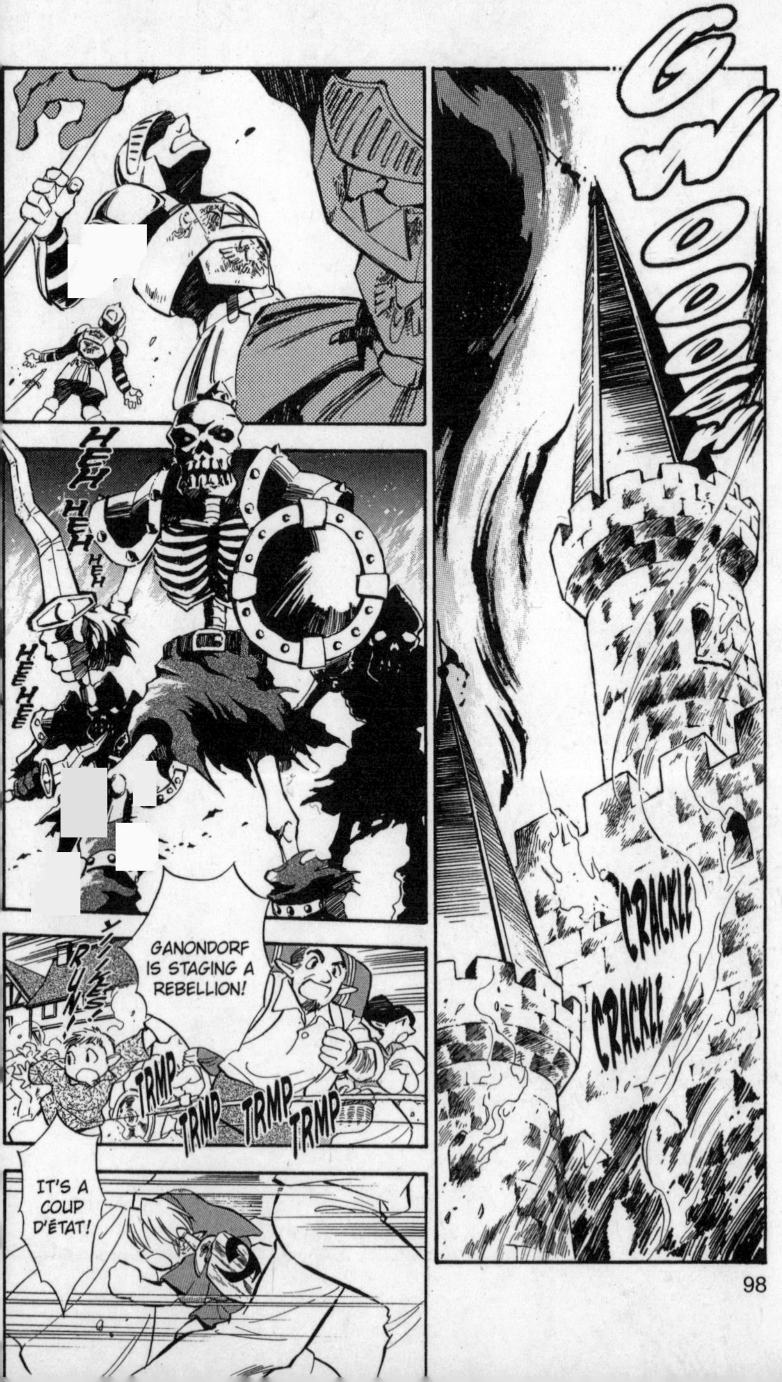
CRACKLE
CRACKLE
HEH HEH HEH
HEHEHE
GANONDORF IS STAGING A REBELLION!
YIKES!
RUN!
TRMP TRMP TRMP TRMP
IT'S A COUP D'ÉTAT!

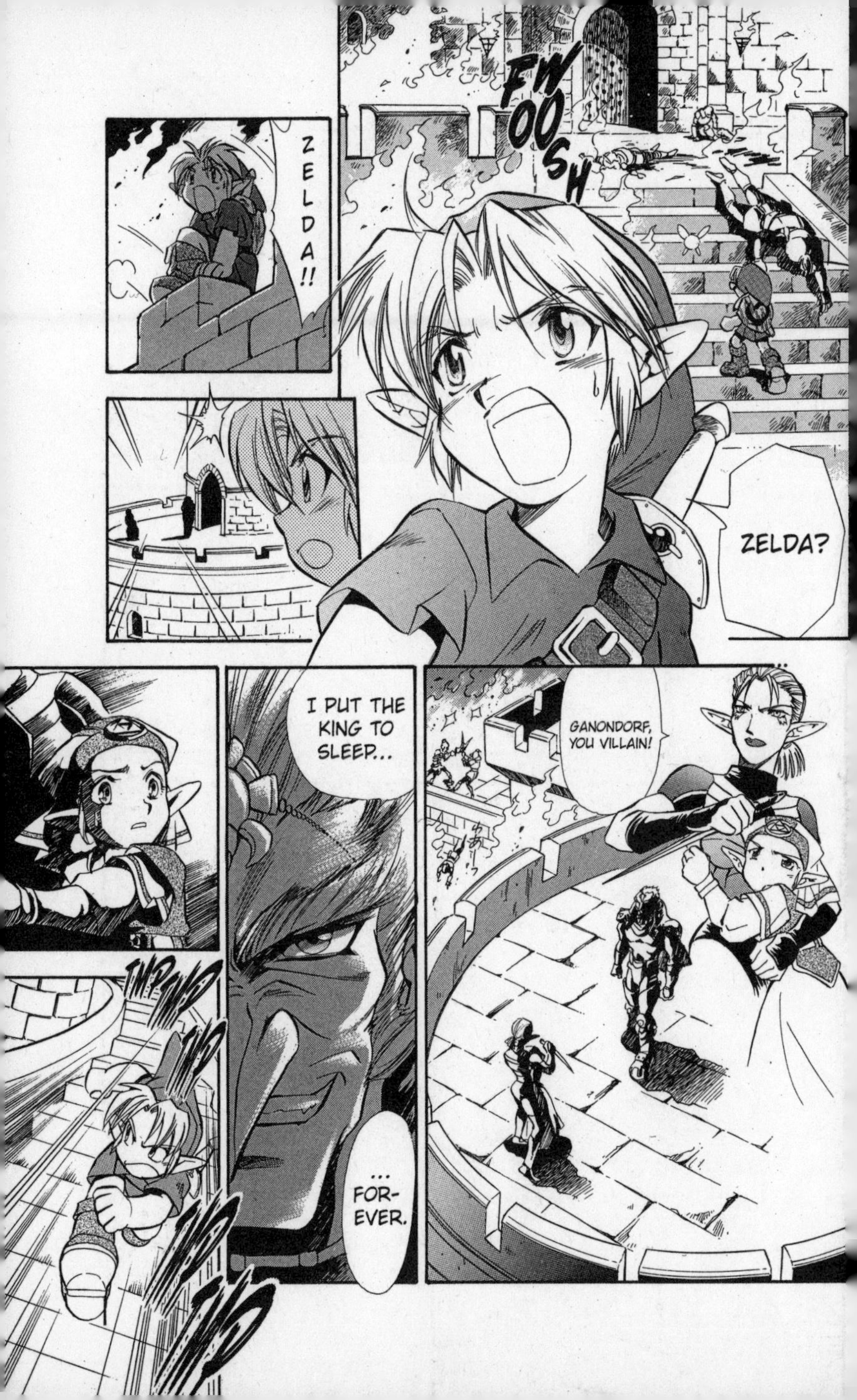
FWOOSH
ZELDA?
ZELDA!!
GANONDORF, YOU VILLAIN!
I PUT THE KING TO SLEEP...
... FOREVER.

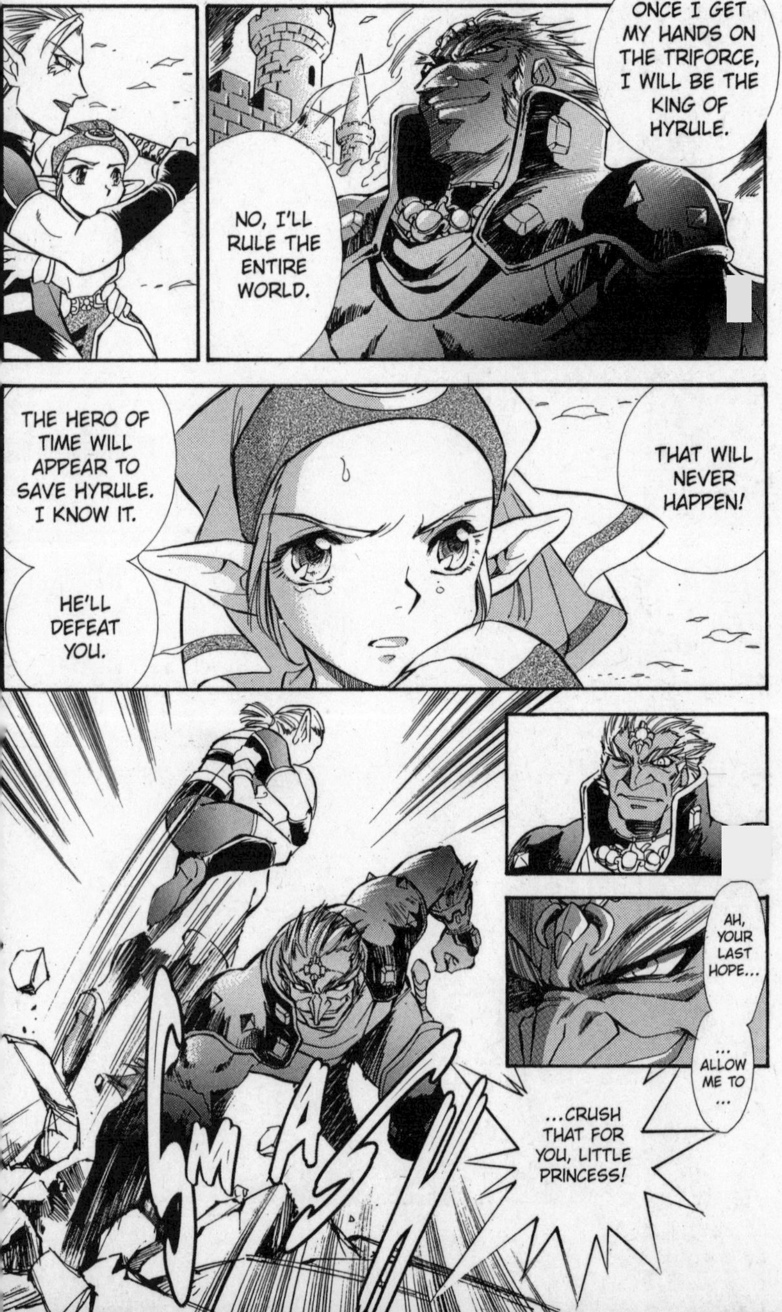
ONCE I GET MY HANDS ON THE TRIFORCE, I WILL BE THE KING OF HYRULE.
NO, I'LL RULE THE ENTIRE WORLD.
THAT WILL NEVER HAPPEN!
THE HERO OF TIME WILL APPEAR TO SAVE HYRULE. I KNOW IT.
HE'LL DEFEAT YOU.
AH, YOUR LAST HOPE...
... ALLOW ME TO ...
...CRUSH THAT FOR YOU, LITTLE PRINCESS!
SMASH

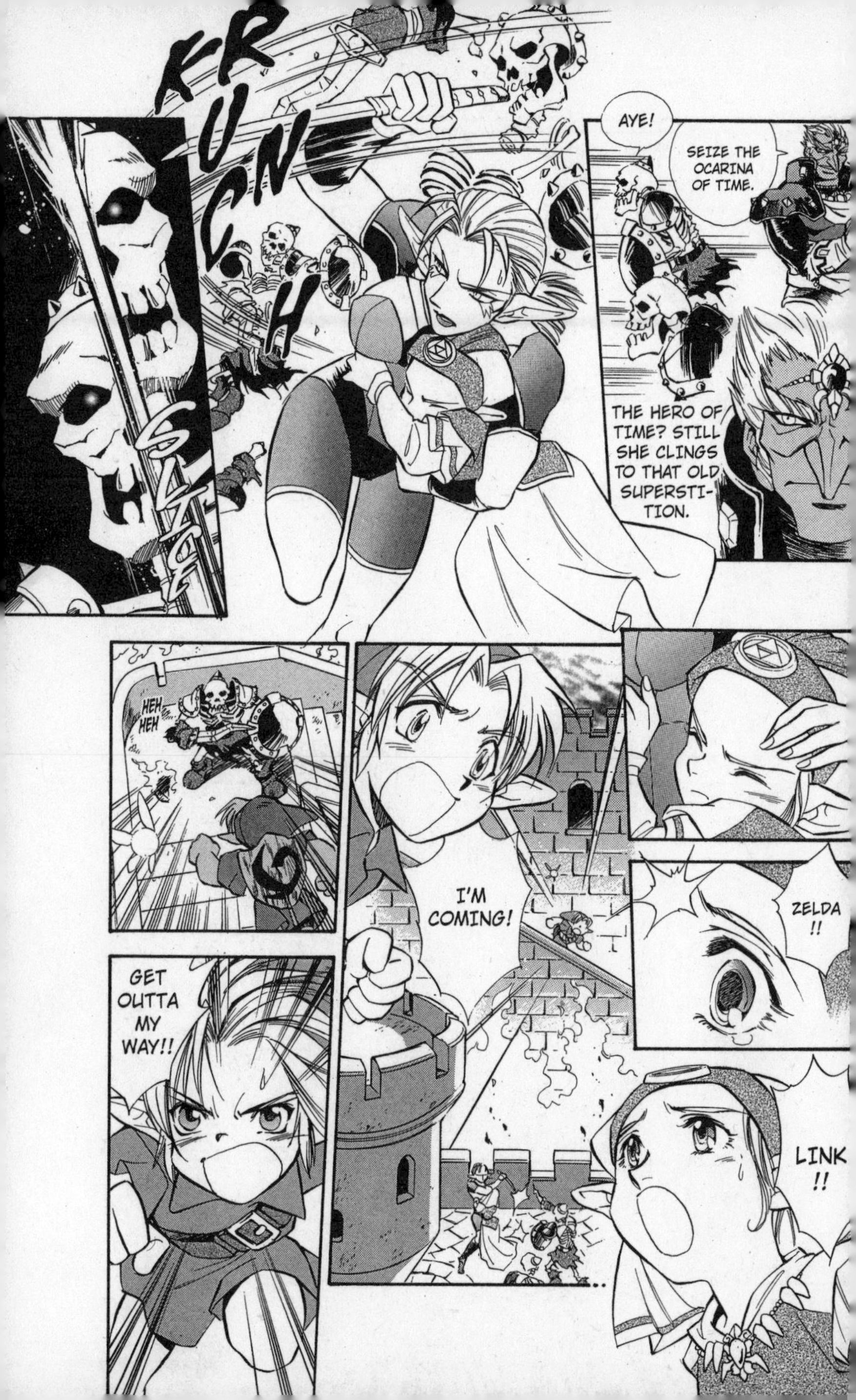
SEIZE THE OCARINA OF TIME.
AYE!
THE HERO OF TIME? STILL SHE CLINGS TO THAT OLD SUPERSTITION.
KRUNCH
SLICE
ZELDA !!
LINK !!
I'M COMING!
HEH HEH
GET OUTTA MY WAY!!

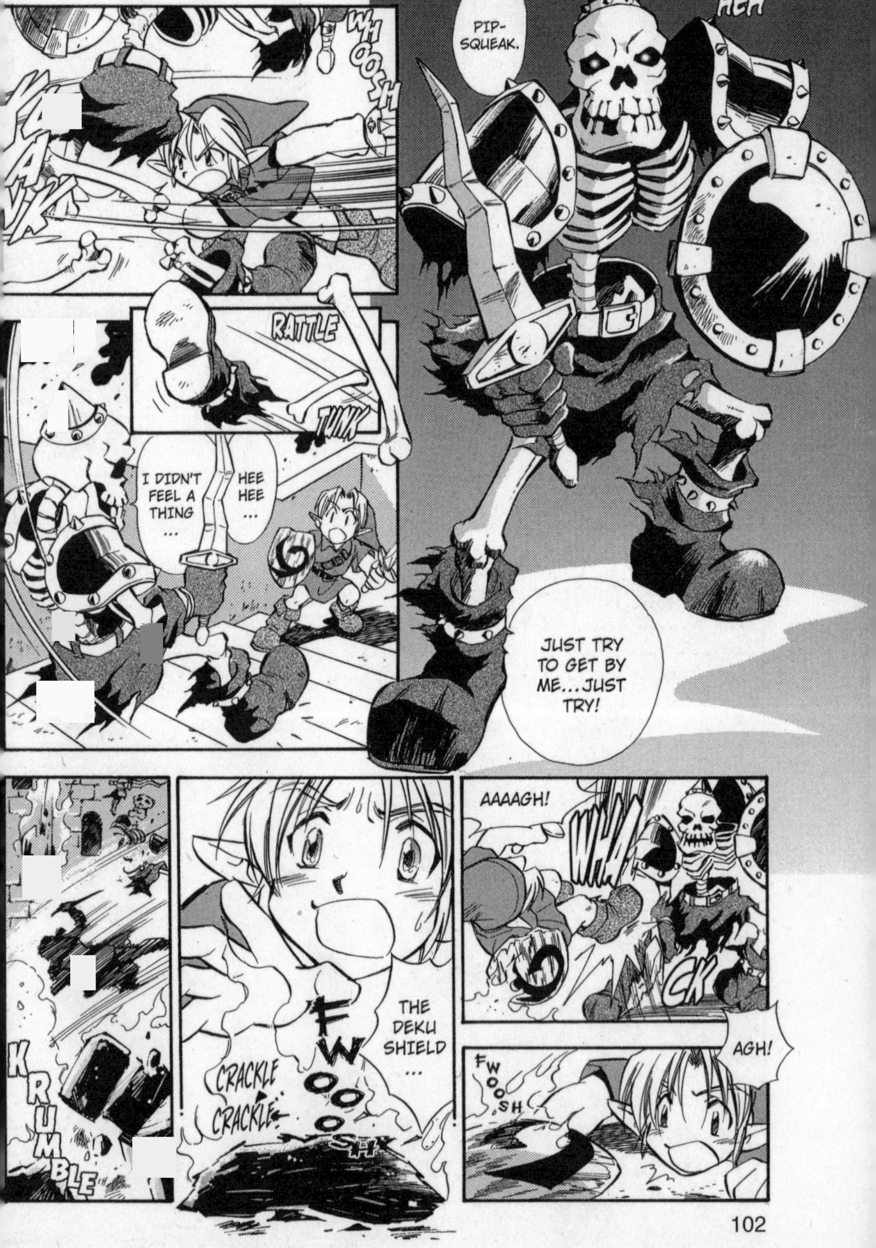
HEH HEH
PIP-SQUEAK.
JUST TRY TO GET BY ME...JUST TRY!
WHOOSH
RATTLE
TUNK
HEE HEE ...
I DIDN'T FEEL A THING ...
AAAAGH!
AGH!
FWOOSH
THE DEKU SHIELD ...
FWOOOOSH
CRACKLE CRACKLE
KRUMBLE

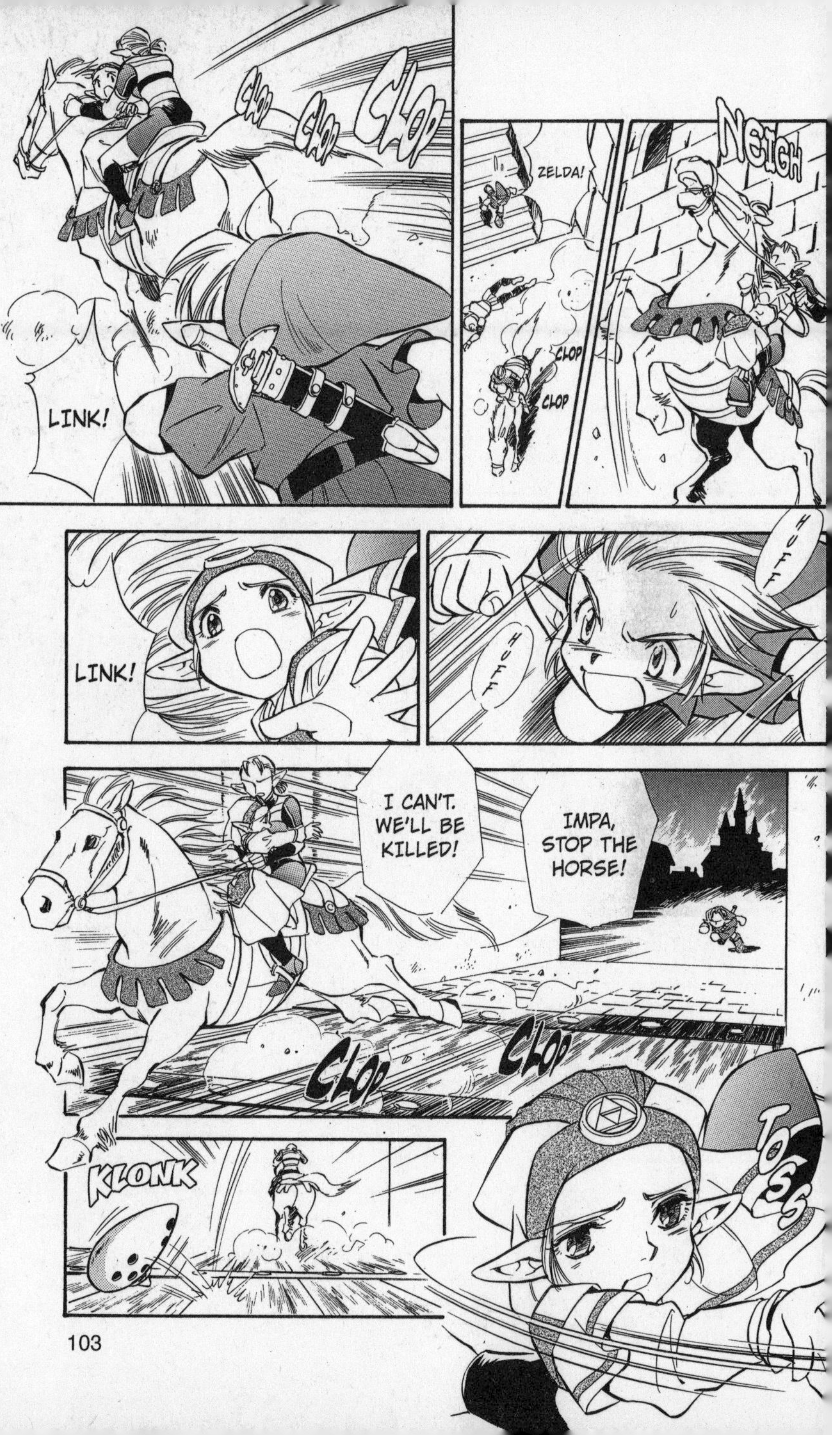
NEIGH
ZELDA!
CLOP
CLOP
CLOP CLOP CLOP
LINK!
HUFF
HUFF
LINK!
IMPA, STOP THE HORSE!
I CAN'T. WE'LL BE KILLED!
CLOP
CLOP
TOSS
KLONK

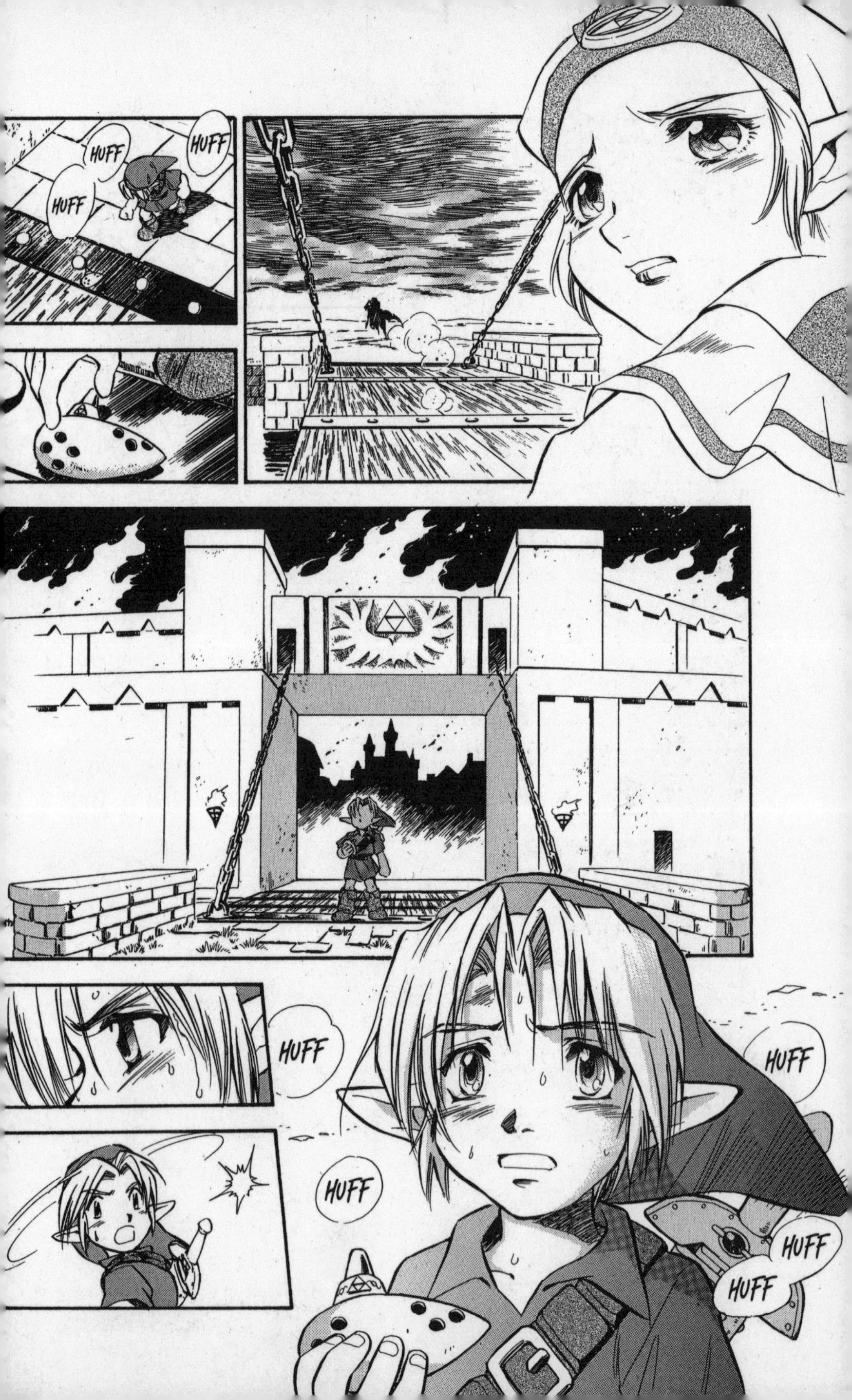
HUFF
HUFF
HUFF
HUFF
HUFF
HUFF
HUFF
HUFF

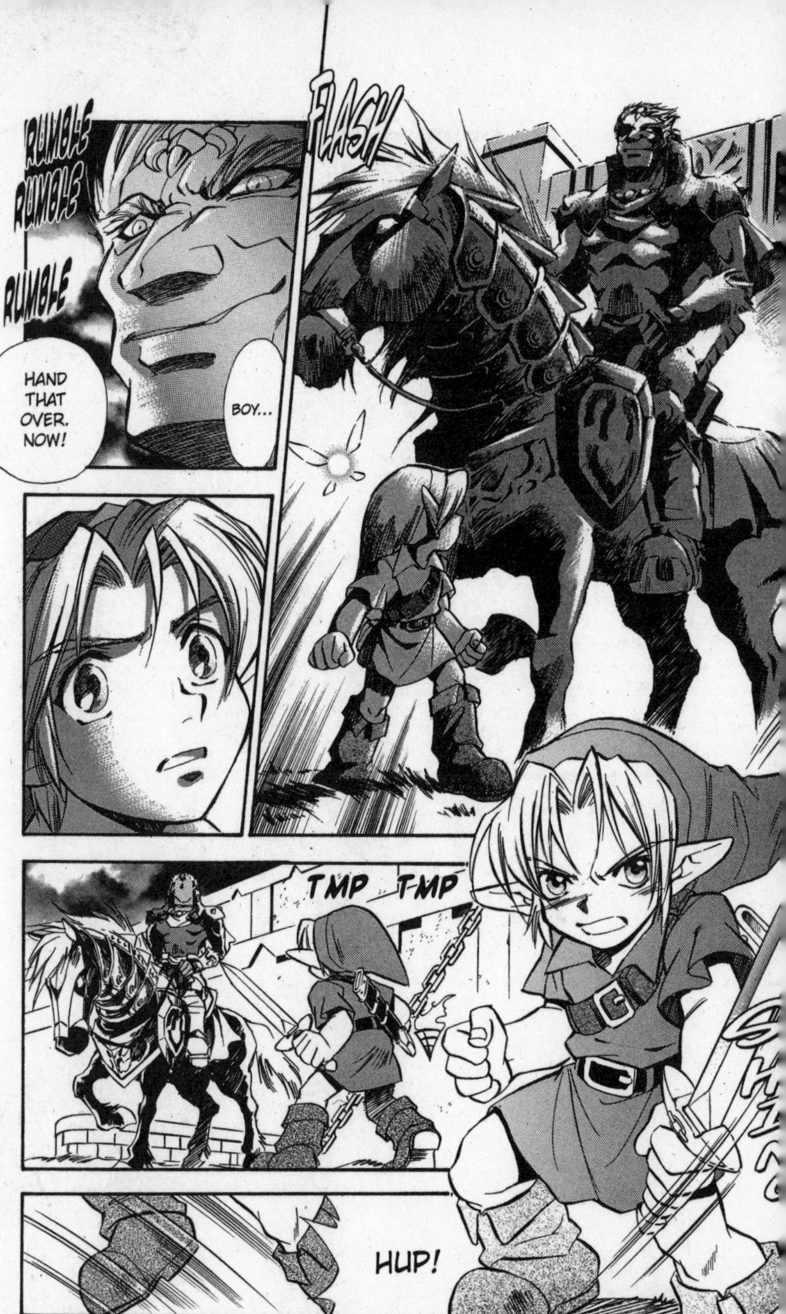
FLASH
RUMBLE
RUMBLE
RUMBLE
BOY...
HAND THAT OVER. NOW!
TMP TMP
HUP!

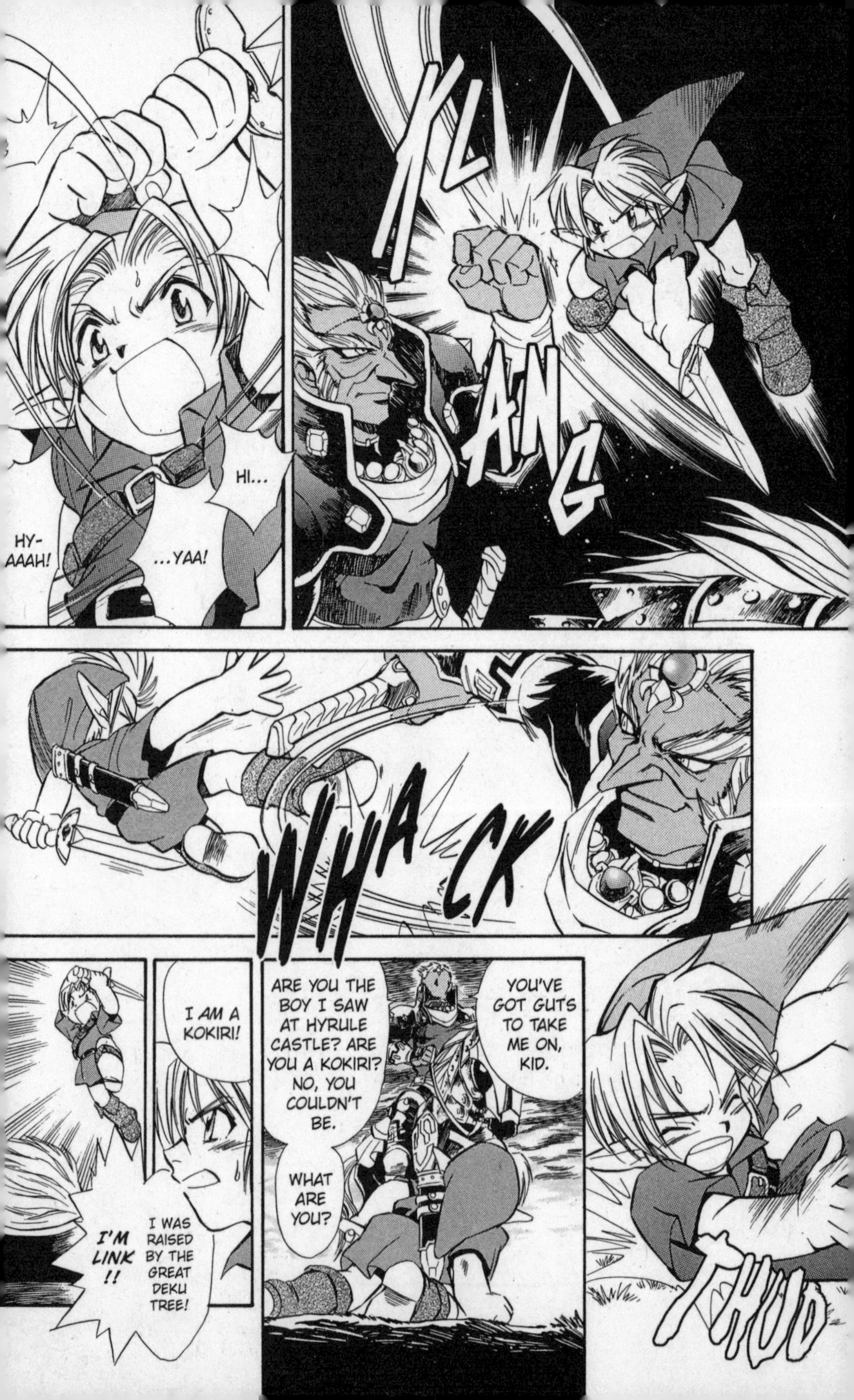
YLANG
HI...
...YAA!
HY-AAAH!
WHACK
THUD
YOU'VE GOT GUTS TO TAKE ME ON, KID.
ARE YOU THE BOY I SAW AT HYRULE CASTLE? ARE YOU A KOKIRI? NO, YOU COULDN'T BE.
WHAT ARE YOU?
I AM A KOKIRI!
I WAS RAISED BY THE GREAT DEKU TREE!
I'M LINK!!

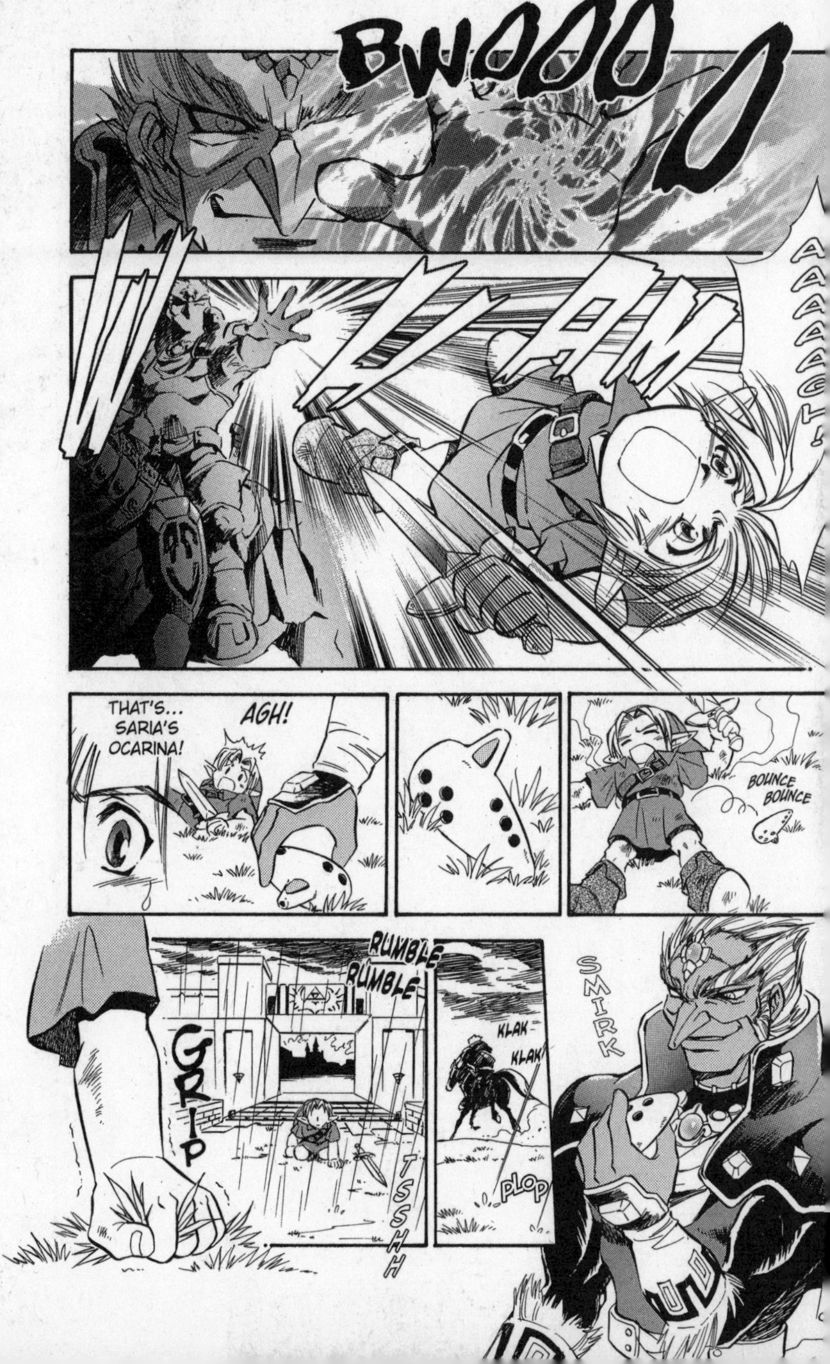
BWOOOO
AAAAAGH!
WHAM
BOUNCE BOUNCE
AGH!
THAT'S... SARIA'S OCARINA!
SMIRK
KLAK-KLAK
PLOP
RUMBLE RUMBLE
TSSHH
GRIP

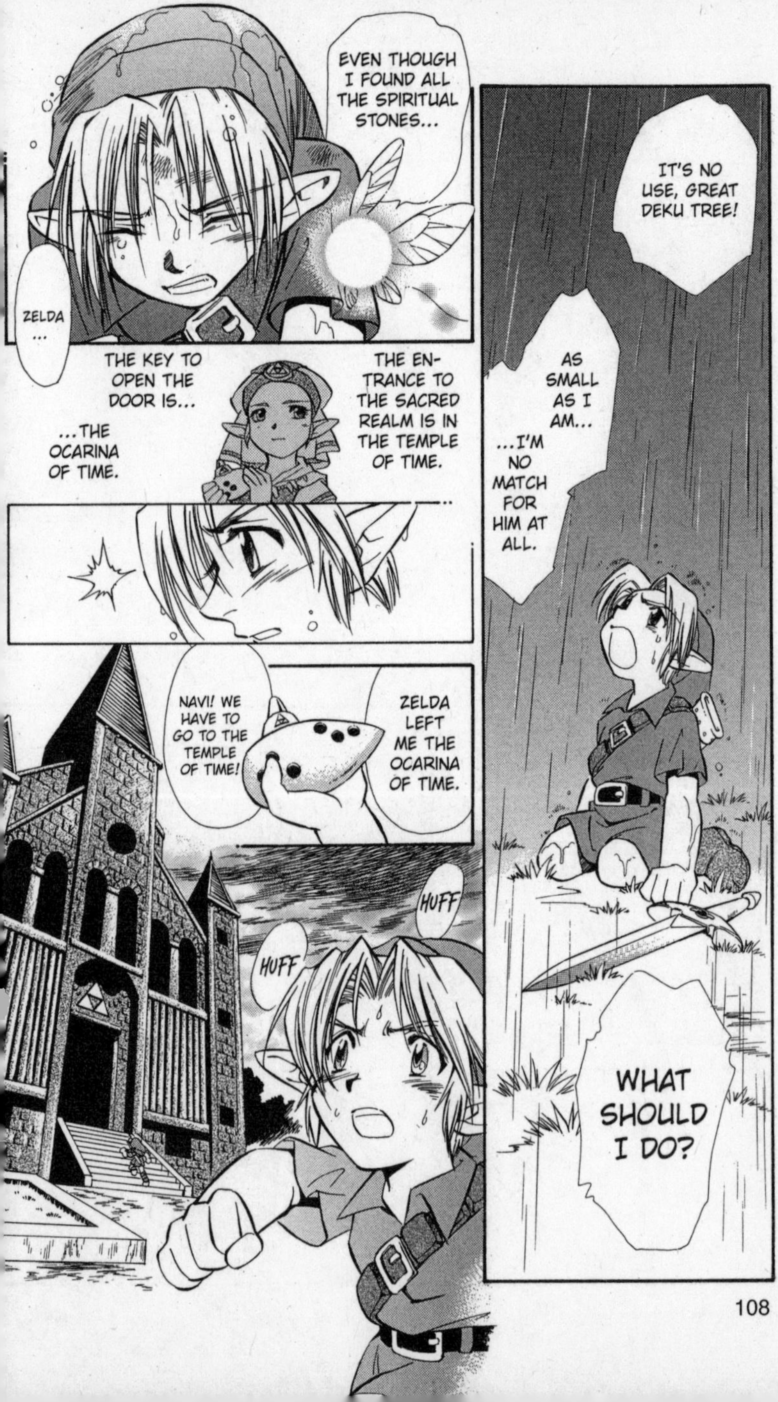
IT'S NO USE, GREAT DEKU TREE!
AS SMALL AS I AM...
...I'M NO MATCH FOR HIM AT ALL.
WHAT SHOULD I DO?
EVEN THOUGH I FOUND ALL THE SPIRITUAL STONES...
ZELDA ...
THE EN-TRANCE TO THE SACRED REALM IS IN THE TEMPLE OF TIME.
THE KEY TO OPEN THE DOOR IS...
...THE OCARINA OF TIME.
ZELDA LEFT ME THE OCARINA OF TIME.
NAVI! WE HAVE TO GO TO THE TEMPLE OF TIME!
HUFF
HUFF

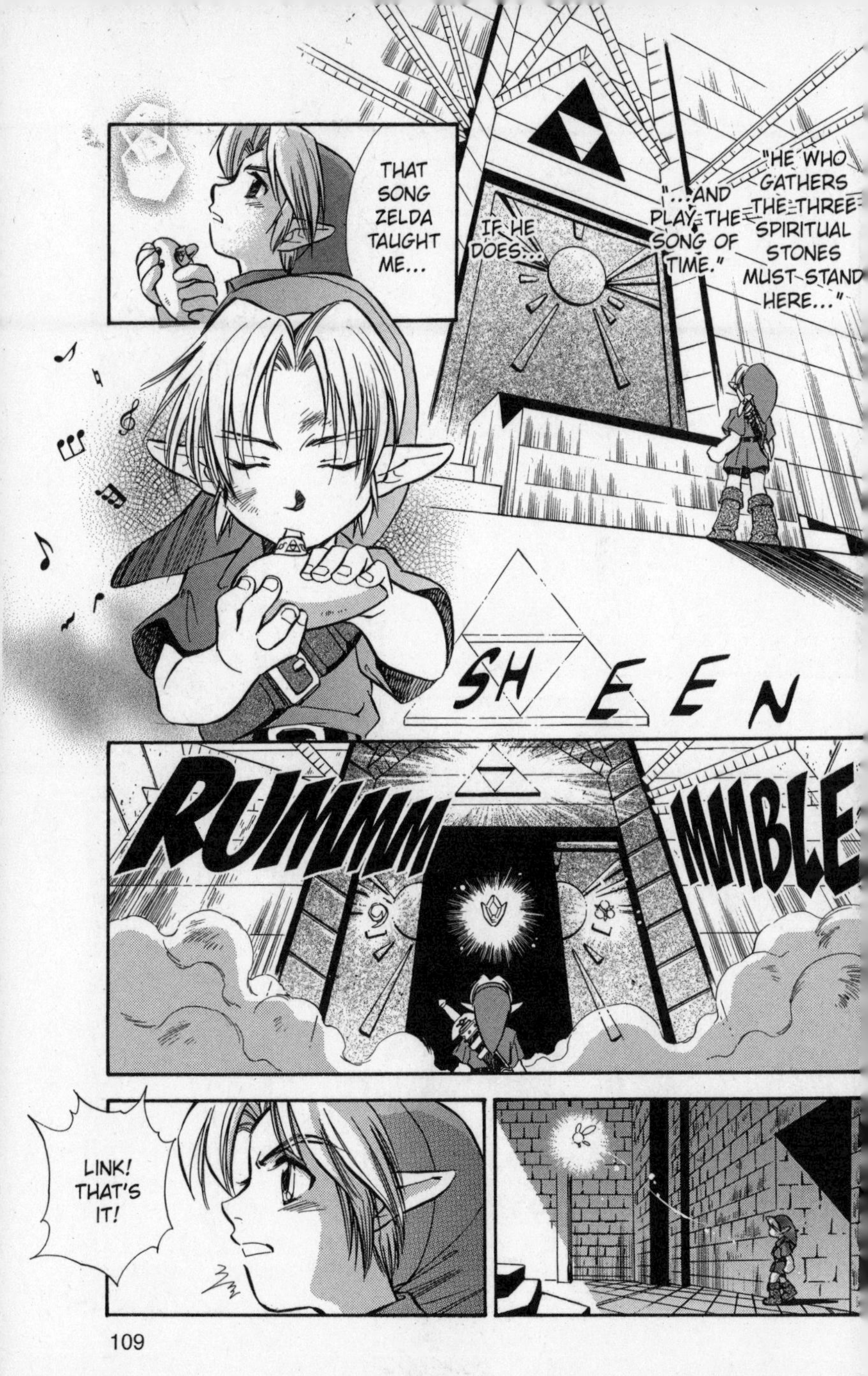
"HE WHO GATHERS THE THREE SPIRITUAL STONES MUST STAND HERE..."
"...AND PLAY THE SONG OF TIME."
IF HE DOES...
THAT SONG ZELDA TAUGHT ME...
SHEEN
RUMMMMMBLE
LINK! THAT'S IT!

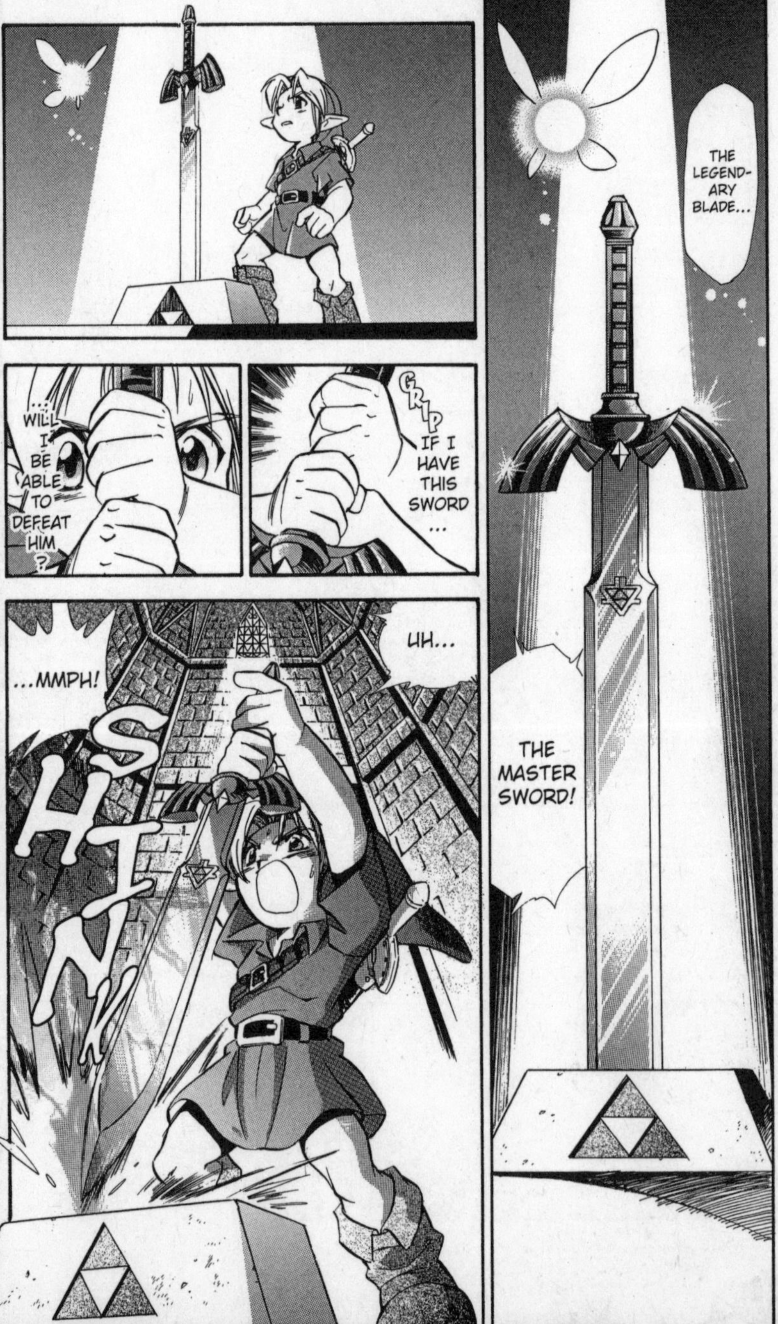
THE LEGENDARY BLADE...
THE MASTER SWORD!
GRIP
IF I HAVE THIS SWORD...
...WILL I BE ABLE TO DEFEAT HIM?
UH...
...MMPH!
SHING

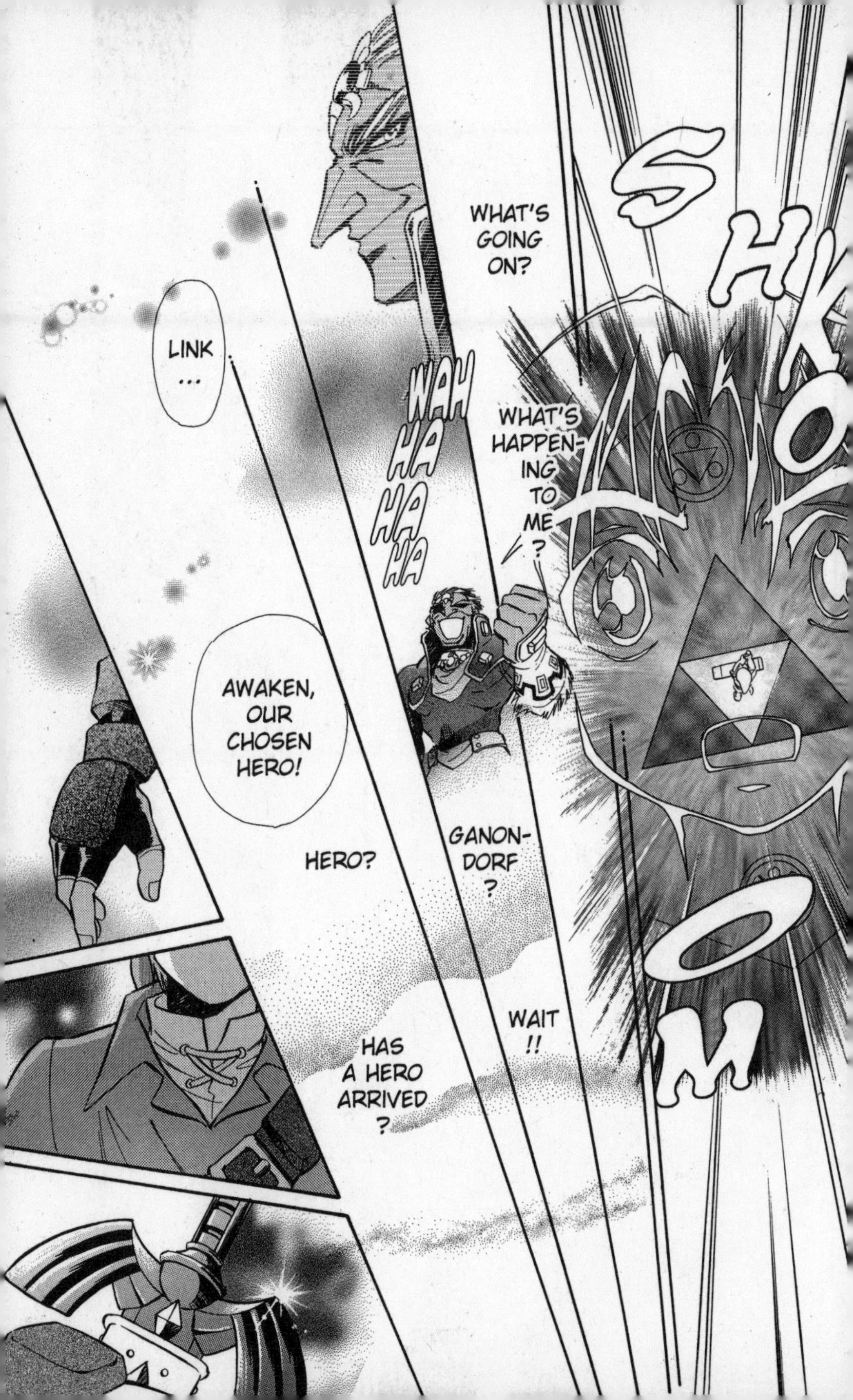
SHKOOM
WHAT'S GOING ON?
WHAT'S HAPPENING TO ME?
GANONDORF?
WAIT!!
WAH HA HA HA HA
LINK ...
AWAKEN, OUR CHOSEN HERO!
HERO?
HAS A HERO ARRIVED?

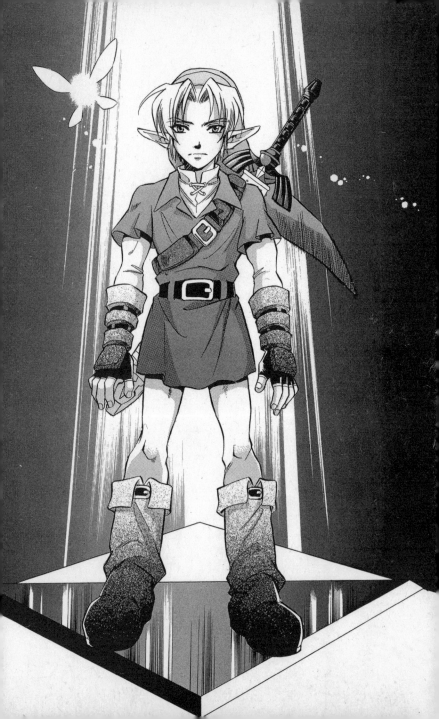

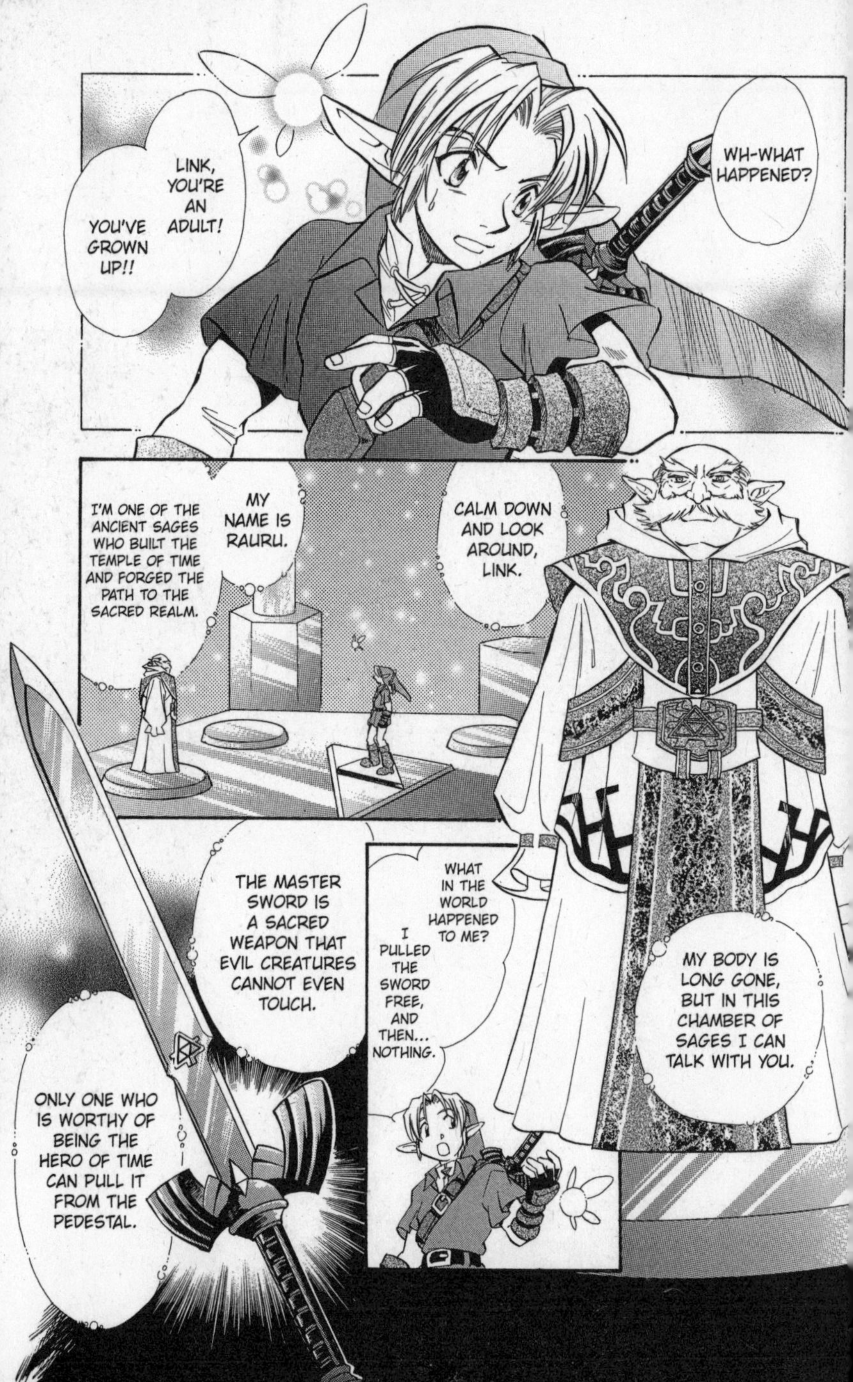
WH-WHAT HAPPENED?
LINK, YOU'RE AN ADULT!
YOU'VE GROWN UP!!
CALM DOWN AND LOOK AROUND, LINK.
MY NAME IS RAURU.
I'M ONE OF THE ANCIENT SAGES WHO BUILT THE TEMPLE OF TIME AND FORGED THE PATH TO THE SACRED REALM.
MY BODY IS LONG GONE, BUT IN THIS CHAMBER OF SAGES I CAN TALK WITH YOU.
WHAT IN THE WORLD HAPPENED TO ME?
I PULLED THE SWORD FREE, AND THEN... NOTHING.
THE MASTER SWORD IS A SACRED WEAPON THAT EVIL CREATURES CANNOT EVEN TOUCH.
ONLY ONE WHO IS WORTHY OF BEING THE HERO OF TIME CAN PULL IT FROM THE PEDESTAL.

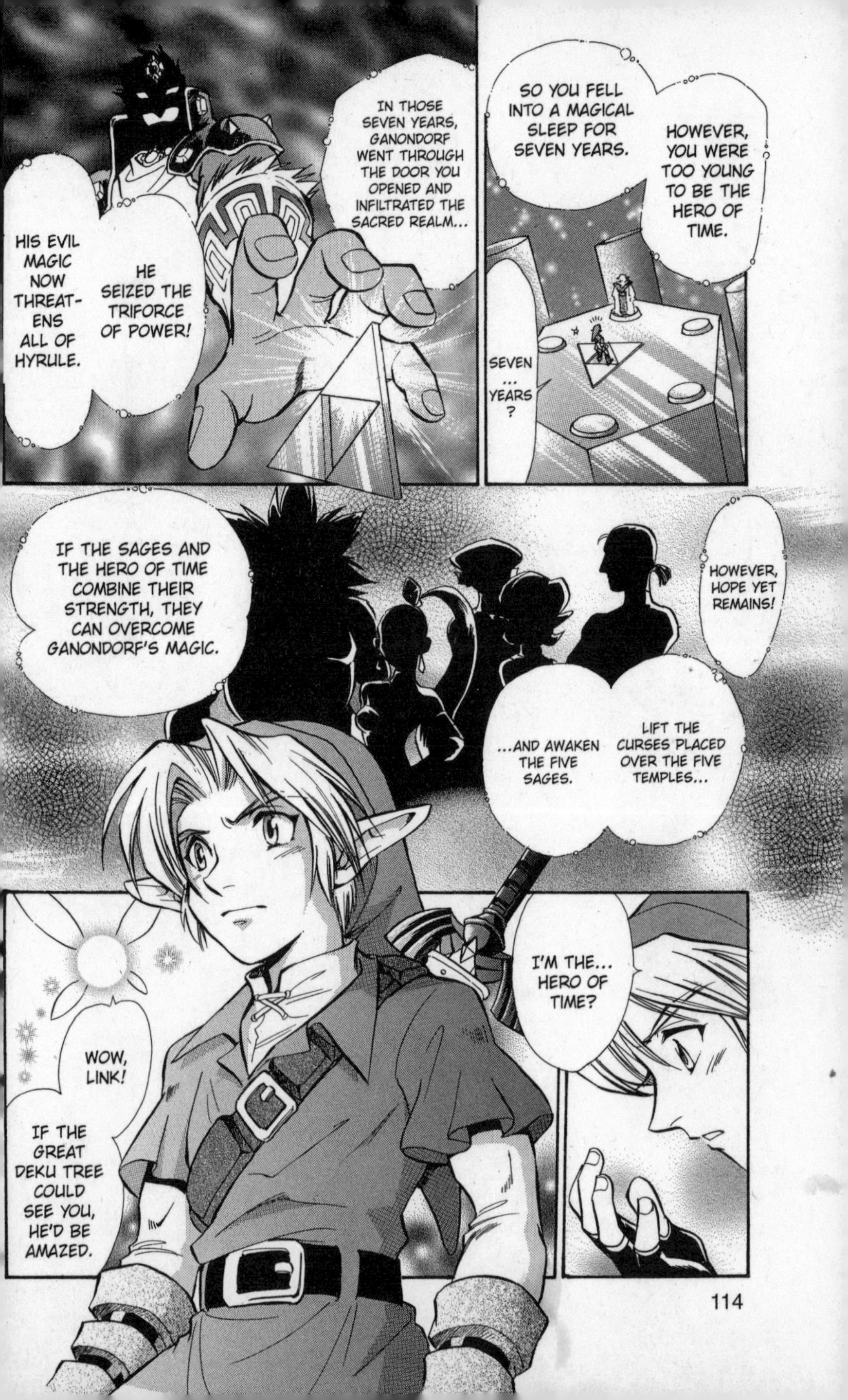
HOWEVER, YOU WERE TOO YOUNG TO BE THE HERO OF TIME.
SO YOU FELL INTO A MAGICAL SLEEP FOR SEVEN YEARS.
SEVEN ... YEARS ?
IN THOSE SEVEN YEARS, GANONDORF WENT THROUGH THE DOOR YOU OPENED AND INFILTRATED THE SACRED REALM...
HE SEIZED THE TRIFORCE OF POWER!
HIS EVIL MAGIC NOW THREAT-ENS ALL OF HYRULE.
HOWEVER, HOPE YET REMAINS!
LIFT THE CURSES PLACED OVER THE FIVE TEMPLES...
...AND AWAKEN THE FIVE SAGES.
IF THE SAGES AND THE HERO OF TIME COMBINE THEIR STRENGTH, THEY CAN OVERCOME GANONDORF'S MAGIC.
I'M THE... HERO OF TIME?
WOW, LINK!
IF THE GREAT DEKU TREE COULD SEE YOU, HE'D BE AMAZED.

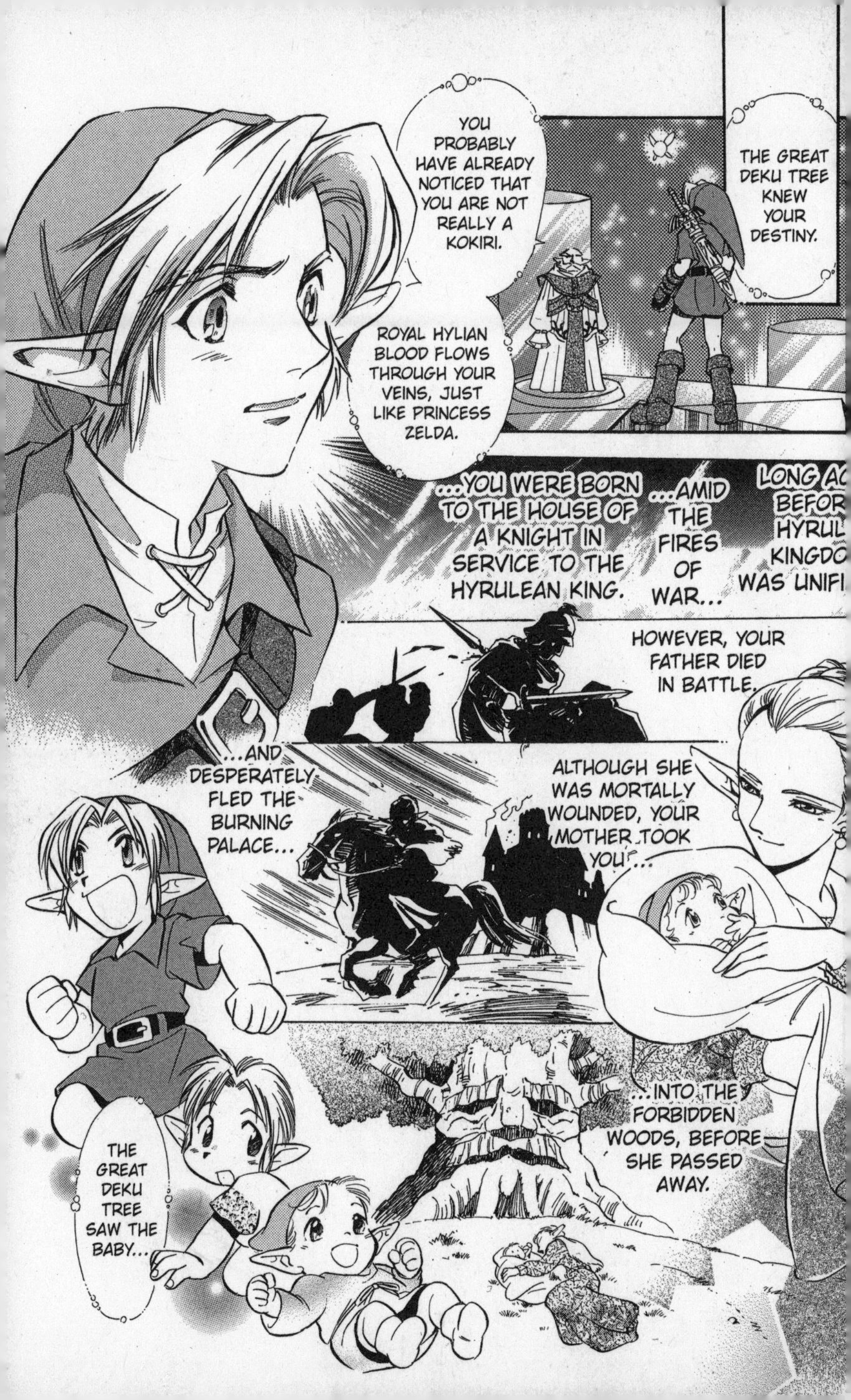
THE GREAT DEKU TREE KNEW YOUR DESTINY.
YOU PROBABLY HAVE ALREADY NOTICED THAT YOU ARE NOT REALLY A KOKIRI.
ROYAL HYLIAN BLOOD FLOWS THROUGH YOUR VEINS, JUST LIKE PRINCESS ZELDA.
LONG AG BEFOR HYRUL KINGDO WAS UNIFI
...AMID THE FIRES OF WAR...
...YOU WERE BORN TO THE HOUSE OF A KNIGHT IN SERVICE TO THE HYRULEAN KING.
HOWEVER, YOUR FATHER DIED IN BATTLE.
ALTHOUGH SHE WAS MORTALLY WOUNDED, YOUR MOTHER TOOK YOU...
...AND DESPERATELY FLED THE BURNING PALACE...
...INTO THE FORBIDDEN WOODS, BEFORE SHE PASSED AWAY.
THE GREAT DEKU TREE SAW THE BABY...

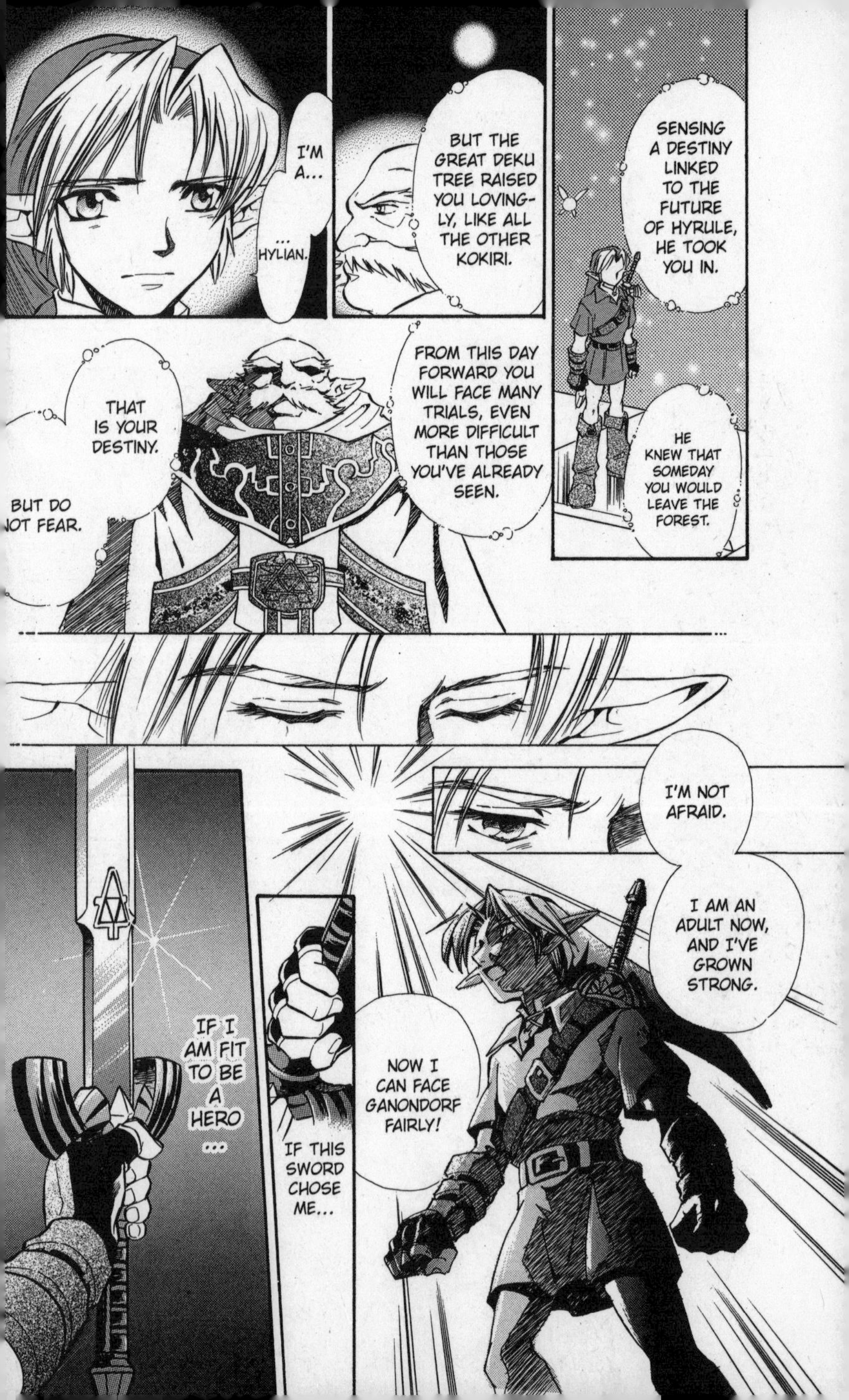
SENSING A DESTINY LINKED TO THE FUTURE OF HYRULE, HE TOOK YOU IN.
HE KNEW THAT SOMEDAY YOU WOULD LEAVE THE FOREST.
BUT THE GREAT DEKU TREE RAISED YOU LOVING-LY, LIKE ALL THE OTHER KOKIRI.
I'M A...
...HYLIAN.
FROM THIS DAY FORWARD YOU WILL FACE MANY TRIALS, EVEN MORE DIFFICULT THAN THOSE YOU'VE ALREADY SEEN.
THAT IS YOUR DESTINY.
BUT DO NOT FEAR.
I'M NOT AFRAID.
I AM AN ADULT NOW, AND I'VE GROWN STRONG.
NOW I CAN FACE GANONDORF FAIRLY!
IF THIS SWORD CHOSE ME...
IF I AM FIT TO BE A HERO...

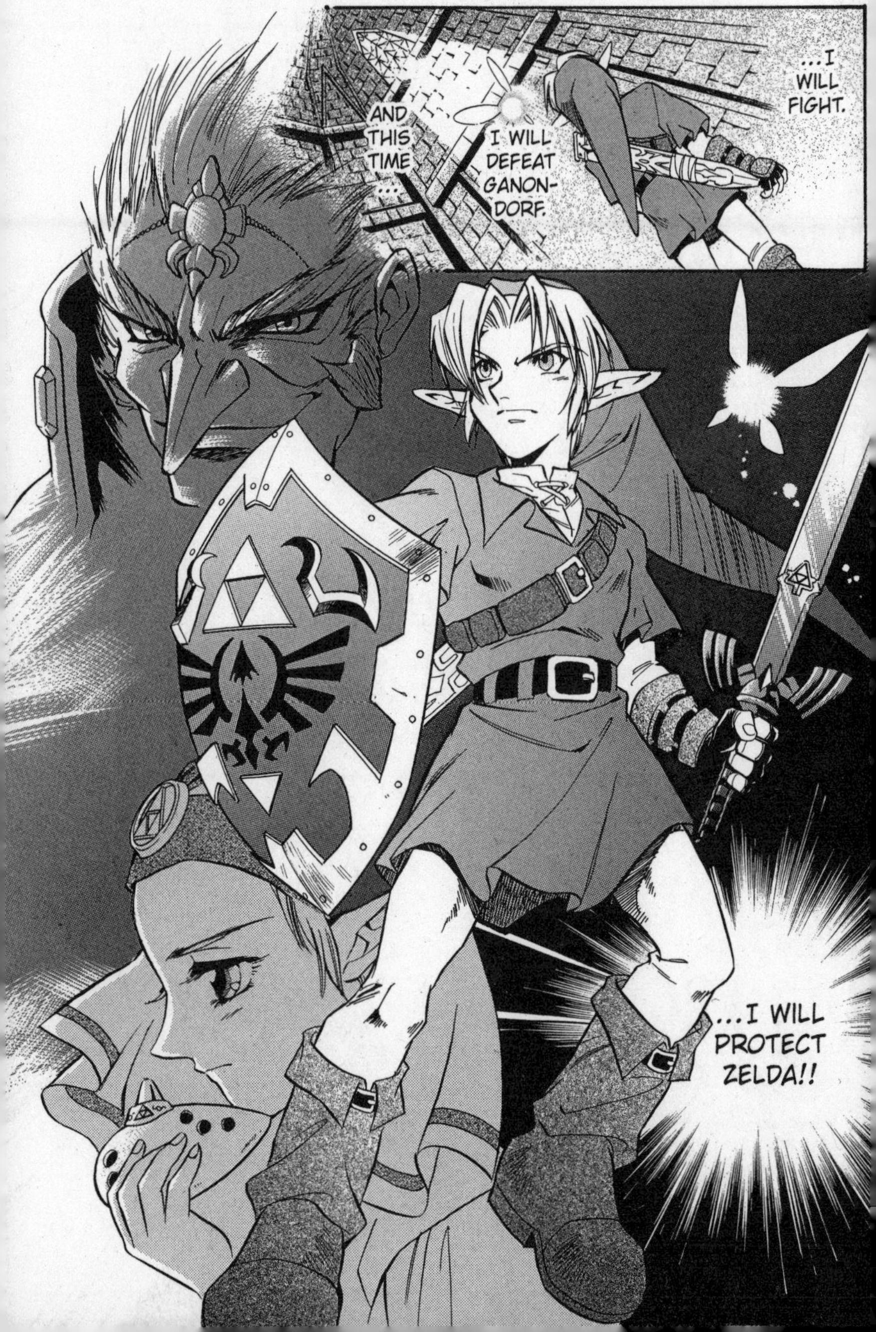
...I WILL FIGHT.
I WILL DEFEAT GANON-DORF.
AND THIS TIME ...
...I WILL PROTECT ZELDA!!

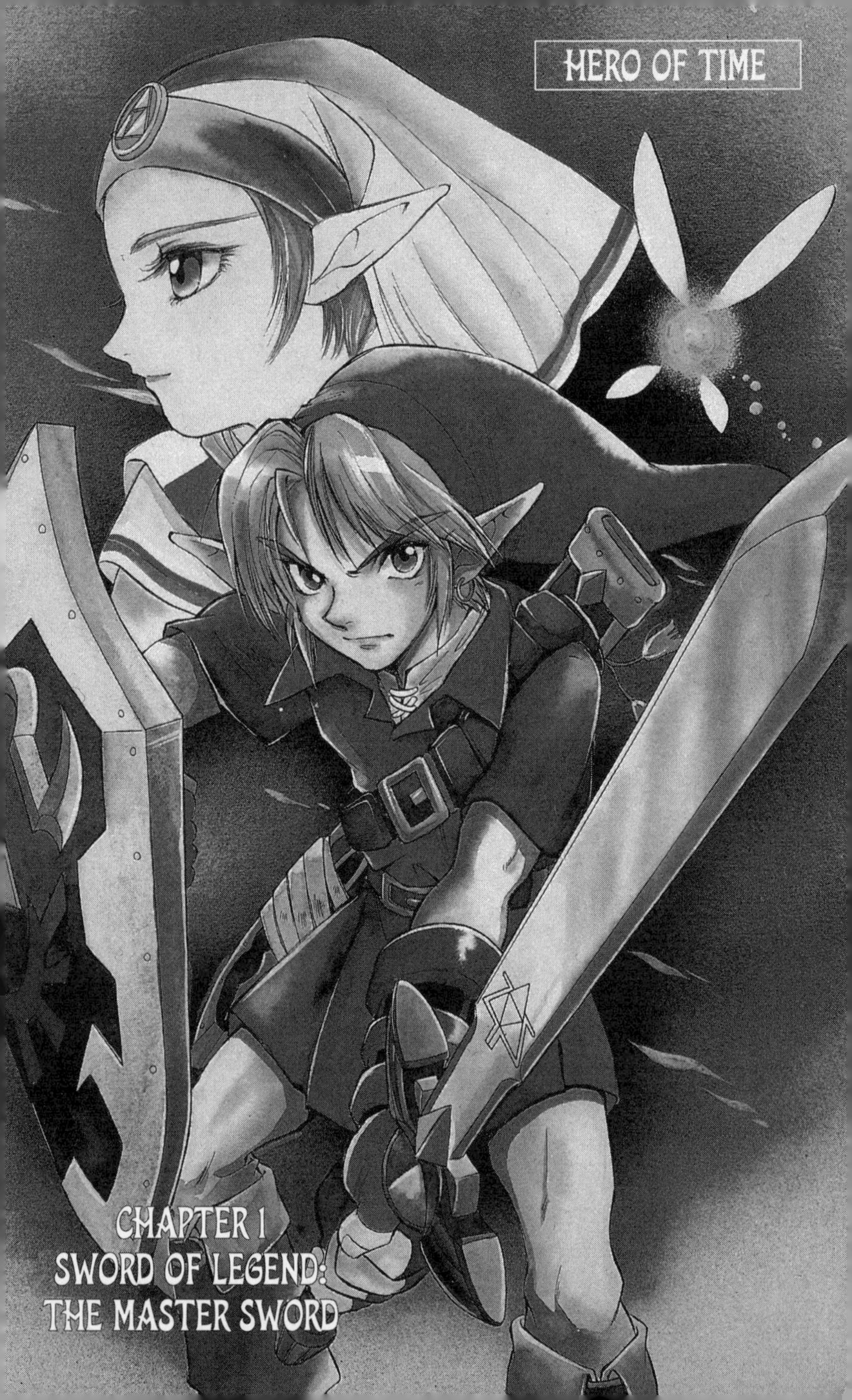
HERO OF TIME
CHAPTER 1
SWORD OF LEGEND:
THE MASTER SWORD

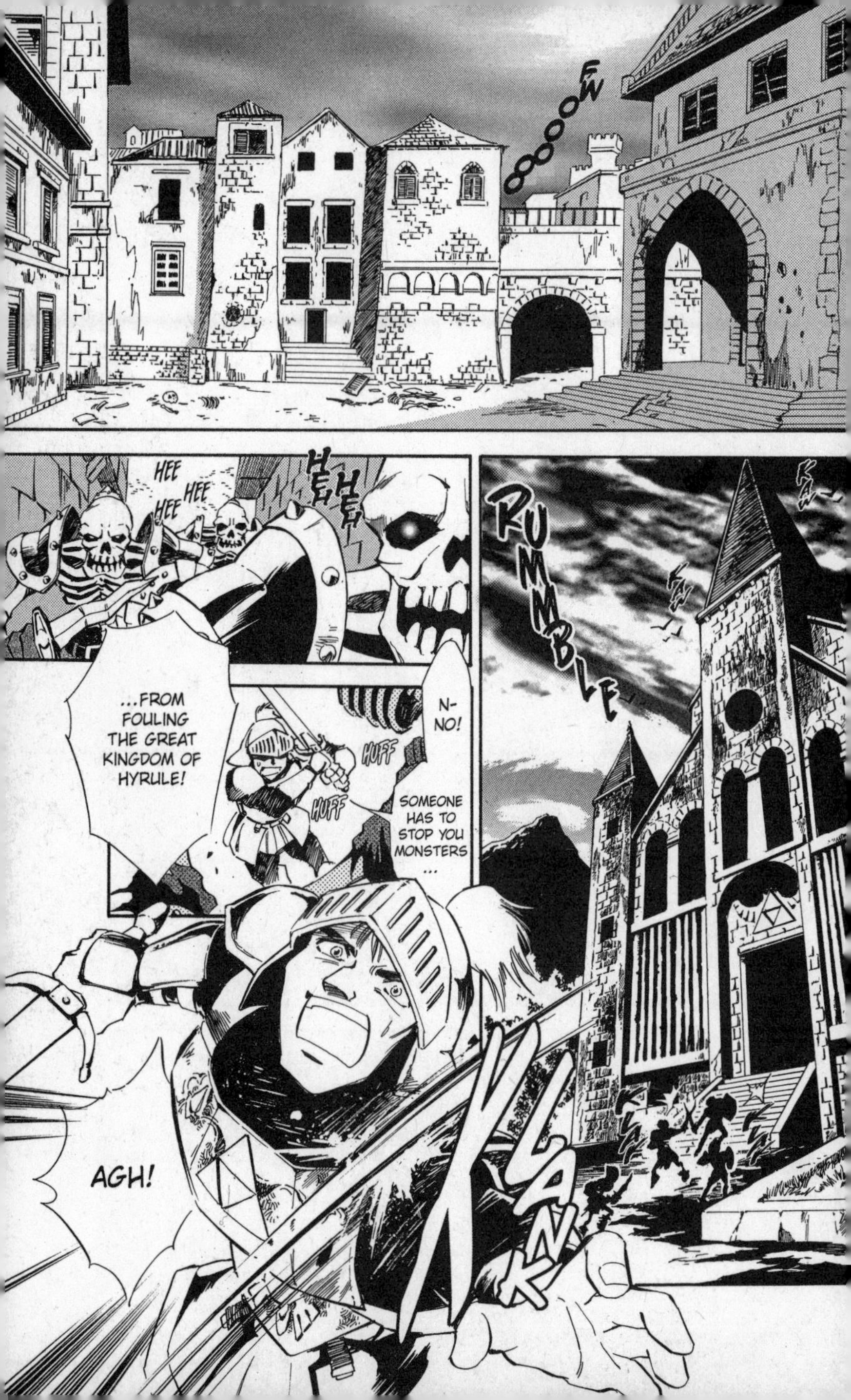
FWOOOOOO
RUMMBLE
KAW
KAW
KLANK
HEE HEE HEE
HEHEH
N-NO!
SOMEONE HAS TO STOP YOU MONSTERS...
...FROM FOULING THE GREAT KINGDOM OF HYRULE!
HUFF
HUFF
AGH!

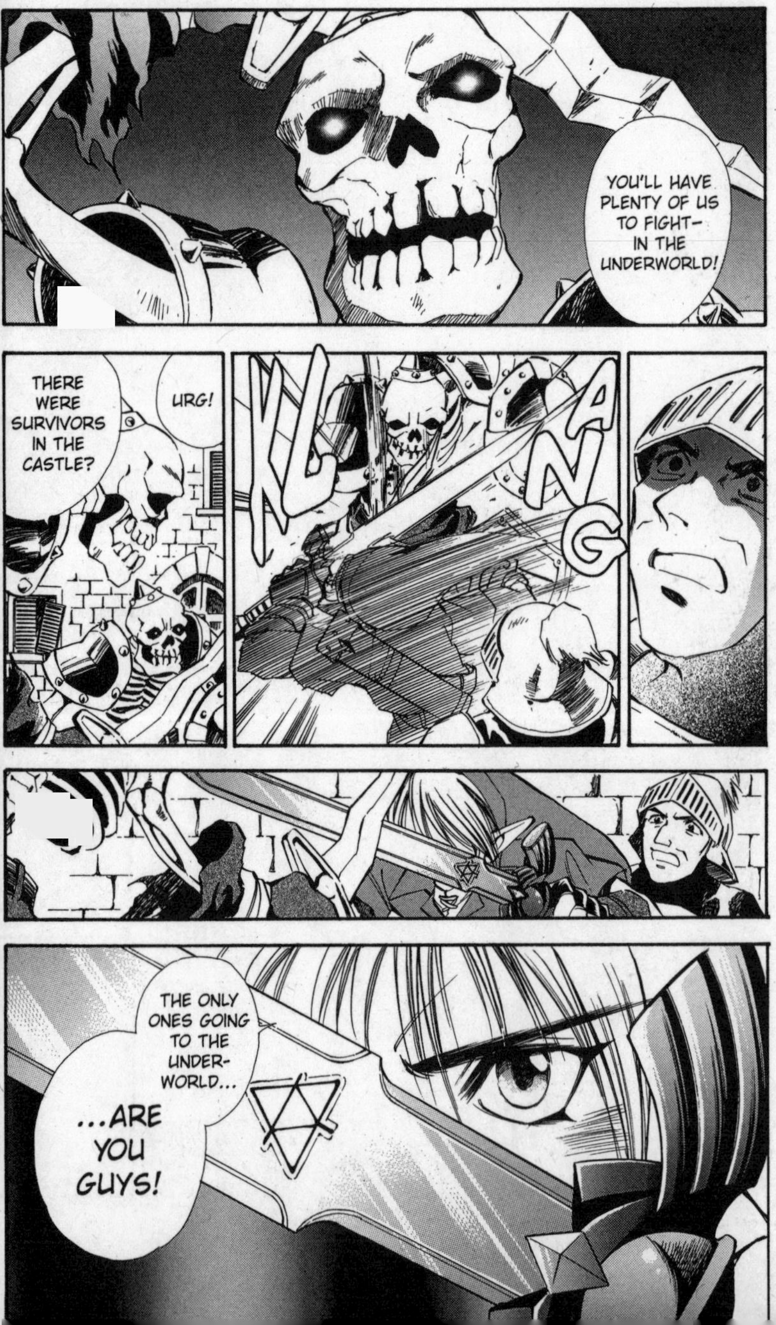
YOU'LL HAVE PLENTY OF US TO FIGHT— IN THE UNDERWORLD!
KLANG
URG!
THERE WERE SURVIVORS IN THE CASTLE?
THE ONLY ONES GOING TO THE UNDER-WORLD...
...ARE YOU GUYS!

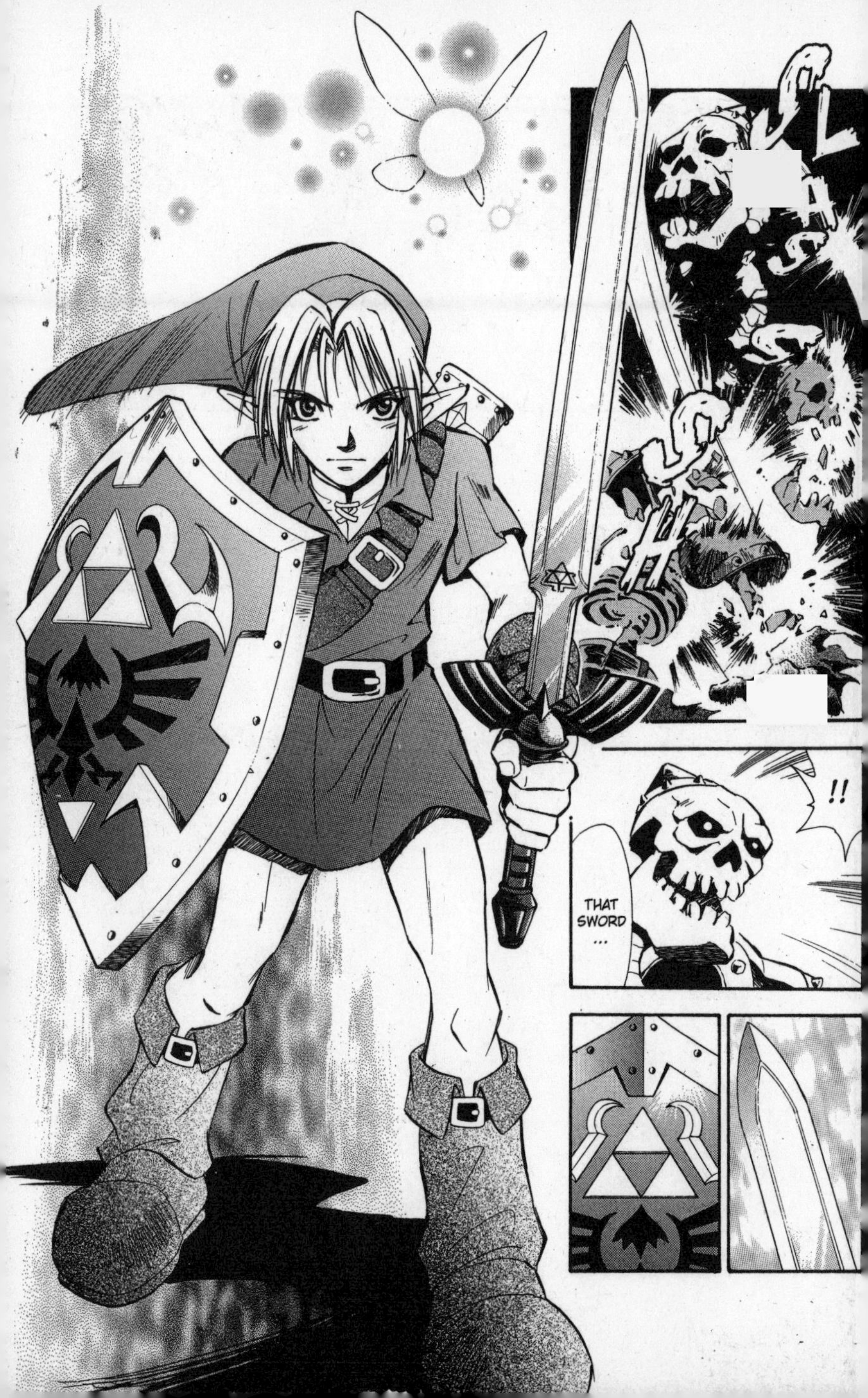
!!
THAT SWORD ...

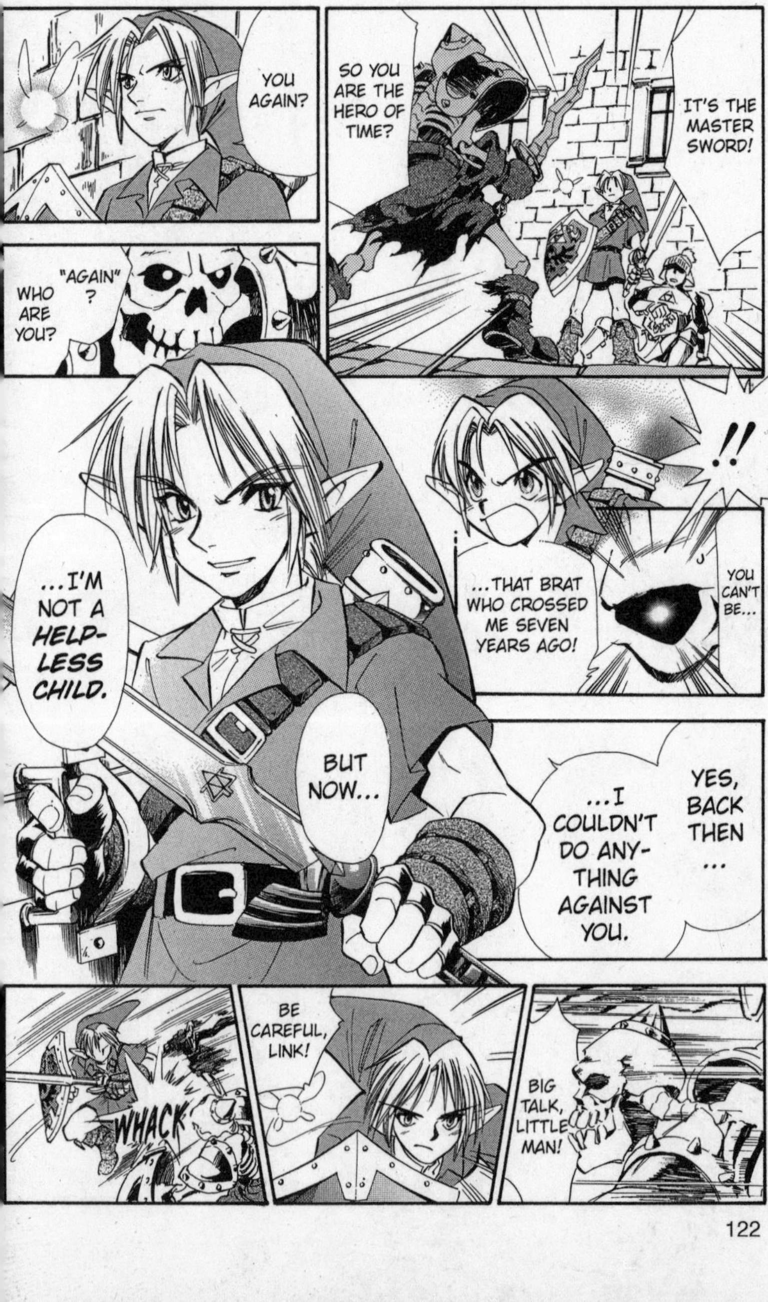
IT'S THE MASTER SWORD!
SO YOU ARE THE HERO OF TIME?
YOU AGAIN?
"AGAIN"?
WHO ARE YOU?
!!
YOU CAN'T BE...
...THAT BRAT WHO CROSSED ME SEVEN YEARS AGO!
YES, BACK THEN...
...I COULDN'T DO ANY-THING AGAINST YOU.
BUT NOW...
...I'M NOT A HELP-LESS CHILD.
BIG TALK, LITTLE MAN!
BE CAREFUL, LINK!
WHACK

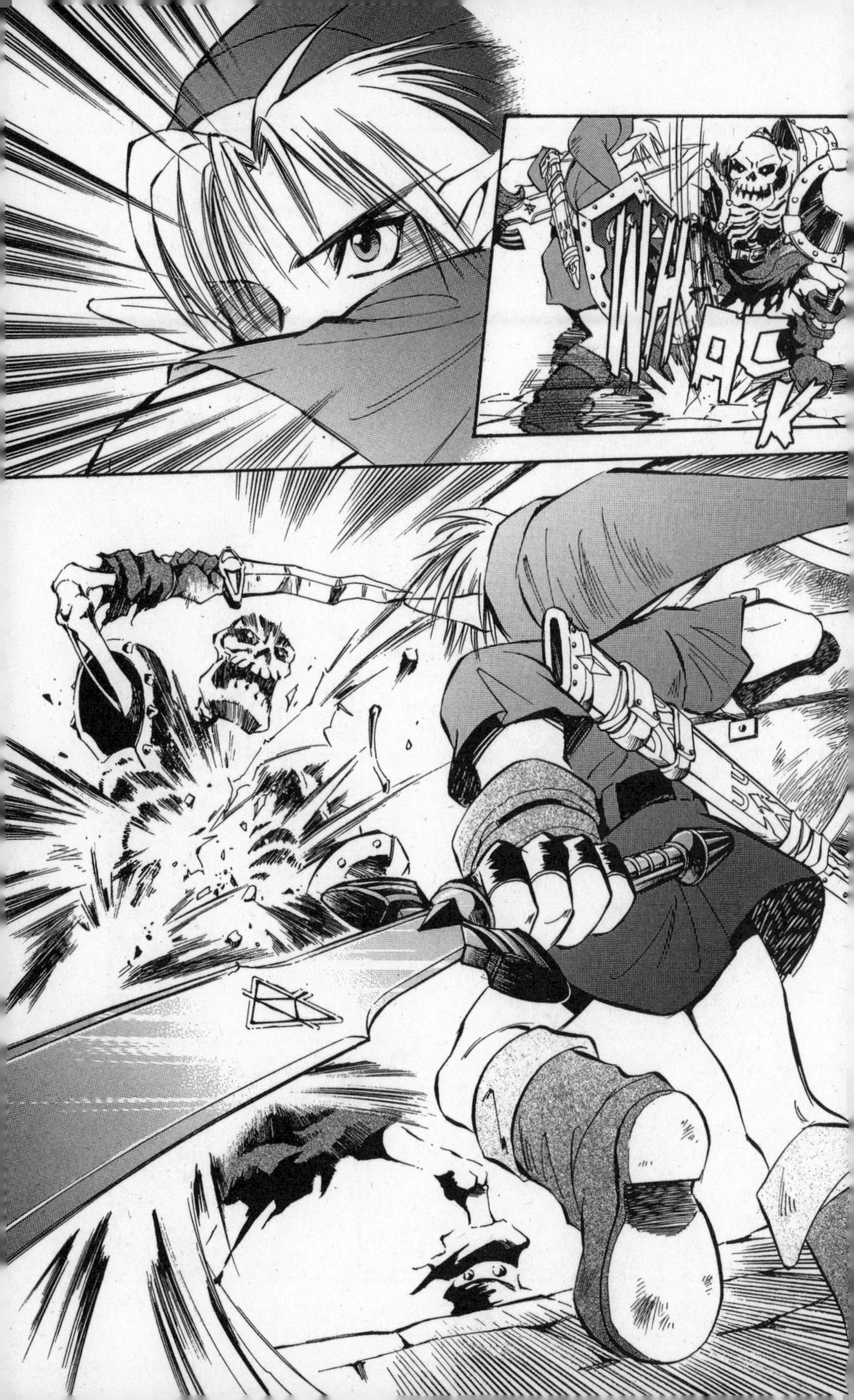
WHACK

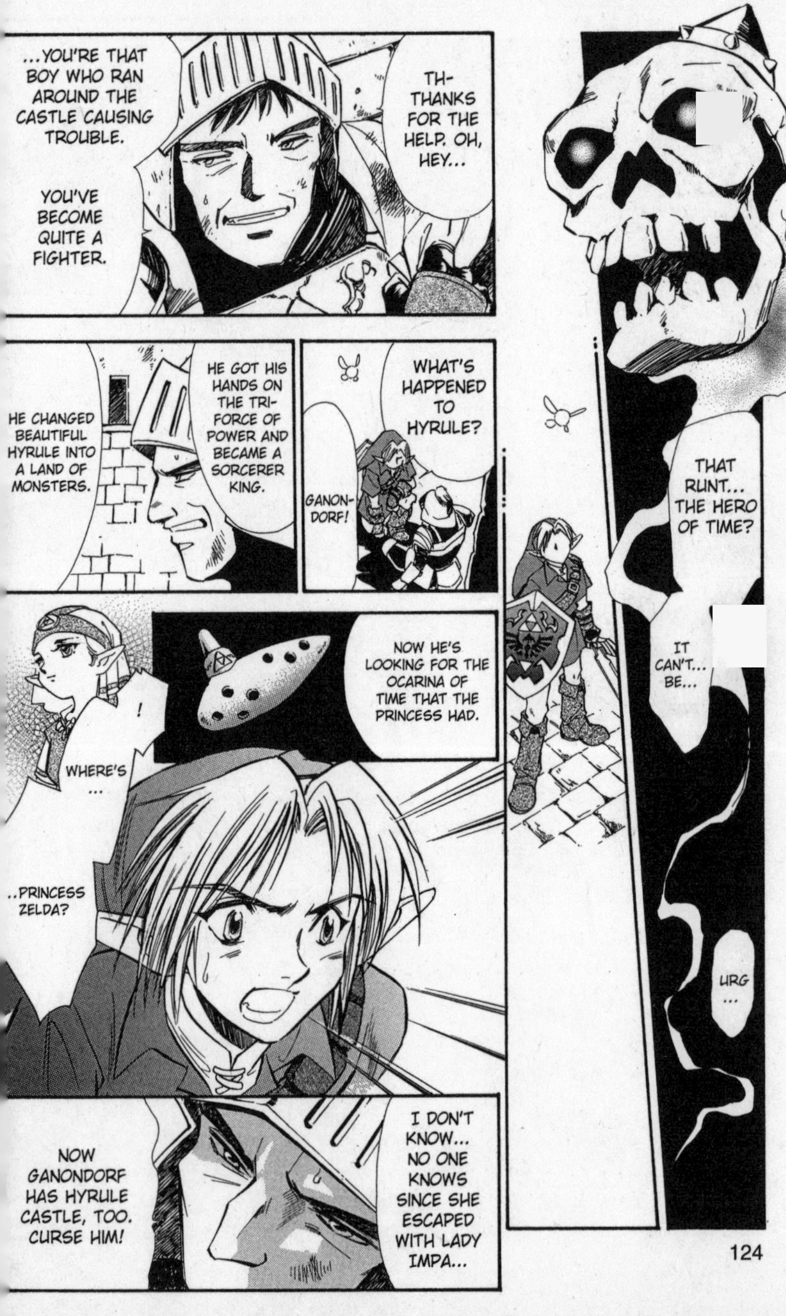
THAT RUNT... THE HERO OF TIME?
IT CAN'T... BE...
URG ...
TH- THANKS FOR THE HELP. OH, HEY...
...YOU'RE THAT BOY WHO RAN AROUND THE CASTLE CAUSING TROUBLE.
YOU'VE BECOME QUITE A FIGHTER.
WHAT'S HAPPENED TO HYRULE?
GANON-DORF!
HE GOT HIS HANDS ON THE TRI-FORCE OF POWER AND BECAME A SORCERER KING.
HE CHANGED BEAUTIFUL HYRULE INTO A LAND OF MONSTERS.
NOW HE'S LOOKING FOR THE OCARINA OF TIME THAT THE PRINCESS HAD.
!
WHERE'S ...
..PRINCESS ZELDA?
I DON'T KNOW... NO ONE KNOWS SINCE SHE ESCAPED WITH LADY IMPA...
NOW GANONDORF HAS HYRULE CASTLE, TOO. CURSE HIM!

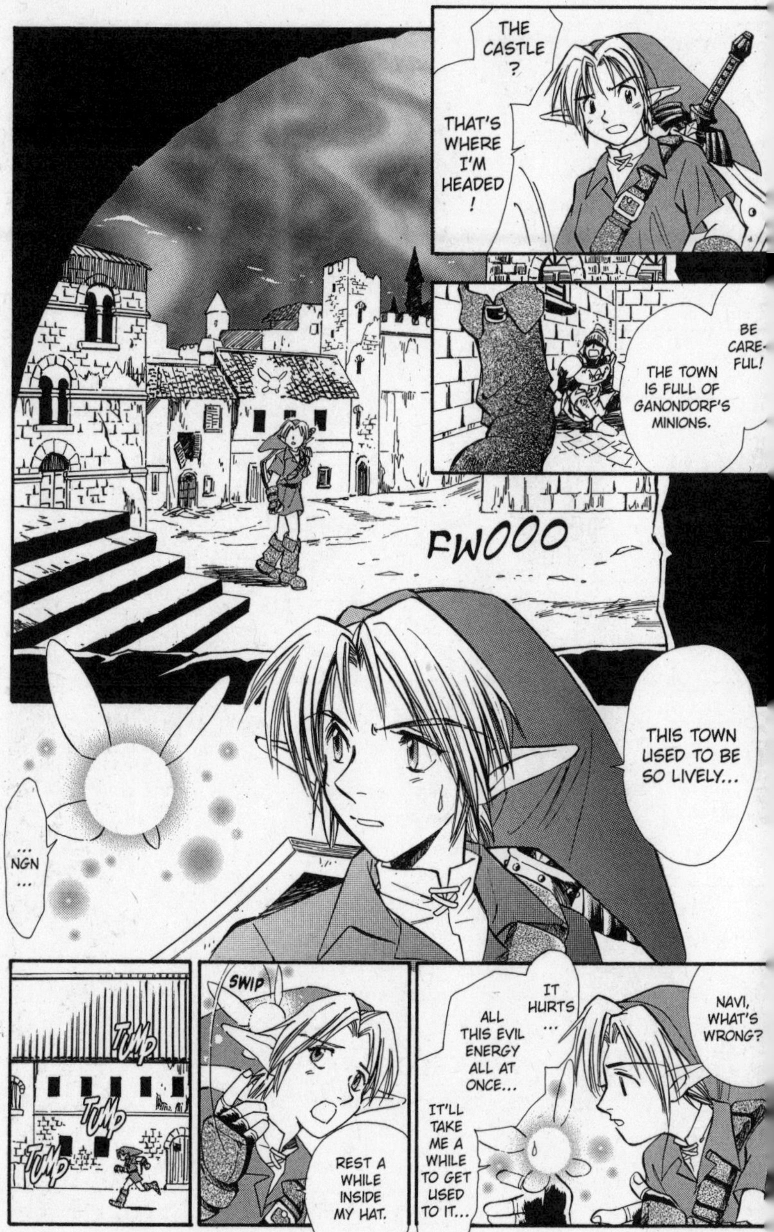

THE CASTLE?
THAT'S WHERE I'M HEADED!
BE CAREFUL!
THE TOWN IS FULL OF GANONDORF'S MINIONS.
FWOOO
THIS TOWN USED TO BE SO LIVELY...
...NGN...
NAVI, WHAT'S WRONG?
IT HURTS...
ALL THIS EVIL ENERGY ALL AT ONCE...
IT'LL TAKE ME A WHILE TO GET USED TO IT...
SWIP
REST A WHILE INSIDE MY HAT.
TUMP
TUMP
TUMP

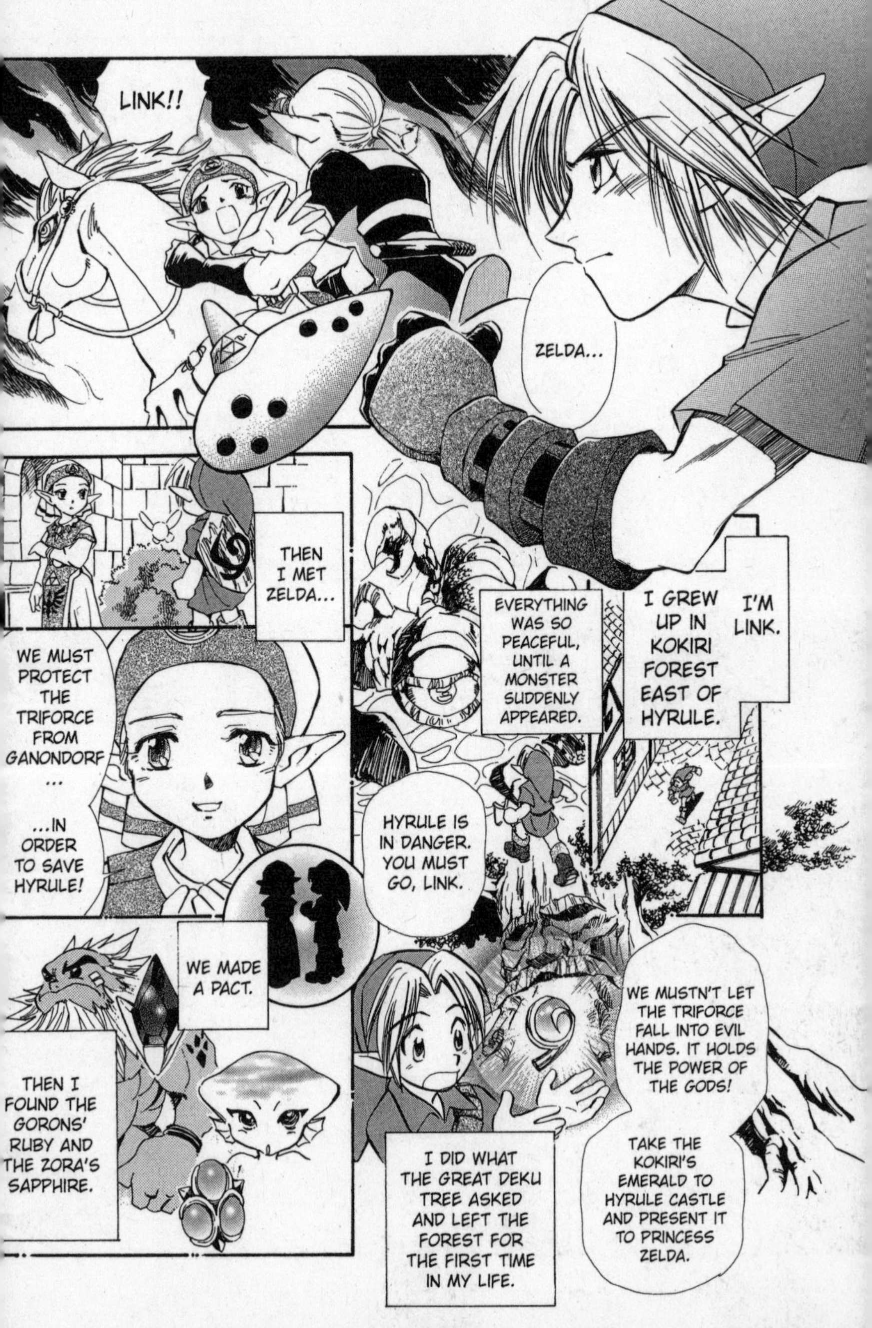
ZELDA...
LINK!!
I'M LINK.
I GREW UP IN KOKIRI FOREST EAST OF HYRULE.
EVERYTHING WAS SO PEACEFUL, UNTIL A MONSTER SUDDENLY APPEARED.
HYRULE IS IN DANGER. YOU MUST GO, LINK.
WE MUSTN'T LET THE TRIFORCE FALL INTO EVIL HANDS. IT HOLDS THE POWER OF THE GODS!
TAKE THE KOKIRI'S EMERALD TO HYRULE CASTLE AND PRESENT IT TO PRINCESS ZELDA.
I DID WHAT THE GREAT DEKU TREE ASKED AND LEFT THE FOREST FOR THE FIRST TIME IN MY LIFE.
THEN I MET ZELDA...
WE MUST PROTECT THE TRIFORCE FROM GANONDORF...
...IN ORDER TO SAVE HYRULE!
WE MADE A PACT.
THEN I FOUND THE GORONS' RUBY AND THE ZORA'S SAPPHIRE.

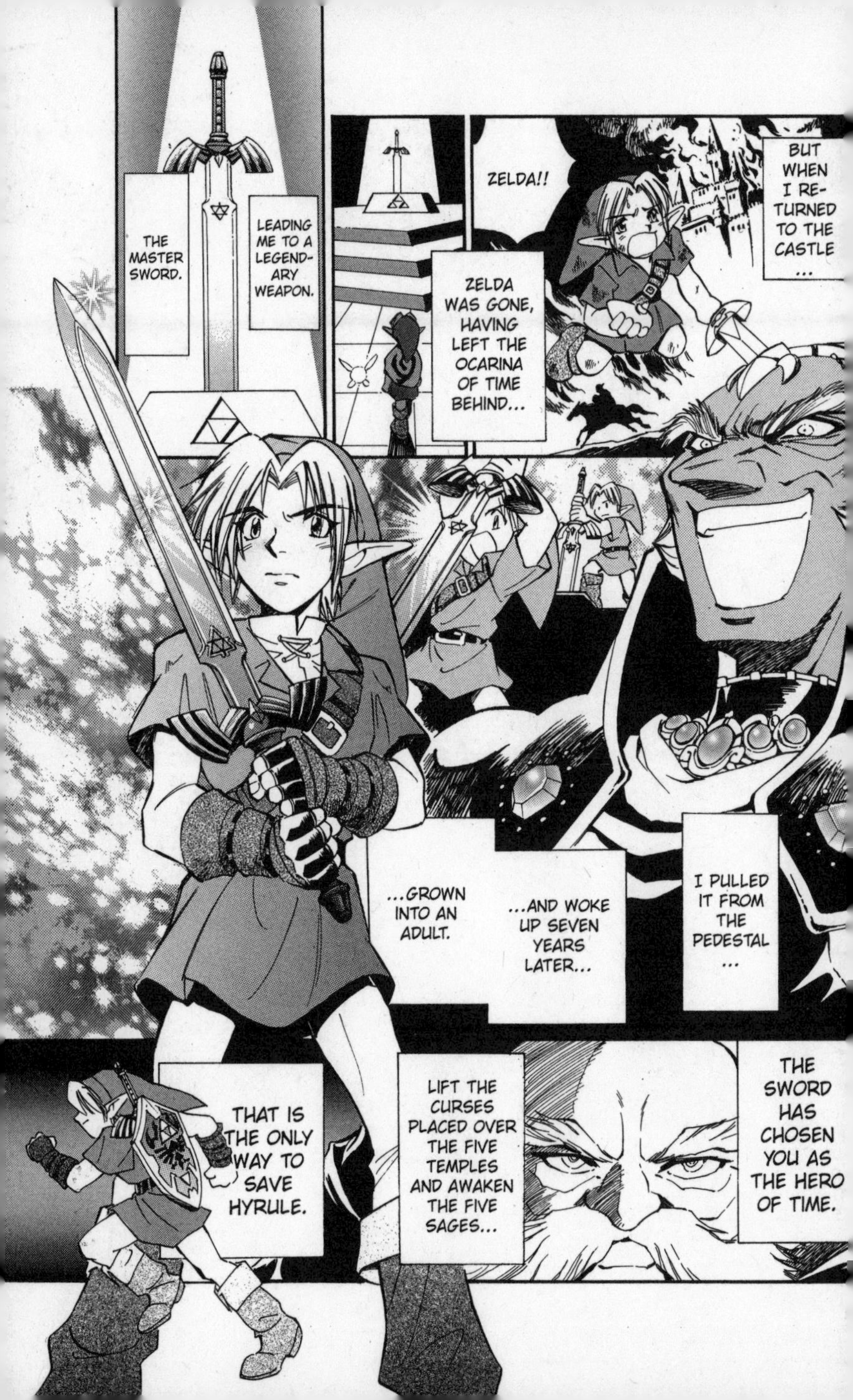

BUT WHEN I RE-TURNED TO THE CASTLE...
ZELDA!!
ZELDA WAS GONE, HAVING LEFT THE OCARINA OF TIME BEHIND...
LEADING ME TO A LEGEND-ARY WEAPON.
THE MASTER SWORD.
I PULLED IT FROM THE PEDESTAL...
...AND WOKE UP SEVEN YEARS LATER...
...GROWN INTO AN ADULT.
THE SWORD HAS CHOSEN YOU AS THE HERO OF TIME.
LIFT THE CURSES PLACED OVER THE FIVE TEMPLES AND AWAKEN THE FIVE SAGES...
THAT IS THE ONLY WAY TO SAVE HYRULE.

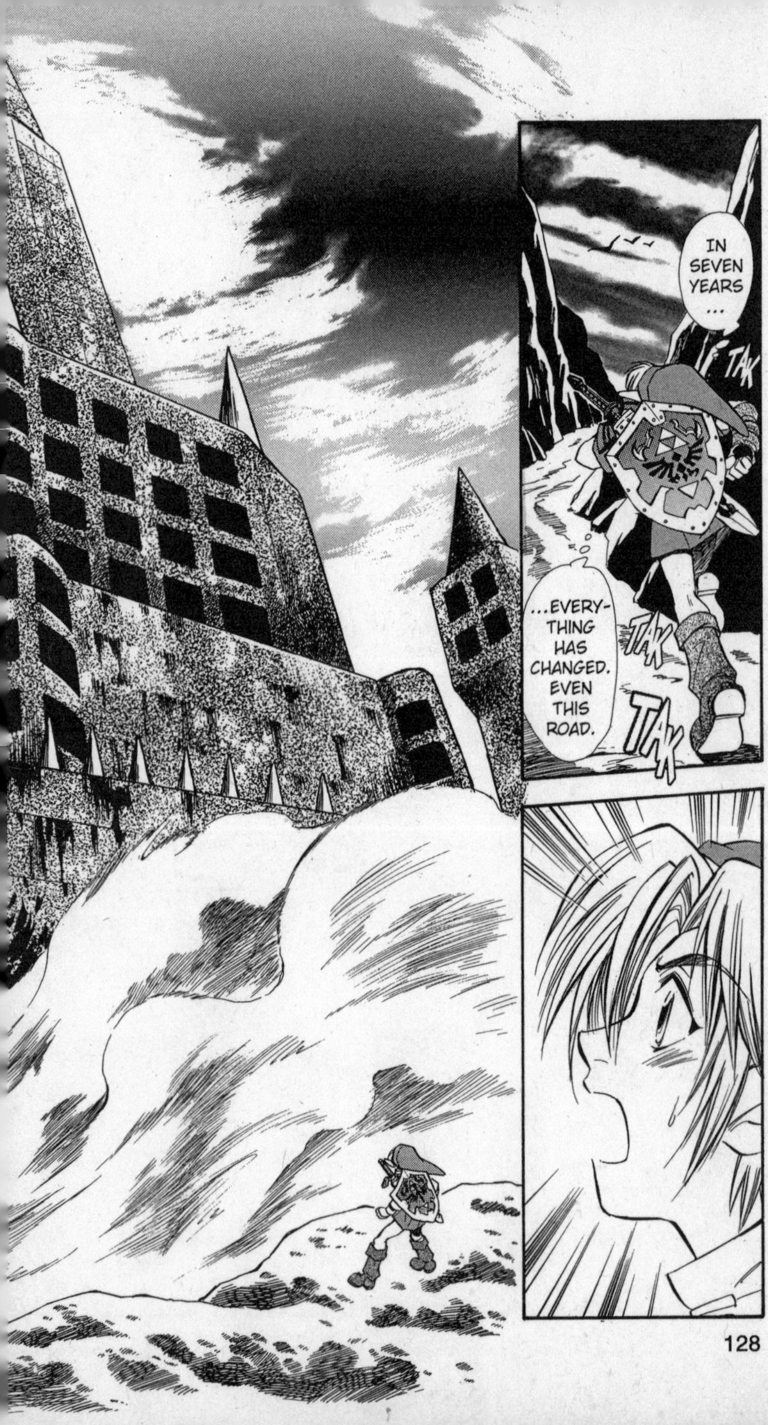
IN SEVEN YEARS ...
TAK
...EVERYTHING HAS CHANGED. EVEN THIS ROAD.
TAK
TAK

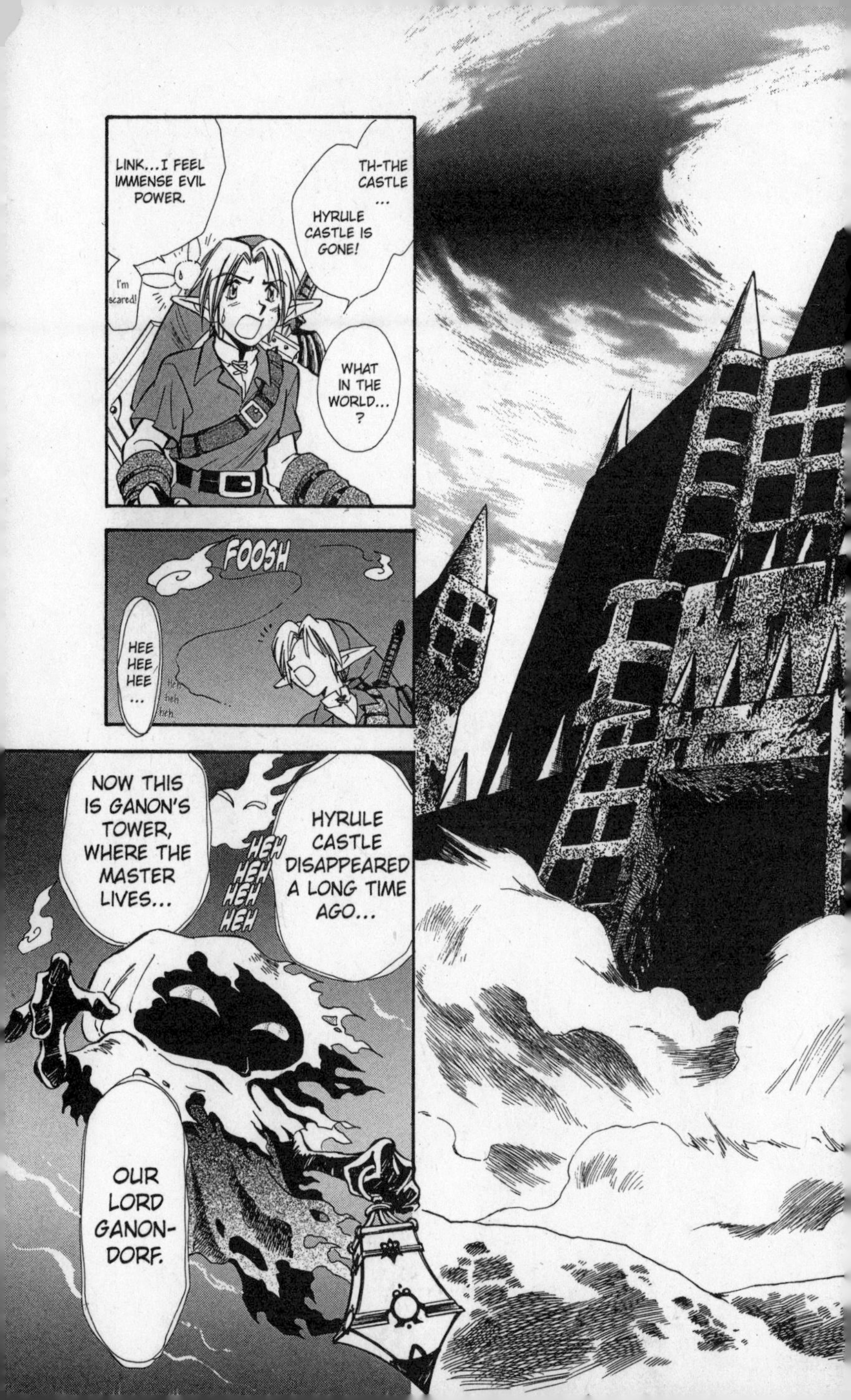

TH-THE CASTLE ... HYRULE CASTLE IS GONE!
LINK...I FEEL IMMENSE EVIL POWER.
I'm scared!
WHAT IN THE WORLD... ?
FOOSH
HEE HEE HEE ...
heh heh heh
HYRULE CASTLE DISAPPEARED A LONG TIME AGO...
NOW THIS IS GANON'S TOWER, WHERE THE MASTER LIVES...
HEH HEH HEH HEH
OUR LORD GANON-DORF.

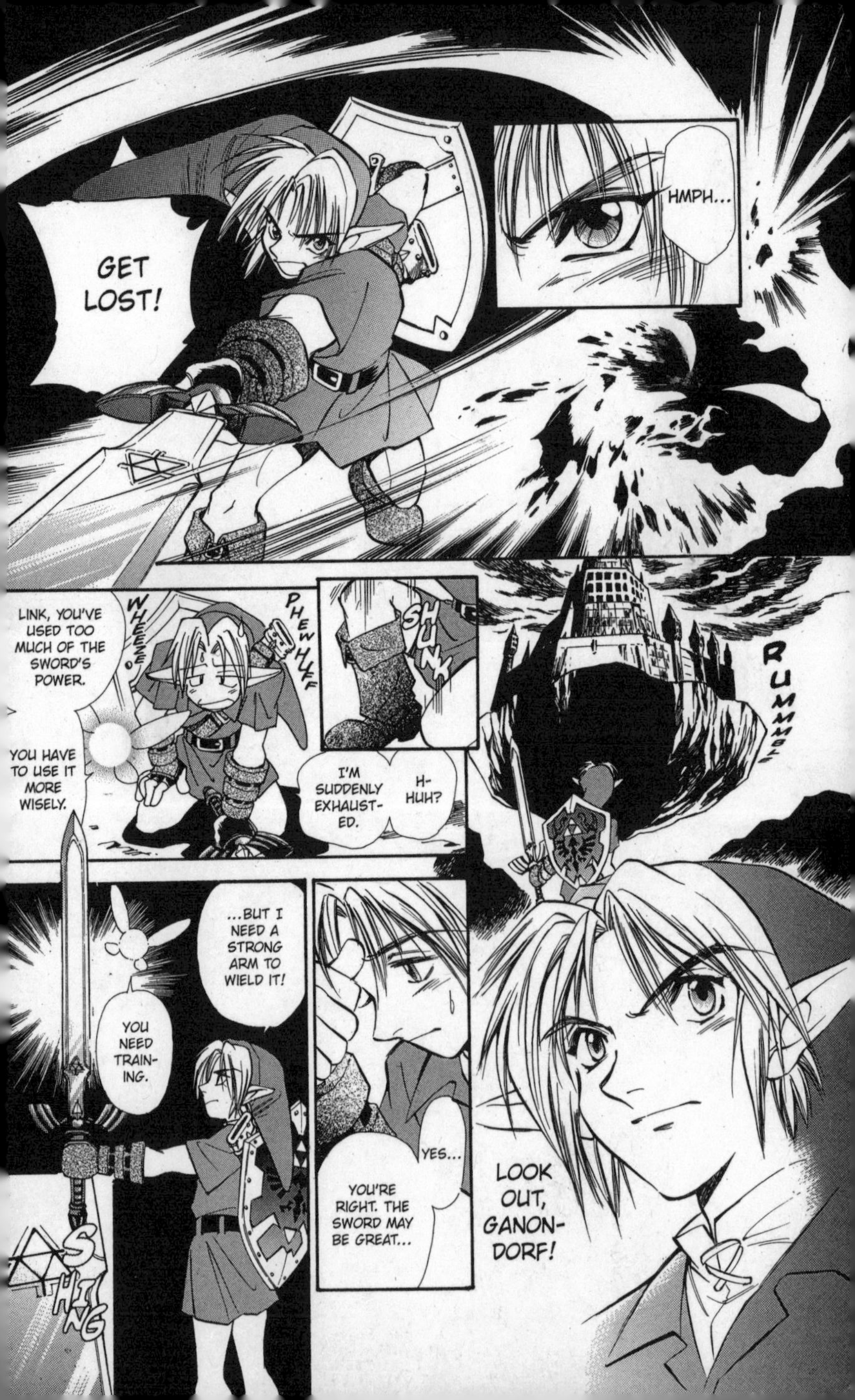
GET LOST!
HMPH...
SHUNK
H-HUH?
I'M SUDDENLY EXHAUSTED.
WHEEZE
PHEWHUFF
LINK, YOU'VE USED TOO MUCH OF THE SWORD'S POWER.
YOU HAVE TO USE IT MORE WISELY.
SHING
YOU NEED TRAINING.
YES...
YOU'RE RIGHT. THE SWORD MAY BE GREAT...
...BUT I NEED A STRONG ARM TO WIELD IT!
RUMMMBLE
LOOK OUT, GANONDORF!

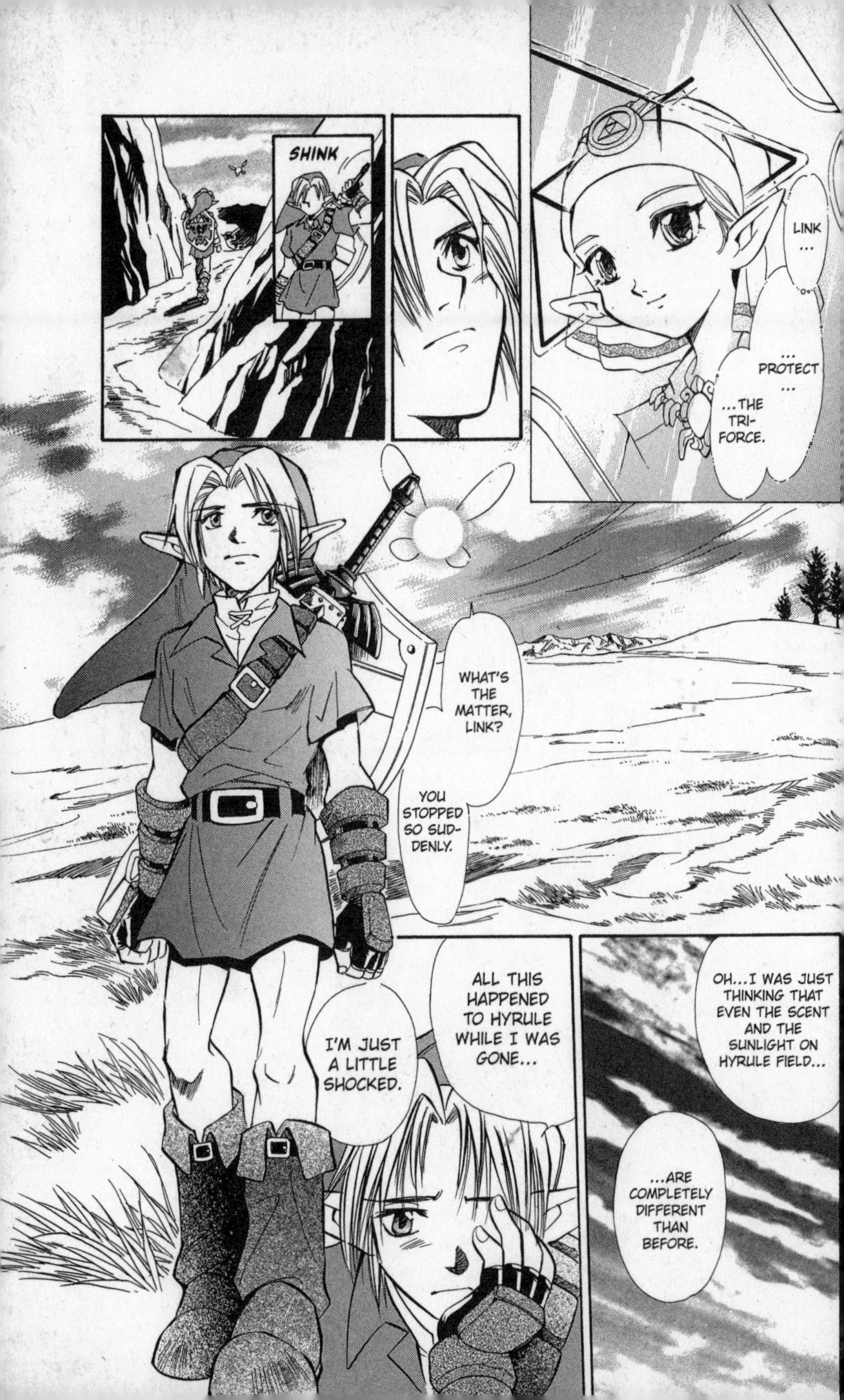
LINK ...
... PROTECT ...
...THE TRI-FORCE.
SHINK
WHAT'S THE MATTER, LINK?
YOU STOPPED SO SUD-DENLY.
OH...I WAS JUST THINKING THAT EVEN THE SCENT AND THE SUNLIGHT ON HYRULE FIELD...
...ARE COMPLETELY DIFFERENT THAN BEFORE.
ALL THIS HAPPENED TO HYRULE WHILE I WAS GONE...
I'M JUST A LITTLE SHOCKED.

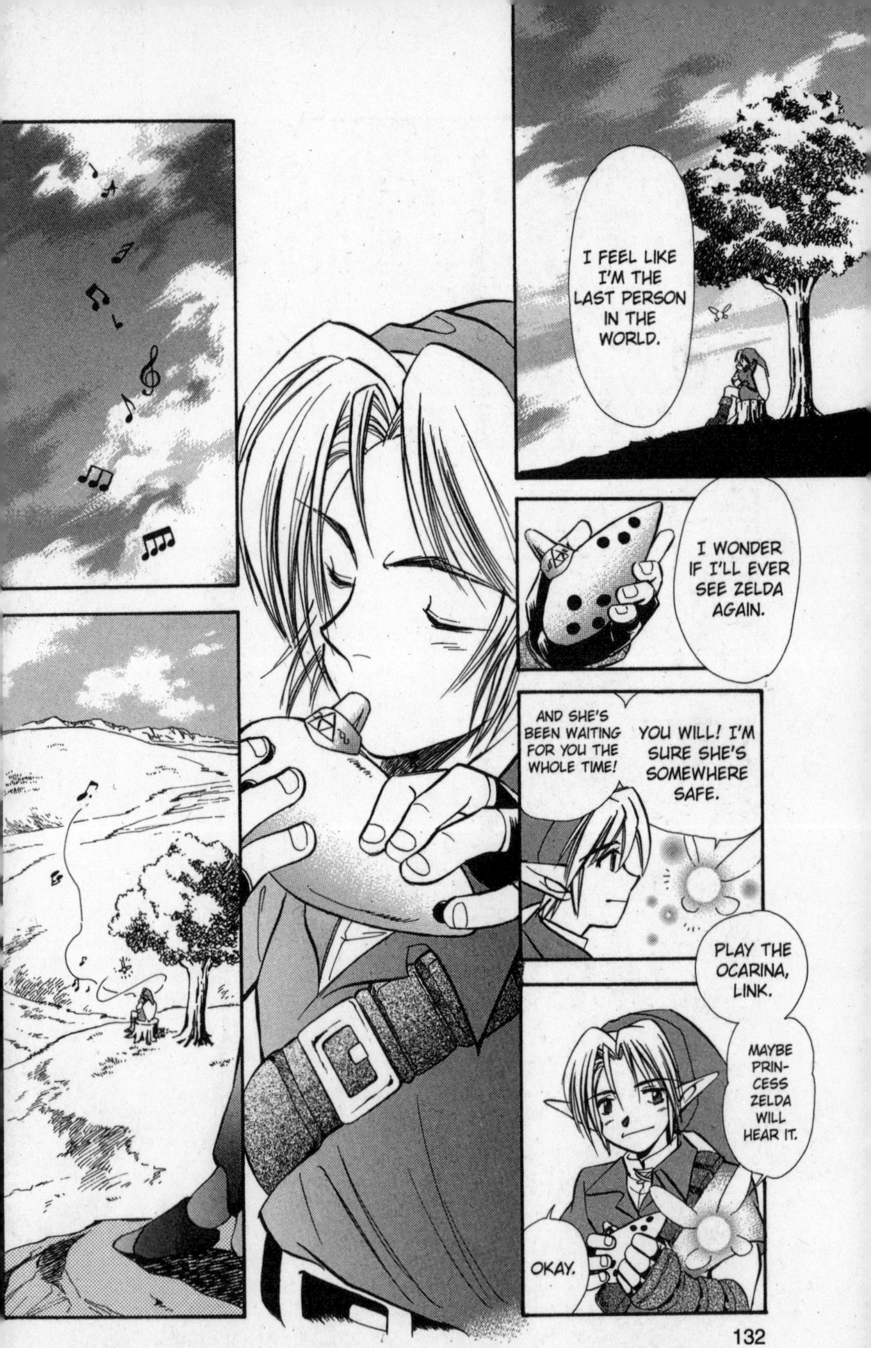
I FEEL LIKE I'M THE LAST PERSON IN THE WORLD.
I WONDER IF I'LL EVER SEE ZELDA AGAIN.
YOU WILL! I'M SURE SHE'S SOMEWHERE SAFE.
AND SHE'S BEEN WAITING FOR YOU THE WHOLE TIME!
PLAY THE OCARINA, LINK.
MAYBE PRINCESS ZELDA WILL HEAR IT.
OKAY.

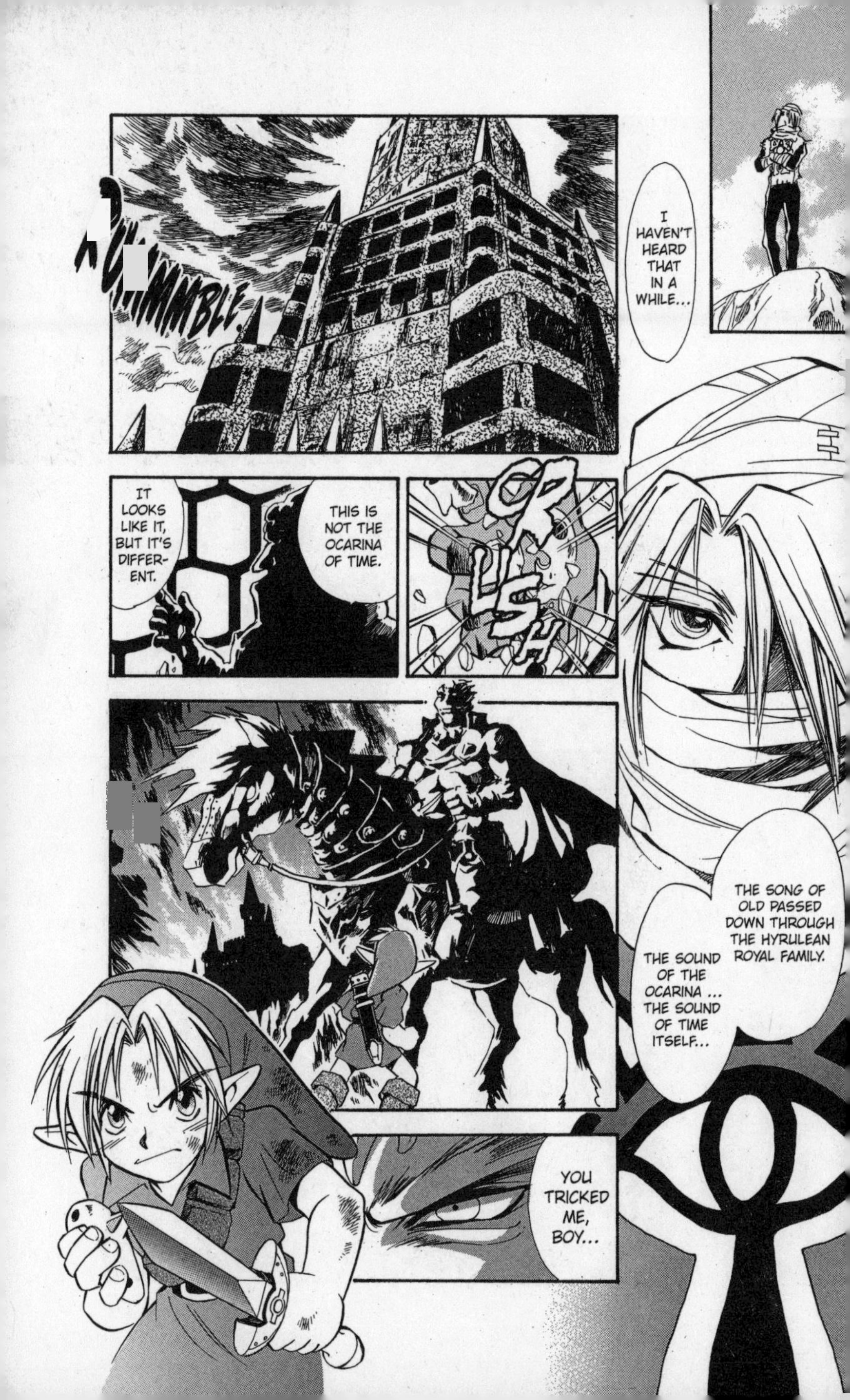
I HAVEN'T HEARD THAT IN A WHILE...
RUMMMMBLE
CRUSH
THIS IS NOT THE OCARINA OF TIME.
IT LOOKS LIKE IT, BUT IT'S DIFFER-ENT.
THE SONG OF OLD PASSED DOWN THROUGH THE HYRULEAN ROYAL FAMILY.
THE SOUND OF THE OCARINA ... THE SOUND OF TIME ITSELF...
YOU TRICKED ME, BOY...

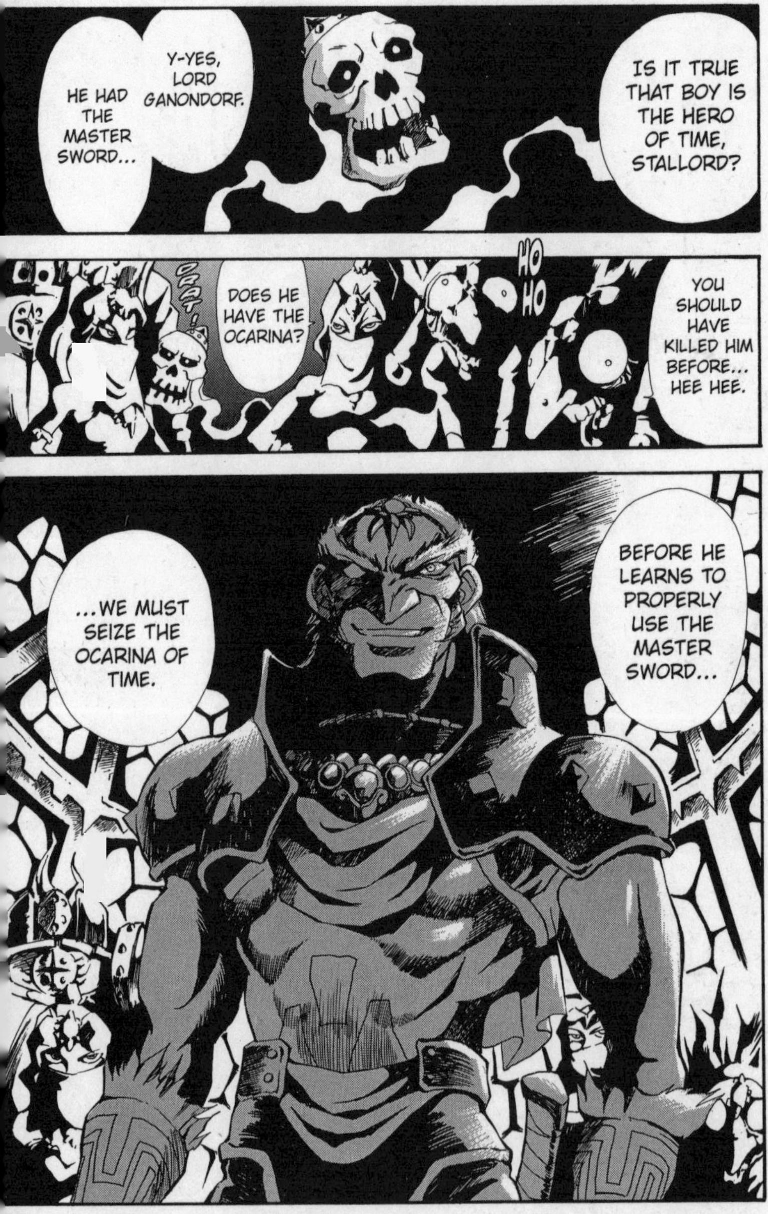

IS IT TRUE THAT BOY IS THE HERO OF TIME, STALLORD?
Y-YES, LORD GANONDORF.
HE HAD THE MASTER SWORD...
YOU SHOULD HAVE KILLED HIM BEFORE... HEE HEE.
HO HO
DOES HE HAVE THE OCARINA?
BEFORE HE LEARNS TO PROPERLY USE THE MASTER SWORD...
...WE MUST SEIZE THE OCARINA OF TIME.

CHAPTER 2 THE SAGE OF THE FOREST: SARIA

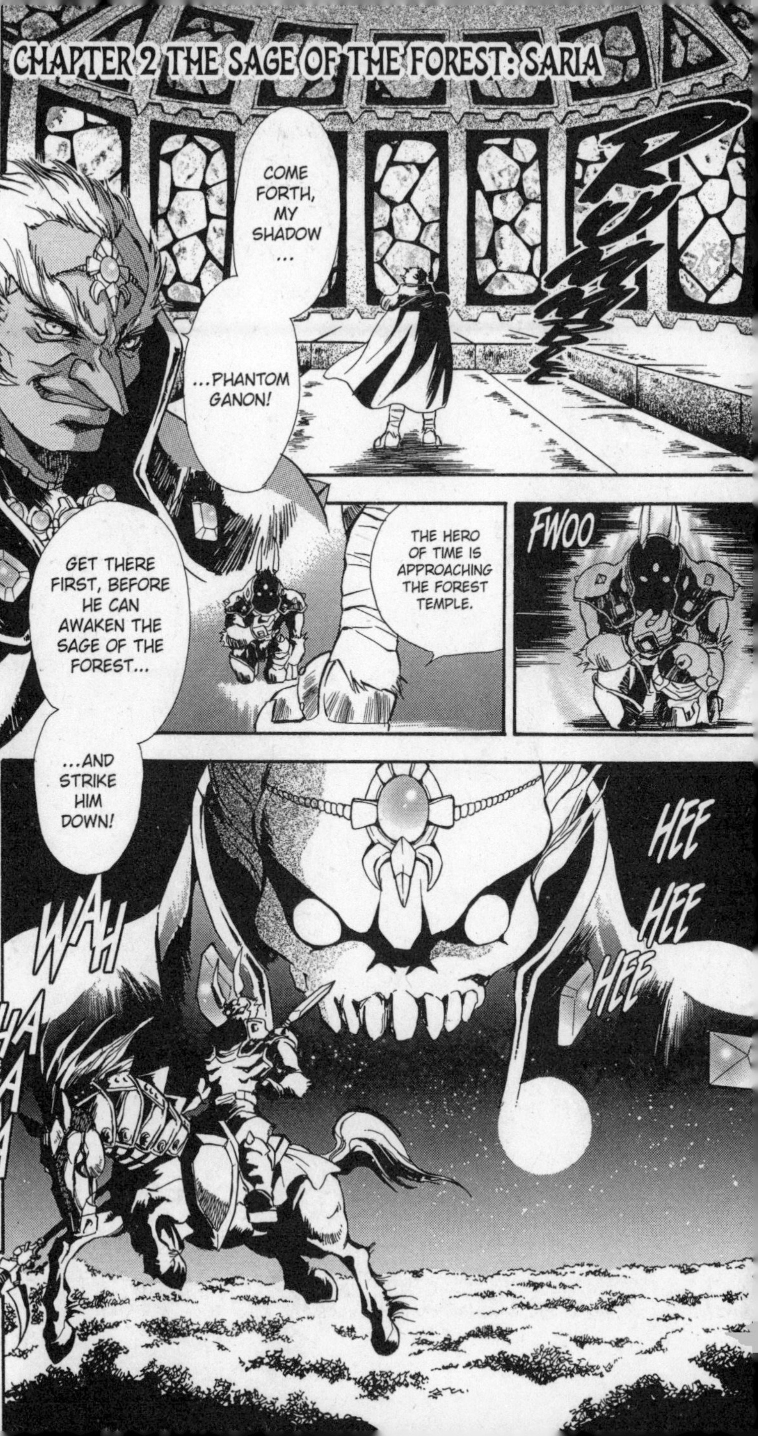
COME FORTH, MY SHADOW...
...PHANTOM GANON!
FWOO
THE HERO OF TIME IS APPROACHING THE FOREST TEMPLE.
GET THERE FIRST, BEFORE HE CAN AWAKEN THE SAGE OF THE FOREST...
...AND STRIKE HIM DOWN!
HEE HEE HEE
WAH HA HA HA HA

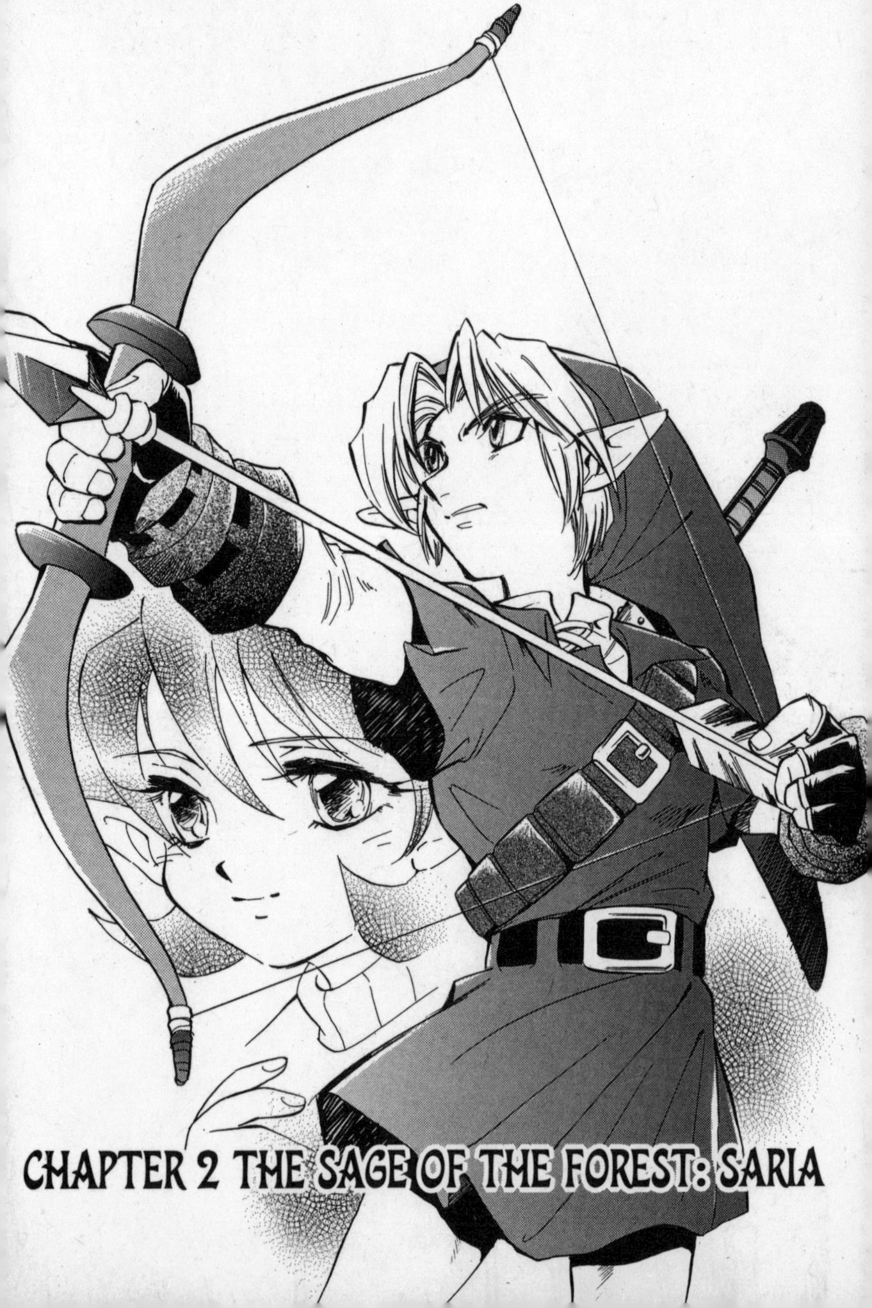

CHAPTER 2 THE SAGE OF THE FOREST: SARIA

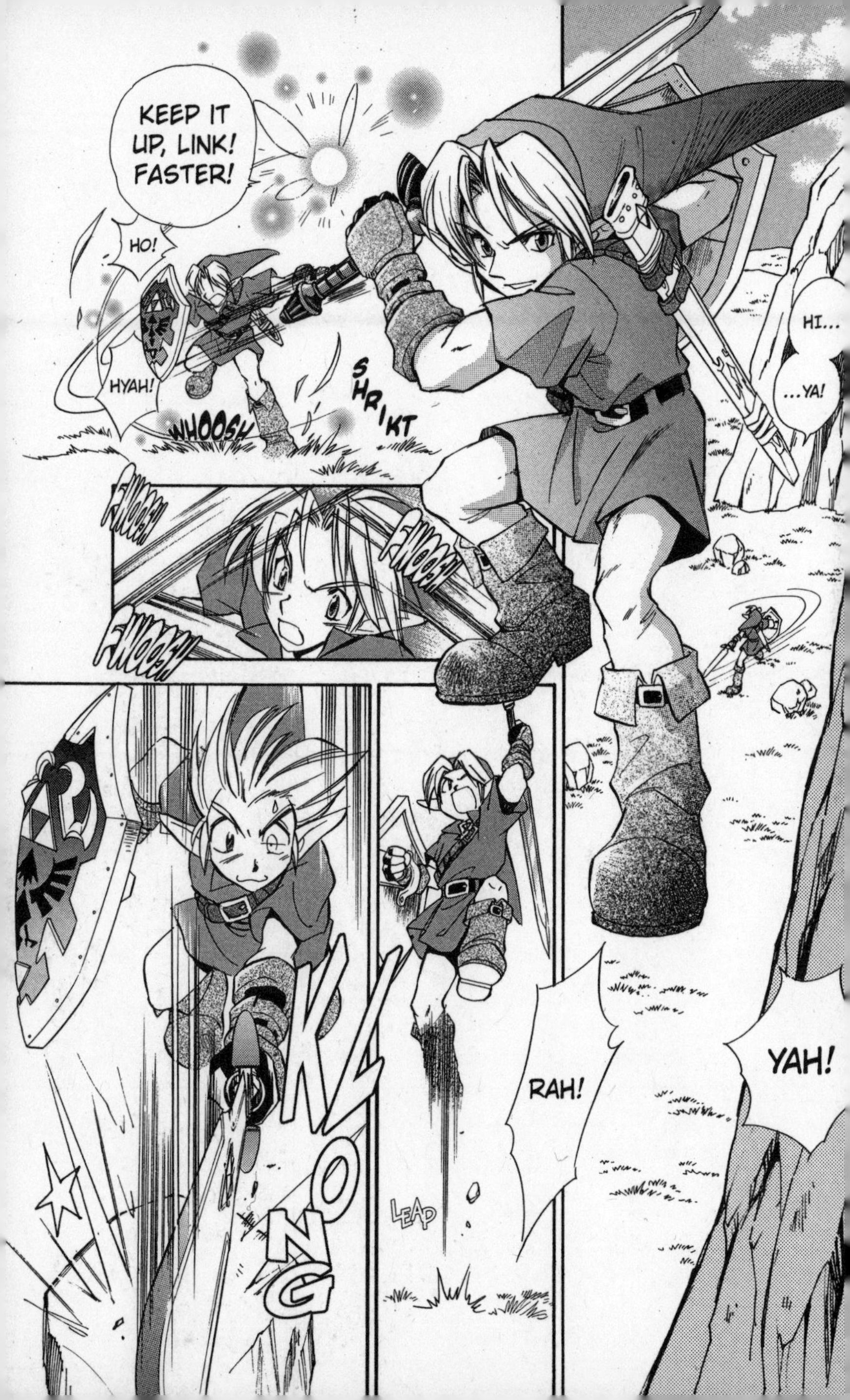
HI...
...YA!
YAH!
RAH!
KEEP IT UP, LINK! FASTER!
HO!
HYAH!
WHOOSH
SHRIKT
FWOOSH
FWOOSH
FWOOSH
LEAP
KLONG

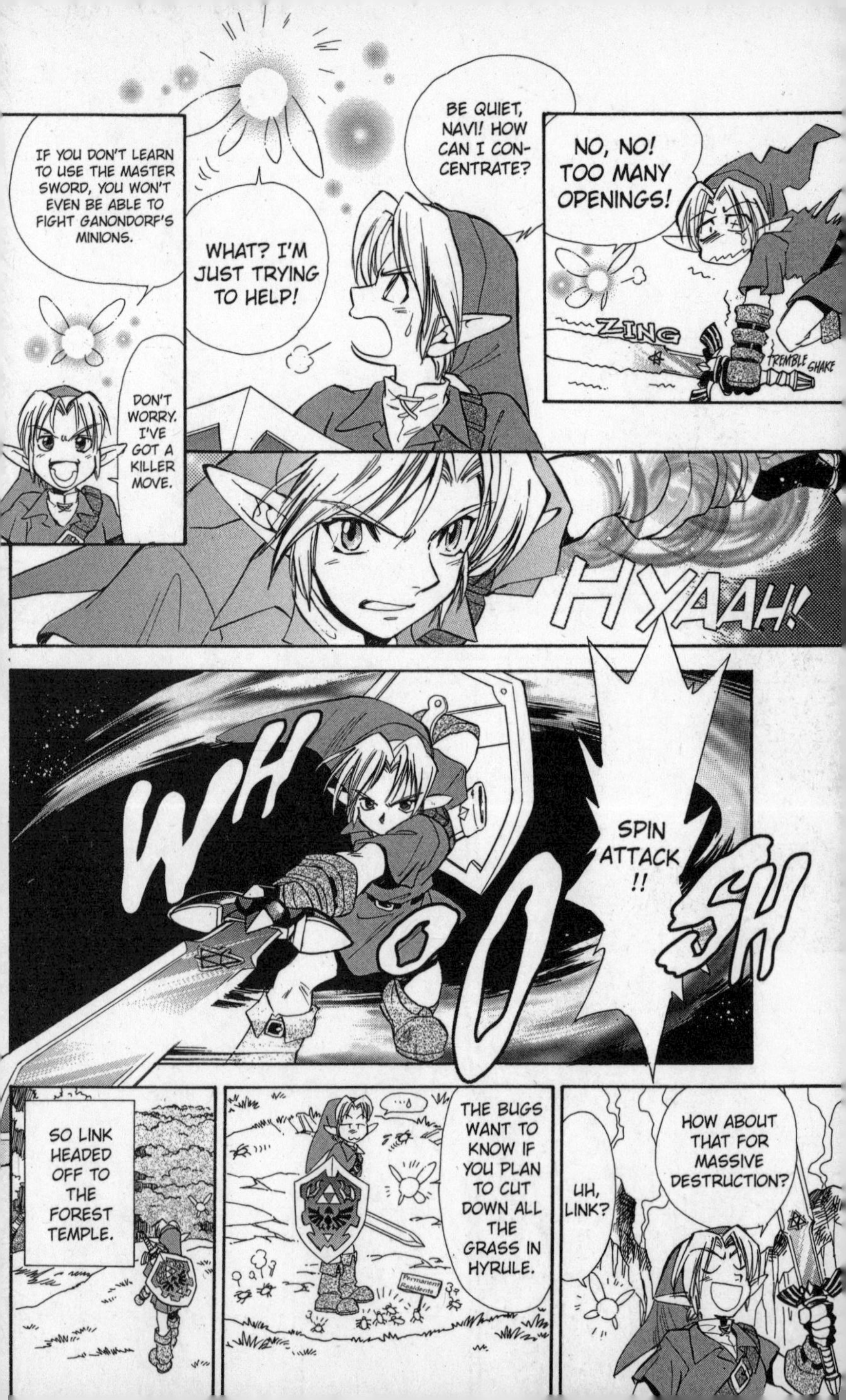
NO, NO! TOO MANY OPENINGS!
ZING
TREMBLE
SHAKE
BE QUIET, NAVI! HOW CAN I CONCENTRATE?
WHAT? I'M JUST TRYING TO HELP!
IF YOU DON'T LEARN TO USE THE MASTER SWORD, YOU WON'T EVEN BE ABLE TO FIGHT GANONDORF'S MINIONS.
DON'T WORRY. I'VE GOT A KILLER MOVE.
HYAAH!
SPIN ATTACK!!
WHOOSH
HOW ABOUT THAT FOR MASSIVE DESTRUCTION?
UH, LINK?
THE BUGS WANT TO KNOW IF YOU PLAN TO CUT DOWN ALL THE GRASS IN HYRULE.
SO LINK HEADED OFF TO THE FOREST TEMPLE.

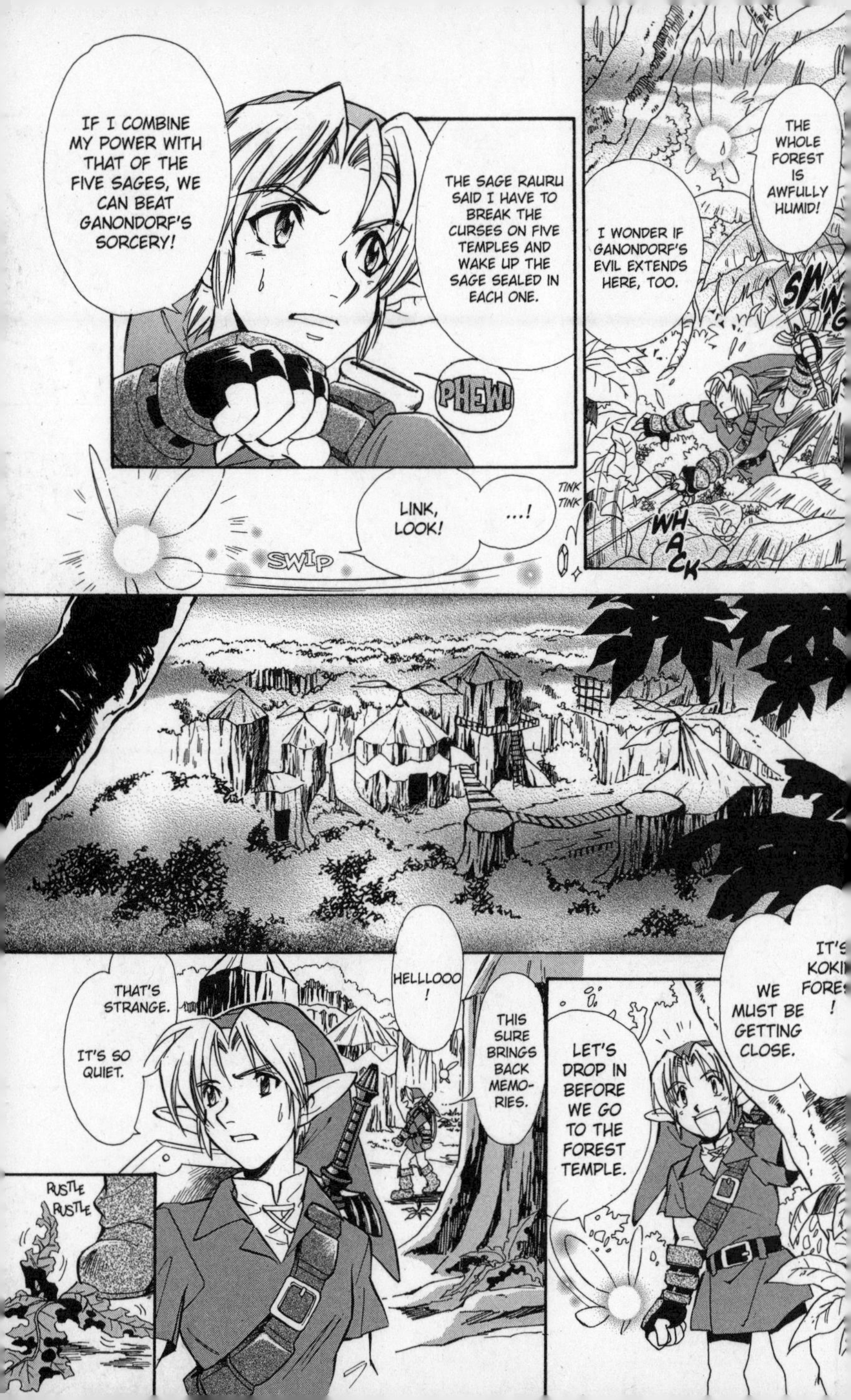
THE WHOLE FOREST IS AWFULLY HUMID!
I WONDER IF GANONDORF'S EVIL EXTENDS HERE, TOO.
SWING
TINK TINK
WHACK
THE SAGE RAURU SAID I HAVE TO BREAK THE CURSES ON FIVE TEMPLES AND WAKE UP THE SAGE SEALED IN EACH ONE.
PHEW!
IF I COMBINE MY POWER WITH THAT OF THE FIVE SAGES, WE CAN BEAT GANONDORF'S SORCERY!
...!
LINK, LOOK!
SWIP
IT'S KOKI FORES !
WE MUST BE GETTING CLOSE.
LET'S DROP IN BEFORE WE GO TO THE FOREST TEMPLE.
THIS SURE BRINGS BACK MEMORIES.
HELLLOOO!
THAT'S STRANGE.
IT'S SO QUIET.
RUSTLE RUSTLE

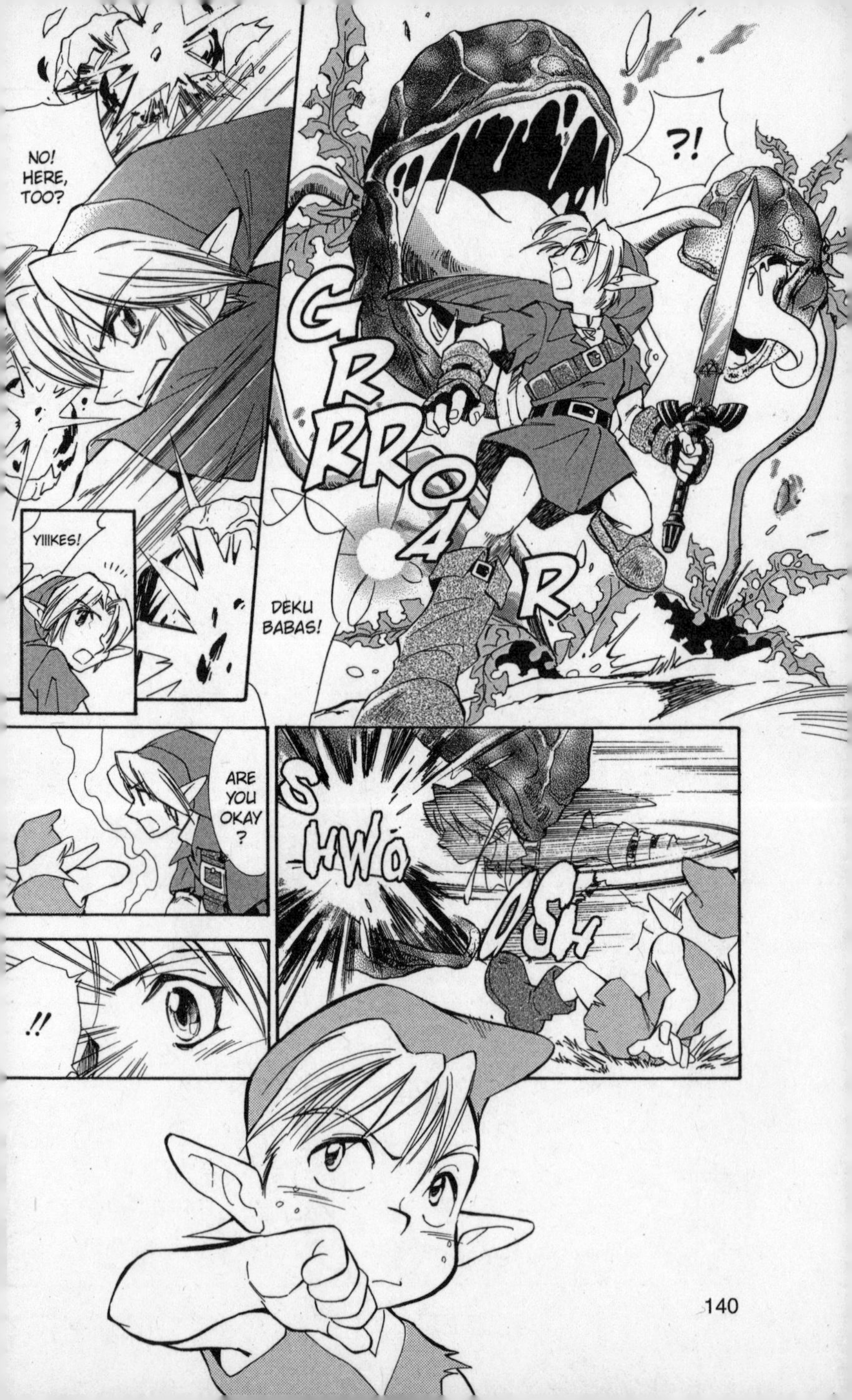
?!
G R BRO O A R
DEKU BABAS!
NO! HERE, TOO?
YIIIKES!
SHWOOSH
ARE YOU OKAY ?
!!

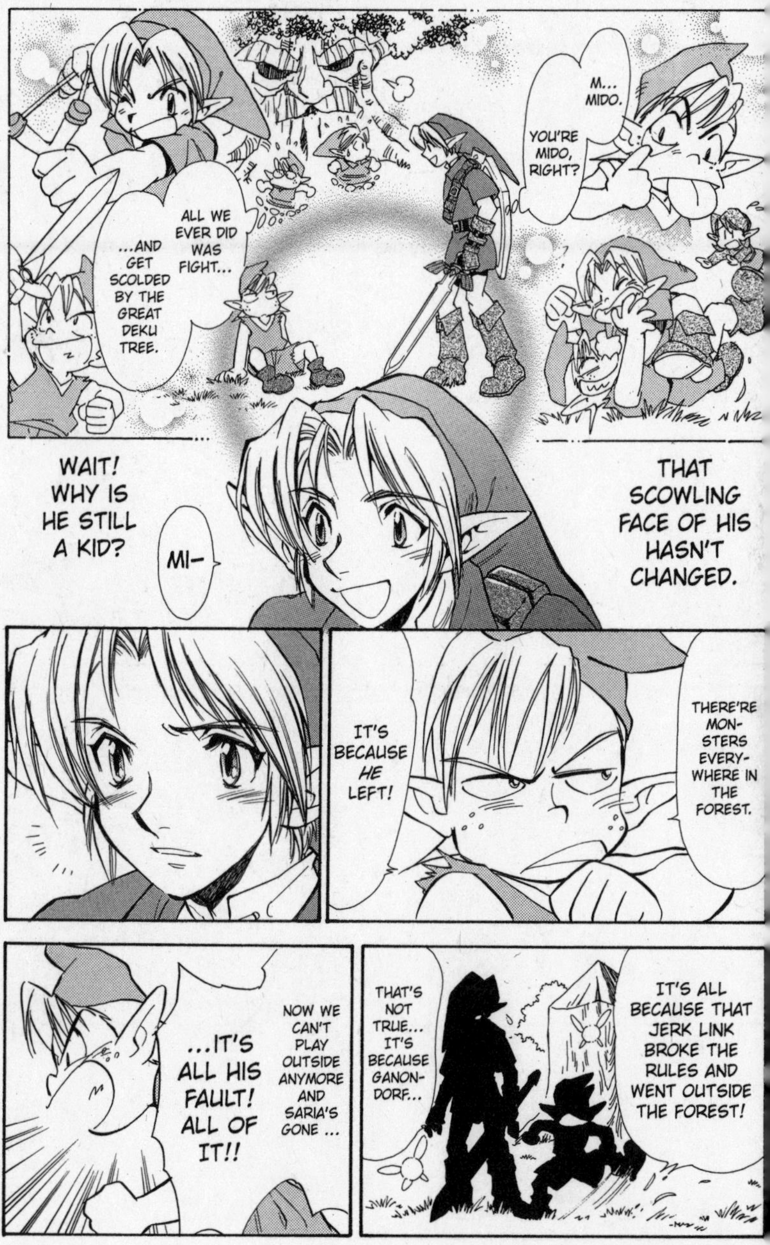
M... MIDO.
YOU'RE MIDO, RIGHT?
ALL WE EVER DID WAS FIGHT...
...AND GET SCOLDED BY THE GREAT DEKU TREE.
THAT SCOWLING FACE OF HIS HASN'T CHANGED.
MI—
WAIT! WHY IS HE STILL A KID?
THERE'RE MONSTERS EVERYWHERE IN THE FOREST.
IT'S BECAUSE *HE* LEFT!
IT'S ALL BECAUSE THAT JERK LINK BROKE THE RULES AND WENT OUTSIDE THE FOREST!
THAT'S NOT TRUE... IT'S BECAUSE GANONDORF...
NOW WE CAN'T PLAY OUTSIDE ANYMORE AND SARIA'S GONE ...
...IT'S ALL HIS FAULT! ALL OF IT!!

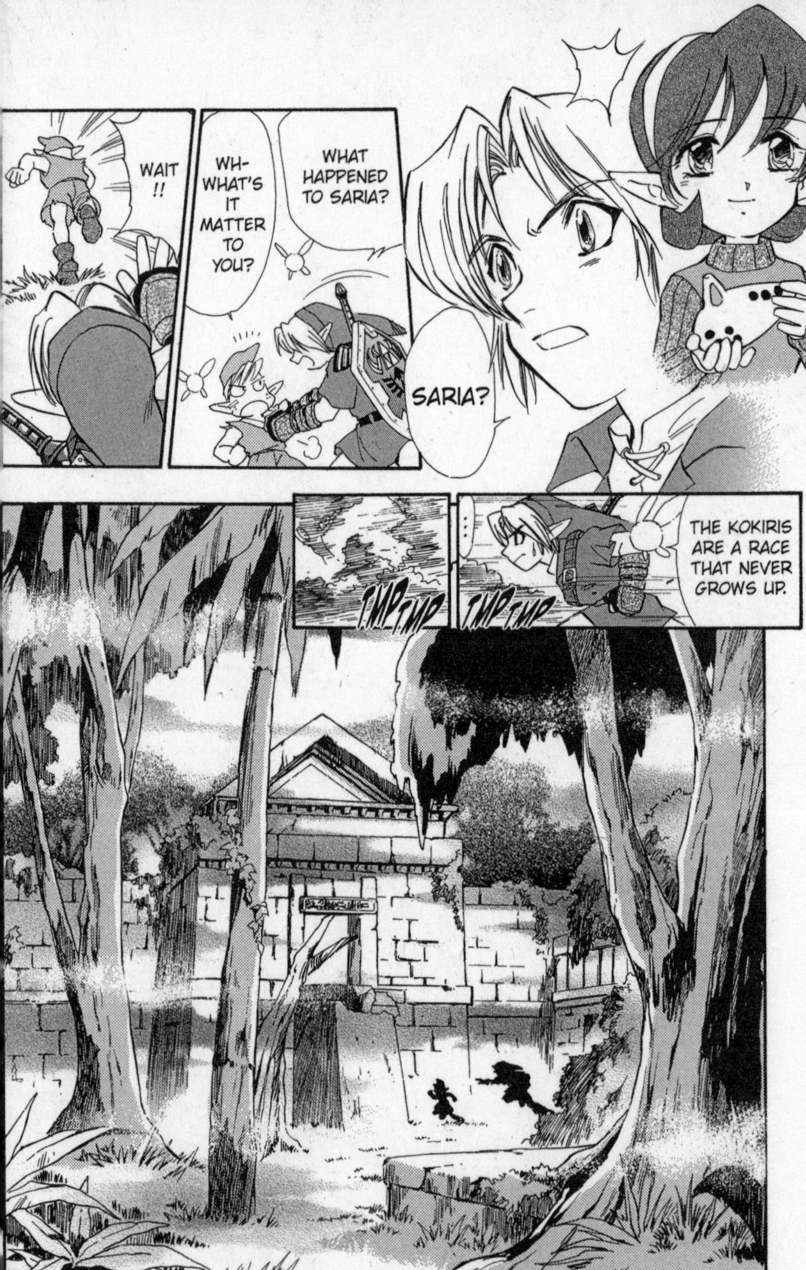
SARIA?
WHAT HAPPENED TO SARIA?
WH- WHAT'S IT MATTER TO YOU?
WAIT !!
THE KOKIRIS ARE A RACE THAT NEVER GROWS UP.
TMP TMP
TMP TMP

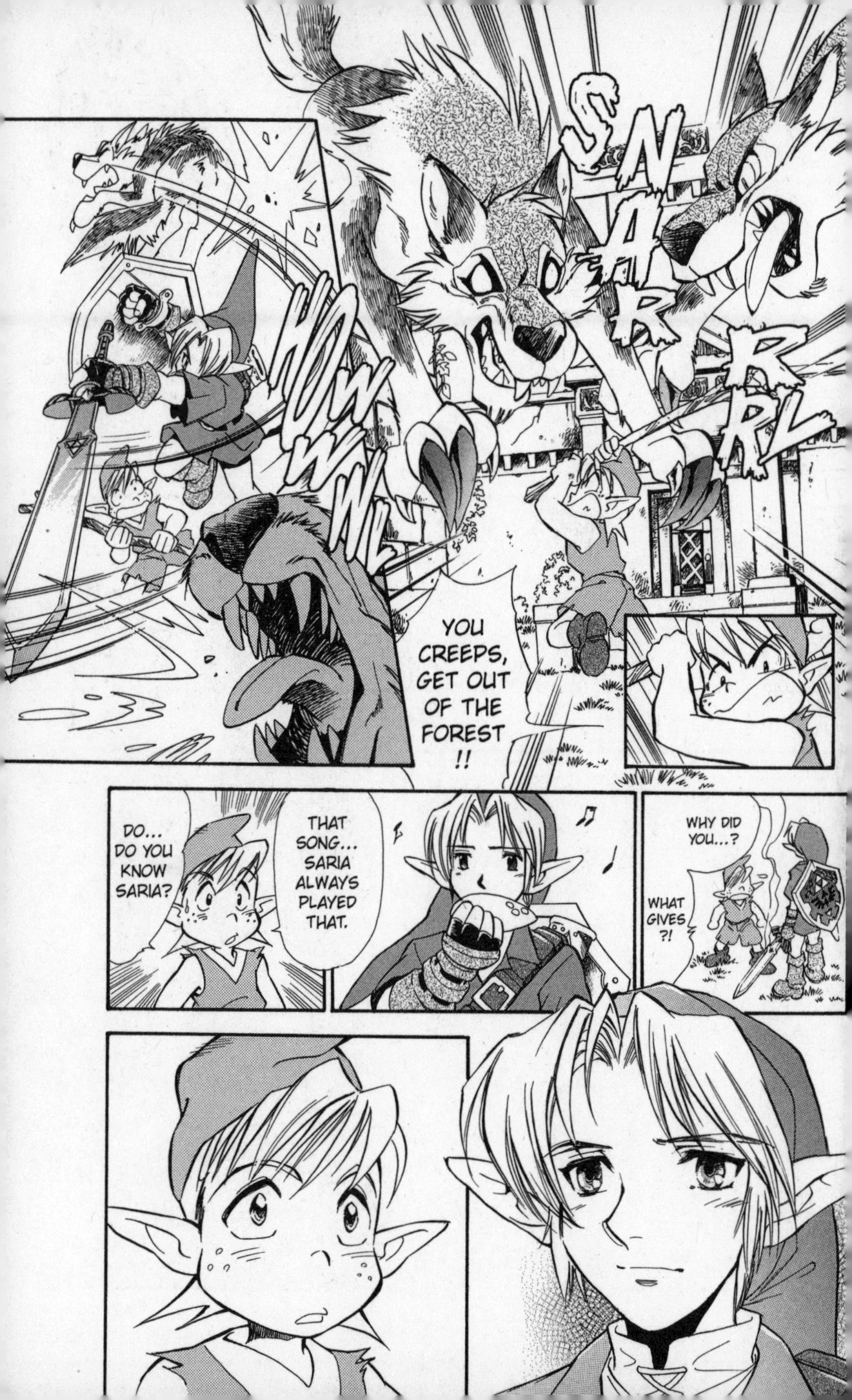

SNARRRL
HOWWWL
YOU CREEPS, GET OUT OF THE FOREST!!
WHY DID YOU...?
WHAT GIVES?!
THAT SONG... SARIA ALWAYS PLAYED THAT.
DO... DO YOU KNOW SARIA?

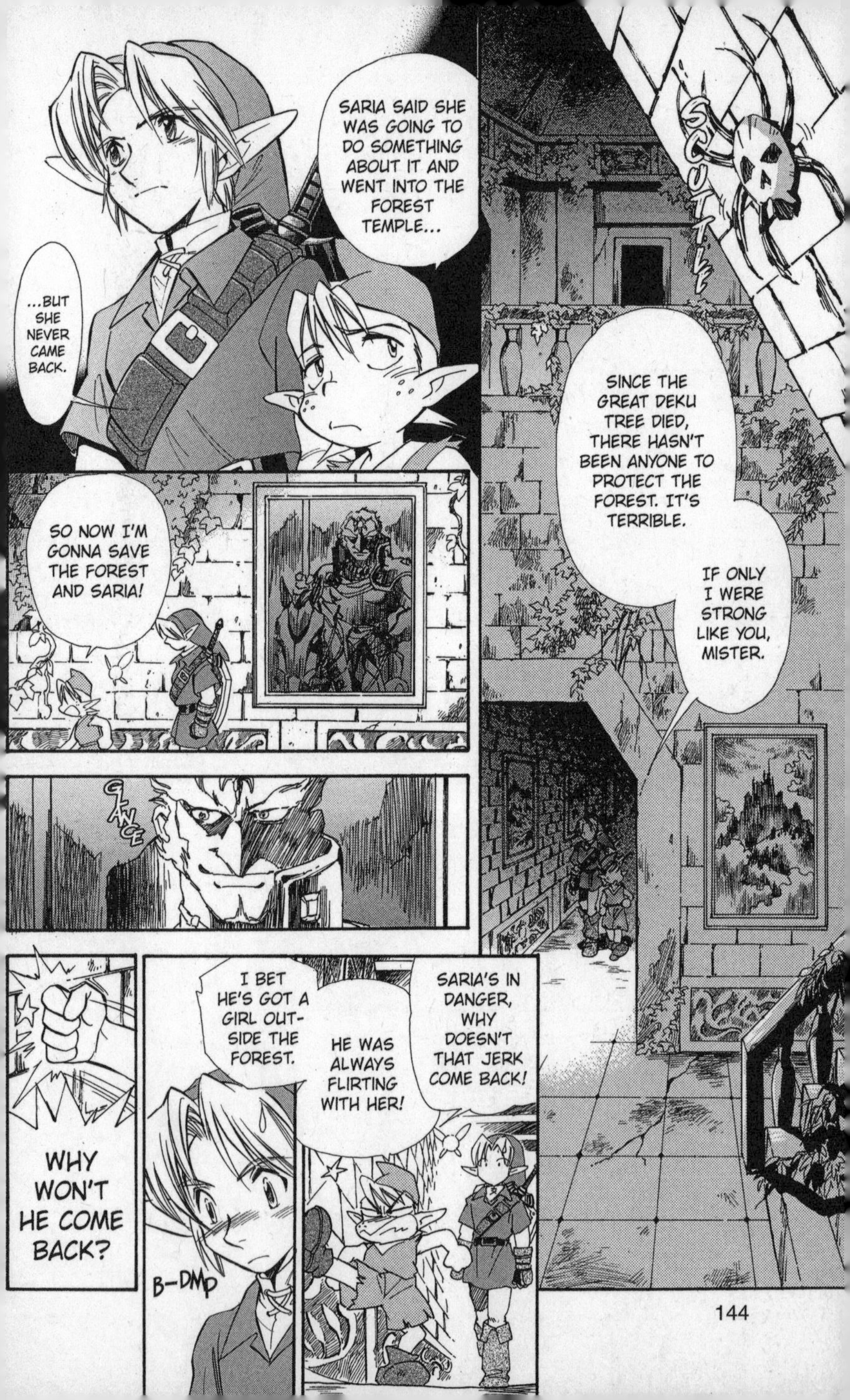
SCUTTLE
SINCE THE GREAT DEKU TREE DIED, THERE HASN'T BEEN ANYONE TO PROTECT THE FOREST. IT'S TERRIBLE.
IF ONLY I WERE STRONG LIKE YOU, MISTER.
SARIA SAID SHE WAS GOING TO DO SOMETHING ABOUT IT AND WENT INTO THE FOREST TEMPLE...
...BUT SHE NEVER CAME BACK.
SO NOW I'M GONNA SAVE THE FOREST AND SARIA!
GLANCE
SARIA'S IN DANGER, WHY DOESN'T THAT JERK COME BACK!
HE WAS ALWAYS FLIRTING WITH HER!
I BET HE'S GOT A GIRL OUT-SIDE THE FOREST.
B-DMP
WHY WON'T HE COME BACK?

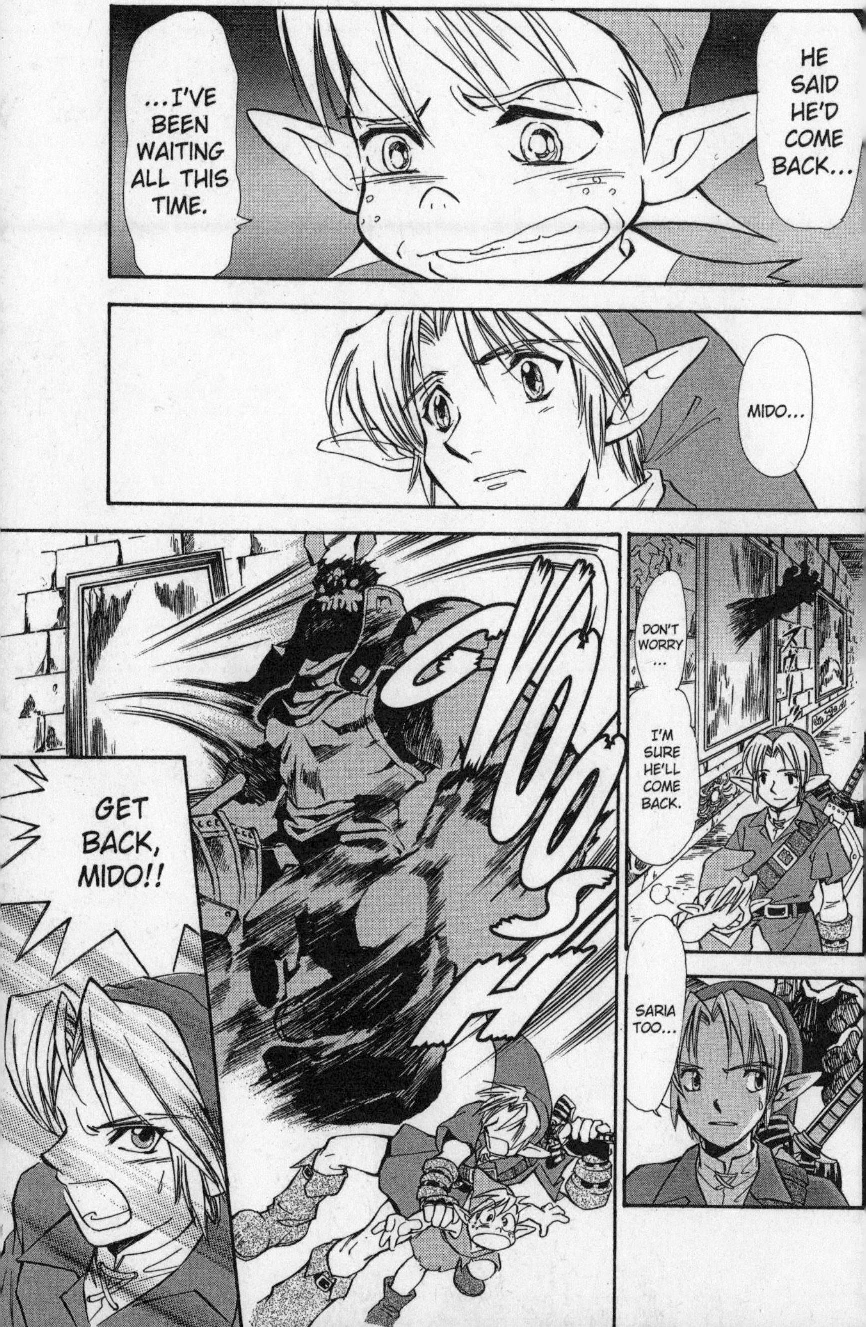
HE SAID HE'D COME BACK...
...I'VE BEEN WAITING ALL THIS TIME.
MIDO...
DON'T WORRY...
I'M SURE HE'LL COME BACK.
SARIA TOO...
GET BACK, MIDO!!

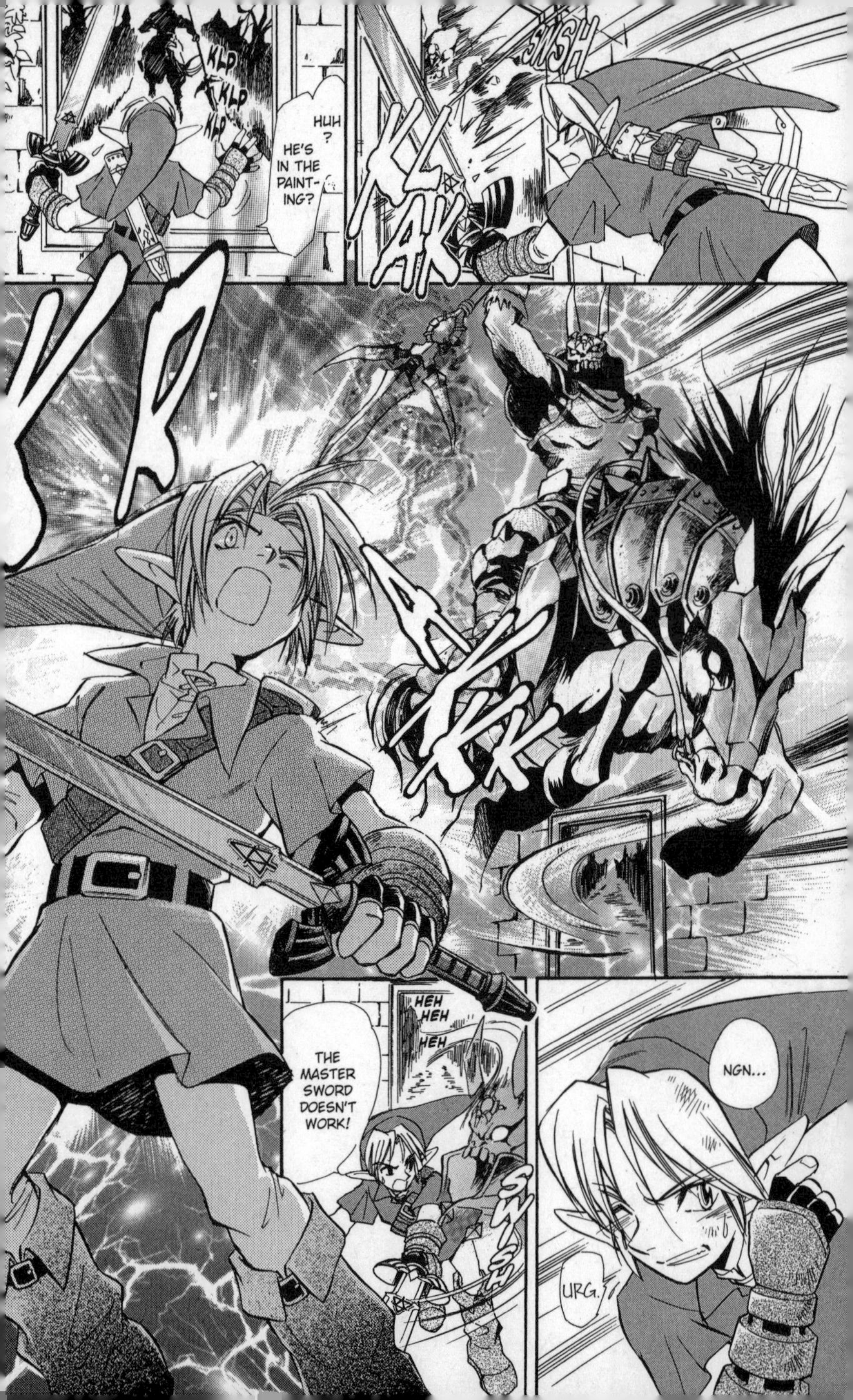
SWSH
KLAK
KLP KLP KLP
HUH?
HE'S IN THE PAINTING?
NGN...
URG.
HEH HEH HEH
THE MASTER SWORD DOESN'T WORK!
SWISH

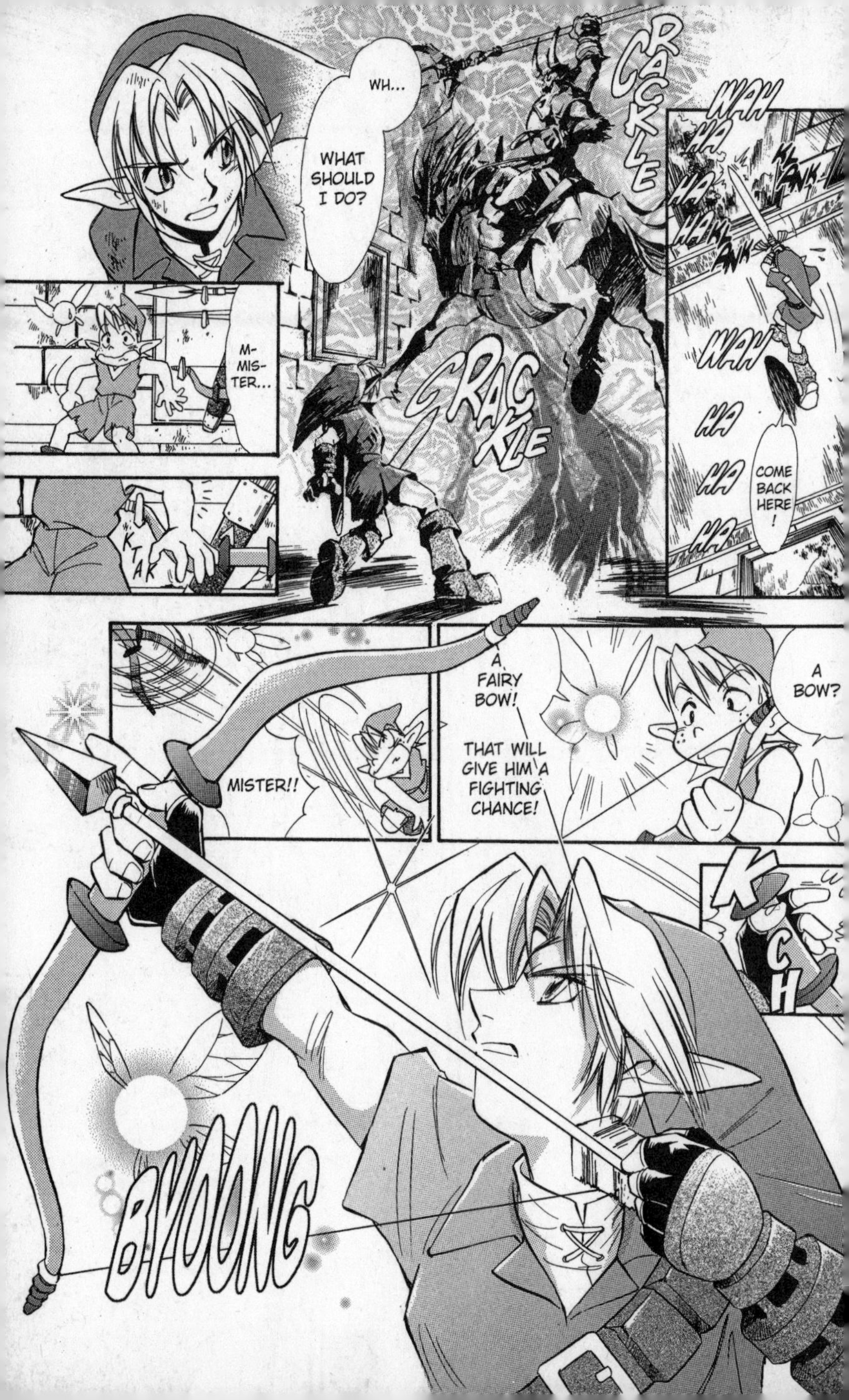
WAH HA HA HAH
KLANK
WAH HA HA HA
COME BACK HERE!
CRACKLE
WH...
WHAT SHOULD I DO?
CRACKLE
M-MISTER...
KTAK
A BOW?
A FAIRY BOW!
THAT WILL GIVE HIM A FIGHTING CHANCE!
MISTER!!
KCH
BYOONG

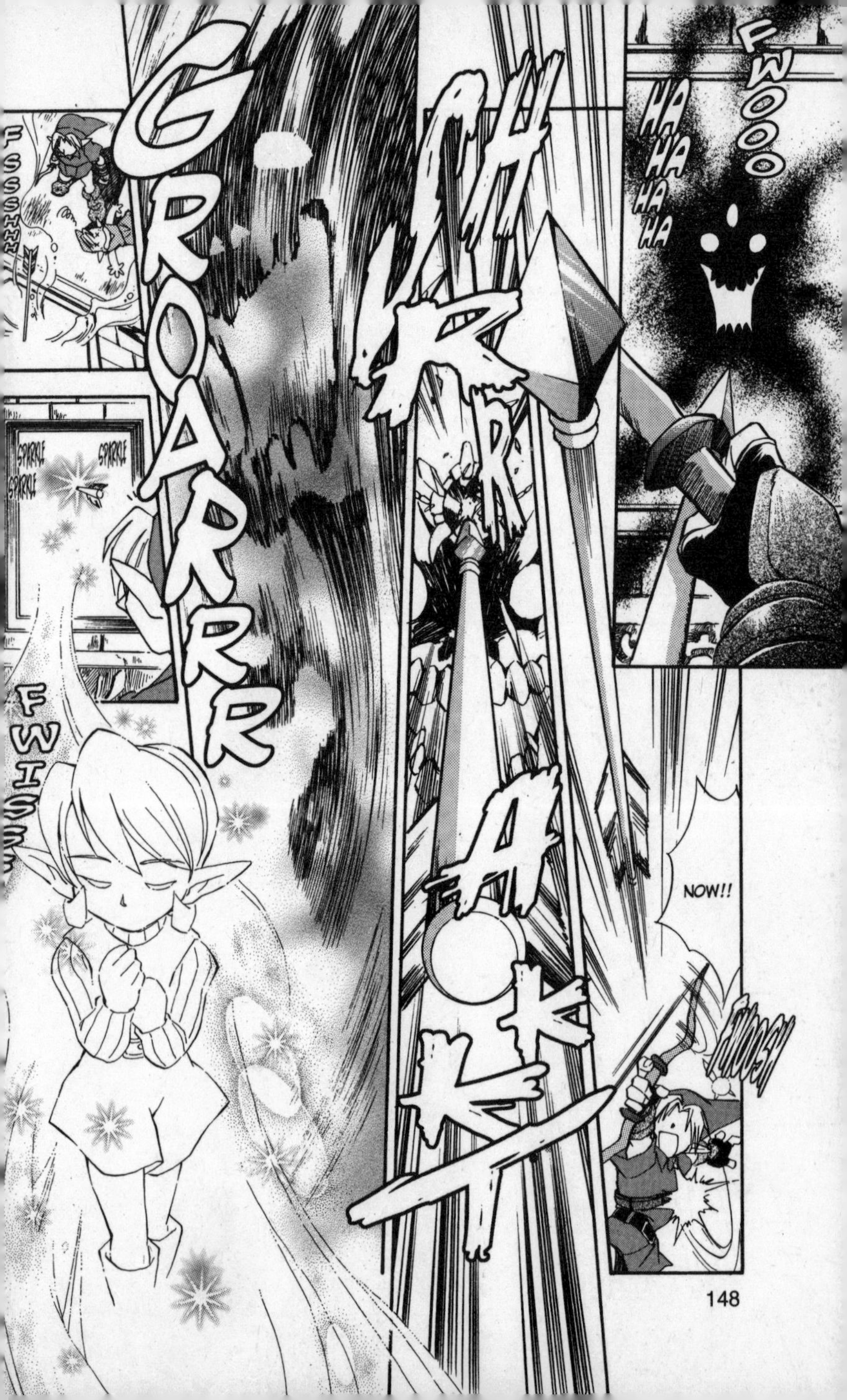
FWOOOO
HA HA HA HA
CHKRAKKK
NOW!!
FWOOSH
GROARRR
FSSSHHH
SPARKLE
SPARKLE
SPARKLE
FWISSS

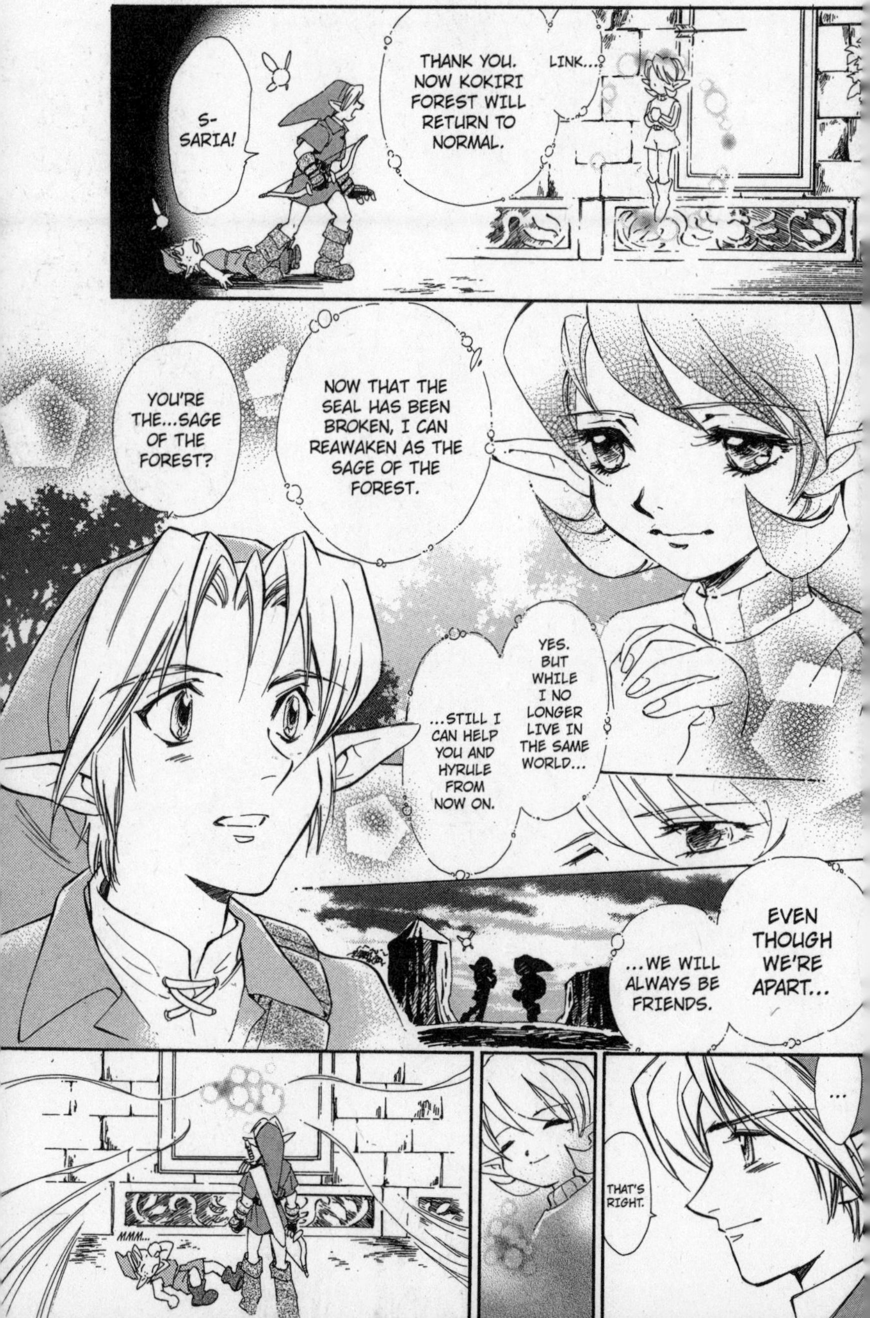
LINK...
THANK YOU. NOW KOKIRI FOREST WILL RETURN TO NORMAL.
S-SARIA!
NOW THAT THE SEAL HAS BEEN BROKEN, I CAN REAWAKEN AS THE SAGE OF THE FOREST.
YOU'RE THE...SAGE OF THE FOREST?
YES. BUT WHILE I NO LONGER LIVE IN THE SAME WORLD...
...STILL I CAN HELP YOU AND HYRULE FROM NOW ON.
EVEN THOUGH WE'RE APART...
...WE WILL ALWAYS BE FRIENDS.
...
THAT'S RIGHT.
MMM...

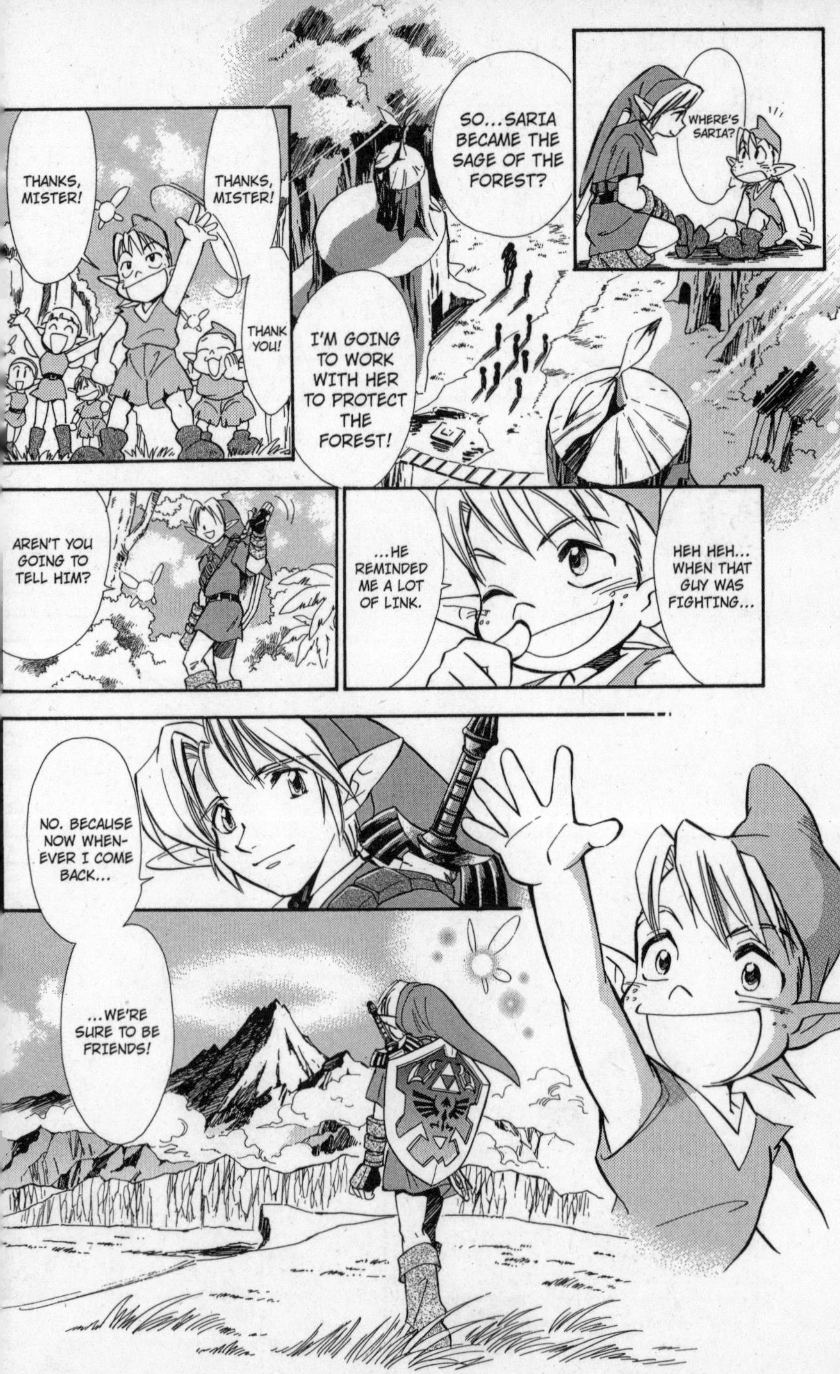
WHERE'S SARIA?
SO...SARIA BECAME THE SAGE OF THE FOREST?
I'M GOING TO WORK WITH HER TO PROTECT THE FOREST!
THANKS, MISTER!
THANKS, MISTER!
THANK YOU!
HEH HEH... WHEN THAT GUY WAS FIGHTING...
...HE REMINDED ME A LOT OF LINK.
AREN'T YOU GOING TO TELL HIM?
NO. BECAUSE NOW WHEN-EVER I COME BACK...
...WE'RE SURE TO BE FRIENDS!

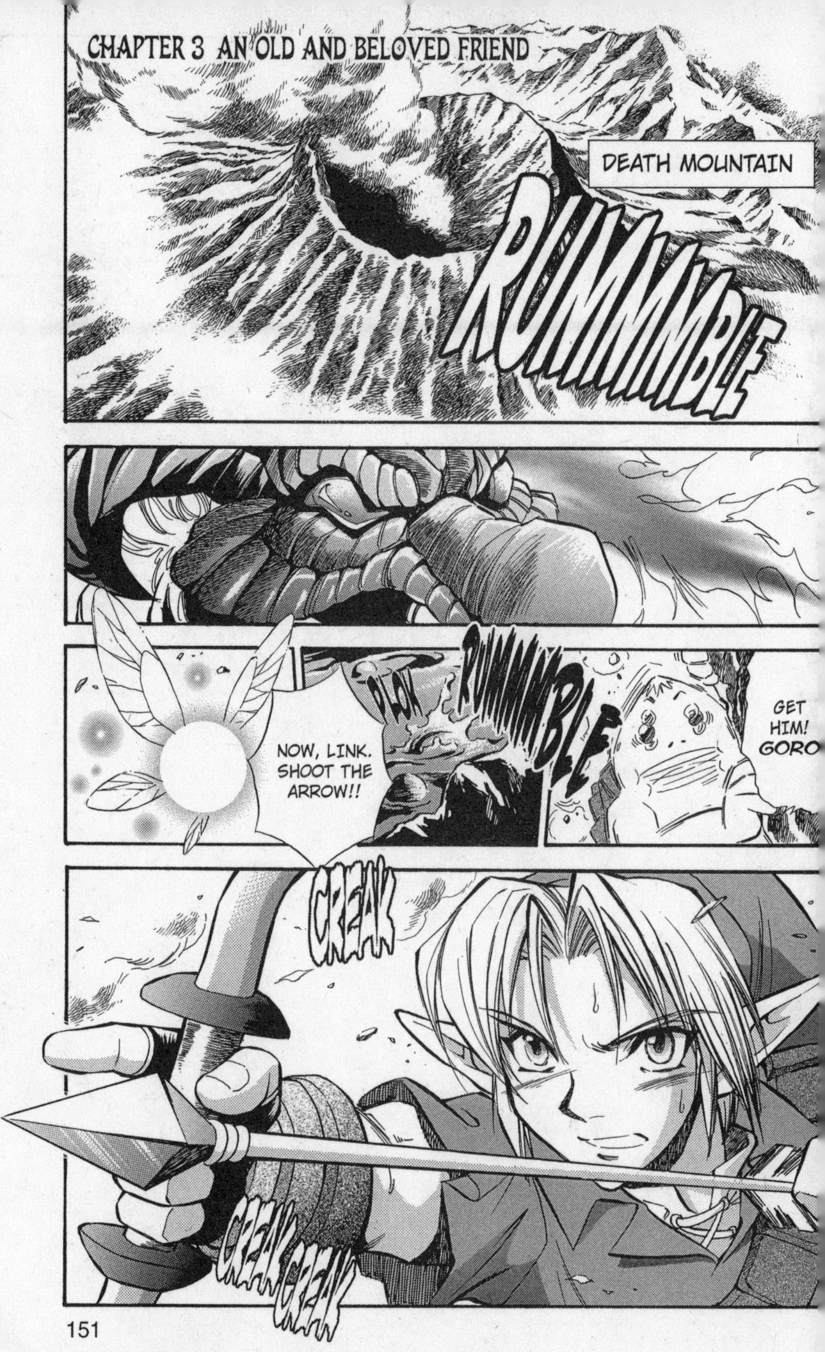
CHAPTER 3 AN OLD AND BELOVED FRIEND
DEATH MOUNTAIN
RUMMMBLE
GET HIM! GORO
RUMMMBLE
DLOK
NOW, LINK. SHOOT THE ARROW!!
CREAK
CREAK CREAK

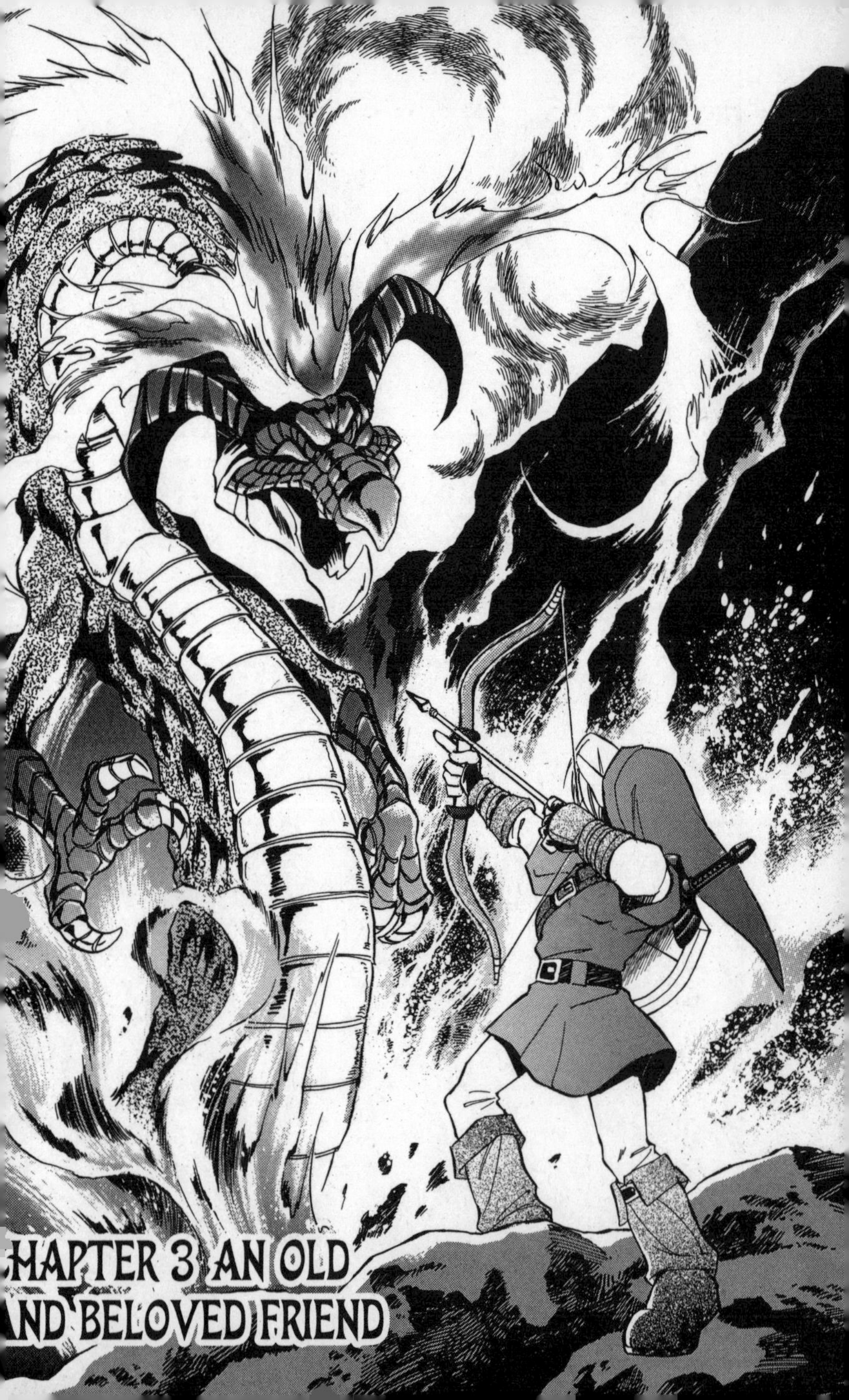
HAPTER 3 AN OLD
ND BELOVED FRIEND

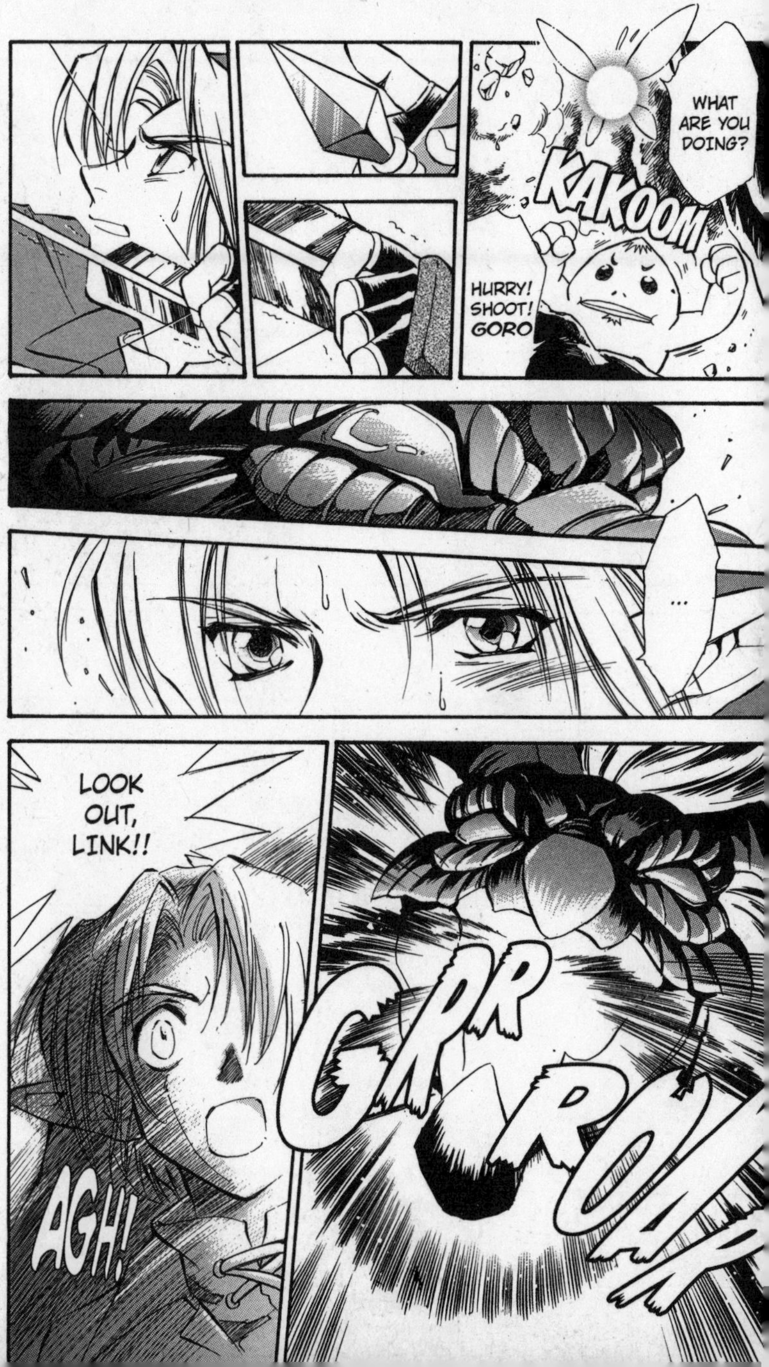
WHAT ARE YOU DOING?
KAKOOM
HURRY! SHOOT! GORO
...
LOOK OUT, LINK!!
GRR
ROAR
AGH!

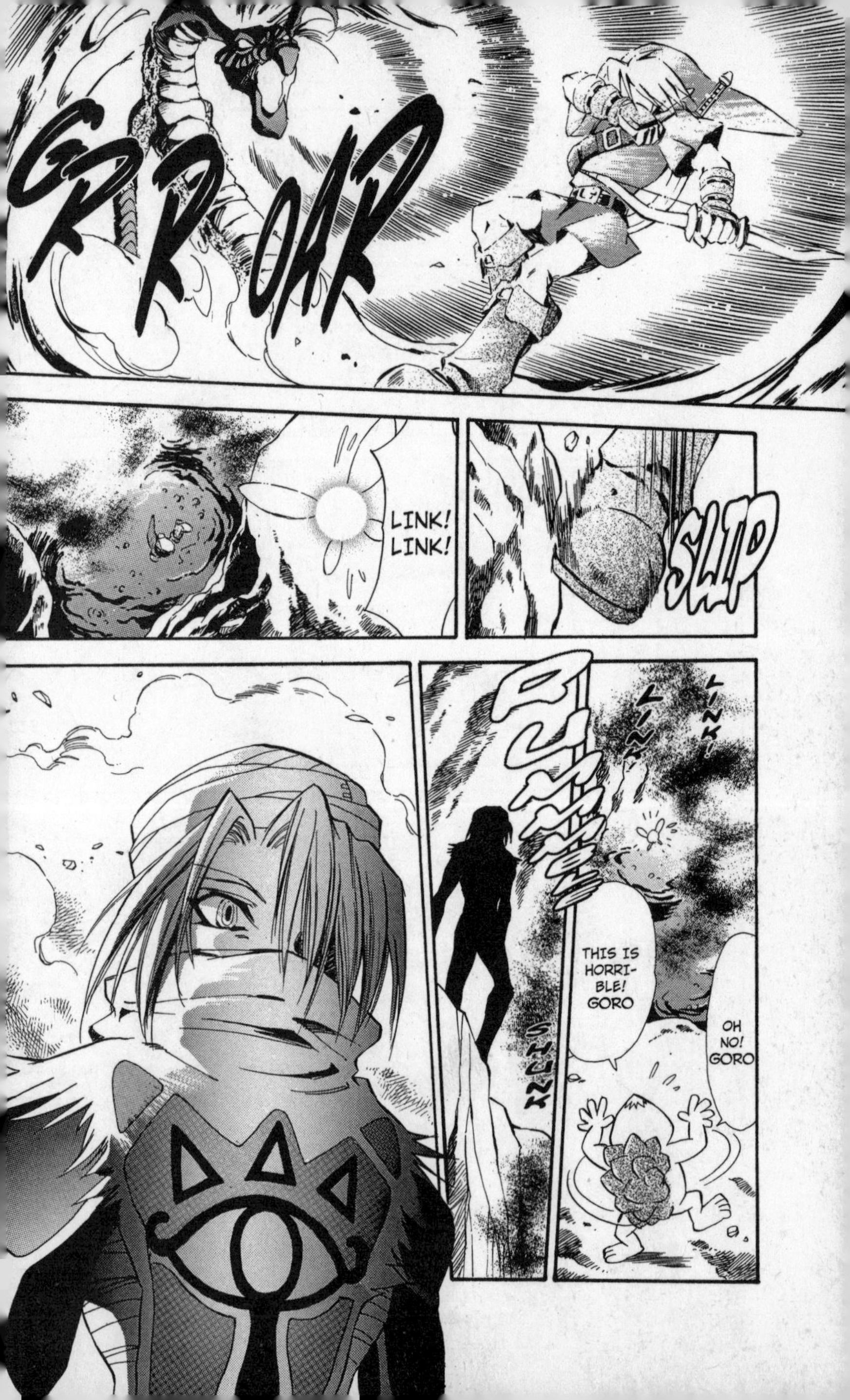
GROAR
SLIP
LINK! LINK!
LINK! LINK!
OH NO! GORO
THIS IS HORRI-BLE! GORO
SHUNK

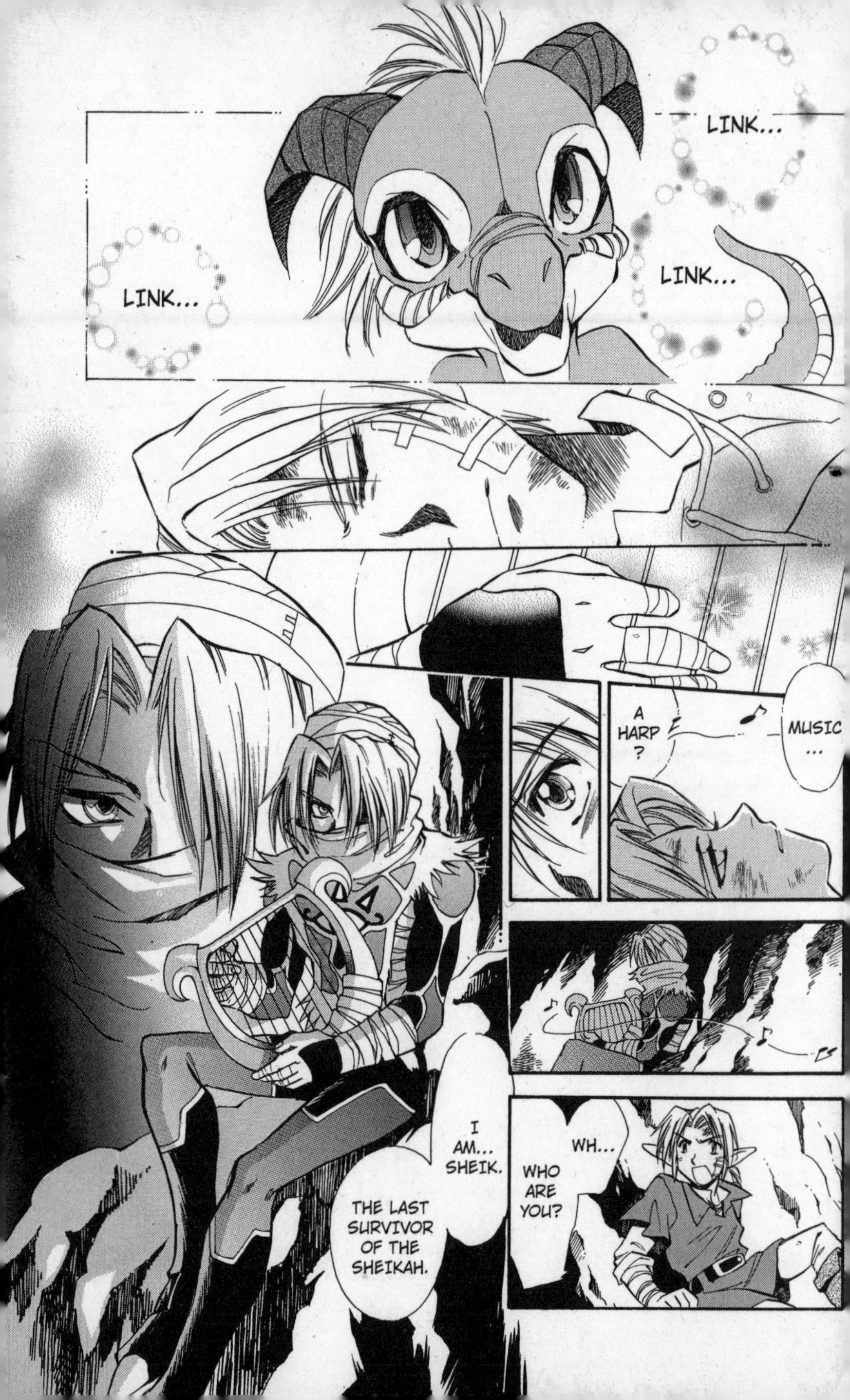
LINK...
LINK...
LINK...
MUSIC...
A HARP?
WH...
WHO ARE YOU?
I AM... SHEIK.
THE LAST SURVIVOR OF THE SHEIKAH.

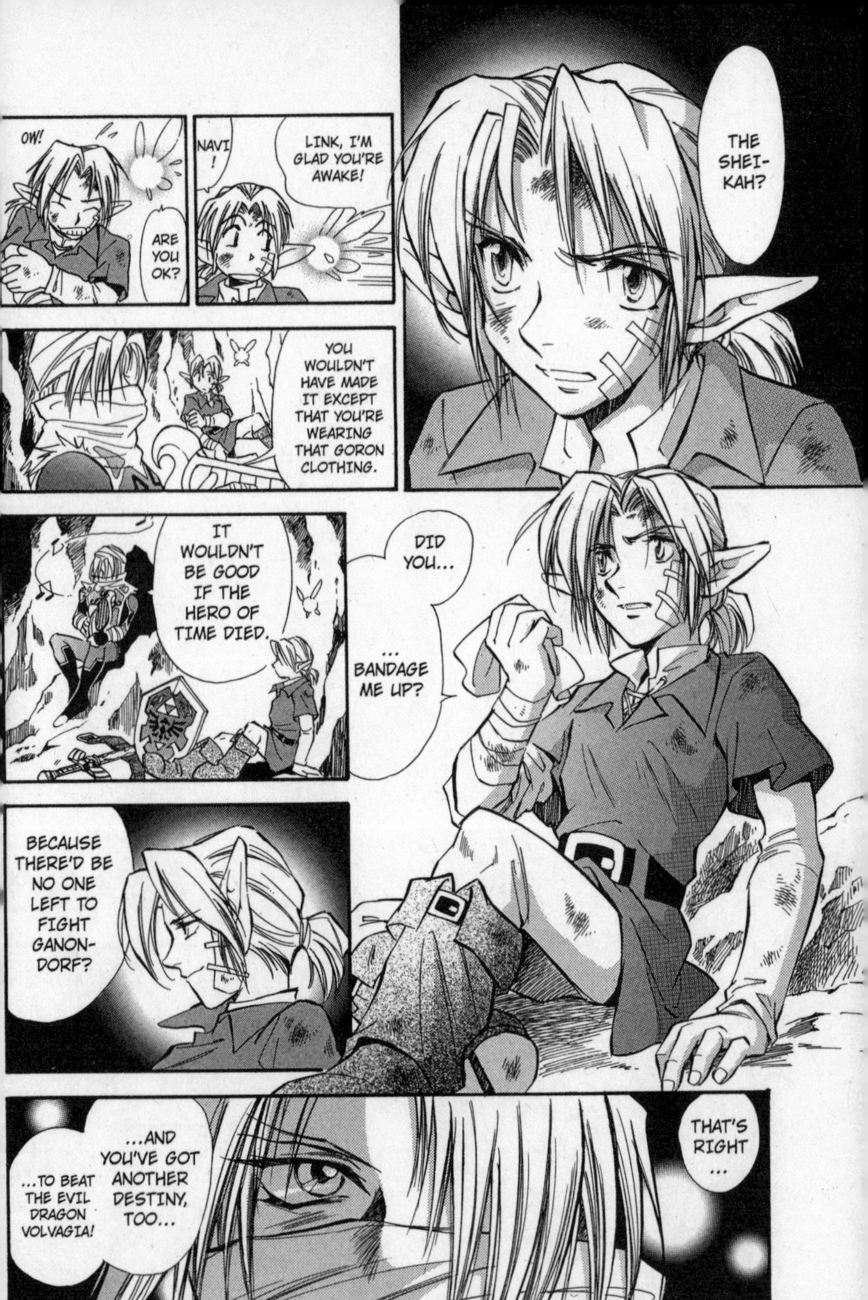
THE SHEI-KAH?
LINK, I'M GLAD YOU'RE AWAKE!
NAVI!
OW!
ARE YOU OK?
YOU WOULDN'T HAVE MADE IT EXCEPT THAT YOU'RE WEARING THAT GORON CLOTHING.
DID YOU...
...BANDAGE ME UP?
IT WOULDN'T BE GOOD IF THE HERO OF TIME DIED.
BECAUSE THERE'D BE NO ONE LEFT TO FIGHT GANON-DORF?
THAT'S RIGHT...
...AND YOU'VE GOT ANOTHER DESTINY, TOO...
...TO BEAT THE EVIL DRAGON VOLVAGIA!

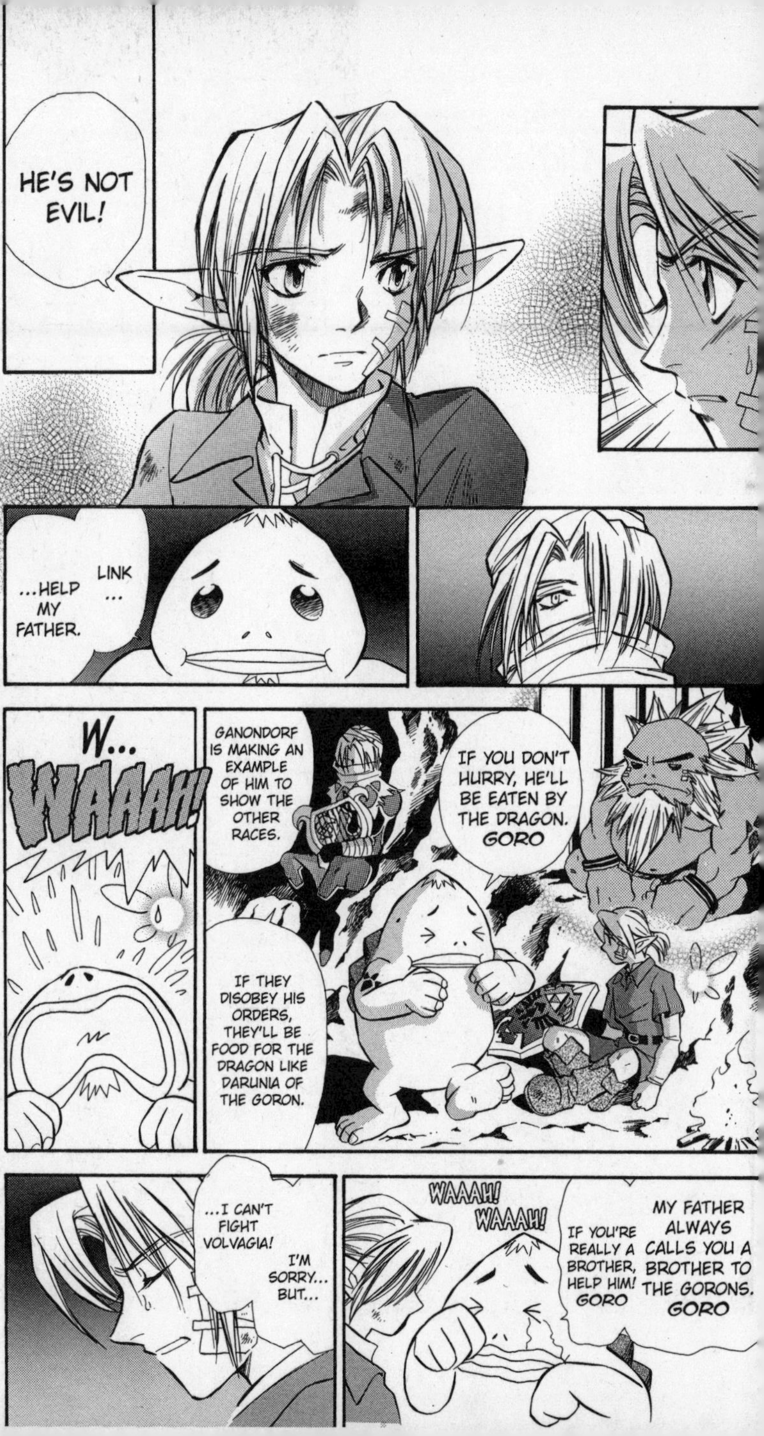
HE'S NOT EVIL!
LINK ...
...HELP MY FATHER.
IF YOU DON'T HURRY, HE'LL BE EATEN BY THE DRAGON. GORO
GANONDORF IS MAKING AN EXAMPLE OF HIM TO SHOW THE OTHER RACES.
IF THEY DISOBEY HIS ORDERS, THEY'LL BE FOOD FOR THE DRAGON LIKE DARUNIA OF THE GORON.
W... WAAAH!
WAAAH! WAAAH!
MY FATHER ALWAYS CALLS YOU A BROTHER TO THE GORONS. GORO
IF YOU'RE REALLY A BROTHER, HELP HIM! GORO
...I CAN'T FIGHT VOLVAGIA!
I'M SORRY... BUT...

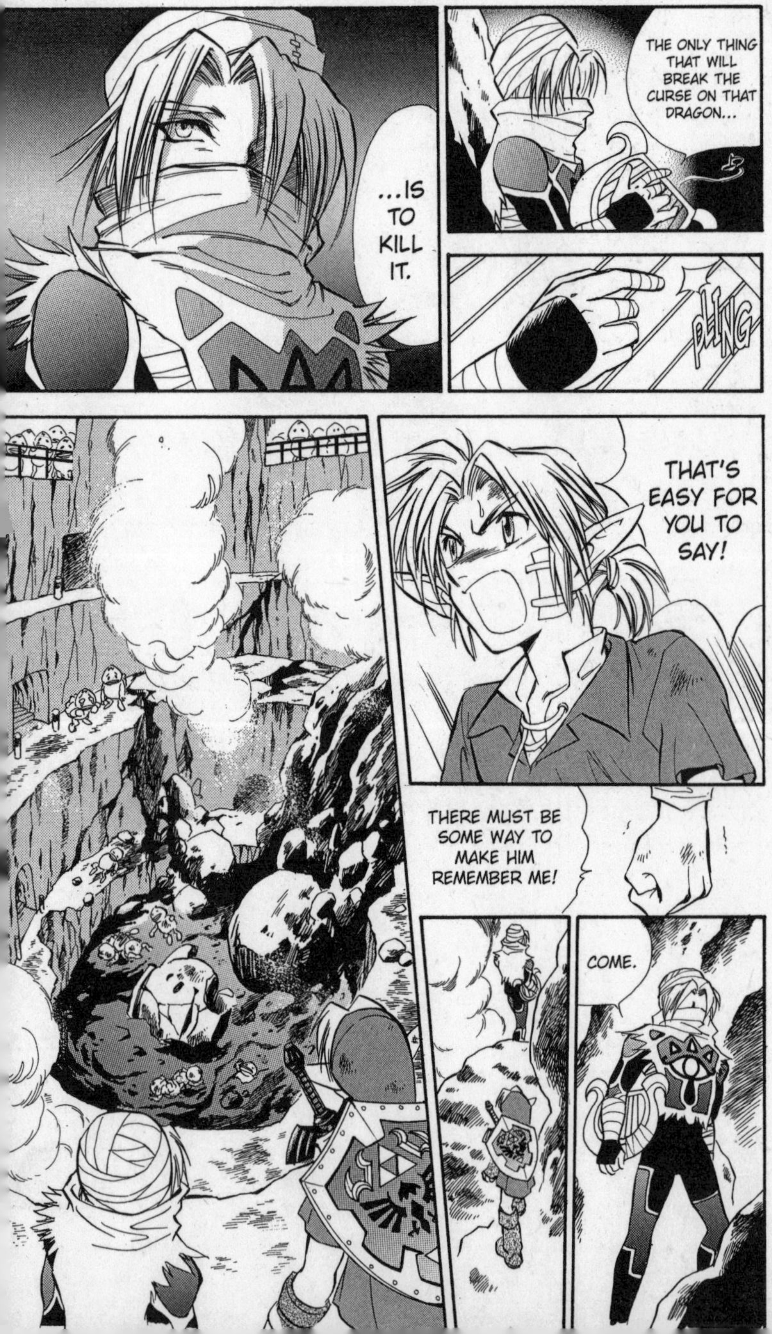
THE ONLY THING THAT WILL BREAK THE CURSE ON THAT DRAGON...
PLING
...IS TO KILL IT.
THAT'S EASY FOR YOU TO SAY!
THERE MUST BE SOME WAY TO MAKE HIM REMEMBER ME!
COME.

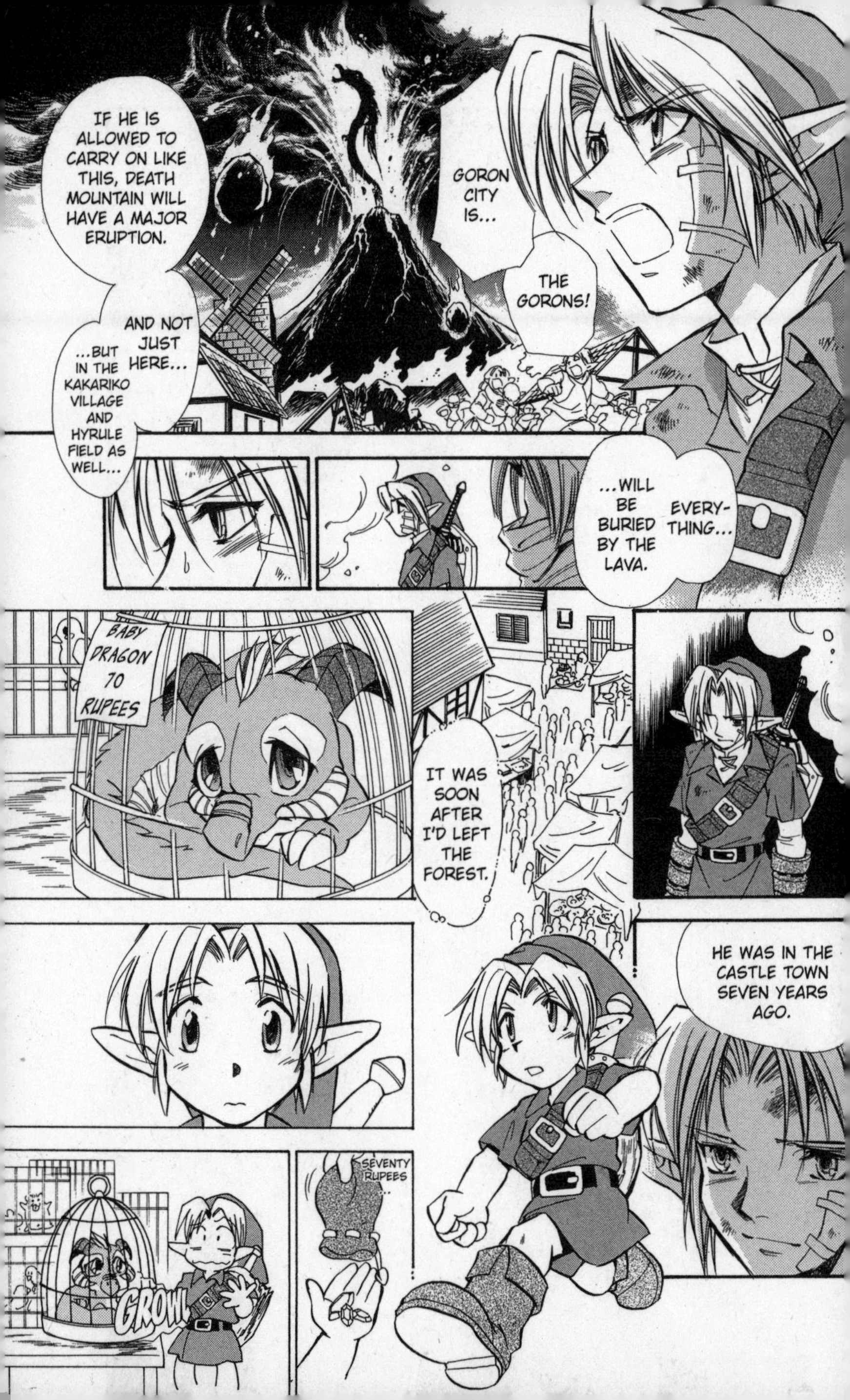
IF HE IS ALLOWED TO CARRY ON LIKE THIS, DEATH MOUNTAIN WILL HAVE A MAJOR ERUPTION.
GORON CITY IS...
THE GORONS!
AND NOT JUST HERE...
...BUT IN THE KAKARIKO VILLAGE AND HYRULE FIELD AS WELL...
EVERY-THING...
...WILL BE BURIED BY THE LAVA.
IT WAS SOON AFTER I'D LEFT THE FOREST.
BABY DRAGON 70 RUPEES
HE WAS IN THE CASTLE TOWN SEVEN YEARS AGO.
SEVENTY RUPEES...
GROWL

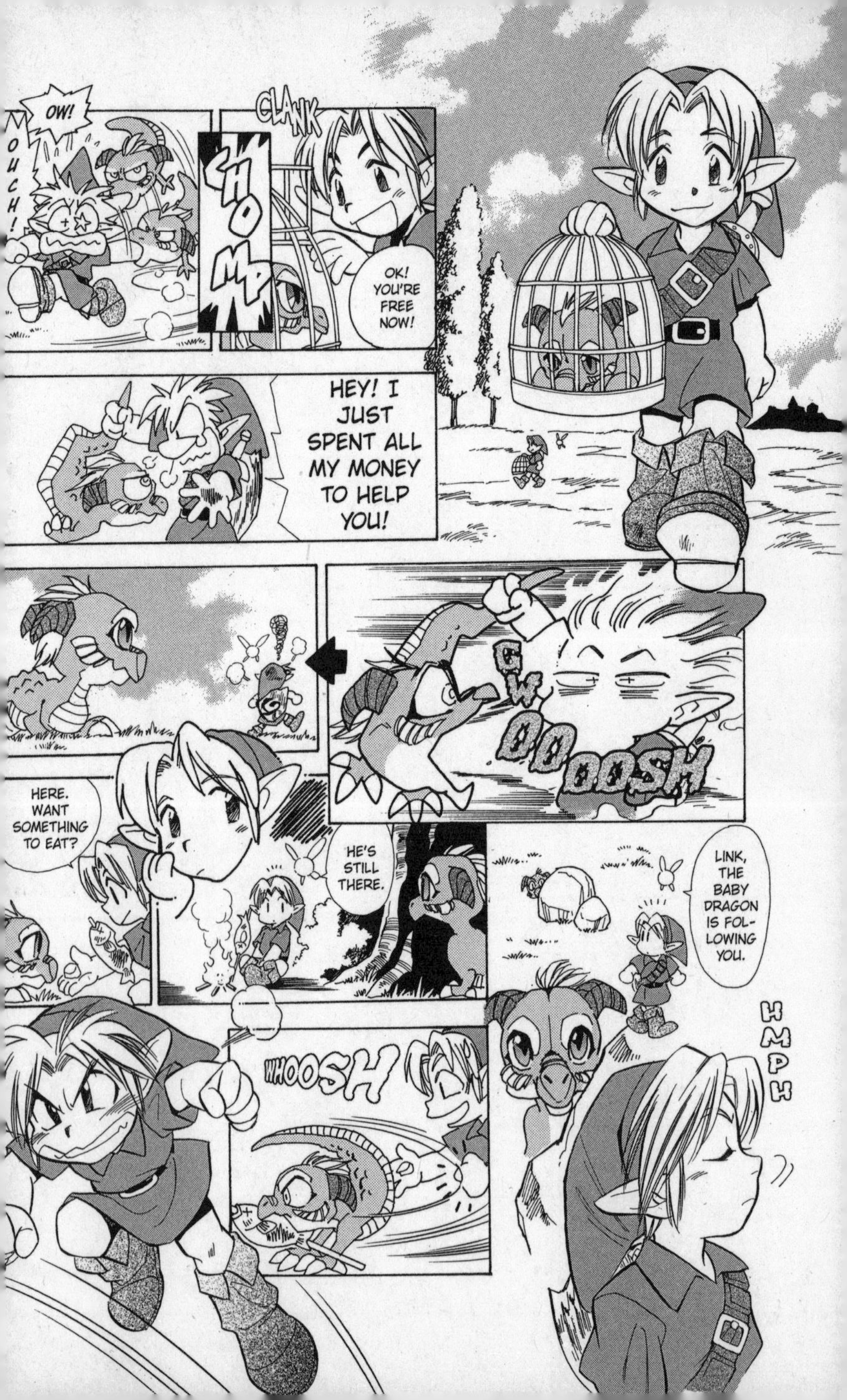
CLANK
CHOMP
OK! YOU'RE FREE NOW!
OW!
OUCH!
HEY! I JUST SPENT ALL MY MONEY TO HELP YOU!
GWOOOOSH
LINK, THE BABY DRAGON IS FOLLOWING YOU.
HMPH
HE'S STILL THERE.
HERE. WANT SOMETHING TO EAT?
WHOOSH

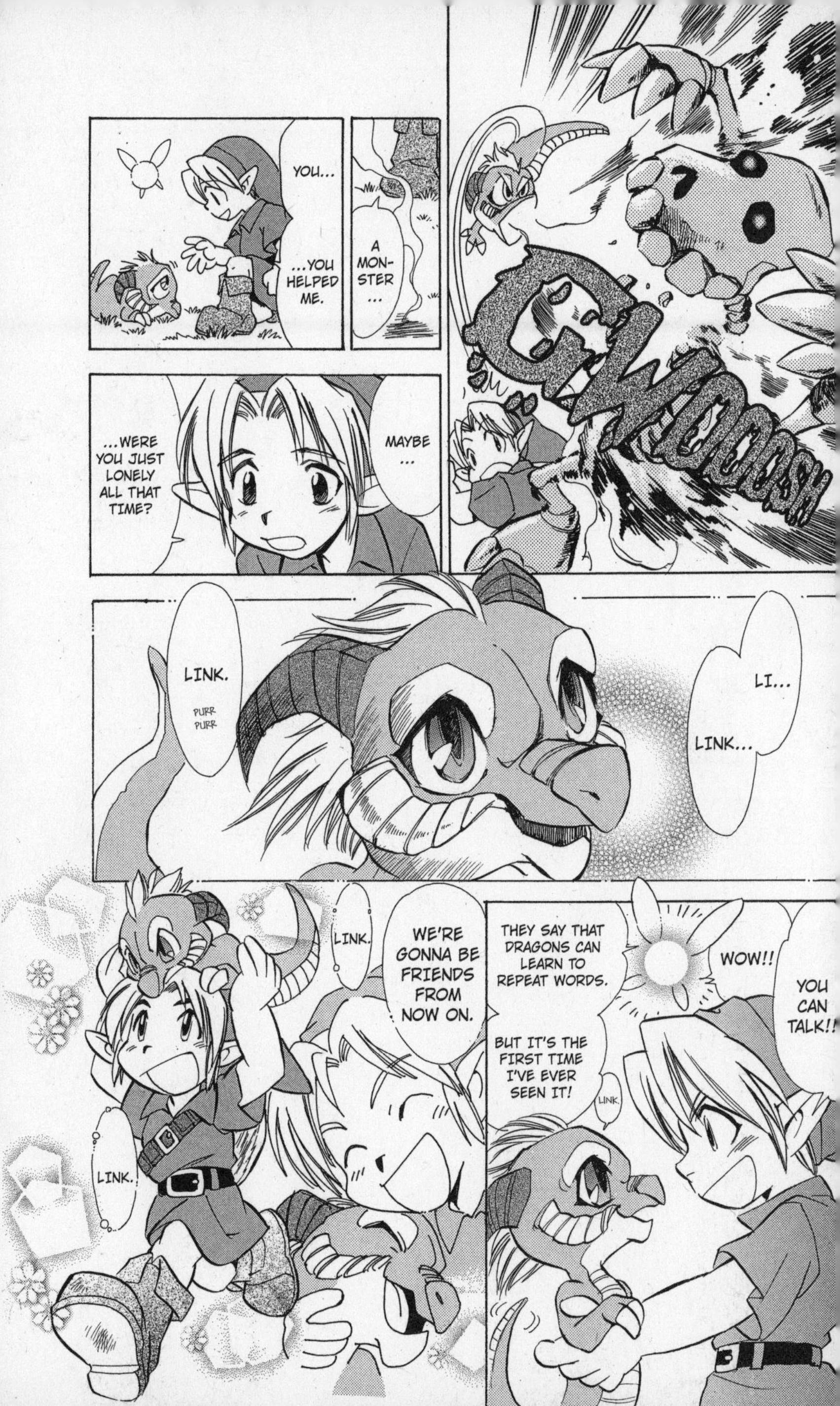
GWOOOSH
A MONSTER...
YOU...
...YOU HELPED ME.
MAYBE...
...WERE YOU JUST LONELY ALL THAT TIME?
LI...
LINK...
LINK.
PURR PURR
WOW!!
YOU CAN TALK!!
THEY SAY THAT DRAGONS CAN LEARN TO REPEAT WORDS.
BUT IT'S THE FIRST TIME I'VE EVER SEEN IT!
LINK.
WE'RE GONNA BE FRIENDS FROM NOW ON.
LINK.
LINK.

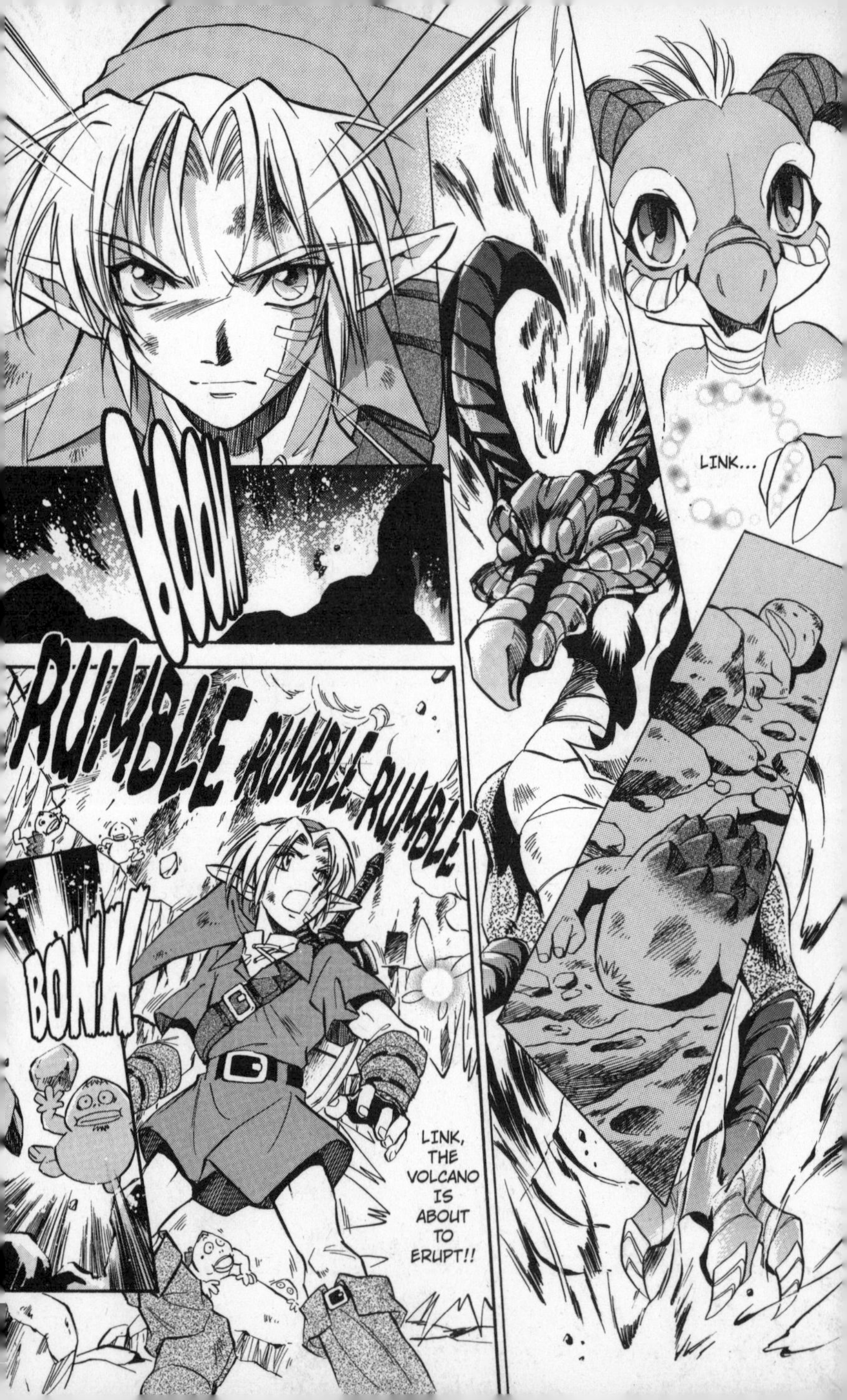

LINK...
BOOM
RUMBLE RUMBLE RUMBLE RUMBLE
BONK
LINK, THE VOLCANO IS ABOUT TO ERUPT!!

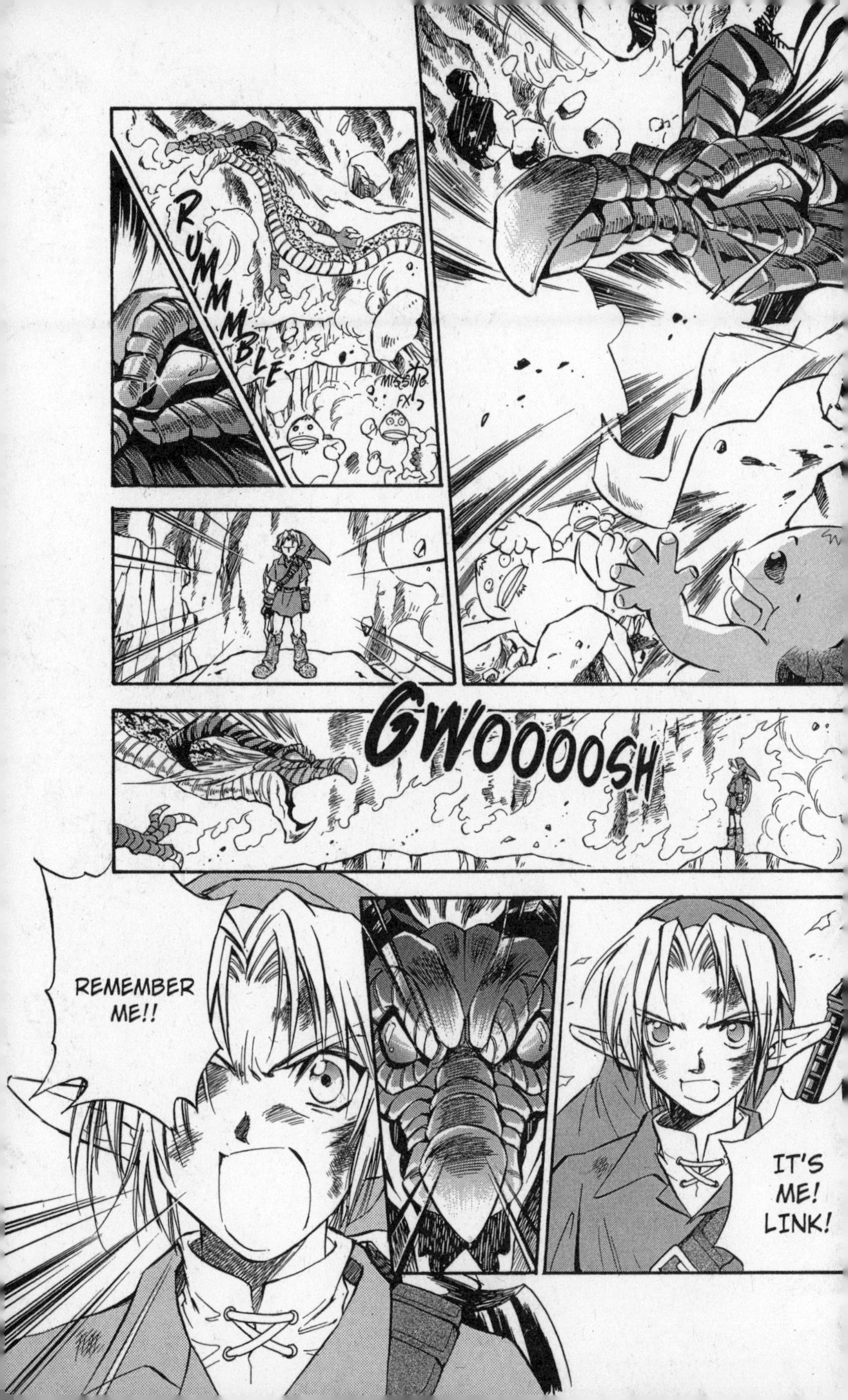
RUMMMBLE
MISSING FX
GWOOOOSH
IT'S ME! LINK!
REMEMBER ME!!

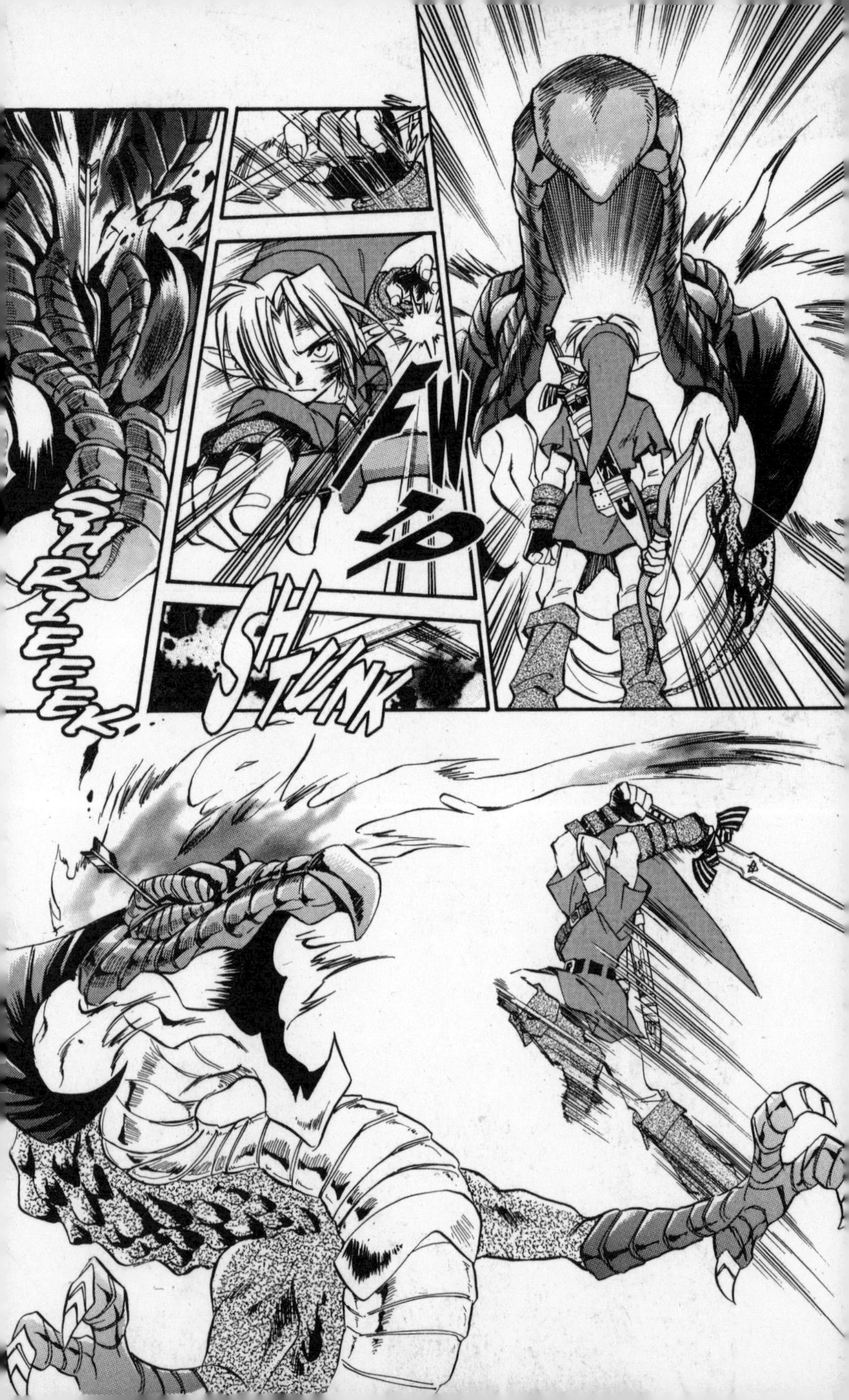
FWIP
SHTUNK
SHRIEEEK

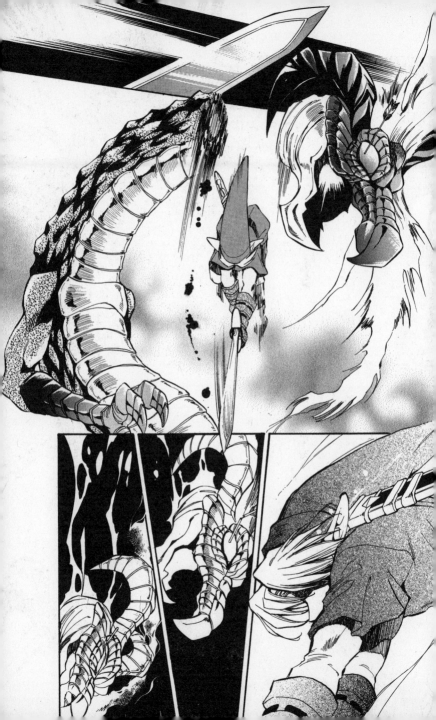

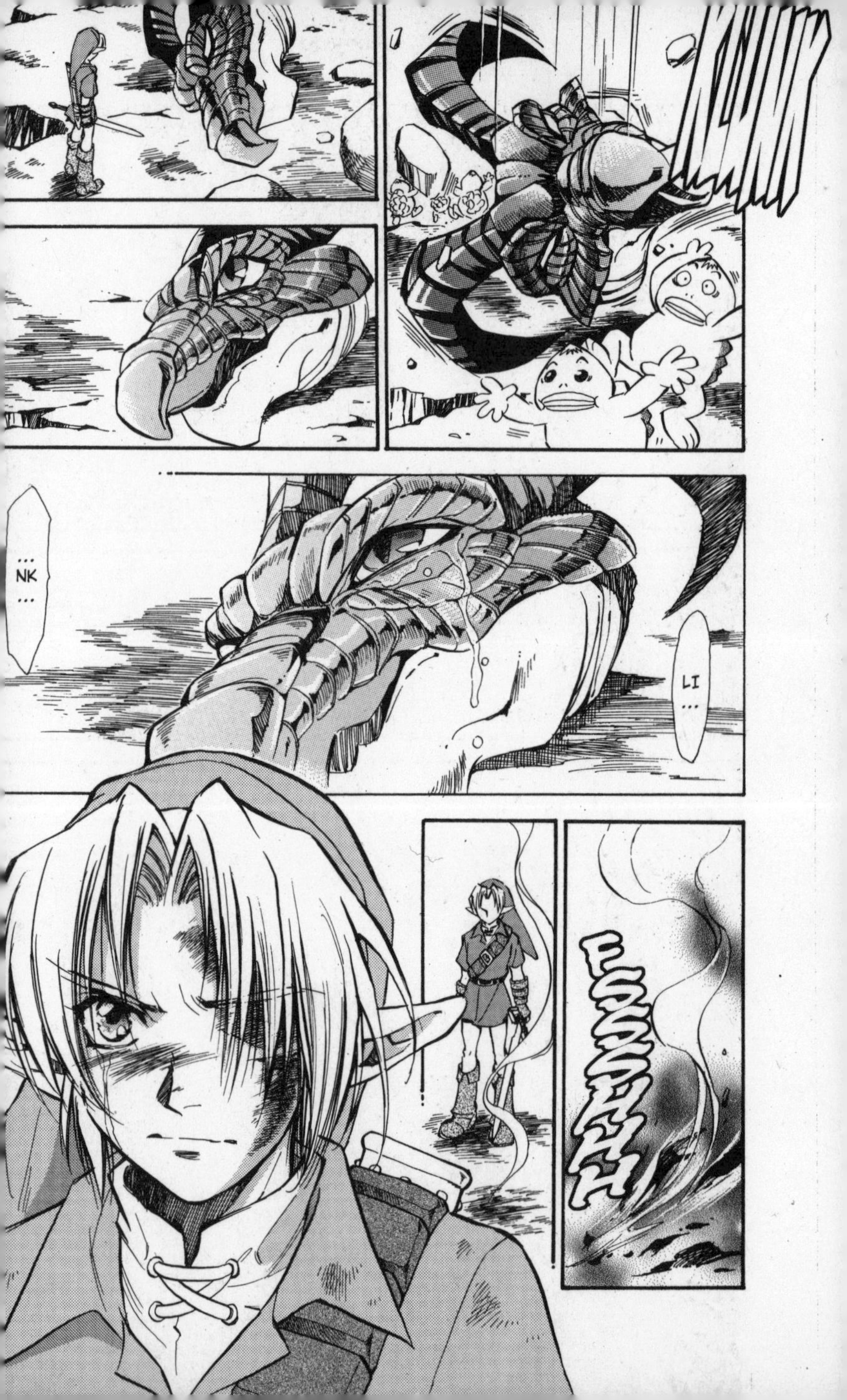
LI...
...NK...

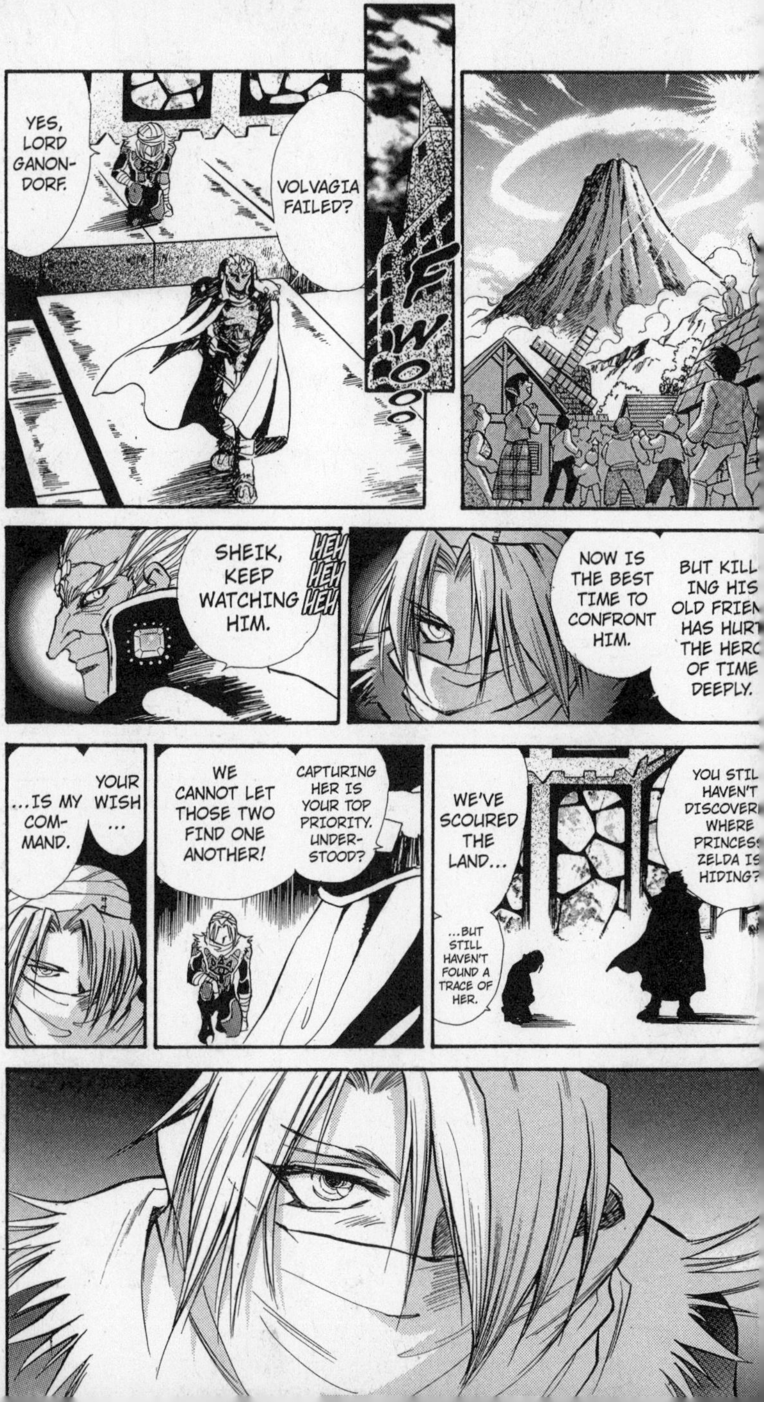
FWOOOO
VOLVAGIA FAILED?
YES, LORD GANON-DORF.
BUT KILL ING HIS OLD FRIE HAS HURT THE HER OF TIME DEEPLY.
NOW IS THE BEST TIME TO CONFRONT HIM.
HEH HEH HEH
SHEIK, KEEP WATCHING HIM.
YOU STIL HAVEN'T DISCOVER WHERE PRINCES ZELDA IS HIDING?
WE'VE SCOURED THE LAND...
...BUT STILL HAVEN'T FOUND A TRACE OF HER.
CAPTURING HER IS YOUR TOP PRIORITY. UNDER-STOOD?
WE CANNOT LET THOSE TWO FIND ONE ANOTHER!
YOUR WISH...
...IS MY COM-MAND.

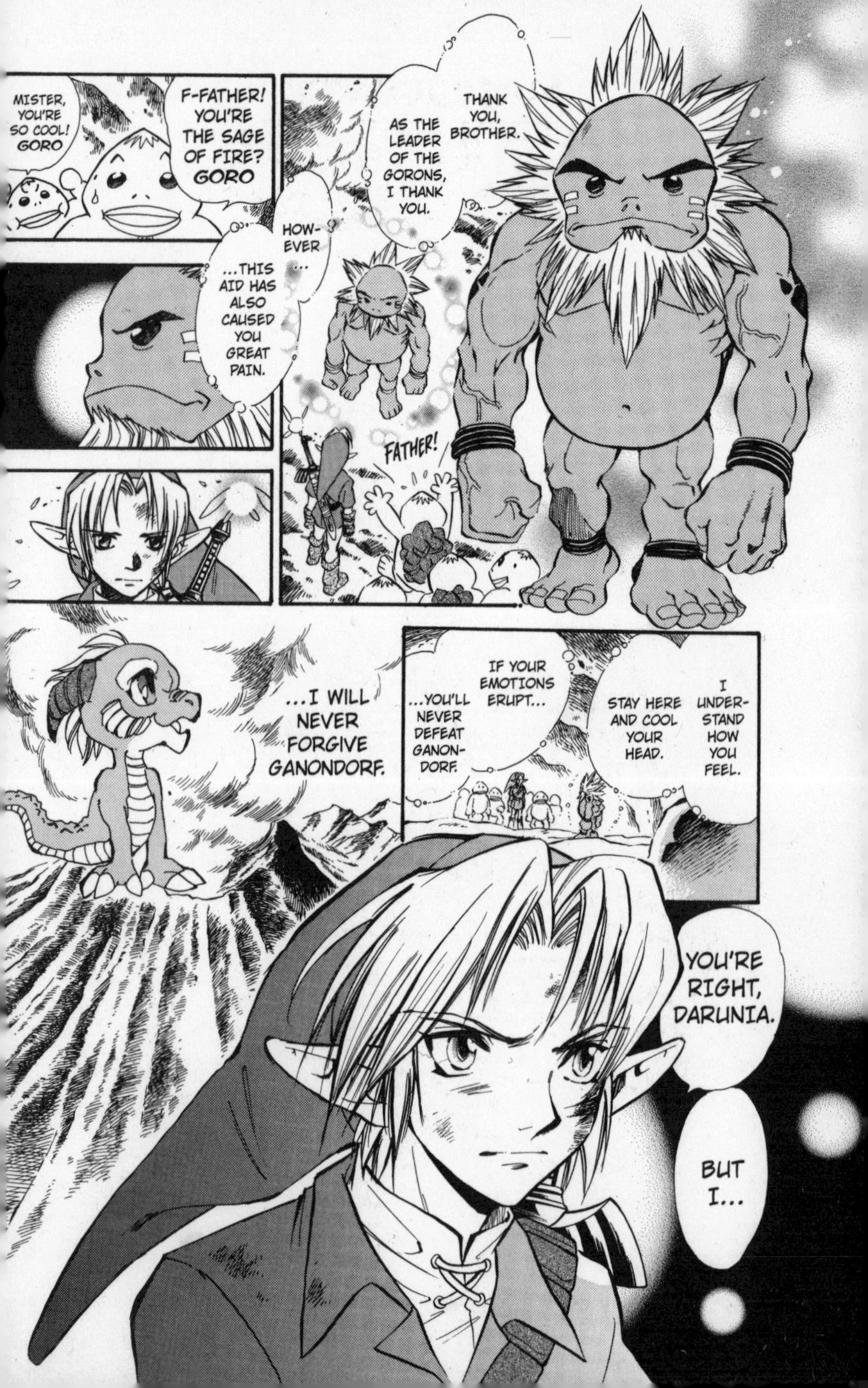
THANK YOU, BROTHER.
AS THE LEADER OF THE GORONS, I THANK YOU.
HOW-EVER...
FATHER!
F-FATHER! YOU'RE THE SAGE OF FIRE? GORO
MISTER, YOU'RE SO COOL! GORO
...THIS AID HAS ALSO CAUSED YOU GREAT PAIN.
I UNDERSTAND HOW YOU FEEL.
STAY HERE AND COOL YOUR HEAD.
IF YOUR EMOTIONS ERUPT...
...YOU'LL NEVER DEFEAT GANONDORF.
...I WILL NEVER FORGIVE GANONDORF.
YOU'RE RIGHT, DARUNIA.
BUT I...

BONUS ILLUSTRATION 3

PRESENTING ANOTHER ROUGH SKETCH DONE BEFORE THE SERIES! IT'S UNUSUAL FOR HIM TO HOLD HIS SWORD IN HIS LEFT HAND.

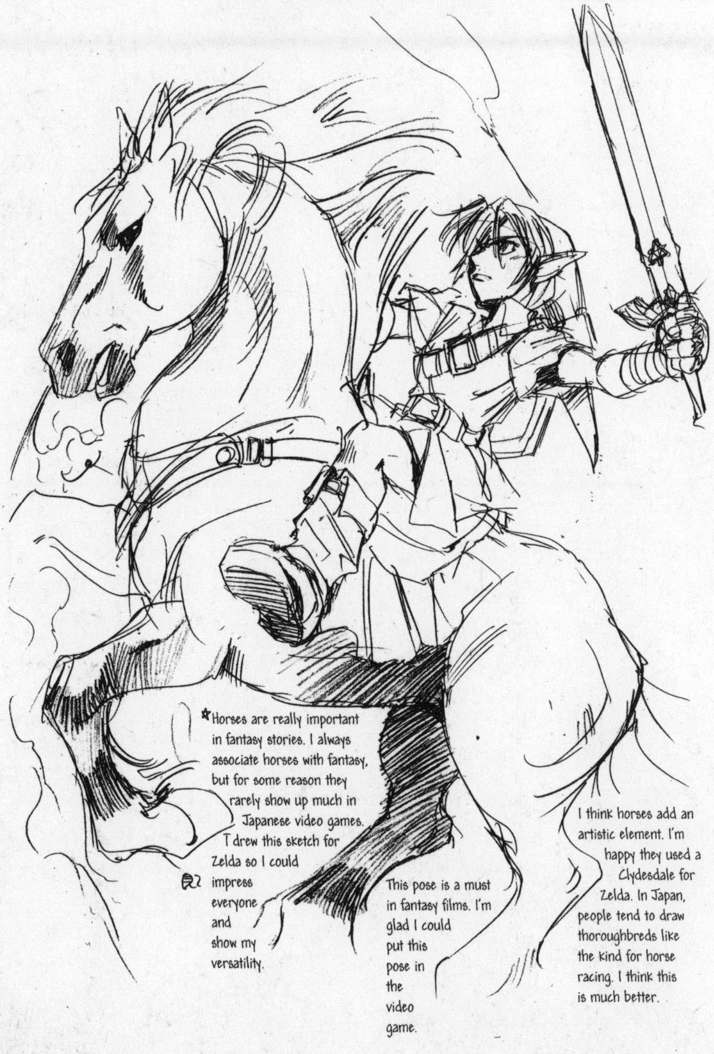

★Horses are really important in fantasy stories. I always associate horses with fantasy, but for some reason they rarely show up much in Japanese video games. I drew this sketch for Zelda so I could impress everyone and show my versatility.
This pose is a must in fantasy films. I'm glad I could put this pose in the video game.
I think horses add an artistic element. I'm happy they used a Clydesdale for Zelda. In Japan, people tend to draw thoroughbreds like the kind for horse racing. I think this is much better.

CHAPTER 4
LINK VS. LINK

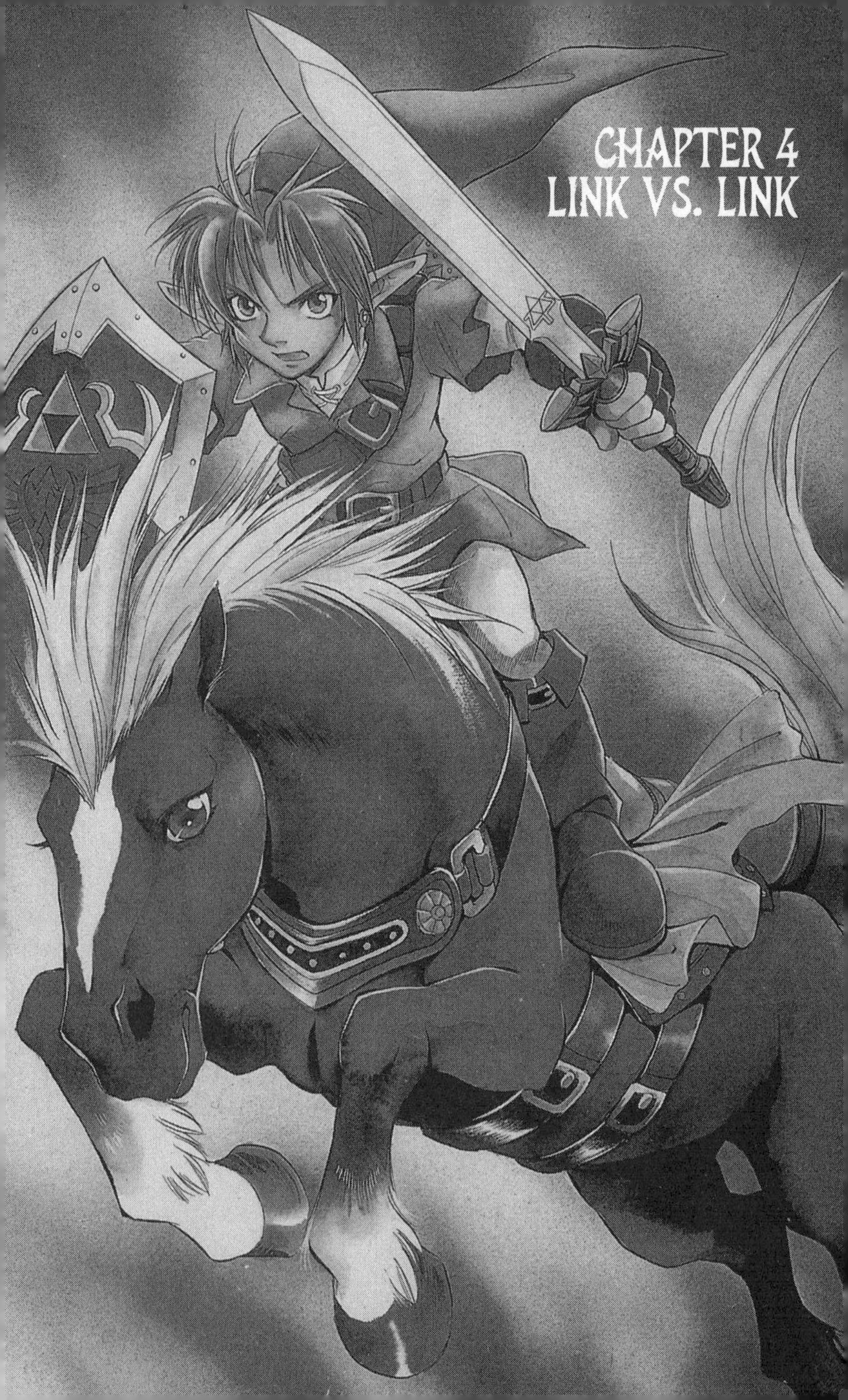

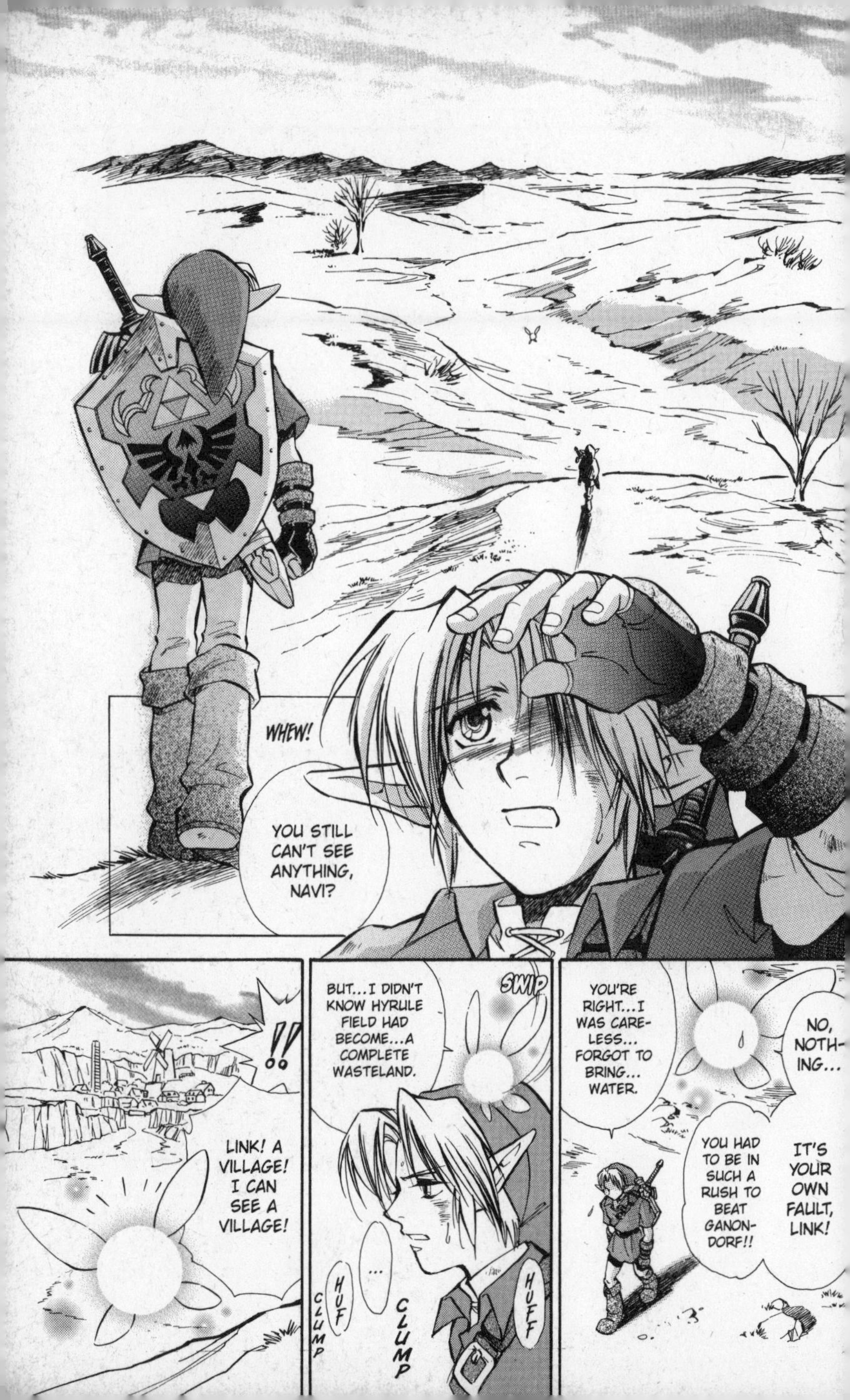
WHEW!
YOU STILL CAN'T SEE ANYTHING, NAVI?
NO, NOTHING...
IT'S YOUR OWN FAULT, LINK!
YOU HAD TO BE IN SUCH A RUSH TO BEAT GANONDORF!!
YOU'RE RIGHT...I WAS CARELESS... FORGOT TO BRING... WATER.
SWIP
BUT...I DIDN'T KNOW HYRULE FIELD HAD BECOME...A COMPLETE WASTELAND.
HUFF
CLUMP
...
HUF
CLUMP
!!
LINK! A VILLAGE! I CAN SEE A VILLAGE!

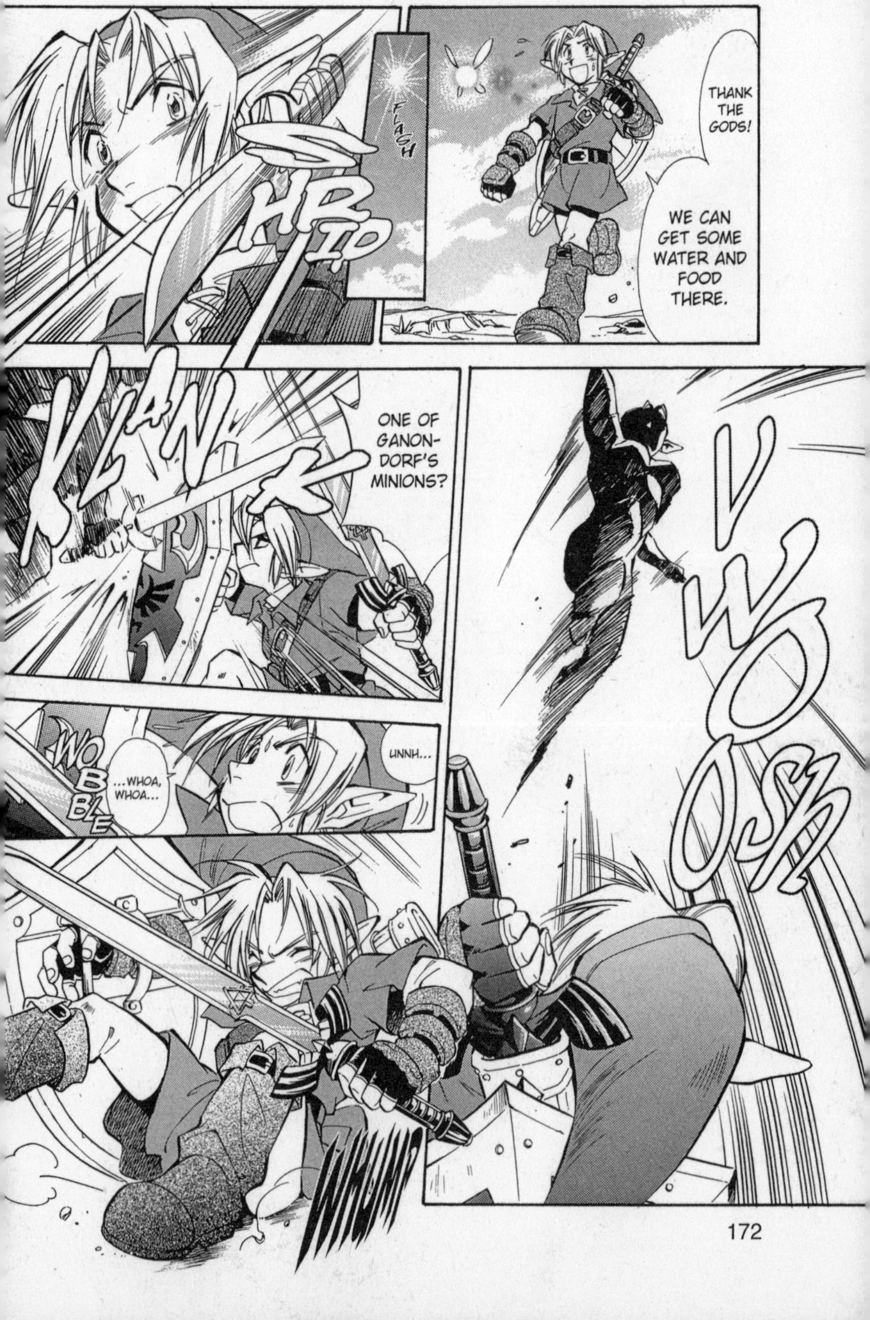
THANK THE GODS!
WE CAN GET SOME WATER AND FOOD THERE.
FLASH
SHRIP
VWOOSH
KLANK
ONE OF GANON-DORF'S MINIONS?
UNNH...
...WHOA, WHOA...
WOBBLE

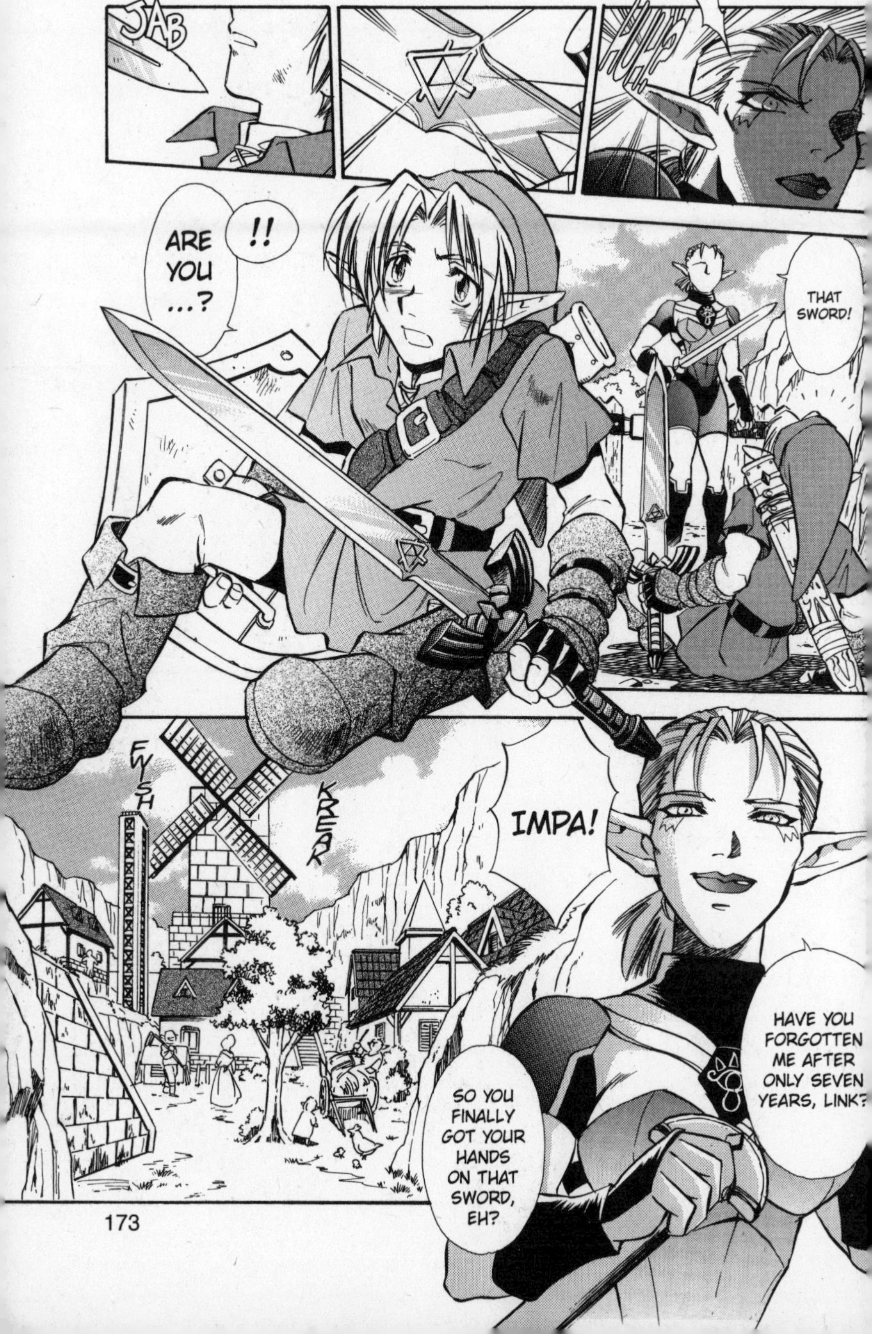
HUP!?
JAB
THAT SWORD!
!!
ARE YOU ...?
IMPA!
HAVE YOU FORGOTTEN ME AFTER ONLY SEVEN YEARS, LINK?
SO YOU FINALLY GOT YOUR HANDS ON THAT SWORD, EH?
KREAK
FWISH

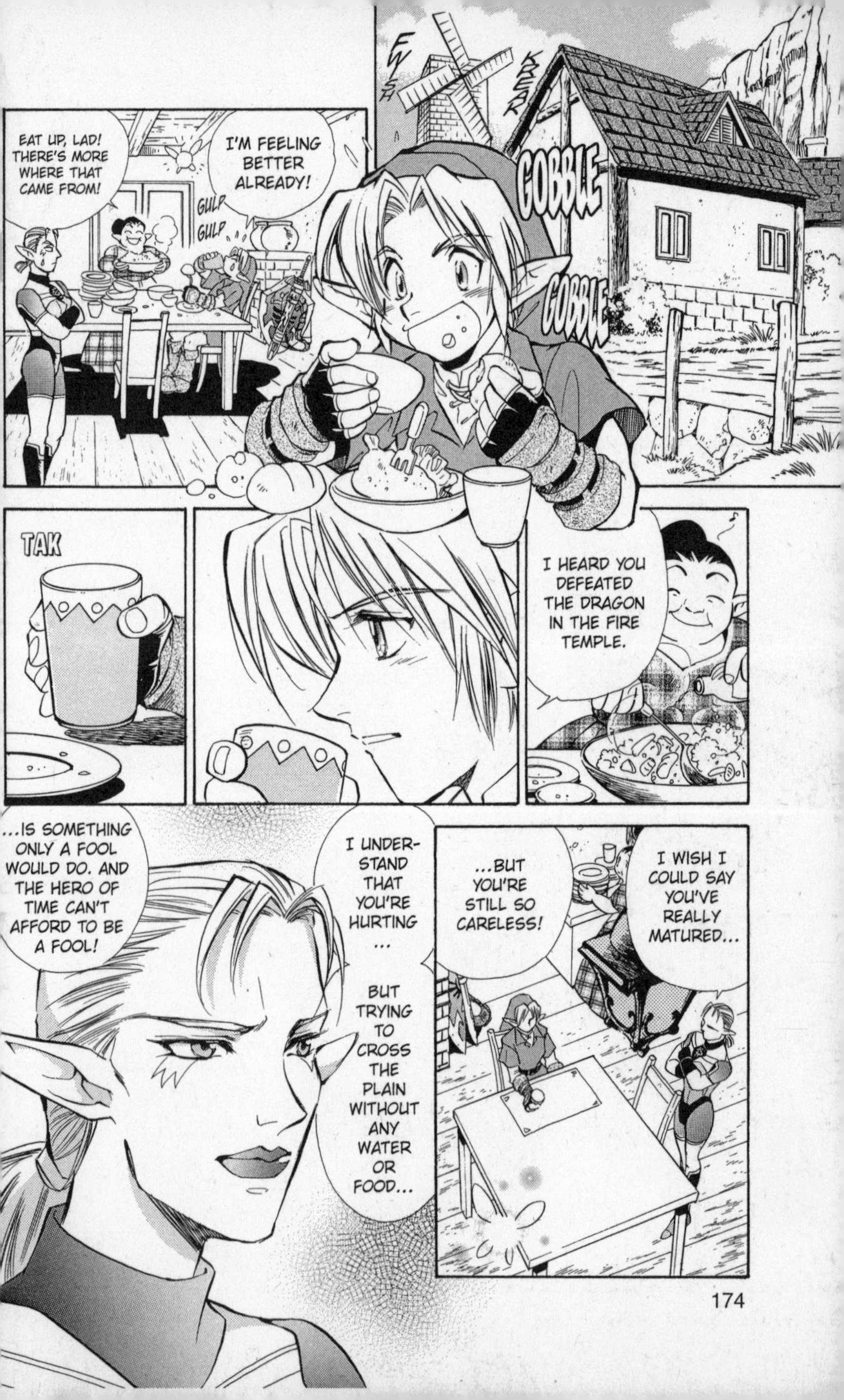
FWISH
KREAK
GOBBLE
GOBBLE
I'M FEELING BETTER ALREADY!
EAT UP, LAD! THERE'S MORE WHERE THAT CAME FROM!
GULP GULP
I HEARD YOU DEFEATED THE DRAGON IN THE FIRE TEMPLE.
TAK
I WISH I COULD SAY YOU'VE REALLY MATURED...
...BUT YOU'RE STILL SO CARELESS!
I UNDER-STAND THAT YOU'RE HURTING...
BUT TRYING TO CROSS THE PLAIN WITHOUT ANY WATER OR FOOD...
...IS SOMETHING ONLY A FOOL WOULD DO. AND THE HERO OF TIME CAN'T AFFORD TO BE A FOOL!

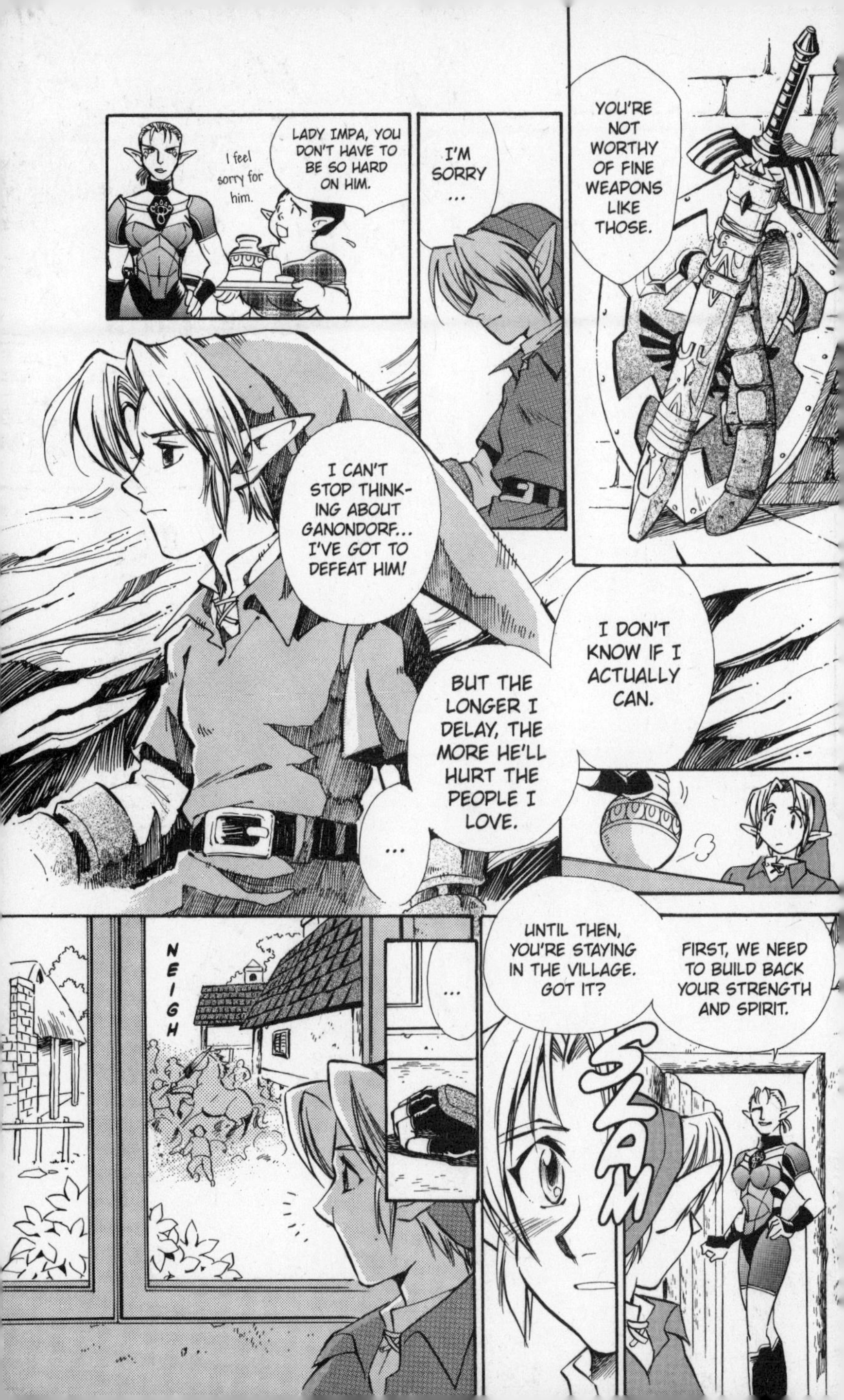
YOU'RE NOT WORTHY OF FINE WEAPONS LIKE THOSE.
I'M SORRY ...
LADY IMPA, YOU DON'T HAVE TO BE SO HARD ON HIM.
I feel sorry for him.
I CAN'T STOP THINKING ABOUT GANONDORF... I'VE GOT TO DEFEAT HIM!
I DON'T KNOW IF I ACTUALLY CAN.
BUT THE LONGER I DELAY, THE MORE HE'LL HURT THE PEOPLE I LOVE.
...
FIRST, WE NEED TO BUILD BACK YOUR STRENGTH AND SPIRIT.
UNTIL THEN, YOU'RE STAYING IN THE VILLAGE. GOT IT?
SLAM
...
NEIGH

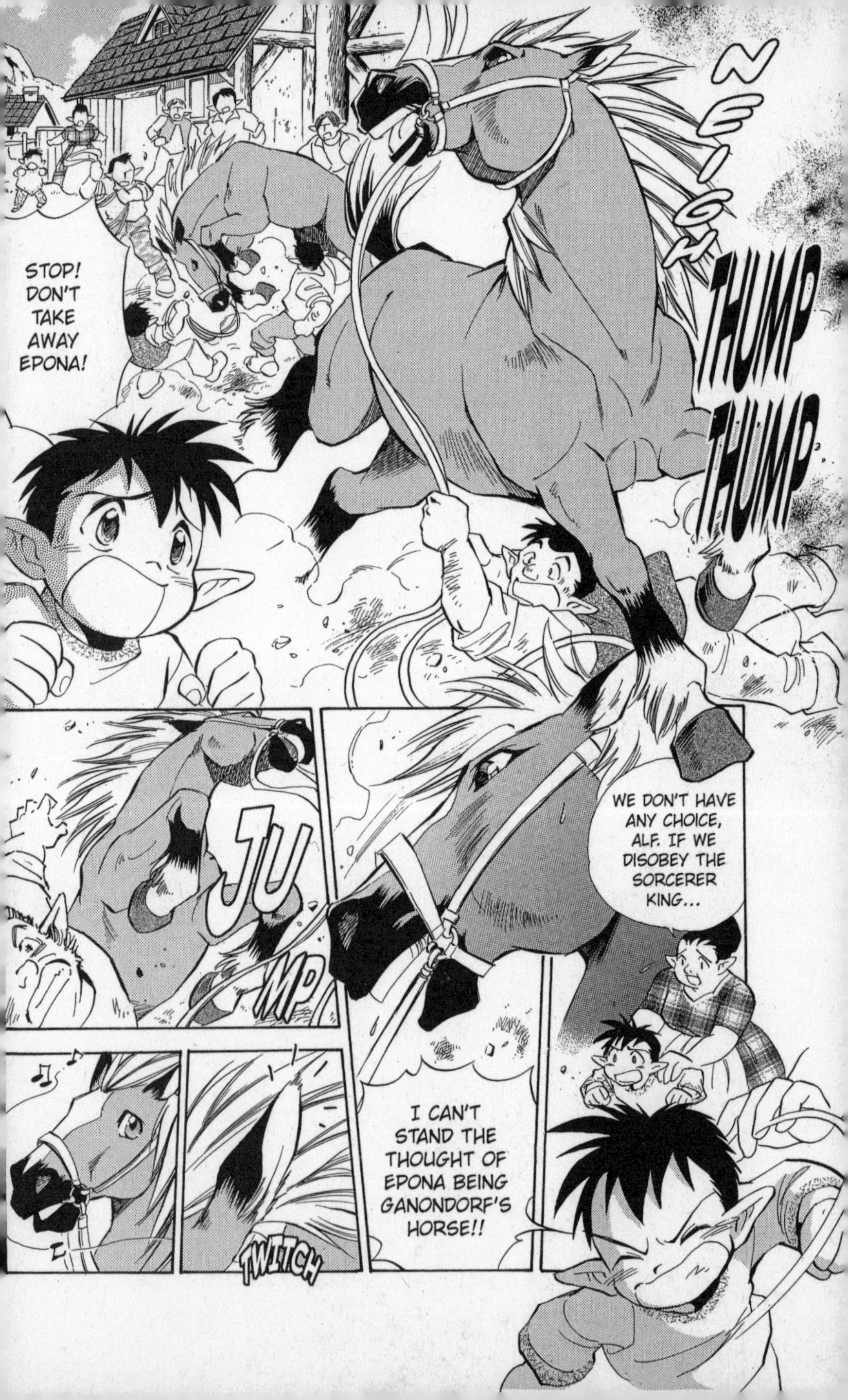
NEIGH
THUMP
THUMP
STOP! DON'T TAKE AWAY EPONA!
WE DON'T HAVE ANY CHOICE, ALF. IF WE DISOBEY THE SORCERER KING...
JUMP
I CAN'T STAND THE THOUGHT OF EPONA BEING GANONDORF'S HORSE!!
TWITCH

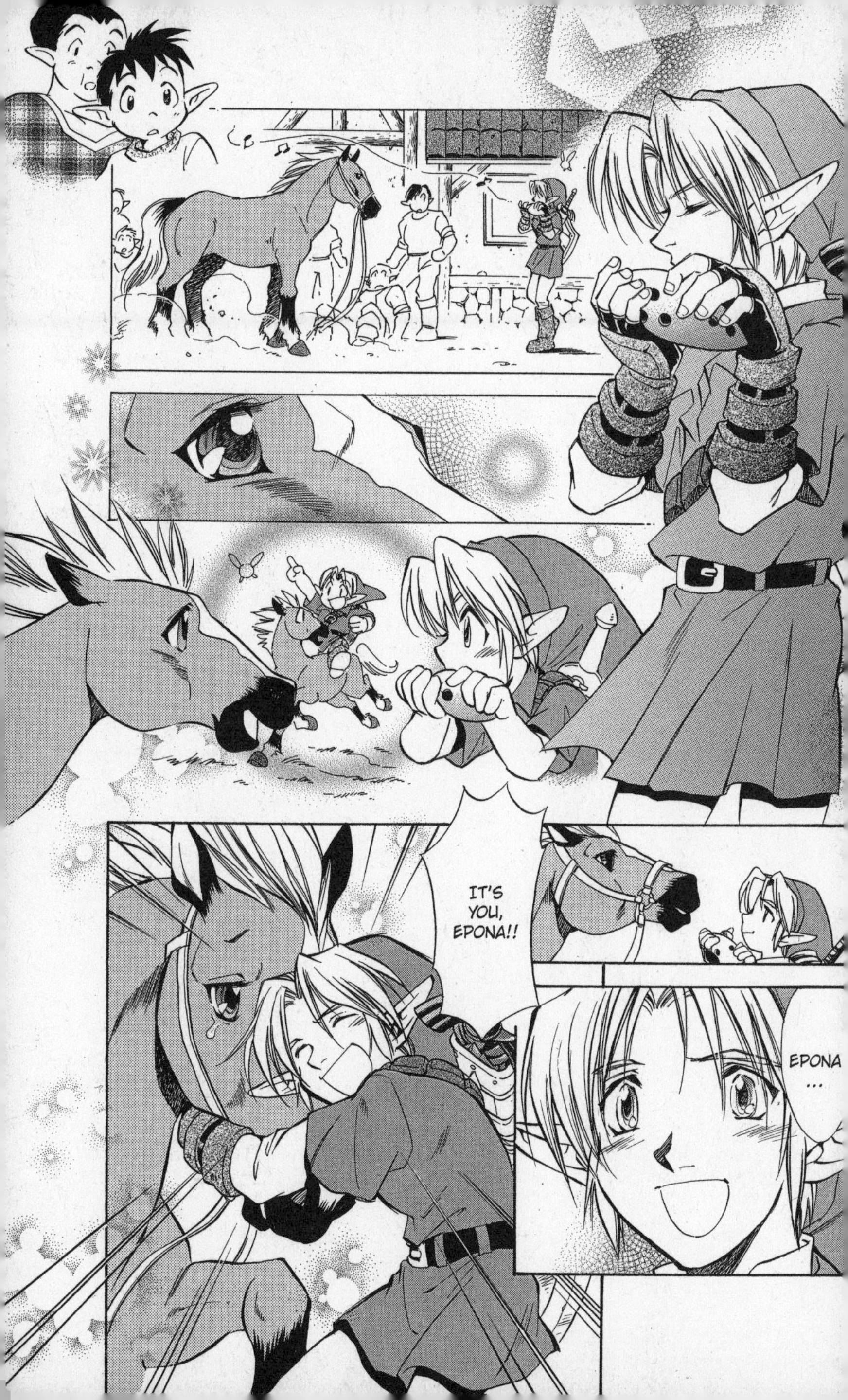
EPONA...
IT'S YOU, EPONA!!

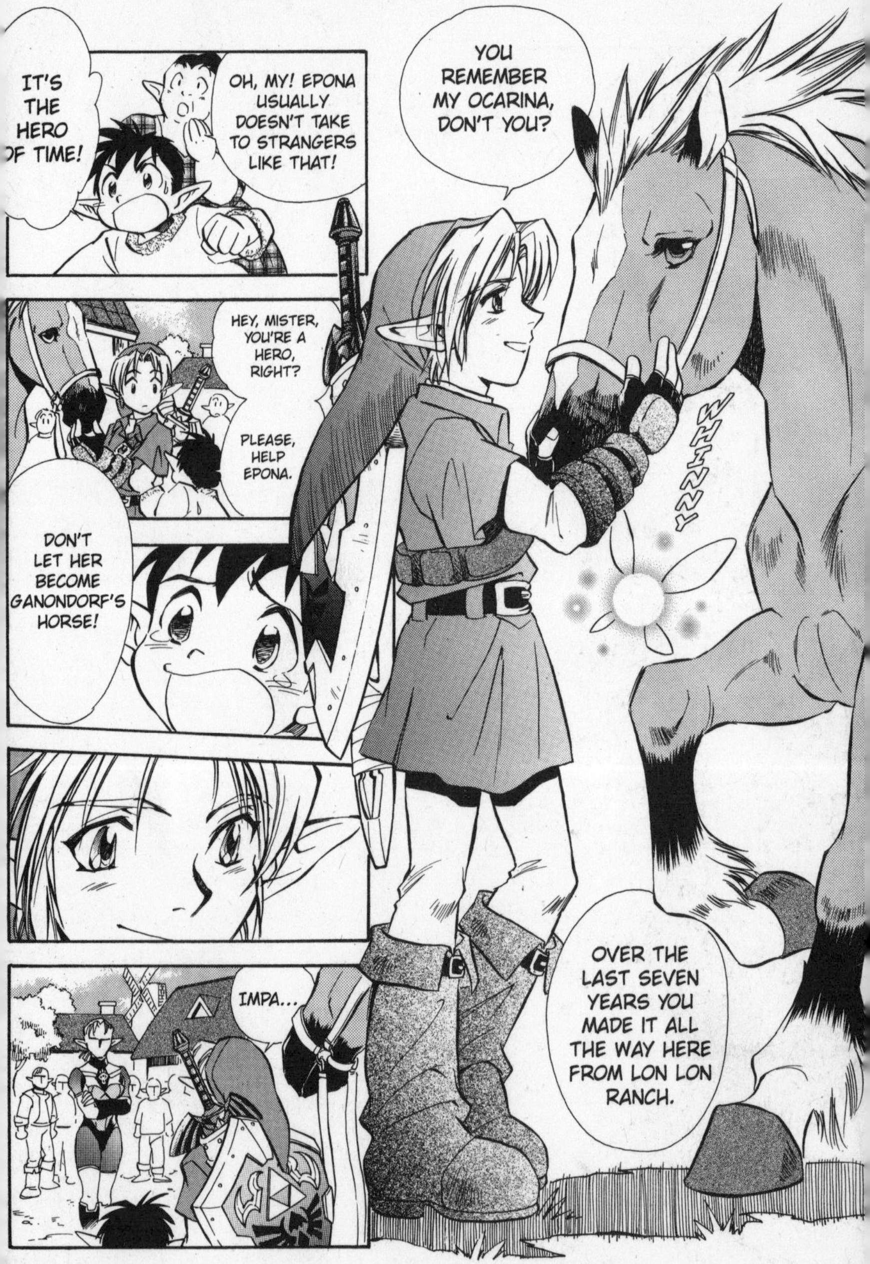
YOU REMEMBER MY OCARINA, DON'T YOU?
WHINNY
OVER THE LAST SEVEN YEARS YOU MADE IT ALL THE WAY HERE FROM LON LON RANCH.
OH, MY! EPONA USUALLY DOESN'T TAKE TO STRANGERS LIKE THAT!
IT'S THE HERO OF TIME!
HEY, MISTER, YOU'RE A HERO, RIGHT?
PLEASE, HELP EPONA.
DON'T LET HER BECOME GANONDORF'S HORSE!
IMPA...

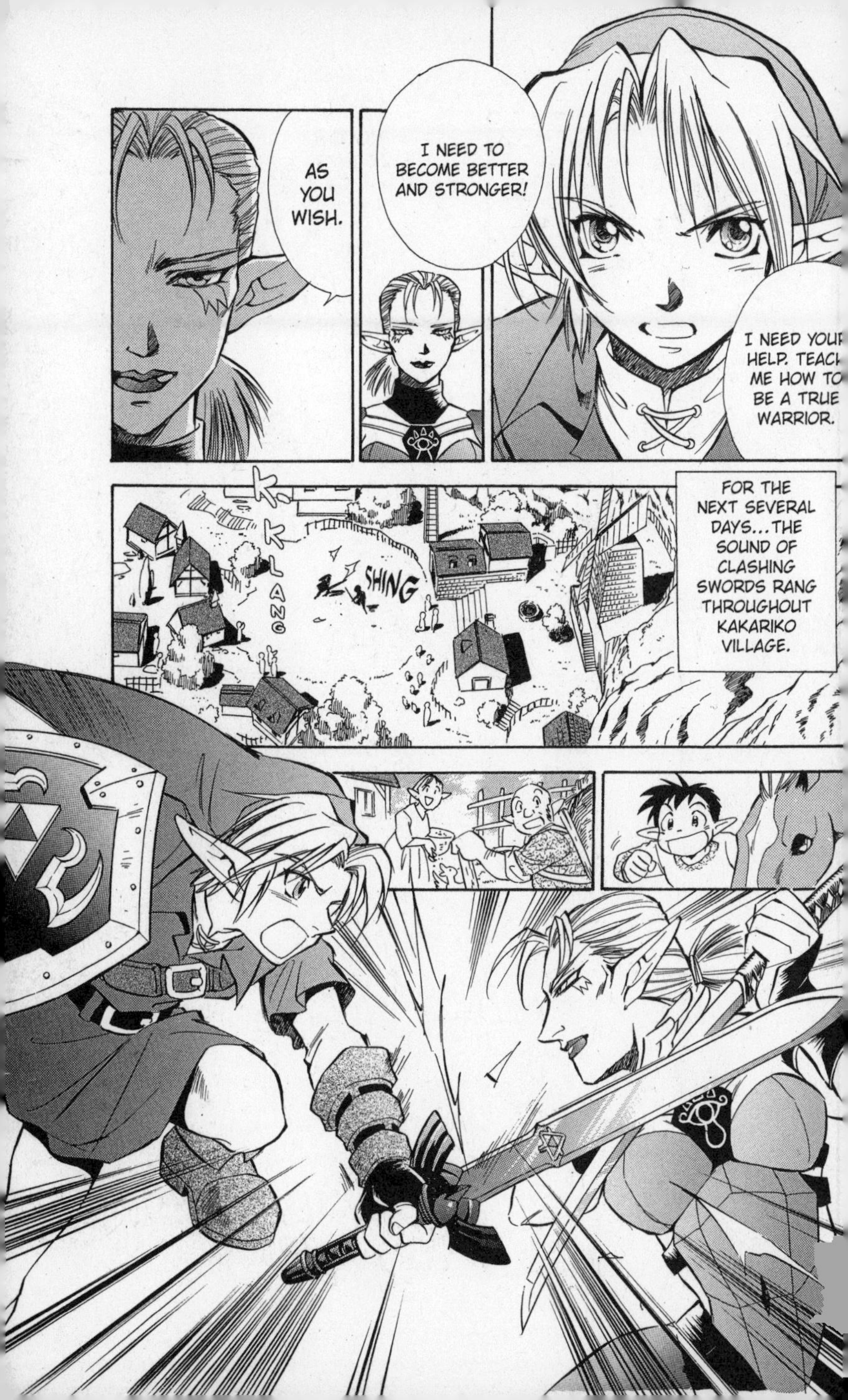
I NEED TO BECOME BETTER AND STRONGER!
I NEED YOUR HELP. TEACH ME HOW TO BE A TRUE WARRIOR.
AS YOU WISH.
FOR THE NEXT SEVERAL DAYS...THE SOUND OF CLASHING SWORDS RANG THROUGHOUT KAKARIKO VILLAGE.
SHING
K-KLANG

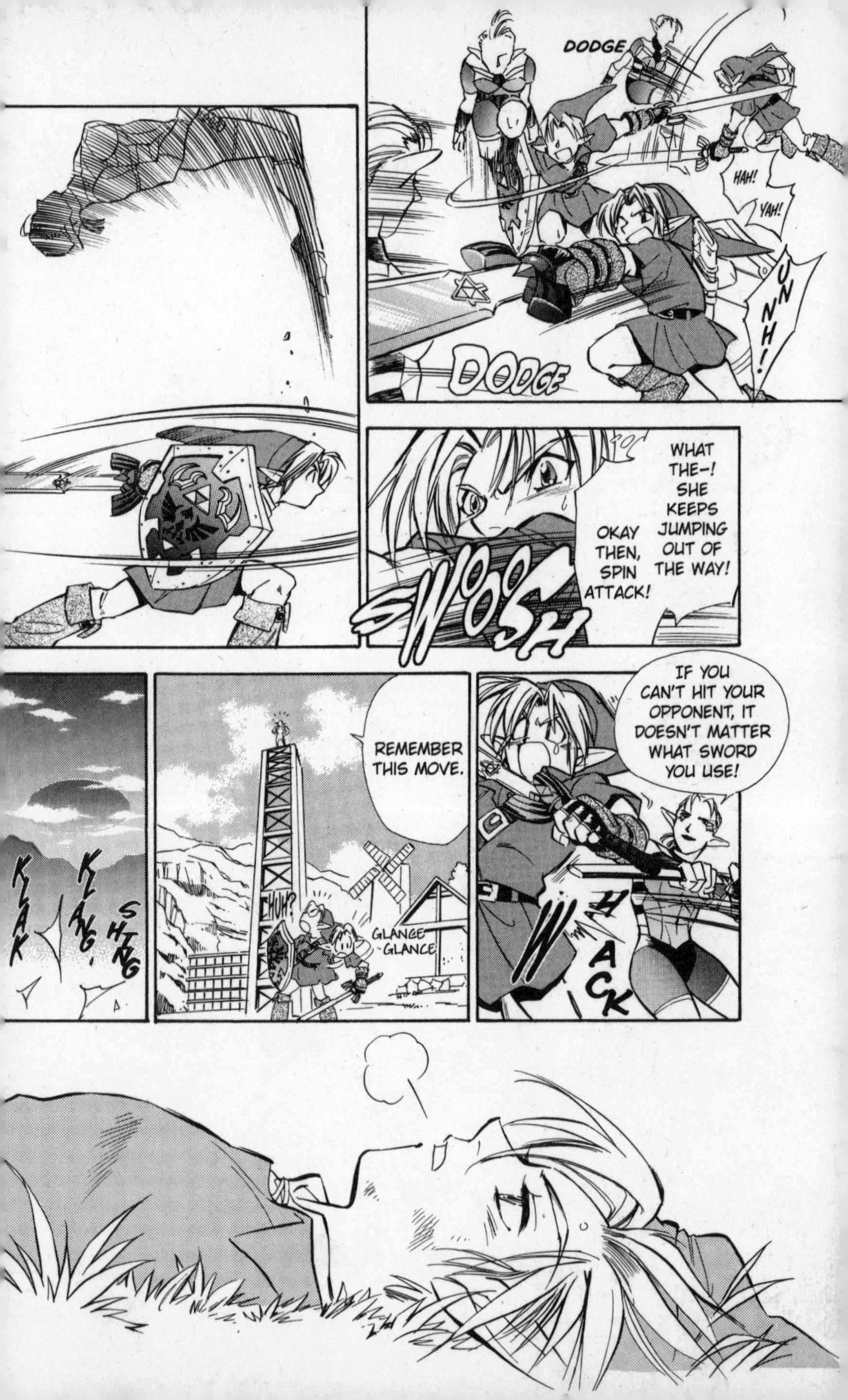
DODGE
HAH!
YAH!
UNNH!
DODGE
WHAT THE-! SHE KEEPS JUMPING OUT OF THE WAY!
OKAY THEN, SPIN ATTACK!
SWOOSH
IF YOU CAN'T HIT YOUR OPPONENT, IT DOESN'T MATTER WHAT SWORD YOU USE!
WHACK
REMEMBER THIS MOVE.
HUH?
GLANCE GLANCE
SHING
KLANG
KLAK

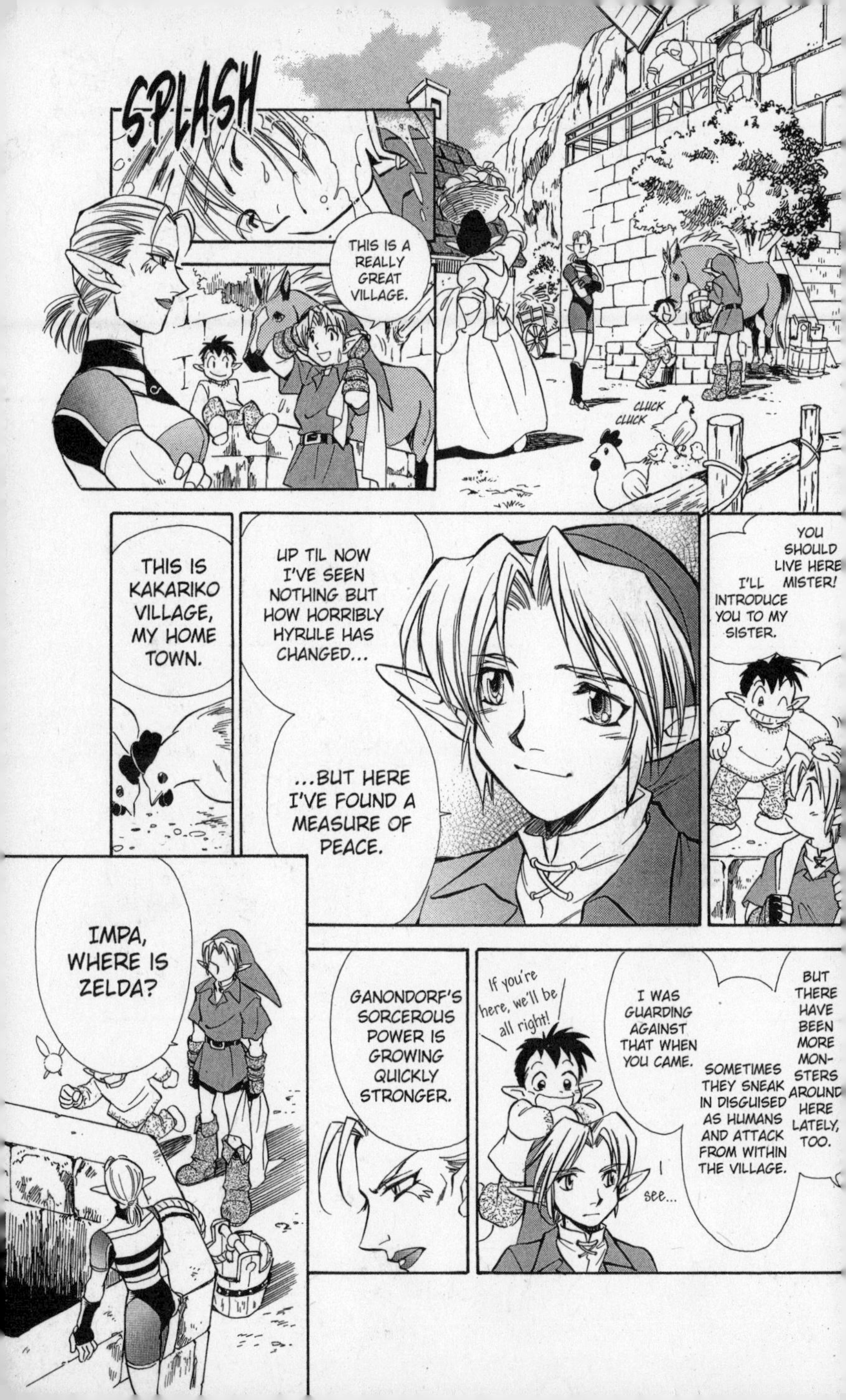
CLUCK
CLUCK
SPLASH
THIS IS A REALLY GREAT VILLAGE.
YOU SHOULD LIVE HERE MISTER!
I'LL INTRODUCE YOU TO MY SISTER.
UP TIL NOW I'VE SEEN NOTHING BUT HOW HORRIBLY HYRULE HAS CHANGED...
...BUT HERE I'VE FOUND A MEASURE OF PEACE.
THIS IS KAKARIKO VILLAGE, MY HOME TOWN.
IMPA, WHERE IS ZELDA?
GANONDORF'S SORCEROUS POWER IS GROWING QUICKLY STRONGER.
BUT THERE HAVE BEEN MORE MON-STERS AROUND HERE LATELY, TOO.
SOMETIMES THEY SNEAK IN DISGUISED AS HUMANS AND ATTACK FROM WITHIN THE VILLAGE.
I WAS GUARDING AGAINST THAT WHEN YOU CAME.
If you're here, we'll be all right!
I see...

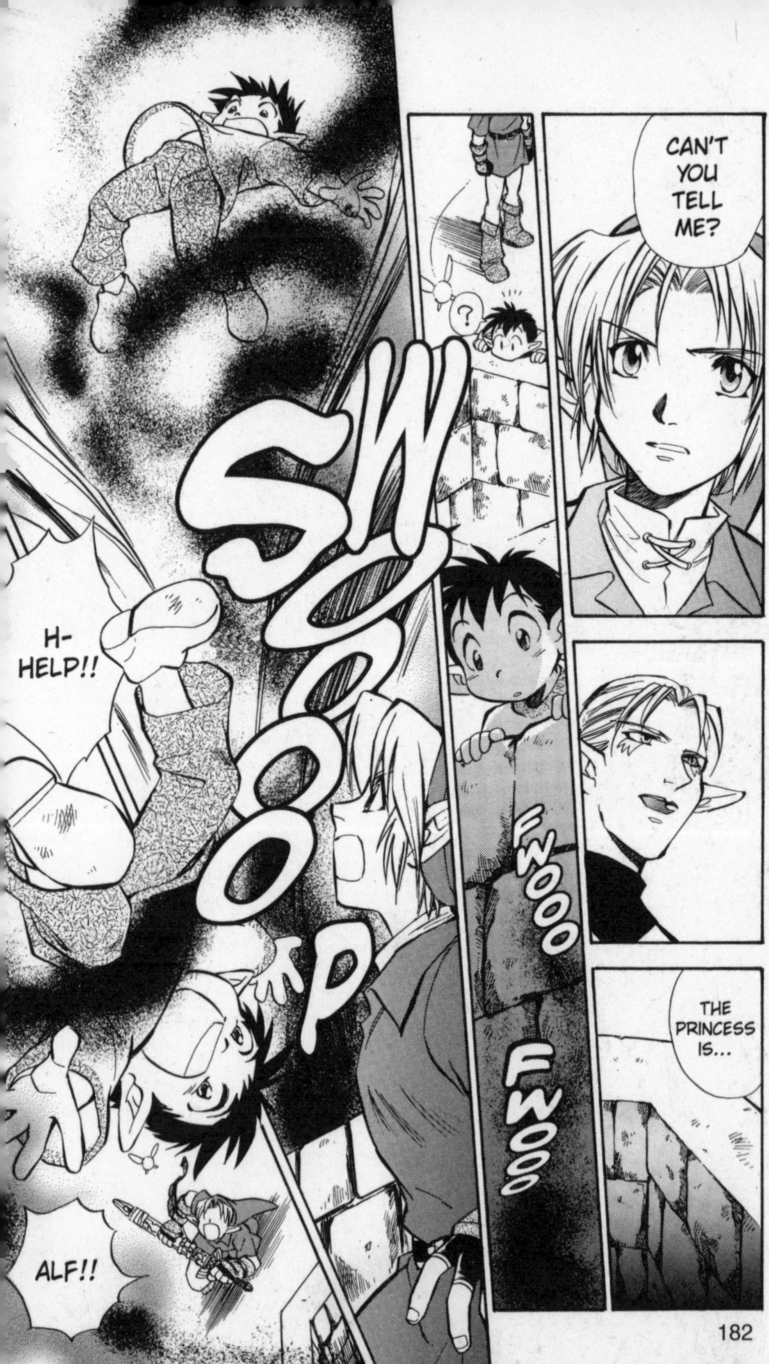
CAN'T YOU TELL ME?
THE PRINCESS IS...
?
FWOOO
FWOOO
SWOOOOP
H-HELP!!
ALF!!

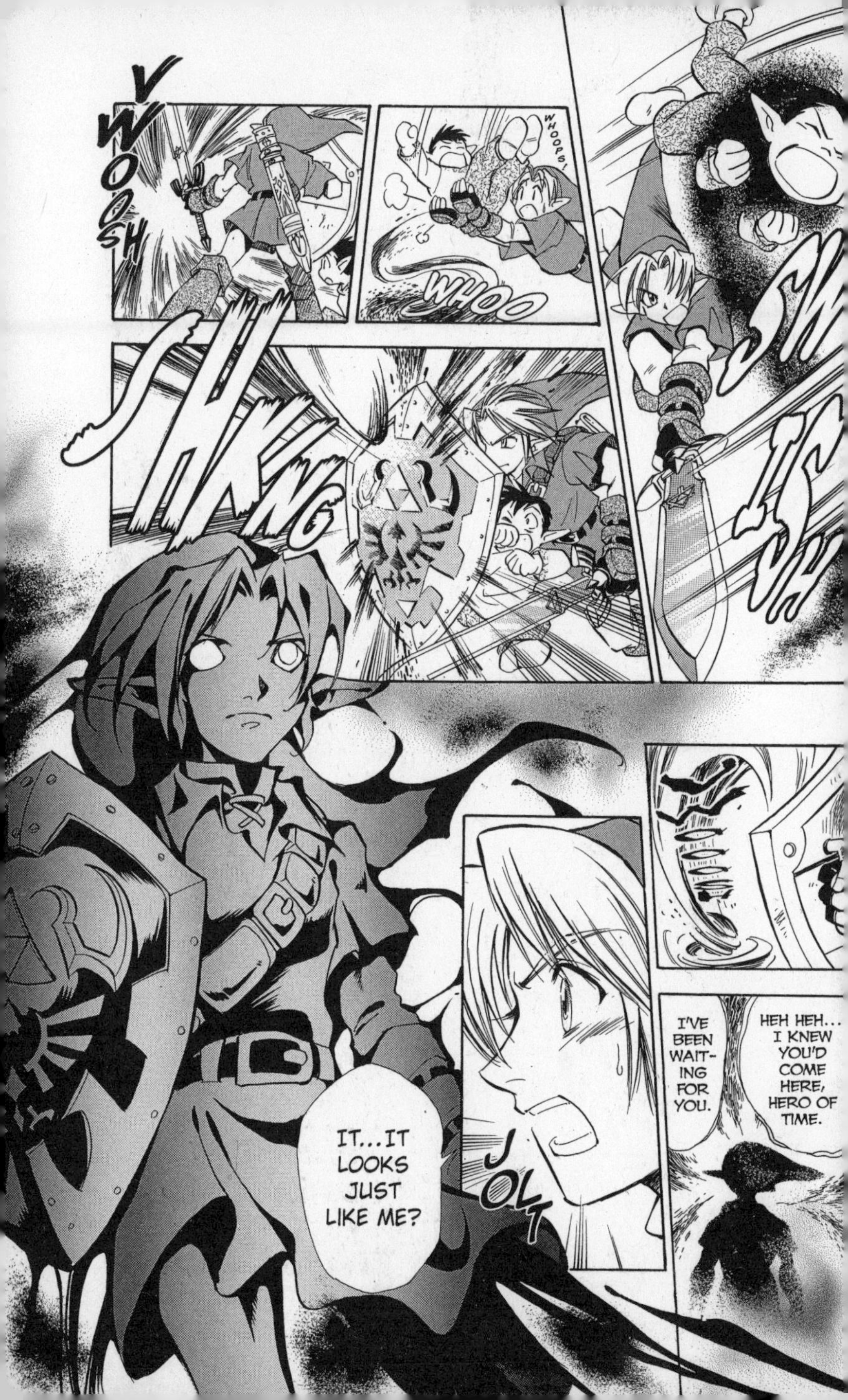
WHOOPS!
WHOO
VWOOSH
HEH HEH... I KNEW YOU'D COME HERE, HERO OF TIME.
I'VE BEEN WAITING FOR YOU.
JOLT
IT...IT LOOKS JUST LIKE ME?

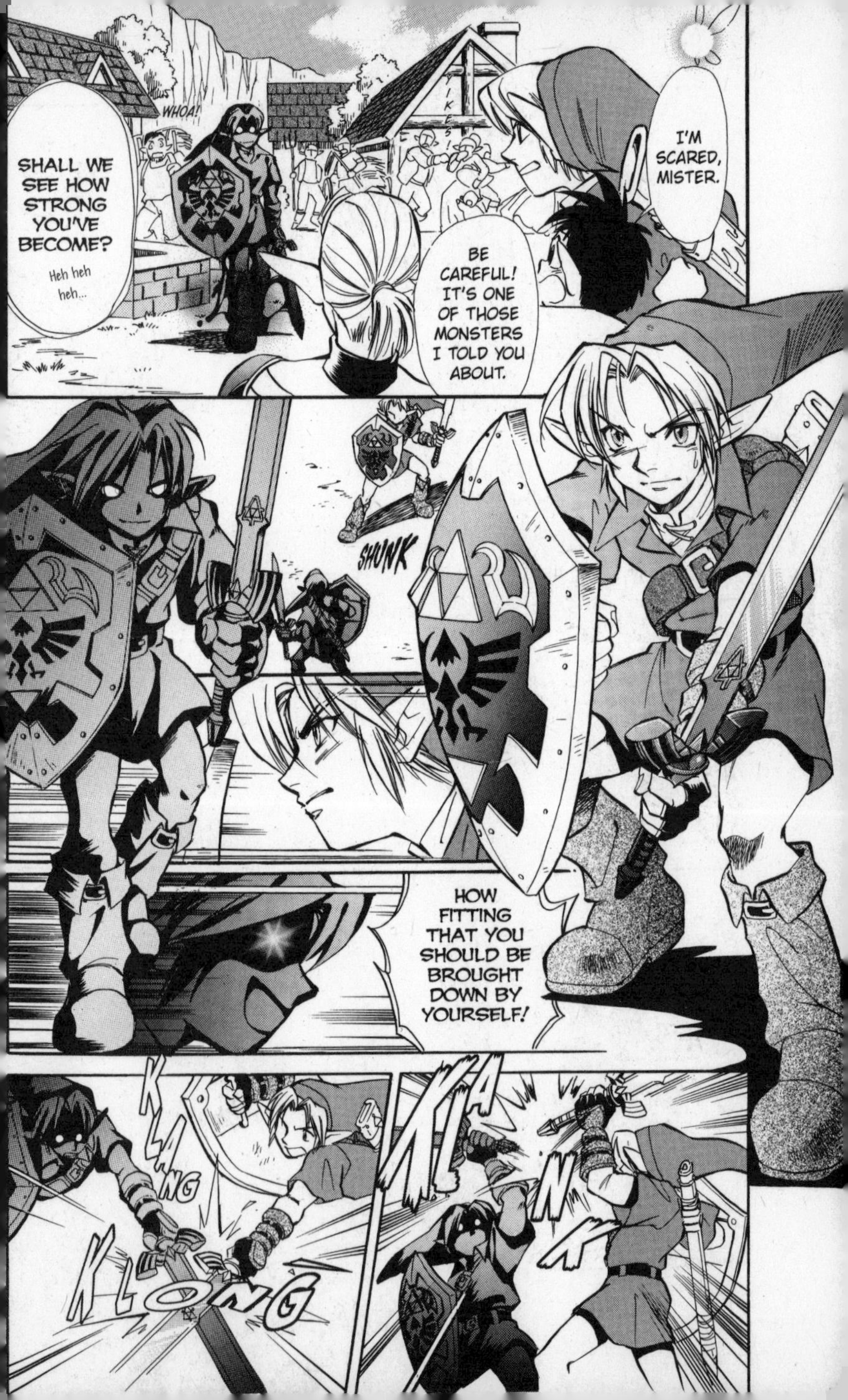
I'M SCARED, MISTER.
BE CAREFUL! IT'S ONE OF THOSE MONSTERS I TOLD YOU ABOUT.
YIKES!
WHOA!
SHALL WE SEE HOW STRONG YOU'VE BECOME?
Heh heh heh...
SHUNK
HOW FITTING THAT YOU SHOULD BE BROUGHT DOWN BY YOURSELF!
KLANK
KLING
KLONG

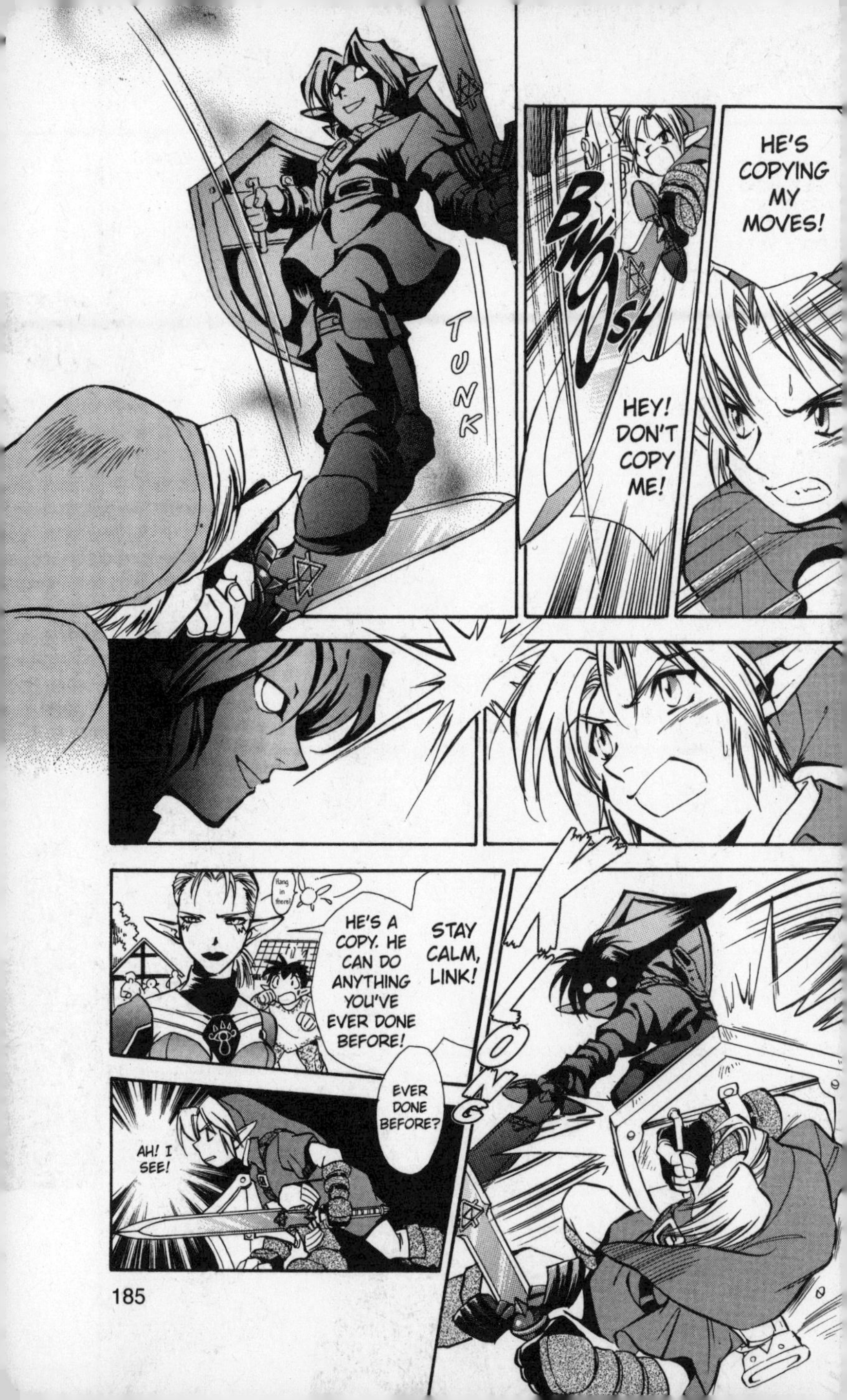
HE'S COPYING MY MOVES!
BWOOSH
HEY! DON'T COPY ME!
TUNK
STAY CALM, LINK!
HE'S A COPY. HE CAN DO ANYTHING YOU'VE EVER DONE BEFORE!
Hang in there!
EVER DONE BEFORE?
AH! I SEE!

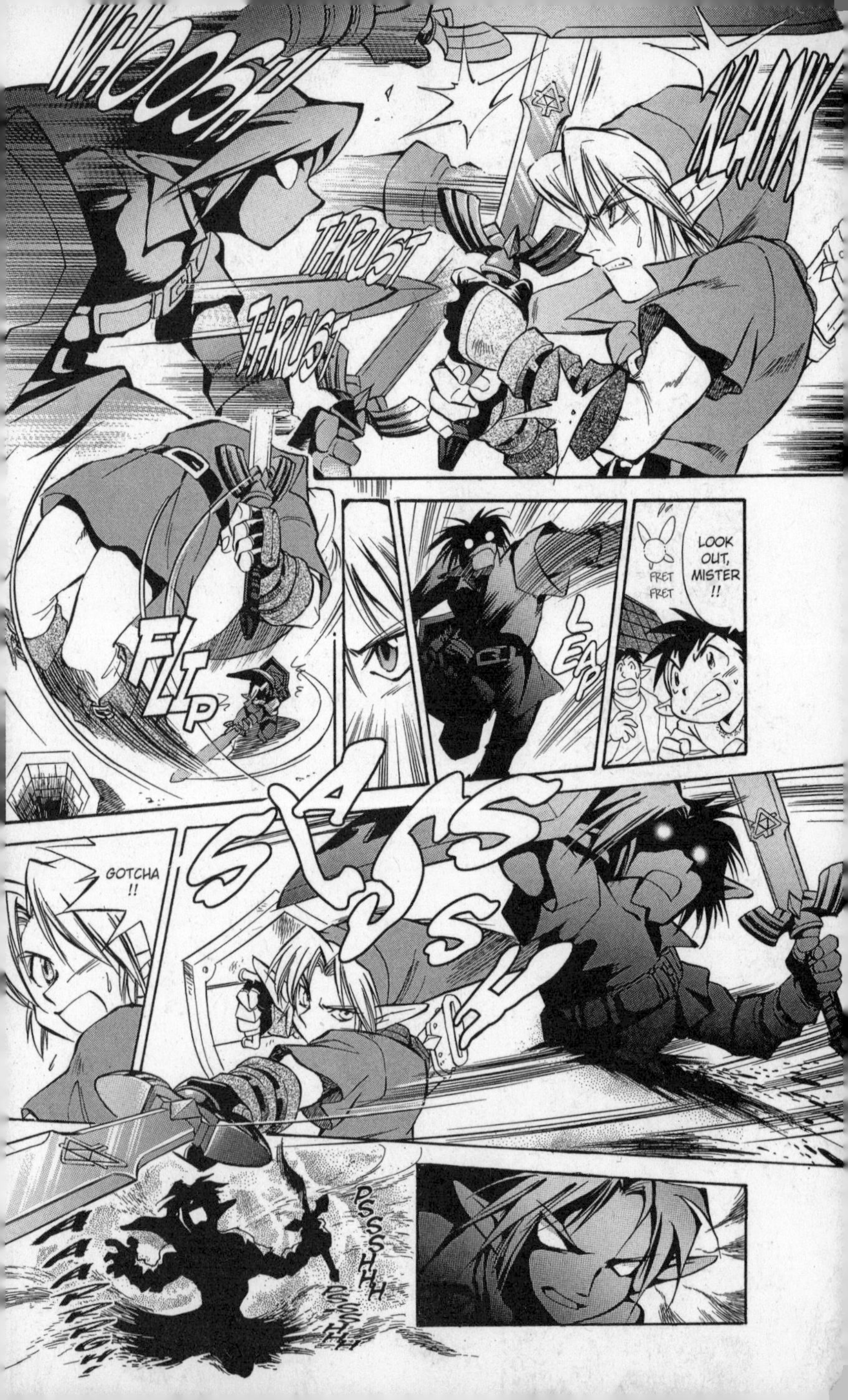
KLANK
WHOOOSH
THRUST
THRUST
LOOK OUT, MISTER !!
FRET FRET
LEAP
FLIP
SLASSS!
GOTCHA !!
PSSSHHH
PSSSHHH
AAAAAAAGH!

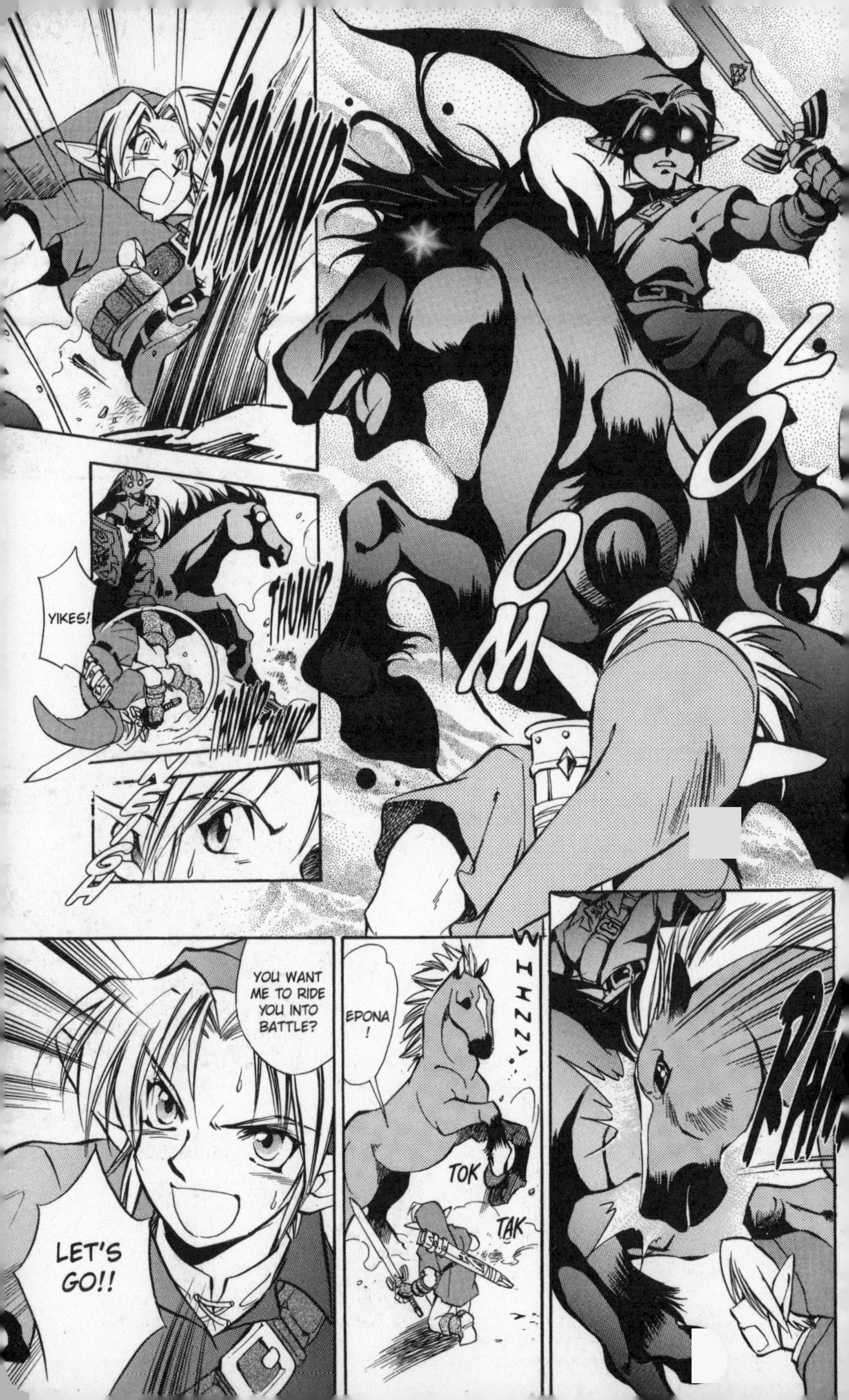
THUMP
YIKES!
WHINNY...
EPONA!
TOK
TAK
YOU WANT ME TO RIDE YOU INTO BATTLE?
LET'S GO!!

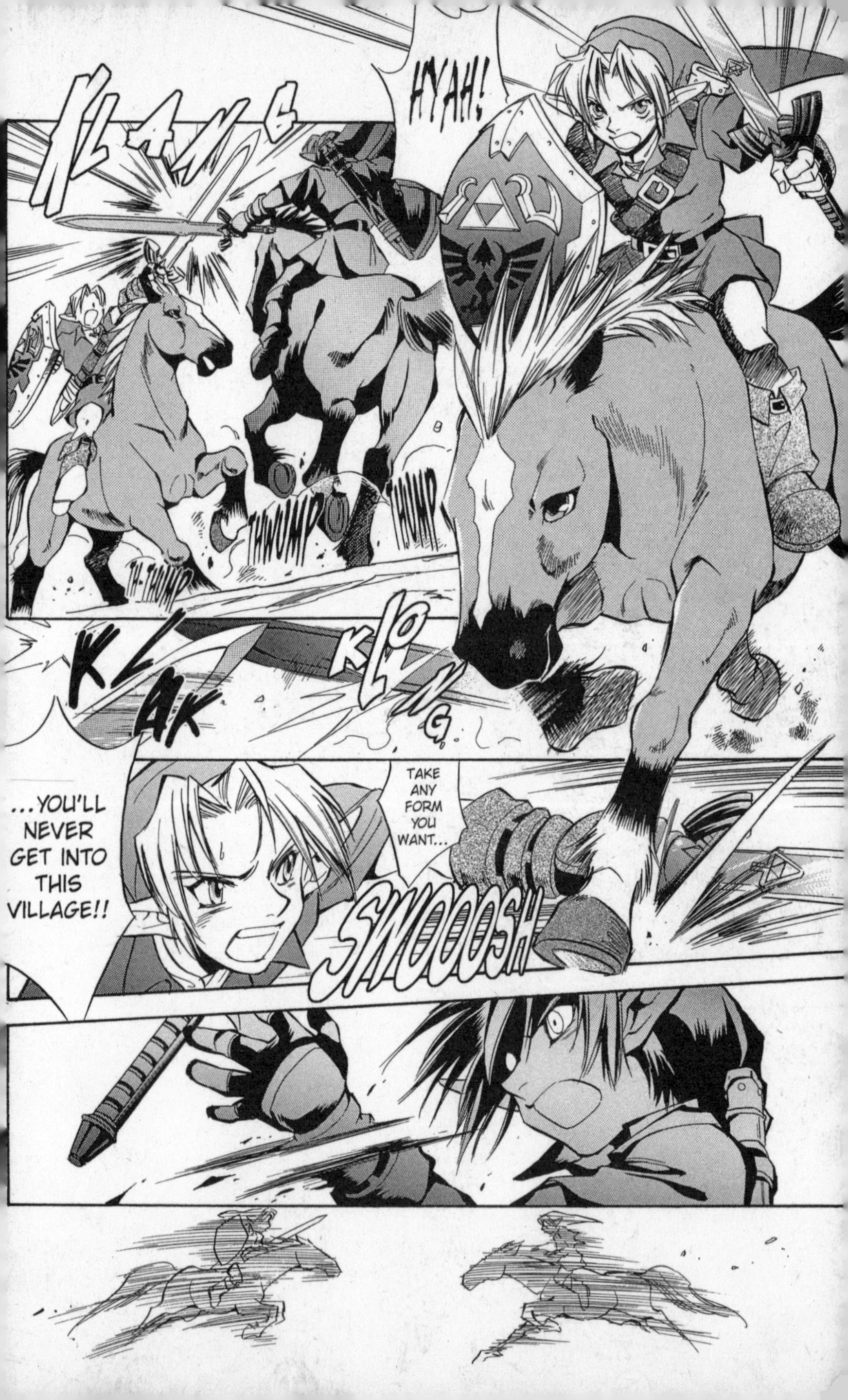
HYAH!
KLANG
THUMP
THWUMP
TH-THUMP
KLONG
KLAK
TAKE ANY FORM YOU WANT...
SWOOOSH
...YOU'LL NEVER GET INTO THIS VILLAGE!!

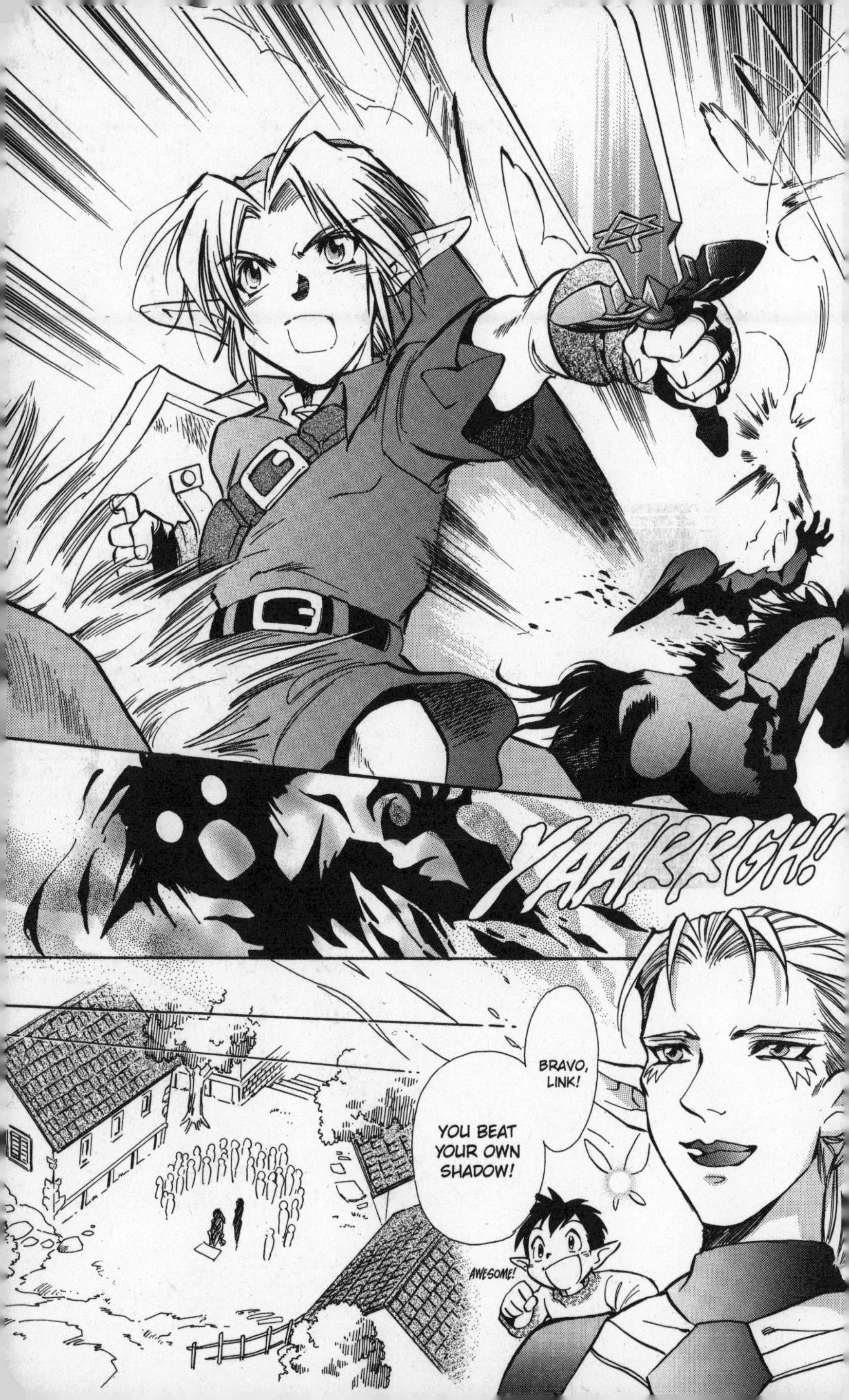
YAARRGH!
BRAVO, LINK!
YOU BEAT YOUR OWN SHADOW!
AWESOME!

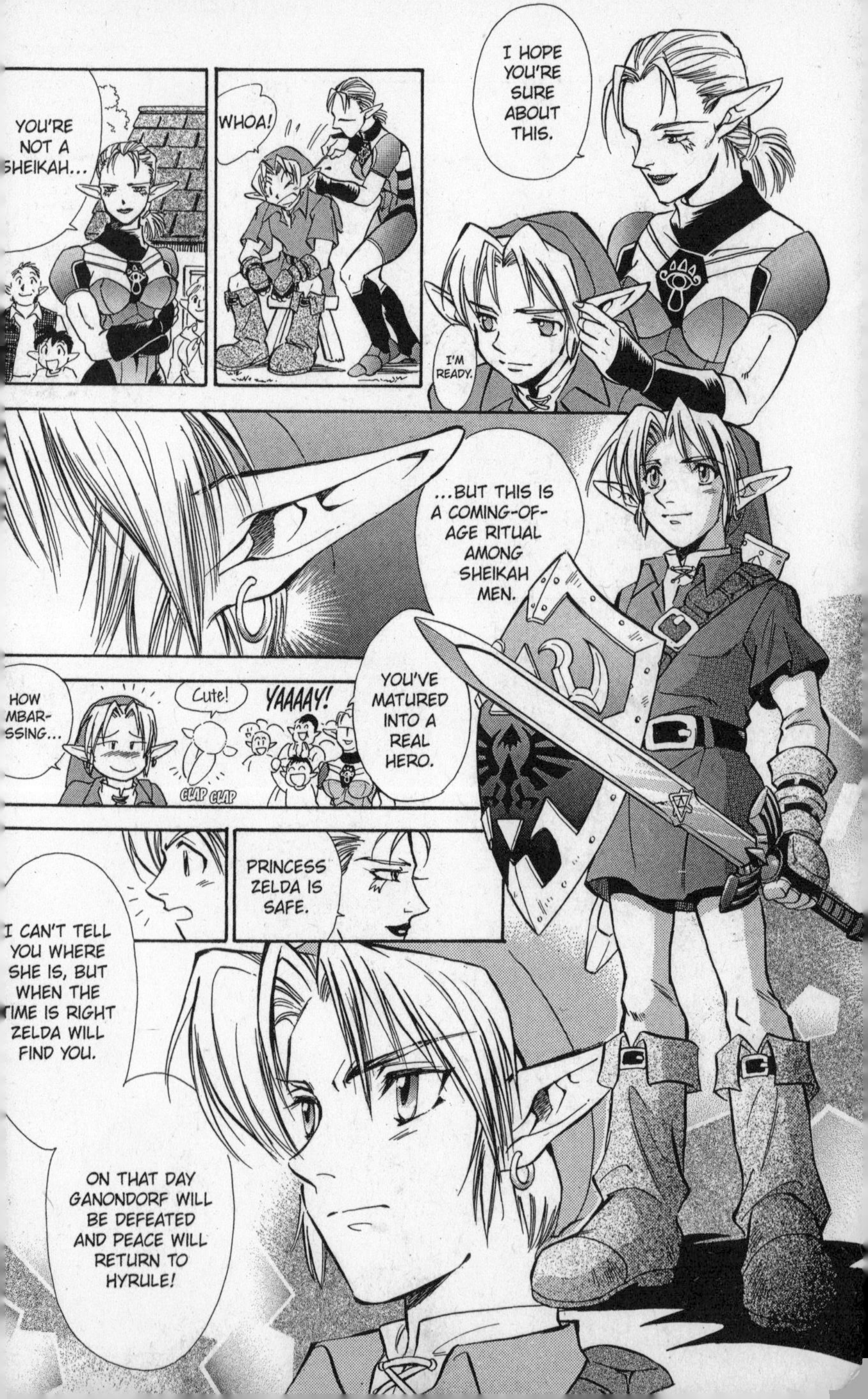
I HOPE YOU'RE SURE ABOUT THIS.
I'M READY.
WHOA!
YOU'RE NOT A SHEIKAH...
...BUT THIS IS A COMING-OF-AGE RITUAL AMONG SHEIKAH MEN.
YOU'VE MATURED INTO A REAL HERO.
YAAAAY!
Cute!
CLAP CLAP
HOW MBAR-SSING...
PRINCESS ZELDA IS SAFE.
I CAN'T TELL YOU WHERE SHE IS, BUT WHEN THE TIME IS RIGHT ZELDA WILL FIND YOU.
ON THAT DAY GANONDORF WILL BE DEFEATED AND PEACE WILL RETURN TO HYRULE!

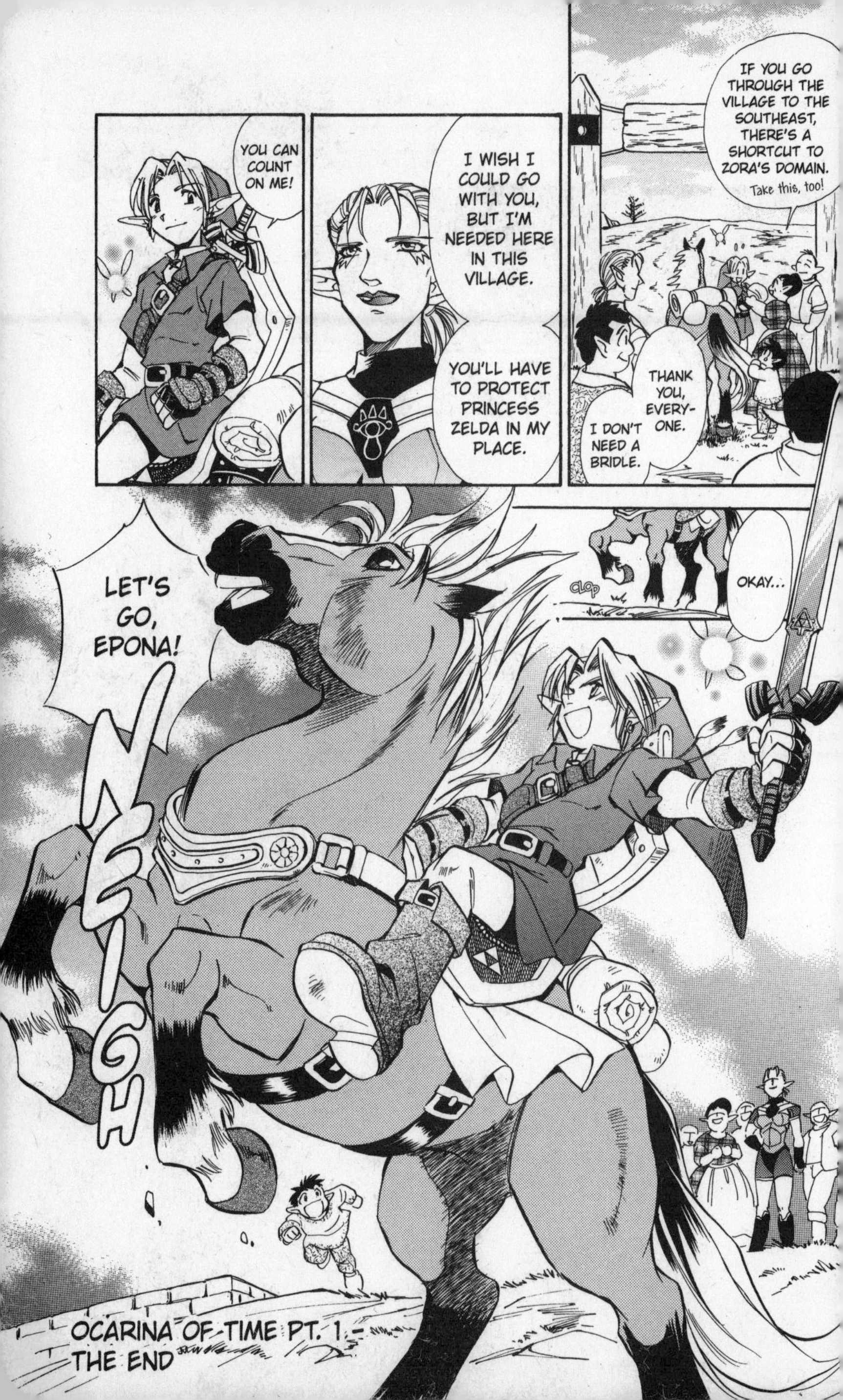
IF YOU GO THROUGH THE VILLAGE TO THE SOUTHEAST, THERE'S A SHORTCUT TO ZORA'S DOMAIN.
Take this, too!
THANK YOU, EVERYONE.
I DON'T NEED A BRIDLE.
I WISH I COULD GO WITH YOU, BUT I'M NEEDED HERE IN THIS VILLAGE.
YOU'LL HAVE TO PROTECT PRINCESS ZELDA IN MY PLACE.
YOU CAN COUNT ON ME!
CLOP
OKAY...
LET'S GO, EPONA!
NEIGH
OCARINA OF TIME PT. 1 - THE END

...ume

Link seeks out the remaining Sages, while Ganondorf searches for Princess Zelda and plots to capture Link with the aid of the witches known as Twinrova. At the urging of the mysterious Sheik, Link enters the Haunted Wasteland to find Zelda. The journey will be dangerous, but Link is determined to overcome Twinrova's traps and survive to face Ganondorf in an epic final battle!

Available Now!